WHAT YOUR COLLEAGUES ARE

BTC just got easier to do in your classroom! We have said for years and years that students need to be doing the thinking and talking in the math classroom. This book gives you the tools to actually do it! Whether you've read the original Building Thinking Classrooms book or not, this book gives you MORE . . . more tasks, more insights, more ideas. If you want to get kids thinking, add this book to your collection.

Christina Tondevold
Founder, Build Math Minds
Orofino, ID

Mathematics Tasks for the Thinking Classroom, Grades K–5 doesn't just offer tasks; it intentionally provides the fuel for transforming classrooms into dynamic critical thinking and collaboration hubs. From task selection to empowering student autonomy, this book equips educators with the tools and knowledge to create vibrant learning environments.

Graham Fletcher
Math Specialist
Atlanta, GA

It was love at first sight when I read *Building Thinking Classrooms in Mathematics: 14 Teaching Practices for Enhancing Learning*. Though it might sound cheesy, it changed my life. While it was a transformational game changer in my classroom, it left me wanting more, especially in regard to the early elementary world. I longed to sit down with Peter and pick his brain concerning how some of the 14 practices might look in my first-grade class. Well, this book answers those questions, and I'm confident it will do the same for all the elementary teachers who have been waiting on the edges of their seats for this book to arrive. Peter and Maegan have hit it out of the ballpark.

Tammy McMorrow
First-Grade Teacher, Indian Creek Elementary
Meridian, ID

This follow-up to *Building Thinking Classrooms in Mathematics* will be a must-have book for every elementary math educator! Not only does it offer a comprehensive guide to a wealth of classroom-tested non-curricular and curricular tasks, and an expansion of many of the practices included in the original book, the presentation for each task takes you from an offered launch to begin the task, to hints and extensions during the task, to examples of student work to help educators consolidate the task, suggested examples of Check-Your-Understanding questions, and even advice from Peter and Maegan on what they have learned during their facilitation of these tasks within classrooms over and over again. Pure gold! This will be such a valuable addition to math educators' professional libraries. I predict facilitation of positive math journeys for each and every student fortunate enough to be in a thinking classroom.

Ann Elise Record
Elementary Math Consultant/Specialist, Ann Elise Record Consulting LLC
Concord, NH

He's done it again! Peter Liljedahl continues to take the math world by storm by answering our most frequently asked questions about building our own thinking classrooms, continuing to share his research findings, and providing us with examples of thinking tasks that fit the criteria of the 14 BTC practices.

Kimberly Rimbey
Chief Learning Officer & CEO, KP Mathematics
Phoenix, AZ

This is the Building Thinking Classrooms companion book that we have been waiting for! From the beginning to the end, readers will absorb every word. This book has the latest and greatest research that is easy to read, understand, and implement right away. This book will be sitting on my desk right beside the original *Building Thinking Classrooms in Mathematics* book so that I can share the information with teachers right away!

Laura Vizdos Tomas
K–5 Math Coach, School District, Palm Beach County
Co-Founder, LearningThroughMath.com
West Palm Beach, FL

Building Thinking Classrooms in Mathematics revolutionized the way I taught mathematics in my fifth-grade classroom. *Mathematics Tasks for the Thinking Classroom* is sure to strengthen teachers' craft as they continue to progress in their own learning journey. The tasks are engaging and detailed. This book is a great follow-up to the first and a must have for every BTC teacher.

Karina Cousins
Fifth-Grade Teacher, School District, Palm Beach County
Co-Founder, LearningThroughMath.com
Lake Worth, FL

This book is a must-read for all K–5 math educators. Whether you are just starting to build thinking classrooms or have been implementing BTC for many years, this book provides valuable insight into the original research along with new moves and practices that have emerged from continued research. The 50 Thinking Tasks included in the book will provide all your students access to engaged learning, while providing you with an increased understanding and framework for continued success in leading a thinking classroom.

Melisa A. McCain
Instructional Coach, Franklin Community Schools
Franklin, IN

This follow-up book to the transformative *Building Thinking Classrooms in Mathematics* is the perfect next step. This book will help teachers continue on the path toward building a thinking classroom, but more importantly, building thinking students.

Jared Sliger
Middle School Math Teacher, Middleton Middle School
Caldwell, ID

For every teacher who had the courage to change.

MATHEMATICS TASKS for the THINKING CLASSROOM

GRADES K–5

PETER LILJEDAHL | MAEGAN GIROUX

ILLUSTRATIONS BY LAURA WHEELER

FOR INFORM

Corwin
A SAGE Co
2455 Tell
Thou

CORWIN **Mathematics**

ΛΡany

ON:

Λmpany
er Road
nd Oaks, California 91320
233-9936
w.corwin.com

SAGE Publications Ltd.
1 Oliver's Yard
55 City Road
London EC1Y 1SP
United Kingdom

SAGE Publications India Pvt. Ltd.
Unit No 323-333, Third Floor, F-Block
International Trade Tower Nehru Place
New Delhi 110 019
India

SAGE Publications Asia-Pacific Pte. Ltd.
18 Cross Street #10-10/11/12
China Square Central
Singapore 048423

Vice President and
  Editorial Director: Monica Eckman
Associate Director and Publisher,
  STEM: Erin Null
Senior Editorial Assistant: Nyle De Leon
Production Editor: Tori Mirsadjadi
Copy Editor: Diana Breti
Typesetters: Integra and C&M Digitals (P) Ltd.
Proofreader: Jennifer Grubba
Indexer: Integra
Cover Designer: Scott Van Atta
Marketing Manager: Margaret O'Connor

Printed in the United States of America

Paperback ISBN 978-1-0719-1329-1

This book is printed on acid-free paper.

24 25 26 27 28 10 9 8 7 6 5

CONTENTS

CHAPTER 6: HOW TO HAVE STUDENTS MAKE MEANINGFUL NOTES 62

CHAPTER 7: HOW TO HAVE STUDENTS DO CHECK-YOUR-UNDERSTANDING QUESTIONS 68

CHAPTER 8: HOW TO USE TASKS AS THE CONTEXT TO IMPROVE STUDENT COMPETENCIES 76

CHAPTER 9: WHAT LESSONS LOOK LIKE IN A THINKING CLASSROOM 86

PART 2 NON-CURRICULAR THINKING TASKS 92

PART 3 CURRICULAR THINKING TASKS 218

Visit the companion website at
https://companion.corwin.com/courses/BTCK5Tasks
for downloadable resources.

ACKNOWLEDGMENTS

ACKNOWLEDGMENTS FROM PETER

I want to thank my wife, Theresa, for her constant companionship as we, together, bring *Building Thinking Classrooms* to teachers around the world. Without your support, none of this would have been possible. I want to thank Erin Null, my editor for all things BTC related. I value your support, your advocacy, your advice, your patience, but most of all your friendship. I also want to thank my co-author, Maegan. Your imagination for creating tasks and love of teaching knows no bounds. Thank you for allowing me to walk alongside you in this project. Finally, I want to thank all the teachers, consultants, and administrators who continue to explore with, trust in, and advocate for Building Thinking Classrooms. You are making a difference in the lives of students.

ACKNOWLEDGMENTS FROM MAEGAN

I first want to thank my husband, Thayne, and two sons, Taylor and Jacob, for their vigorous love and support throughout this project and in life. You are all my personal spark and inspiration for so much of my professional work. I want to thank my co-author, Peter. Your continued guidance and belief in me has shown me that I can achieve more than I thought possible. Thank you for your steadfast counsel and trusting me with your vision. I'd also like to thank Kyle Webb and all the consultants and administrators within the Regina Catholic School Division for their championship of BTC. So many educators and students have discovered the magic of BTC because of you. Finally, I need to thank Diana Shuba and all the teachers and students I've worked with over the past few years. Your willingness to embrace BTC and transform your classrooms energizes me daily. These tasks couldn't have been created and tested without open-minded people like you.

ACKNOWLEDGMENTS FROM PETER AND MAEGAN

We want to acknowledge the entire team at Corwin beginning with (again) our editor and Corwin Mathematics publisher, Erin Null. Your ongoing support and advocacy for all things *Building Thinking Classrooms* is what keeps the work moving forward. We want to thank Laura Wheeler for illustrating this book. You have, again, found ways to give life to our words through your artistry. And we thank Senior Editorial Assistant Nyle DeLeon and Senior Project Editor Tori Mirsadjadi, who helped with many technical aspects of turning a manuscript into an actual book. Finally, we are grateful to Senior Marketing Manager Margaret O'Connor, who worked so hard to get this book into your hands.

PUBLISHER'S ACKNOWLEDGMENTS

Corwin gratefully acknowledges the contributions of the following reviewers:

Karina Cousins
Fifth-grade teacher, School District, Palm Beach County
Co-founder of LearningThroughMath.com
Lake Worth, FL

Melisa A. McCain
Instructional coach, Franklin Community Schools
Franklin, IN

Tammy McMorrow
First-grade teacher, Indian Creek Elementary
Meridian, ID

Chase Orton
Math change agent, chaseorton.com
Culver, CA

Ann Elise Record
Elementary math consultant/specialist, Ann Elise Record Consulting LLC
Concord, NH

Kimberly Rimbey
Chief Learning Officer & CEO, KP Mathematics
Phoenix, AZ

April Strom
Mathematics faculty, Chandler-Gilbert Community College
Phoenix, AZ

Laura Vizdos Tomas
K–5 math coach, School District, Palm Beach County
Co-founder, LearningThroughMath.com
West Palm Beach, FL

ABOUT THE AUTHORS

Dr. Peter Liljedahl is a professor of mathematics education in the Faculty of Education at Simon Fraser University and author of the best-selling book, *Building Thinking Classrooms in Mathematics (Grades K–12): 14 Teaching Practices for Enhancing Learning.* Peter is a former high school mathematics teacher who has kept his research interest and activities close to the classroom. With a passion for fostering deep mathematical thinking and problem-solving skills, Peter has dedicated his career to reshaping classroom environments. His work emphasizes thinking, collaborative learning, and problem solving, leading to more effective and meaningful mathematics education experiences for students of all ages. Through his research-based innovative teaching methods, Peter continues to inspire educators worldwide to create dynamic and thought-provoking learning spaces. He consults regularly with teachers, schools, school districts, and ministries and departments of education on issues of teaching and learning, problem solving, assessment, numeracy, and building thinking classrooms. Peter has authored or co-authored 13 books, 45 book chapters, and 45 research articles on a wide range of topics including creativity in mathematics, the role of beliefs in teaching and learning mathematics, and building thinking classrooms. He is the recipient of the Cmolik Prize for the Enhancement of Public Education (2017), The Margaret Sinclair Memorial Award Recognizing Innovation and Excellence in Mathematics Education (2018), and the Læringsprisen for Changing the Way We Think About Education in Denmark (2022).

Maegan Giroux is an accomplished mathematics teacher, instructional coach, and educational consultant, currently working in Regina Catholic Schools. Having taught for more than a decade at every grade level from kindergarten to Grade 8, Maegan's teaching philosophy is rooted in innovative and student-centered approaches, with a strong emphasis on thinking classroom pedagogy, fostering student autonomy, and implementing robust assessment practices. Maegan also works in Canada as a valuable member of the Building Thinking Classrooms professional development team. In this capacity, she plays a key role in facilitating workshops related to Building Thinking Classrooms methodologies, sharing her expertise and insights with educators who are interested in implementing these innovative teaching practices. She speaks frequently at various educational conferences, where she imparts her knowledge on a wide range of math teaching concepts, further contributing to the advancement of mathematics education in Canada and beyond. In addition to her role as an educator, Maegan is actively engaged in academic pursuits. Her current research focuses on decolonizing mathematics education by challenging power dynamics through the framework of the 4 Rs of Indigenous research.

INTRODUCTION

If you have picked up this book, you are likely already familiar with the pedagogical framework known as Building Thinking Classrooms (BTC; Liljedahl, 2021). You probably also know that BTC is the result of more than 15 years of research grounded in the classroom practices that either support or hinder student thinking. The original research—done in mathematics classrooms—was a reaction to a recognized reality that the majority of students spend the majority of their time in a math classroom not thinking. And this is a problem. Thinking is a necessary precursor to learning and if students are not thinking, they are not learning. Something is broken and many who work in math education have been trying to repair it for more than half a century. Since the introduction of the National Council of Teachers of Mathematics *Principles and Standards* (2000), math teachers and leaders, organizations, school districts, and departments and ministries of education around the world have been trying to change this reality. But, for the most part, they have been trying to make this change while keeping the classroom the same. Teaching through problem solving, problem-based learning, project-based learning, and inquiry initiatives coupled with changes to assessment, the introduction of competencies, mathematical processes, and mathematical mindset work have dominated curriculum reform for the last 50 years. But students are still sitting, and teachers are still standing. Students are still writing on paper, while teachers are still writing on whiteboards. And as much as collaboration has permeated education, learning has largely been seen as a solitary activity.

The work on BTC changed all this. It began by looking at the core routines that every teacher does:

- the types of tasks we use;

- how we form collaborative groups;

- where students work;

- how we arrange the furniture;

- how we answer questions;

- when, where, and how tasks are given;

- what homework looks like;

- how we foster student autonomy;

- how we use hints and extensions;

- how we consolidate a lesson;

- how students take notes;

- what we choose to evaluate;

- how we use formative assessment; and

- how we grade.

These routines account for 90% of what every teacher does (Kaplinsky, 2022). My (Peter's) question was, then, can these routines, individually and collectively, be enacted differently so as to maximize student thinking? And thus began a journey that—so far—has taken more than 20 years—a journey in pursuit of optimal ways to enact each of these core routines in such a way as to maximize student thinking.

The results of this research were transformative. Classrooms went from spaces where students sat working in their individual notebooks to spaces where they stood in random groups of three working on vertical whiteboards. They went from spaces where we, as teachers, pre-taught students how to do things like add two-digit numbers, multiply fractions, and order decimals, to places where students figured these things out on their own with the support of their random groups and the groups around them. Classrooms went from spaces where students were told meaning to spaces where they were making meaning. And they went from spaces where only 20% of students were thinking for 20% of the time to spaces where upwards of 90% of students were thinking for 100% of the time. And the 10% who weren't thinking for 100% of the time were still thinking for more than 50% of the time.

What BTC did that so many other initiatives had not was examine the role that environment plays on student behavior. By examining the core institutional structures, BTC revealed that so many of the things about classrooms that have been invariant for more than a century have outlived their utility. Having students sit in their desks worked well in the post-industrial model of education when the goals of education were conformity and compliance, and school served as a vehicle for preparing factory workers. But if the goal is to think, we are going to have to do things differently. What BTC showed us was that to achieve 21st century goals we needed to get away from the 19th century classroom—we needed new practices. The research into how to build a thinking classroom told us that if we want our students to think, then we need to

- use thinking tasks;

- frequently form random groupings;

- use vertical nonpermanent surfaces;

- defront the classroom;

- only answer keep-thinking questions;

- give tasks early, standing, and verbally;

- give check-your-understanding questions;

- be intentionally less helpful;

- create and manage flow;

- consolidate from the bottom;

- use meaningful notes;

- evaluate what you value;

- communicate to students where they are and where they are going; and

- report out based on data (not points).

Each of these empirically deduced practices is a response to the question of how we can enact our core classroom routines so as to maximize student thinking. The research into BTC began in 2003. By 2014, some of the optimal thinking practices had begun to emerge from the data, each of which was obvious and surprising, liberating and frightening, simple and complex. And this pattern continued. Each thinking practice that emerged from the data was forehead-slapping obvious (if we want students to think, then we have to give them something to think about) and complex (what constitutes a good thinking task and how do we find and/or make them)—far too complex to be captured in the list above, a keynote, or an article. This is not to say that efforts were not made. I gave talks and wrote articles—neither of which could fully encapsulate the complexity of each practice. The only ways teachers could really learn about the nuances was through workshops—access to which were hampered by vastness of geography and the limits of time.

In October 2020, the book *Building Thinking Classrooms in Mathematics: 14 Teaching Practices for Enhancing Learning* (Liljedahl, 2021) was released. For the first time, research that had taken, to that point, more than 15 years to collect, analyze, and make sense of now lived in a form that allowed teachers to access it without having to be in a workshop. And access it they did. Since publication, BTC has taken on a life of its own. Teachers have begun building their own thinking classrooms and students have begun experiencing math as something to be thought about—in groups and on their own. Students are more often now standing rather than sitting, writing on whiteboards rather than paper, working in groups rather than individually, and even working in groups of groups, rather than groups working in isolation (see Figures i.1 and i.2).

Figure i.1 | Kindergarten students working together in groups of two at whiteboards.

Photo credit: **Erin Null**

Figure i.2 | Fifth-grade students working together in groups of three at Wipebook whiteboards.

Photo credit: **Erin Null**

More classrooms have been defronted, tasks are being given verbally to groups of students huddled around the teacher, and flow is being maintained through hints and extensions. And so much more. The book—and the book clubs, Facebook groups, and PLCs that have sprung up around BTC—enabled teachers all over the world to build their own thinking classroom without having to attend a workshop with me. This is not to say that I became obsolete. Countless requests to visit book clubs, to lead workshops, and to give talks started pouring in. Teachers had questions and assumed I had all the answers.

At the same time, school districts, divisions, and boards the world over began systematically supporting teachers in their pursuit to implement thinking classrooms. Some did this on their own, using only the book and publicly available podcasts, interviews, and presentations I had given over the years. Others asked me to provide workshops to their teachers—including a collection of school divisions in and around Regina, Canada, whom I partnered with starting in the fall of 2021 to provide ongoing workshops to groups of teachers wanting to implement the BTC practices. This is where I met Maegan Giroux.

Maegan was the math instructional coach for the Regina Catholic School Division and worked hard to support elementary teachers in their implementation of BTC in their K–8 classrooms. In this work, Maegan spent three years walking along side teachers as they implemented the 14 BTC practices. She taught and cotaught countless lessons and gave numerous workshops.

Across these many interactions—myself more globally and Maegan more locally—one of the questions we encountered the most was, *"Where can we get more tasks?"* The *Building Thinking Classrooms in Mathematics* book had some, and it referenced where teachers could find additional tasks. Maegan, together with Kyle Webb, had compiled a further 800+ tasks (https://tasks.kylewebb.ca/). But teachers wanted more. And until now, our response to this has been, "No, you don't." We are drowning in tasks. Our textbooks are full of them, tasks are posted on X (Twitter) and Facebook in droves, and if we do a Google search for "problem of the day" we get 7 trillion hits. We do not need more tasks. And yet the requests kept coming.

After some time, we began to realize that the request for more tasks was not to be taken literally—it was a proxy. Teachers weren't asking where they could get more tasks. They were asking

1. where they could find more good tasks—tasks that had been tested in classrooms, with real students, and had been shown to work;

2. where they could find tasks that could help them build their own thinking classroom;

3. where they could find tasks that address specific curriculum outcomes or standards; and

4. where they could learn how to implement specific tasks to ensure they were successful.

That's what this book is about—tasks. Lots of tasks—tasks that have been tested in diverse classrooms with real students and have been shown to be effective at shifting student engagement, transforming student thinking and learning behavior, and promoting learning of specific curricular outcomes and standards. Lots of tasks—but not so many that you have difficulty deciding which ones to choose.

Here's the thing, though: tasks are inert and incapable of achieving any of these goals on their own. They need pedagogy to bring them to life. So, although this book is ostensibly about tasks, what this book is *really* about is how to use these tasks to achieve the pedagogical goals of BTC and the curricular goals set by your jurisdiction. As such, this book also offers a deep dive into several of the BTC practices and discusses how to use these practices to breathe life into each of the tasks in this book. At the same time, these tasks also become the context through which we can work on enhancing our familiarity and competency with these BTC practices.

> What this book is *really* about is how to use these tasks to achieve the pedagogical goals of BTC and the curricular goals set by your jurisdiction.

WHO IS THIS BOOK FOR?

This book has been written for five distinct, but related, audiences. First, this book is for the teacher who has read *Building Thinking Classrooms in Mathematics: 14 Teaching Practices for Enhancing Learning*, has used the macro- and micro-moves detailed in each chapter to build their own thinking classroom, and is now looking for more tasks to feed their thinking classroom. Second, this book is for the teacher who has read the BTC book, has not yet begun to implement the BTC practices in their classroom, but is looking for more tasks in anticipation of doing so.

If you have read the main BTC book, you are aware that it contains very good tasks for building and maintaining your thinking classroom. And if you have been following the BTC movement through social media, you may also be aware that although the tasks in the main BTC book are good, these are now tasks that are "out there," and many students have already seen them. This was unlikely when the BTC book was first released in 2020, but as BTC has become more and more popular, there is greater likelihood that your students have previously been in a thinking classroom in some shape or form, and there is greater likelihood that they have been exposed to the tasks in the BTC book. Maybe last year's teacher used them in an effort to build their thinking classroom. Or maybe, you were last year's teacher, and you have, for example, shifted from teaching Kindergarten to Grade 1 or from teaching a 2/3 blended class to a 4/5 blended class. Regardless, tasks like The Answers Are (BTC, p. 168) or Farmer John (BTC, p. 184) have become very popular among K through Grade 5 teachers and are being used in classrooms all over the world—whether in a thinking classroom or not. More good tasks are needed for you to build and sustain your thinking classroom. If this is what you are looking for, then this book is for you.

The third audience, like the first two, is teachers who have read the BTC book and used the macro- and micro-moves detailed in each chapter to build their own thinking classroom. Unlike the first two audiences, however, they are looking not for more tasks—although more tasks are nice—but for more ideas on how to implement the BTC practices, including how to implement curricular tasks, more examples of thin-slicing, more examples of consolidation, more ideas for check-your-understanding (CYU) questions, and more in-depth information on implementing meaningful notes.

Although the BTC book was published in 2020, the ideas that are in it were, so to say, locked in in 2019. Since that time, the research on BTC has not stood still. I have continued to work in classrooms with real teachers and real students. And new practices have emerged. These practices are mostly in the form of micro-moves—important micro-moves that are proving to make the macro-moves easier to implement and more effective in engaging students in thinking. Some of these new practices are in this book. If this is what you are looking for, then this book is also for you.

The fourth audience is the teachers who may know little to nothing about thinking classrooms, have not read the BTC book, but who have been working on crafting a student-centered, problem-based classroom and are in search of good tasks. If this is what you are looking for, then this book is also for you. However, you will find more than what you were looking for as each of the tasks in this book is wrapped in BTC practices that may help you to be more successful in achieving your goals and may move you to want to learn more about *Building Thinking Classrooms*.

Finally, this book is also for the "middle children" (Vardabasso, 2023) of education—the consultants, coaches, coordinators, numeracy leads, and so on. It is for those who are not teachers but work with teachers and, as such, are in need of tasks they can use to introduce and showcase the best and most authentic picture of a thinking classroom.

STRUCTURE OF THE BOOK

To be able to address each of the five aforementioned audiences, this book contains four parts:

- Part 1: BTC Practices: In Review and in the New
- Part 2: Non-Curricular Tasks
- Part 3: Curricular Tasks
- Part 4: From Page to Practice

Part 1: BTC Practices: In Review and in the New

Part 1 of the book provides a brief review of the eight BTC practices that are most relevant to the use of tasks:

1. What kinds of tasks to use (BTC, Chapter 1);

2. How, when, and where to give tasks (BTC, Chapter 6);

3. How to build and utilize student autonomy (BTC, Chapter 8);

4. How to use hints and extensions to maintain flow (BTC, Chapter 9);

5. How to consolidate the task(s) (BTC, Chapter 10);

6. How to have students make meaningful notes (BTC, Chapter 11);

7. How to have students do check-your-understanding questions (BTC, Chapter 7); and

8. How to use tasks as the context to improve student competencies (BTC, Chapter 12).

Each chapter culminates with answers to some frequently asked questions (FAQ). Part 1 of the book ends with a chapter on how to pull all these practices together into a lesson—What Does a Lesson Look Like in a Thinking Classroom (BTC, Chapter 15).

Part 1 is both more and less than what the corresponding chapters in the BTC book offer. More because it offers new research results leading to new nuances and insights in some of these practices. Less because, new insights aside, it is still just a review. To get a full depth of understanding of each of these practices you really need to have read the corresponding chapters in the primary BTC book. Regardless, what Part 1 does is set you up to best be able to extract the full affordances that each of the tasks in Parts 2 and 3 of the book have to offer.

Part 2: Non-Curricular Thinking Tasks

Part 2 is a collection of 20 non-curricular tasks, each of which goes *way* beyond just the task. Each begins with a statement of the task in its simplest form, followed by five specific indicators that will help you quickly select which non-curricular tasks are right for you and your students at this specific point in your journey to build a thinking classroom:

- Grades—what grade level(s) the task is appropriate for

- Content Potential—what mathematics topics students may encounter while solving this task

- Perseverance Scales—how much perseverance the students will need to solve this task for a variety of suitable grades

- Macro-Moves—which of the 14 BTC practices are specifically supported by the task

- Competencies—what student competencies can be introduced and/or enhanced by engaging in this task

TASK 1: HEXAGON HAVOC

TASK

Write the numbers 1, 1, 2, 2, 3, 3 into 6 connecting hexagons without having hexagons with the same number touching one another.

Grades: K–1

Content Potential: patterning, counting, writing numbers

Perseverance Scale:

Grade Level	K	1
Perseverance Level	1	1

Macro-Moves: using hints and extension to maintain flow, consolidating from the bottom

Competencies: looking for patterns

After these indicators comes the actual task presented in a comprehensive format that will help you launch, facilitate, and consolidate the task.

This includes the following:

- Launch Script—a detailed script on how to launch the task with your students

- Creating Access—a set of notes about how to create access to the task for different grade or ability levels

- Extension Script—a detailed script on how to extend groups when they have solved the original, and subsequent, problems

- Author Solutions—a discussion of the ideas central to the solution of the task

- Student Solutions—a set of possible student solutions

- Suggested Hints—a set of hints that can be used to help move students from one solution to another

- Consolidation—a discussion of what is critical to pull out of the solutions during consolidation as well as (embedded within the sequence of student solutions) the order in which the task can be consolidated, with key solution elements highlighted

- Check-Your-Understanding Questions—new types of CYU questions (discussed in Part 1 of the book) that can be used to help students assess and consolidate their individual understanding from the task

- Author Notes—helpful comments, suggestions, tips, and tricks about the launch, facilitation, and consolidation of the task gleaned from multiple experiences using the task with students

- Notes to My Future Forgetful Self—a space for you to add your own helpful comments, suggestions, tips, and tricks about the launch, facilitation, and consolidation of the task gleaned from your own experiences using the task with your students

Taken together, these tasks provide you with the comprehensive information you need, regardless of why you are reading this book. Whether you are just looking for good tasks, more tasks for your BTC classroom, or wanting to refine and enhance your BTC teaching practices, the detailed presentation of each task will give you what you need. And if you want more tasks, Part 4 of the book provides a catalog listing resources for more tasks along with access to a task template for you to explore and build out your own indicators.

Part 3: Curricular Thinking Tasks

In Part 3, we share a collection of 30 curricular tasks. Each of these is built out from an initial task into a sequence of tasks that get progressively more challenging as students abilities increase (called *thin-slicing*). Unlike non-curricular tasks, however, by the time you get to these curricular tasks, there is an assumption that most of the BTC practices are well established within your classroom norms and routines. As such, the focus on curricular tasks is less on how we teach (BTC practices) and more on what we teach (content and competencies). This is not to say that you should stop working on the BTC practices. These take months for both you and your students to become proficient and comfortable with. But in this part of the book, the focus is more on the content.

To this end, in order to help you decide whether the content of a particular task is appropriate for you and your students, each task begins with a brief description of what the task sequence is. This is followed by four salient indicators to help you locate the task sequence within your curriculum and your progress in a thinking classroom:

- Content—the mathematics topics the task covers
- Competencies—which student competencies can be introduced and/or enhanced by engaging in this task sequence
- Seen Before—a list of topics that students have previously seen
- Before You Launch—tips to be aware of before you launch

TASK 21: STAR, STAR, MOON

TASK
This task will have students extending and completing repeating shape patterns.

Content: recognizing and completing a repeating pattern

Competencies: collaboration, communication, willingness to take risks

Seen Before: a basic AB repeating pattern

Before You Launch: Use the images available for download to create slips of paper that you give to groups to keep them in flow.

After the content and competency indicators comes the actual task sequence presented in a format that will help you launch, facilitate, and consolidate the sequence:

- Launch Script—a detailed script on how to launch the task with your students

- Task Sequence—a list, broken into three types, of progressively more challenging tasks (thin-sliced tasks) that the students can move through within one lesson or concept

- Hints—occasional hints that can be used to help move students' thinking as you move them from one type of task to another

- Consolidation Tasks—a set of three tasks that can be used to facilitate a new type of consolidation specific to these types of (thin-sliced) curricular tasks (discussed in Chapter 5)

- Student Notes to Their Future Forgetful Selves—a new template (discussed in Chapter 6) for having students make meaningful notes as a way to organize their thinking from the activity as well as to create a record of this thinking

- Check-Your-Understanding Questions—the task concludes with a new format of related CYU questions (discussed in Chapter 7) that can be used to help students assess and consolidate their individual understanding from the task

- Author Notes—helpful comments, suggestions, tips, and tricks about the launch, facilitation, and consolidation of the task gleaned from multiple experiences using the task with students

- Notes to My Future Forgetful Self—a space for you to add your own helpful comments, suggestions, tips, and tricks about the launch, facilitation, and consolidation of the task gleaned from your own experiences using the task with your students

Although each of these curricular tasks can be used to take students through specific topics across a wide range of grades and curricula, this list is not comprehensive. That is, there is no grade or curricula that is entirely covered by these 30 examples. This means that you are going to have to start making your own (thin-sliced) sequences— either from scratch or from existing resources—of tasks to use with students on topics that you teach. Part 4 of the book will provide you with help to do this.

Part 4: From Page to Practice

Part 4 is going to help you move beyond the book and shows you where else you can find good tasks—both curricular and non-curricular. More importantly, Part 4 will teach you how to make your own thin-sliced sequences of curricular tasks. This part of the book has five sections:

- Where to Find More Tasks

- How to Thin-Slice From Scratch

- How to Thin-Slice Existing Curriculum Resources

- How to Thin-Slice Word Problems

- How to Thick-Slice

Each of these sections is about finding and/or making tasks for the thinking classroom—both curricular and non-curricular. Each section ends by providing you with task templates into which you can embed your work to build a living archive of tasks for your—and others'—thinking classrooms.

HOW TO READ THIS BOOK

Who you are will determine, to a great extent, how you should read this book. Regardless, we urge all of you to read Part 1. Whether you are new to BTC or a seasoned user, there are new things in Part 1 that you need to understand to make sense of Parts 2 and 3.

If you are just beginning, go to Part 2, which contains all the non-curricular tasks you need to build a culture of thinking in your classroom. The indicators at the beginning of each task will help you decide which tasks are appropriate for your students. Keep in mind that these indicators are only a guide, and you need to reflect realistically about where you and your students are in your journey to build a thinking classroom. Also keep in mind that your class is not a homogeneous collection of students all in possession of the same interests, curiosities, and prerequisite abilities. When in doubt, start easier and allow the class as a whole to show you what they are capable of and ready for. Once you have done four to six non-curricular tasks with your students, move on to Part 3.

If you already have a thinking classroom, then Part 2 still has value to you—just not right now. But it will be useful at the start of a new school year when you need to build up a culture of thinking anew, or when your already thinking students come back from an extended break and they need to be re-immersed into a culture of thinking. For the time being, however, you may want to jump to Part 3.

If you already have a culture of thinking, or have just recently developed one, and you want to leverage this culture toward curriculum, go to Part 3. As in Part 2, the indicators will help you to find appropriate thin-sliced sequences of tasks for your students. There are 30 tasks spread across six grades, which means that although you will for sure find curricular thin-sliced tasks you can use in your classroom, you will not find nearly enough to sustain you for an entire school year, but that is the point. These are designed to be examples to give you models to make your own. This is what Part 4 of the book is for. But before you jump to Part 4, we urge you to examine each of the 30 curricular thinking task sequences. There are patterns in these tasks that will help make Part 4 make sense. In fact, we are confident that if you do examine each of the 30 curricular tasks and the patterns within the structures of the task, you will be able to build your own curricular task sequences without too much help from Part 4.

Once you have looked at all of the curricular task sequences, go to Part 4 for helpful tips and resources on how to build your own curricular task sequences. Here you will come to see that it really is not as difficult as you have made it out to be, and you will quickly realize that you have the knowledge and the ability to sustain your thinking classroom through a whole year of curriculum.

In the meantime, enjoy the journey to building, sustaining, and leveraging your own thinking classroom. It will re-invigorate you as a teacher and you will find joy in watching students think, make meaning, and learn.

Peter Liljedahl & Maegan Giroux

PART 1

BTC PRACTICES: IN REVIEW AND IN THE NEW

"Given the enormity of the problems we all face, I am especially eager for teachers to implement the ideas and techniques in *Building Thinking Classrooms*. Could there be anything more important and pressing than teaching students how to think?"

—Tracy Johnston Zager
Author of *Becoming the Math Teacher You Wish You'd Had: Ideas and Strategies From Vibrant Classrooms*

When the main *Building Thinking Classrooms in Mathematics* book (hereafter referred to as the BTC book or the main BTC book) was published, it contained the results of 15 years of research with more than 400 teachers and the results of thousands of micro-experiments on what works in real classrooms to get students to think. But this was not the culmination. The research continued. In this part of the book, we summarize some of the results of the original research as well as some of the results of the new research to bring you up to speed on the practices that are relevant to Parts 2 and 3 of this book.

As mentioned in the introduction, Part 1 is both *less than* and *more than* the details in the main BTC book. It is *less than* in that this is, to some degree, a summary. We go into only eight of the 14 BTC practices, and we do not go into the same level of detail that the main BTC book does. We do not revisit the FAQ that are in the main BTC book. So, as you read Part 1 of this book and you find yourself with questions or you find yourself saying "yeah, but ..." we strongly urge you to read, or reread, the relevant chapters in the original BTC book.

At the same time, this summary is *more than* the original book in that it presents exciting new results around consolidation (BTC, Chapter 10), meaningful notes (BTC, Chapter 11), and check-your-understanding questions (BTC, Chapter 7). Some of these results are relevant to both non-curricular tasks (Part 2 of this book) and curricular tasks (Part 3 of this book). Others are relevant to only curricular tasks. But these new results are built on the same foundational realizations that are presented in the main BTC book and the same FAQ are relevant. So, as you read about these new results, if you find yourself with questions or saying "yeah, but ..." we again urge you to read, or reread, the relevant chapters in the original BTC book.

With that in mind, what follows is a summary of the eight BTC practices and one lesson framework that are most relevant to this book with its focus on tasks:

1. What kinds of tasks to use (BTC, Chapter 1);

2. How, when, and where to give tasks (BTC, Chapter 6);

3. How to build and utilize student autonomy (BTC, Chapter 8);

4. How to use hints and extensions to maintain flow (BTC, Chapter 9);

5. How to consolidate the task(s) (BTC, Chapter 10);

6. How to have students make meaningful notes (BTC, Chapter 11);

7. How to use check-your-understanding questions (BTC, Chapter 7);

8. How to use tasks as the context to improve student competencies (BTC, Chapter 12); and

9. What does a lesson look like in a thinking classroom? (BTC, Chapter 15)

Missing from this list are summaries of the original BTC book's Chapter 2 (how we form collaborative groups—frequent visibly random groups) and Chapter 3 (where students work—vertical non-permanent surfaces). In this book, we are taking as shared that we should be using visibly random groups every period and that students should be working at vertical non-permanent surfaces (VNPS). Nothing has changed with respect to these practices. They are cornerstones of BTC, and all other practices are built on the foundation that they anchor. If you are not familiar with these practices, we suggest you read Chapters 2 and 3 in the main BTC book.

The same is true for BTC Chapter 4 (how we arrange furniture—we defront the classroom) and Chapter 5 (how we answer questions—only answer keep-thinking questions). As with random groups and vertical surfaces, these are practices that are vital to building and sustaining a thinking classroom and are not to be disregarded. Students don't listen to what we say. They listen to what we do. And holding onto the aesthetics of an overly organized classroom tells students that perfection is what matters. Thinking is not perfect. It is full of errors and wrong turns. And it is messy. A defronted classroom tells students that this is OK. Likewise, not answering students' proximity and stop-thinking questions tells students that you have confidence in them—that they are all capable and all equal. Students listen to what we do. The principles of Chapters 4 and 5 are not dispensable. If you have further questions about these practices, we suggest you read Chapters 4 and 5 in the main BTC book.

Also omitted are summaries of Chapters 13 and 14 on formative and summative assessment of content, respectively. Like the other chapters, these are important practices and are not dispensable. But, they are different. Unlike the rest of the practices in the main BTC book, formative and summative assessment have way more institutional constraints on them. How you assess can be dictated by outside forces. This is not true of how you form groups or how you answer questions. Further, assessment is a practice that occupies time at the scale of the unit. The other practices in the main BTC book occupy time at the scale of the lesson. This is not to say that assessment does not happen in the context of a lesson, but it does not happen every lesson. The focus in this book is on the lesson; consequently, we have not woven assessment of content into it. Having said that, we still review and use rubrics for the assessment and development of student behaviors (BTC, Chapter 12). Unlike assessment of content, assessment of behaviors can happen in every lesson.

Having discussed what is not included in this book, what follows is a review of the eight practices and a lesson framework that are particularly relevant to the use of tasks—at the lesson level. Importantly, the reviews include some critical evolutions, updates, and nuances about these particular practices that are important to consider when getting students to think about mathematics using both non-curricular and curricular tasks. At the end of each short chapter, you will also find answers to the most frequently asked questions (FAQ) we get from educators, as well as some questions for you to think about.

CHAPTER 1

WHAT KINDS OF TASKS TO USE

If we want our students to think, we need to give them something to think about. And that something is a task. This seems obvious—maybe too obvious. But there is irony in this obviousness. There has been a huge movement in mathematics education for the last 30 years to make and find the ideal tasks. Much of this movement is predicated on the assumption that a good task will solve all our issues in math education—that what is missing are good tasks. It is very easy to get swept up in this idea. In fact, you may recall from the main BTC book, Peter's first encounter with Jane was around this very issue—good tasks. Jane wanted to introduce problem solving to her students and she assumed that all she needed was good tasks. Peter's response was to provide her with good tasks. The ensuing disastrous lessons proved that good tasks were not enough to get students to think—we need other things as well, and the main BTC book and the remainder of Part 1 of this book are all about what these other things are. But, we still need good tasks. Although insufficient on its own, a good task is a necessary condition for building a thinking classroom. Let's look closer at three elements of a good thinking task and what can enhance their use:

1. Hallmarks of a good thinking task

2. Manipulatives as support for thinking tasks

3. The use of technology with thinking tasks

HALLMARKS OF A GOOD THINKING TASK

So, what makes a good task? It turns out there are three distinct qualities that make a mathematical task a good thinking task:

1. It has a low floor.

2. It has a high ceiling.

3. It is novel.

Again, this may sound obvious, but there are some important things to understand about these traits. First, a good task has a low floor (Papert, 1980)—a way for every student to be able to start. This is incredibly important. But why? Every jurisdiction that we have worked in for the last several years is striving to achieve equity within and through education. But what does this mean? How does this affect teachers' day-to-day practice?

When we talk to teachers about this, they have a difficult time articulating what they are meant to be doing differently in their classroom and they often default to saying things like "making things equal," "inclusion," and "this is important." It is important.

> Equity is what we want to achieve. Creating access is one of the ways we achieve it.

They are having difficulty because equity is a goal and equity is an outcome—but the day-to-day work of achieving the outcome of equity lies in creating access. Equity is what we want to achieve. Creating access is one of the ways we achieve it. This is something that is much easier for teachers to think about as they plan and execute their day-to-day teaching. "How can I create access for my students?" is a question teachers can answer. And this is why a good task needs to have a low floor. It creates access. To do otherwise would exclude some students in the classroom—it would make mathematics inaccessible. And inequitable.

Having a low floor doesn't mean that the task should be trivial. The second trait of a good task is that it also has a high ceiling (Papert, 1981)—meaning that everyone will meet challenge at some point in the task. When and where this happens is dependent on the student, their past experience, and their prior knowledge, but everyone needs to meet some level of challenge at some point in the task. It is through challenge that thinking is really unlocked. It is in the moments when we are stuck that we think.

There is a strong correlation between the thinking that occurs when we are stuck and the idea of *productive struggle* (SanGiovanni et al., 2020), which can be loosely defined as the willingness to persist through challenge and to keep trying even when progress is stalled. The work on BTC has shown that productive struggle is more of a state than it is a trait. Certainly, some students are more persistent than others, but even the most persistent student will give up under the wrong circumstances and even the most vulnerable student will persist under the right circumstances. What are the right circumstances? When a student meets challenge on the heels of success, they are more likely to enter into a state of productive struggle—to persist, to endure, and to eventually overcome. If students meet challenge without prior success—or worse, on the heels of failure—they are more likely to give up. Early success is key to later perseverance and productive struggle.

> Early success is key to later perseverance and productive struggle.

This further justifies the need for a good thinking task to have both a low floor and a high ceiling. The low floor not only ensures access, it creates opportunities for early success. And the high ceiling creates the opportunity for productive struggle.

The third quality of a good thinking task is novelty—it has to be something that the students have not seen before. This is because thinking is what we do when we don't know what to do. If we know what to do, we just do it—we mimic. Novelty ensures that the students can't mimic. It also ensures that, at some level and in some way, they will get stuck. And that is when they will think. They will try and they will fail and then they will try again. And then they will get unstuck. And when they do, they will learn. They will learn about mathematics, they will learn about themselves, and they will learn how to think. Along the way, they will also learn that being stuck is not a bad thing; it is just part of mathematics.

Teacher:	So, what's going on?
Student:	We're stuck.
Teacher:	So, what happens now?
Student:	We try to get unstuck.

This is not to say that all of this—low floor, high ceiling, and novelty—needs to be achieved within one big meaty task. By and large, most good thinking tasks are actually composed of a series of smaller tasks that get progressively more challenging. This progression allows for both a low floor and a high ceiling and ensures that novelty can be achieved, even if the initial task may be familiar to the students. This will be discussed more in Chapter 4 and is the basis of all of the non-curricular and curricular thinking tasks in Part 2 and Part 3, respectively, of this book.

Because of the diversity of the classrooms in which we teach, even the best tasks need extensions. Consider, for example, the following *Open Middle* task (Kaplinsky, 2019) intended for Grade 2 students:

> Using the digits 1 to 9 at most one time each, place a digit in each box to create an expression with the greatest possible value.
>
> $\square\square + \square\square - \square\square =$

This is a rich curricular task that has a low floor, high ceiling, and is likely novel to the students. Some students may start with trial and error—just plugging in digits to see if their new answer is more or less than their previous answer. Eventually, they may arrive at the conclusion that they need to make the first two two-digit numbers as large as possible and the third as small as possible. If they think about the first two two-digit numbers together and that one needs to be 90-something and the other 80-something, then they are off to a good start. But if they think of the first two-digit number on its own, they might start thinking that 98 is the best choice. Regardless, there is much to think about here, places to get stuck, and ways to get unstuck. But what to do with the students who eventually get the answer of 97 + 86 − 12 = 171 or 96 + 87 − 12 = 171?

> One of the main tenets of a thinking classroom is that no one ever gets to be done.

One of the main tenets of a thinking classroom is that no one ever gets to be done. We will talk more about this throughout Part 1. In the meantime, we give students who "finish" an extension:

> Using the digits 1 to 9 at most one time each, place a digit in each box to create an expression with a value close to 50.
>
> $\square\square + \square\square - \square\square =$

It doesn't matter how rich the original task is. All tasks need extensions—something that requires the students to do more thinking, to persist longer, and to keep struggling. And they will. The success on the first task makes it more likely that they will enter into a state of productive struggle on the next one. And so on. Consequently, all the tasks in this book contain extensions.

MANIPULATIVES AS SUPPORT FOR THINKING TASKS

Another facet of good thinking tasks worth exploring is that they can be brought to life through manipulatives. Manipulatives are central to the teaching and learning of mathematics.

> The evidence indicates, in short, that manipulatives can provide valuable support for student learning when teachers interact over time with the students to help them build links between the object, the symbol, and the mathematical idea both represent. (National Research Council, 2001, p. 354)

This is especially true in Grades K–5. And this truth is not diminished in a thinking classroom where manipulatives should be just as ubiquitous as they are in any other math classroom. In fact, in a thinking classroom, the thinking tasks we use are sometimes inseparable from manipulatives. Whether we are using 10-frames, pattern blocks, Unifix cubes, multiplex cubes, attribute blocks, fraction disks, Dienes blocks, Cuisenaire rods, or counters, manipulatives support students' early development of number, quantity, and shape. With respect to thinking tasks, manipulatives serve three distinct purposes:

1. Students think about the manipulatives.

2. Students think with the manipulatives.

3. Students represent their thinking with manipulatives.

Sometimes the manipulative is the context from which our tasks emerge. For example, consider pattern blocks (see Figure 1.1) and the following tasks:

Figure 1.1 | Pattern blocks

1. If the green triangle is worth $5, how much is the red trapezoid worth?

2. If the yellow hexagon is worth $12, what is the blue parallelogram worth?

3. If the blue parallelogram is with $8, how much is the red trapezoid worth?

Source: **Teacher Created Resources**

These three tasks emerge out of the manipulatives themselves—they are thinking about the manipulatives. Note that this task leverages both the color of each shape (as they are traditionally manufactured), the name of the shape, and the value of each one. Mentioning the color in addition to the shape is a low-floor tactic to help all children access the task if they don't yet have the mathematical vocabulary and is also a way of introducing new vocabulary.

Alternatively, they might use manipulatives to solve a task. For example, students might use Dienes blocks to solve tasks (see Figure 1.2).

Figure 1.2 | Dienes blocks

1. $8 + 7 =$
2. $24 + 35 =$
3. $85 + 37 =$

Source: EdxEducation

For these tasks, Dienes blocks allow the students to regroup ones into tens and tens into hundreds—they are thinking with the manipulatives.

A very particular form of thinking with manipulatives is for students to use manipulatives to help them *see* what the task is asking. For example, cubes (see Figure 1.3) are a good way to help students *see* the painted cube problem.

Figure 1.3 | Painted cube

A 3 × 3 × 3 cube is dipped in green paint and then left to dry. Once dry, the cube is taken apart into its 27 original smaller cubes. How many of those smaller cubes have black paint on 3 sides, 2 sides, 1 side, and 0 sides?

If students have access to cubes, they can build the $3 \times 3 \times 3$ shape to help them *see* what is being asked. And the ability to take the $3 \times 3 \times 3$ cube apart will help them to think about what the task is asking—they are thinking with the manipulatives.

The third way in which manipulatives are used with tasks is to help students represent and communicate their thinking. Solving tasks in groups requires copious amounts of communication, negotiation, and persistence. It is sometimes difficult for students to make themselves understood using only their words, and manipulatives can be used to mediate this process. For example, a student who is having difficulty explaining why the 49th term in ABCABCABC . . . is going to be A might grab some red (A), blue (B), and green (C) Unifix cubes to build the sequence RBGRBGRBGRBG. Using these 12 cubes they can show that the 12th cube is green, as are the 24th, the 36th, and 48th cubes. And so, the 49th cube is red. In this case, the student is not using manipulatives to think with—they have already done the thinking. Instead, they are using manipulatives to help their groupmates understand what they are trying to communicate—they are helping their groupmates to think with the manipulatives.

Regardless of the use, however, it is important that students have either explicit or implicit access to the manipulatives. Explicit access means you, as the teacher, decree that they are to use the manipulatives, and maybe even use them in a specific way. Explicit access to manipulatives is needed when students are solving tasks that require them to think about the manipulative—like the previous pattern block tasks. Implicit access means, most often, that there are several different manipulatives available to students should they need them. Students who want to use manipulatives to communicate their thinking—like the previous ABC pattern task—would then decide which ones they want and go get them. To think with manipulatives—like the painted cube example—students can have either explicit or implicit access to manipulatives.

Whichever purpose manipulatives are being used for, however, it is important to remember that manipulatives are only one form of mathematical representation—one of five representations as seen in the Lesh Translation Model (Lesh et al., 2003):

1. Manipulatives
2. Pictures
3. Written symbols
4. Verbal symbols
5. Real-life situations

It is important that what students learn is how to translate between these different representations. One of the best ways to ensure that translation between these five forms of mathematical representation is to make sure that they are doing more than one at the same time. This means that while they are manipulating, we also need them to be talking and drawing and writing. A thinking task gives students something to talk about and visibly random groups give students someone to talk with. But where is the best workspace when students are using manipulatives? Traditionally, this kind of work, along with most student work, has been done with students sitting at their desks. BTC showed us that working on a VNPS was far superior to working at a desk, and that turns out to be true when incorporating manipulatives as well. This is most easily achieved by having a group manipulate on the floor or a chair next to a VNPS (see Figure 1.4), on a desk or table pulled close to a VNPS (see Figure 1.5), or on a ledge or shelf at the VNPS (see Figure 1.6). The manipulatives give the students models to think about, think with, and communicate with while the VNPS provides a workspace that has been proven to create better engagement, enthusiasm, perseverance, knowledge mobility, time on task—and thinking. Together they work to help students translate between representations.

Figure 1.4 | Manipulating on the floor

Photo credit: **Maegan Giroux, 2023**

Figure 1.5 | Manipulating on a table

Photo credit: **Maegan Giroux, 2023**

Figure 1.6 | Manipulating on a ledge

Photo credit: **Maegan Giroux, 2023**

For very young students (Grades K–2), it is also possible to have them using manipulatives and writing on a horizontal non-permanent surface (HNPS) like a whiteboard lying on a table. In the original BTC research, it was clear that VNPSs were far superior to HNPSs (see BTC, Chapter 3). One of the reasons for this was that when students are sitting, they feel anonymous—and when students feel anonymous, they are more likely to disengage. This, it turns out, is an encultured response to sitting. That is, it is a phenomenon that becomes more and more prevalent the more years students have experienced normative classrooms. The power of VNPSs is in the standing. Standing takes away anonymity—and with it, the pull to disengage.

Primary students have not been encultured in this way . . . yet. So having them work at HNPSs does not elicit the same response as having high school students working at HNPSs. It also allows for ease of manipulating and talking, writing, and drawing in the same space at the same time—something that helps students to translate between representations. We recommend using HNPSs only with primary students. Even intermediate students will be lulled into disengagement if given the opportunity to sit while they work, even when working at an erasable surface.

THE USE OF TECHNOLOGY WITH THINKING TASKS

As with manipulatives, technology should be ubiquitous in a thinking classroom. And as with manipulatives, there are three main uses of technology in a thinking classroom. Whether we are using calculators, mathigon, microbits, or bee bots, students use technology as

1. a computational tool,

2. an exploratory tool, or

3. a coding tool.

The first of these involves students using technology to calculate results for expressions, to plot data, or to measure a geometric figure—all for the purposes of computing something. We found that for tasks that require computation, one device—preferably handheld—in each group is sufficient. This promotes collaboration in the same way that one marker per VNPS promotes collaboration. If everyone had their own marker and/or their own device, students would drift away from each other rather than toward each other. We further found that everything that goes into the device and comes out of the device must be written on the VNPS. The reason for this is twofold. First, students often make mistakes when keying something into a device. Writing down what they key in as well as the result that the technology gives makes it easier to spot input errors. Second, the person with the device can become separated from the group as they begin to do their own thing. By having the group, as a whole, decide what goes into the device, the technology becomes a communal tool rather than a tool that only one person uses.

Technology can also be an exploratory tool. For example, students can explore what happens to

- the remainder as you increase the dividend,
- the area of a triangle as you move one of the corners of the triangle to different points on a grid, or
- the average of four numbers as you increase one of the numbers.

All of these activities require students to work in a cycle of observing, conjecturing, and testing, and technology provides them with both outcomes to think about and a tool to test conjectures. As with technology as a computational tool, this works best when there is one device per group. And, although there is too much happening to record everything they do on the VNPS, this works best if they, at least, record their conjectures and the results of these conjectures. Having multiple data points on the VNPS is what will allow them to begin to see patterns.

Finally, technology can be used as a coding tool. Whether students are telling a turtle where they want it to go, programming a robot, directing a programmable car, or writing code to get a computer to complete some task, the technology is inseparable from the task—they are thinking about the technology. Coding, by its very nature, is exploratory. This is how we learn new functionality and how we debug our code, and both are achieved by making note of inputs and outputs. The difference between coding and the exploration we described is that, while exploration is often constrained to one or two variables, coding is more comprehensive, requiring students to bring together multiple routines. The other difference is that coding is rarely done on handheld devices; it is usually done on laptops and, as such, is difficult to do solely at a VNPS. We found that what worked best for coding was to have students work in groups of two, have access to both a VNPS and a desk or table where they can sit, and have one device for every group. Students can use the VNPS to plan out their code and to record some of their explorations.

It is important to remember that technology, like manipulatives, does not make a task good. A bad task with manipulatives is still a bad task. Likewise, it doesn't matter how good the animations are, or how many badges you get, technology does not make a bad task good. For a task to be good, it will still need to have a low floor, high ceiling, and novelty. In Chapter 4, we will look at how to achieve this through a sequence of tasks.

 What is the difference between a rich task and a non-curricular task?

 A rich task is any task that requires students to draw on a wide diversity of mathematical knowledge and to put this knowledge together in different ways in order to solve the problem. If some of this diverse knowledge happens to map onto the curriculum you are teaching, then the rich task can also be considered a curricular task—but only for those students who happen to use this curricular knowledge. For students who do not, this rich task is a non-curricular task.

The similarity between non-curricular tasks and rich tasks lies not in what they are as much as what they do—and what they both do well is engage. Consider the *Open Middle* task from earlier in this chapter:

> Using the digits 1 to 9 at most one time each, place a digit in each box to create an expression with the greatest possible value.
>
> $\square\square + \square\square - \square\square =$

For a Grade 3 student learning how to add and subtract two-digit numbers, this is a curricular task. For everyone else, this is a non-curricular task. Regardless, this is a rich task with the potential to tap into a variety of different ways to think about and represent numbers, to perform addition and subtraction, and what it means to regroup and decompose multi-digit numbers. And, for most, it is a highly engaging task that can be used in the early days of building a thinking classroom.

 Are all manipulatives good?

 Manipulatives are inert. They are neither good nor bad. What makes a manipulative good or bad is how it is used and for what purpose. Manipulatives, at their core, are a model to help mediate a connection between concrete and abstract ways of learning. Manipulatives that can be used to do this well are good manipulatives in that context and for that purpose. For example, popsicle sticks and rubber bands are a great manipulative when used to help students understand how regrouping and decomposing works when adding or subtracting two-digit numbers. Pattern blocks could not be used to achieve the same outcome to the same effect.

You use the word *tool* when talking about technology but not when talking about manipulatives. Why is that?

For us, a tool is something that you will always use to achieve a task. Just like a hammer will always be used to drive a nail, a calculator will always be used to perform arithmetic with very large or very small numbers. A calculator is a tool—you will always use it. Manipulatives are models. A model is useful for students to get from point A to point B, but with time, they will move past them. Consider, for example, popsicle sticks and rubber bands. This is a great model for how place value works. But a student will eventually move beyond the model and onto other models for adding and subtracting. Tools stay with us. As we acquire more abstract ways of thinking, we leave our models behind us.

Q If some members of a group are using manipulatives on the floor or a desk and one member is standing at the board, won't the group become fractured?

A Yes—but only if there is no communication between group members. The same can be said for having only one marker—one student is engaged in writing, the other two are not. The fact that one is writing while others manipulate can drive really good multi- and intra-representational conversation. But just like with the whiteboard marker, the roles should switch and switch frequently.

Q I don't like using manipulatives because the students just play with them rather than using them how I want. The same is true of technology. How do I prevent this?

A Don't prevent it. Trying to get children to not play is like trying to hold back the ocean with a broom. Know that whenever you give students a new manipulative or a new technology, they need 20 minutes to get the yaya's out. They need to play. Let them. If you do not, they will anyways. But you can use this to your advantage. Let them play and then vector that play as the means through which they become familiar with the manipulative and/or technology.

Q You talk about the use of manipulatives as something they can think with. The example you gave was blocks to help students think about the painted cube problem. Wouldn't they think more if we didn't give them a manipulative?

A Students are still thinking even with the manipulative. What they are doing, however, is *visualizing*. Visualizing is what we do when we don't have a visual. If we have a visual, we tend not to visualize. So, if the type of thinking you want students to do is visualize, then do not give them a visual—whether that comes in the form of a manipulative or technology. To be clear, we are not saying to not use visuals. Use them. And use them a lot. But recognize that if you want to develop the skill of visualization, you need to withhold the visual from time to time.

> Visualizing is what we do when we don't have a visual.

Alternatively, when we do the painted cube task, for example, we show them a $3 \times 3 \times 3$ cube. We use it to explain the task. And then we put it away. Then, while the students are working on the task at their whiteboards, we carry the cube with us and let groups use it to explain their thinking. But then we take it away. And if there is a group that is really struggling to visualize, we would leave the cube with them for a while. In this fashion, we are using the visual to support visualizing rather than replace visualizing.

Questions to Think About

1. What in this chapter feels immediately correct?

2. What in this chapter challenges you?

3. Think about a task that you have used in the past that really got students to think. Reflect on this task through the lens of some of the things you learned in this chapter. What were the things about the task that made it good?

4. In this chapter you learned about the different purposes for manipulatives. Think about the last time you used manipulatives in your classroom. Which purpose were you using them for?

5. In this chapter you also learned about the three uses of technology. Think about the last time you used technology in your classroom. What were you using it for?

6. Think about a task that will be made better with the use of manipulatives and/or technology. Why will it get better with the use of manipulatives and/or technology?

7. Now think about a task that would not be made better with the use of manipulatives and/or technology. Why will it not get better with the use of manipulatives and/or technology?

CHAPTER 2
HOW, WHEN, AND WHERE TO GIVE TASKS

This book has 50 tasks in it—20 non-curricular and 30 curricular. All of them have been tested in the classroom and all have been proven to be very good. Now that you have these 50 tasks, let's discuss how, when, and where you are going to give them to your students.

HOW TO GIVE THINKING TASKS

In a normative classroom, the most common methods teachers use to give a task are to either write the task on the board or project it on the screen, to give it as a handout or worksheet, or to ask students to do a specific task out of the textbook. The BTC research revealed that, of these, the textbook produced the least amount of thinking because textbook tasks are viewed by students as tasks that they are asked to do after they have been shown how. Textbook tasks are mimicking tasks. Students did not bring that same assumption to a task handwritten on the board.

However, the BTC research also revealed that we got the most thinking out of students when the task was given verbally—perhaps with some gestures, modelling, and details written on the board. This result shocked us—so much so that we trialed and verified this result over and over again. The data spoke clearly, telling us that verbal was best in every grade and every context—even in classrooms with large multilingual learner populations. Yet, despite all of the data, we still had a tough time believing it. Here are some things that helped us understand why that is:

1. We already know, at a visceral level, that verbal instructions are better than textual instructions. Case in point—if you have a student who is struggling to decode a word problem, your first intervention is, and always has been, to go over it with them verbally.

2. From an evolutionary biology perspective, we have been verbal for much longer than we have been literate.

This does not explain everything about these results, but the results are still clear—verbal is better. This is not to say that you don't have individual students who will have difficulty processing verbal instructions—every class does. But you have far fewer students who have difficulty processing verbal instructions than have challenges processing instructions in text form. The odds are that some of the students who have difficulty processing verbal instructions also have difficulty processing written instructions.

In normative classrooms we have always operated on the idea that it is a principle of efficiency to have every individual student understand the instructions. And because of this we write them, say them, model them, do turn-and-talk, Q&A, and then do it again with feeling for those who still did not understand. Ironically, this is hugely inefficient. In a thinking classroom, we do not need everyone to understand the instructions when we first tell them what we want them to do. We just need *enough* students to understand the instructions. The power of collaboration that is fostered in a thinking classroom will take care of the rest. Students are not working alone. They are embedded in a group that is surrounded by other groups. And you are still a teacher in the room who can intervene as necessary. We call it the "firefighter approach." Give the instructions verbally. Then go out and put out any fires. It is much more efficient than trying to prevent the fires.

> We call it the "firefighter approach." Give the instructions verbally. Then go out and put out any fires. It is much more efficient than trying to prevent the fires.

Now, to be clear, being verbal does not mean that you are *exclusively* verbal. We are trying to reduce cognitive load, not increase it. If you are talking about a table of data, give them the data on a piece of paper. If you are talking about a pattern, write the pattern on the board. If there is a detail in the problem you are talking about—"there are 125 students"—then write that detail on the board. What you want them to do with this data, pattern, or detail, however, you verbalize.

This, of course, does not explain how we prepare students to cope with the word problems that are a staple of standardized assessment. If you work in such a setting, then you need to prepare your students to be tolerant of, and competent with, information given textually. To do this, you need to first recognize that there is a difference between *building* a thinking classroom and *having* a thinking classroom.

For the first three to four weeks, you are still building a thinking classroom. During this time, be verbal. Once the norms and routines of a thinking classroom have been established, if you need to prepare students to know what to do with written problems, you can begin to give tasks in textual form—slowly and occasionally at first and then with more regularity. When doing so, you can simply give a group the task on a slip of paper. However, the research shows that when doing this, you should use small font and very limited white space. This, it turns out, is true any time you give the students information on paper at their VNPSs—whether it is a table of values, a drawing, a geometric figure, or a word problem. This is because when students are given larger paper with larger fonts and diagrams, they tend to attach the paper to the VNPS and then work on the paper. We also know that students behave differently when writing on paper than when writing on erasable surfaces. When the font and diagrams are small with limited white space, they recreate the information on the VNPS and proceed with the same risk-taking and engagement they normally would.

Even if you offer tasks in written form from time to time because you *have* a thinking classroom, recognize that being verbal is still better for your students, so you should not make written tasks the norm. Verbal instructions give more, and immediate, access to the majority of your students. As a result, every task in this book comes with a launch script that details what you say and what you show. If you need students to engage with some of these through written instructions, it will be easy enough for you to turn part of the script into a written version of the task.

WHEN TO GIVE A THINKING TASK

The research shows us that we need to get our students thinking within the first five minutes of the lesson. To be clear, this is from when you declare the lesson is starting, not from when the bell rings. As a teacher, there are often a lot of things to take care of in the first few minutes of class. You may need to take attendance, collect consent forms, do show-and-tell, and/or have circle time. In K–5 classrooms, the lesson doesn't begin when the bell, if there is a bell, rings. It begins when you transition to math time. From that point, you have five minutes.

> One of the key things to getting students to think is to get out of their way. To stop assuming that they can't and start assuming that they can.

For those of us who are used to demonstrating and lecturing to our students at the beginning of the lesson before we turn them loose to do things on their own, this is difficult to comprehend. We are used to a method of teaching that assumes that the students don't know much and are incapable of making connections and figuring things out on their own. But they know things, and they are capable. They can make connections and they can figure things out if we can get them to think. One of the key things to getting students to think is to get out of their way. To stop assuming that they can't and start assuming that they can. We need to stop sucking the thinking out of the tasks we give them.

The longer we talk, the more we give away. We can't help it. As teachers we know so much, and we just want to ensure their success by removing all the anticipated barriers.

"If they use a T-chart it will be so much easier for them."

"Adding the ones digits first is more efficient."

"This task is faster to solve if you work backwards."

All of these statements are true—it will be easier, more efficient, and faster. And it will remove opportunities for students to think, to get stuck, to productively struggle, to succeed, and to learn. In North America, people talk about helicopter parents—the parents who hover over their children. In Sweden they don't talk about helicopter parents; they talk about curling parents—parents who sweep the path for their children, smoothing the way by removing any potential barriers and obstacles. But it's the rough patches where the learning happens. We need to avoid being curling teachers. And one of the best ways to do that is to not say too much before getting the students up to their VNPSs working in their random groups.

The other reason we need to get students thinking early into the lesson is that the transition from being a passive receiver of knowledge to being an active creator of knowledge is a difficult transition to make. And the longer we leave them in the role of passive receiver of knowledge, the more passive they become and the more difficult that transition becomes.

This is not to say that students can figure everything out on their own. There are things we need to tell them. Sometimes direct instruction is the correct thing to do when introducing a new concept or a new topic. Fine . . . you have five minutes. You have five minutes! What are you going to say in that time? When we give direct instruction, we are used to talking and demonstrating until we have prepared the students to do the most complex and nuanced variation of the task. To do this, we have to talk for a long time. But what if we only need to prepare them to do the first task in our sequence of increasingly complex tasks? Then they learn something from the first task that helps them to do the second task, and so on. We need to say less. We can always say more later in the form of a hint (see Chapter 4). To help you with this, the sequences of tasks we provide in this book come with hints that you can use when students have difficulty moving from one concept to another while moving through the sequences of tasks.

WHERE TO GIVE A THINKING TASK

Now that we know that the task should be given verbally in the first five minutes of the lesson, the next question is where should you and the students be when giving the task? The research shows that having the students stand in loose formation around you when you give the task is better than having them sitting in their desks as you tell them the instructions. The reasons for this, as with everything in BTC, turned out to be nuanced and varied.

First, the research on having the students stand and work on vertical whiteboards revealed something interesting about why having them sit and work on horizontal surfaces was so ineffective. As mentioned in Chapter 1, when students are sitting, they feel anonymous—they feel invisible. And the further they sit from the teacher the more anonymous they feel. When students feel anonymous, they disengage. This is both a conscious and a subconscious act. Also, when students feel invisible, they just aren't as attentive.

Having students stand near us, for the few minutes that we gave the instructions—whether we were just telling them the task or doing some direct instruction—made a huge difference. When the students were in their seats, only 50% were visibly engaged in what was being said and the teacher received 10 to 15 clarifying questions in the first few minutes of the activity. When the students were standing around the teacher, 90% of the students were visibly engaged and the teacher only got three clarifying questions in the first few minutes. The students were just more attentive when standing around the teacher. And teachers reported feeling like they were more connected to their students in these moments, saying that they felt like they were talking *with* their students rather than *at* their students.

Another benefit to having the students standing with you when giving the instructions is that the toughest part of the transition—getting students out of their desks—has already been achieved. Once the instructions have been given, you need only to randomize your students and get them going. Finally, having students standing around a table, regardless of grade, is the best way to demonstrate how to use a specific manipulative that you want them to have explicit access to for a task.

**FAQ**

Q I have a student who is not good at processing verbal instructions. Wouldn't a good adaptation for them be to also give the task in text form?

A Perhaps. But students who have difficulty processing verbal instructions often have difficulty when those instructions are given to the whole class and given well before they need to take action. They are often much more capable when the instructions are given directly to them, come in smaller packets of information, and come just in time to take action—all of which are things that happen within small groups in a thinking classroom. Begin by observing how this new environment supports them. And remember—you are still the teacher in the room and can intervene to provide more support whenever needed.

Q For years we were hearing about learning styles and how we should work toward students' specific strengths. What happened to those ideas?

A The early work on learning styles created an assumption that we have to cater to each and every learner's preferred learning style, and with equal intensity. Not only is this untenable, but it creates contradictions. For example, you are going to do some group work in your classroom—a thinking classroom or otherwise. You have a student who is not good at processing verbal information. So, you make sure you provide them (and maybe the whole class) with written instructions for what is to be done. Now the group work begins. How are the students communicating in those groups? Verbally. Even if we can use the ideas of learning styles to shape the way information flows from us to each student, we cannot control how information flows between students. Our response, in education, to the learning styles literature has been a little backwards.

Imagine that you are coaching a basketball team, and you have a player who is good at shooting, but bad at dribbling. What are you going to work on? We think you know the answer is dribbling. In all things in life, we work on our weaknesses. This does not mean that we do not play to our strengths. But we work on our weaknesses. We often do not get to choose how information comes to us in life. It could be verbal, textual, visual, or kinesthetic. Yes, we have strengths, but we need to also be able to be competent in the other forms. To develop competencies, students need time and opportunity to experience information coming at them in multiple forms. And they need support. These are all things that thinking classrooms offer.

Q What if I need to teach the students something before they can start their first task? How do I do that?

A First, you need to ask yourself whether what you want to teach is review or new information. If it is review, odds are that enough students in the room already know enough for a thinking classroom to begin without any direct teaching. Knowledge mobility (see Chapter 3) will take care of the rest. If you are not sure, ask a question in the launch, do a turn-and-talk, and see what comes out.

If it is truly new information, then teach it. But, keep in mind that you have five minutes. Also keep in mind that you want to say only enough to help them do the first task in your task sequence. Say what you need to say and maybe do one example. Do not repeat yourself endlessly and do not do multiple examples. Doing either will only serve to suck the thinking out of the room. Students don't learn well from us talking and showing more. They learn by doing, by making mistakes and correcting their mistakes. Students need to have opportunities to make meaning, not have meaning made for them.

> Students need to have opportunities to make meaning, not have meaning made for them.

Q Is the launch a good time to present vocabulary to students?

A Yes and no. If you are discussing things they encountered the lesson before, then it is a great time to introduce vocabulary—"The red shape is called a trapezoid," "Those are called prime numbers." Vocabulary makes sense when we are giving them words that name experiences they have already had with objects and ideas—we want to name their experiences. This works well at the end of the lesson as well.

If we are giving them the names of things they have yet to experience, the words are arbitrary and meaningless to them. They aren't anchored to anything. Hearing the phrase "order of operation" before they understand why it matters has no personal meaning. It is a name waiting for an experience. Let them experience ideas and objects first. Then name them.

Q If the goal is to reduce the transition time between the students getting the tasks and getting to work, wouldn't it be better to send the students to the boards first and then give them the instructions?

A In the original research, we tried this. It didn't work. Once the students were in their groups at the whiteboard, they were more interested in each other than anything we had to say. There are a lot of social dynamics to work through—both individually and collectively—when groups first come together. Students are nervous, excited, and sometimes disappointed with the group they have been randomly placed in. They are not listening to you while they are processing this. When we give students the task first and then randomize them, they are thinking about the task much more than what group they are in.

> When we give students the task first and then randomize them, they are thinking about the task much more than what group they are in.

Q I teach kindergarten. If I have my students standing around me, they touch each other. Can we have them sitting?

A Having students stand around the teacher during the launch is something we have seen work well in every grade. This is not to say that this is equally manageable in all grades. Primary students can get very goofy if you have them standing in close proximity to each other for too long. But, they are capable of standing and paying attention. It will take time to develop, but it will not develop if we do not work on it. For young students, less is more. Say less. Spend less time standing during the launch. Get them going.

Questions to Think About

1. What in this chapter feels immediately correct?

2. What in this chapter challenges you?

3. Think about a student you know will struggle with verbal instructions. Now think about the last time you worked with that student one-on-one to provide some support. What was your primary medium of communication?

4. Think about the last time you gave your students a set of instructions detailing what you wanted them to do. How long did it take? And how many times did you say the same thing by repeating yourself, modeling, and/or giving examples?

5. Think about a place in your room from where you can launch a task with all the students standing. Now think about a second space that you can launch from. Now think about a third. What kind of work do you need to do in your classroom to make sure that you have multiple places you can launch from with all the students standing in close proximity to you?

CHAPTER 3
HOW TO BUILD AND UTILIZE STUDENT AUTONOMY

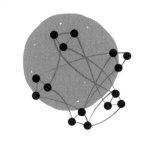

The autonomy students have to seek help from and give help to peers is an incredibly useful tool in the thinking classroom. There is so much knowledge in a classroom—the smartest person in the room is the room. When developed properly, student autonomy will help to mobilize the knowledge and get it into the hands and minds of other students. A thinking classroom, with its highly visible work surfaces and strong community, will naturally develop some degree of student autonomy. But this autonomy can be further developed with some direct attention to it.

A NEW WAY OF DEVELOPING STUDENT AUTONOMY

The BTC research showed that if we, as the teachers, are always the ones who give the next task, or are the only source of help when students get stuck, then we are stunting the development of student autonomy and limiting knowledge mobility—we become the knowledge keepers in the room. We need every student and every group of students to be, and to be seen as, knowledge keepers in the room. The way to develop this is to actively push students to seek out others' knowledge when they are stuck or they are done.

> We need every student and every group of students to be, and to be seen as, knowledge keepers in the room.

When a group is stuck, rather than stepping in and helping them, first see if there is a group that you can direct them to for help, either passively—"Look what they are doing"—or actively—"Let's go talk to this group." This may not always be the case. There may be no group that has the knowledge that can help the group that is stuck, and you will have to do it. But whenever possible, see if there is knowledge in the room that you can direct them to if a group is stuck.

The same is true if a group is done with a task. Rather than swooping in and giving them the next task, direct them to a group where they can get the next task—either passively or actively. To help with this, we developed something called the *banner*.

The banner is the top 6–8 inches (15–20 cm) of the whiteboard. There are three rules associated with the banner:

1. Whatever task a group is working on, and only the task they are currently working on, is written on the banner. Their work happens below the banner.

2. When a group is finished with their current task, they look around at other groups' banners and see if there is a task on one of them that they have not done yet, and they steal it for themselves. This new task then gets written on their own banner (see Rule #1).

3. A group is never to make up their own task and write it on the banner. They can make up their own task, but they are not to write it on the banner. This is because their task is likely not in line with the task sequence that you have in mind (see Chapter 4).

Figure 3.1 illustrates how a pair of first-grade students on the left have *stolen* the next task in the sequence from their neighbors on the right. In Figure 3.2, their teacher adds the next task in the sequence to a different group's banner.

Figure 3.1 | A pair of first-graders (left) has borrowed the next task from their neighbor's banner (right)

Photo Credit: Erin Null

Figure 3.2 | A first-grade teacher adds a new task to a banner

Photo Credit: **Erin Null**

The banner was developed after the publication of the main BTC book, and it has proven to be very useful for helping classes move through sequences of progressively more challenging tasks—especially tasks that can be given verbally. Most of the tasks in this book—non-curricular and curricular—work well with the banner. Once your thinking classroom becomes proficient with the banner, you only have to give out a new task once and the rest of the students get this task from each other's banners. This gives you more time to work on providing hints to groups that need it. As you will see in the next chapter, the ability to efficiently give extensions so you have more time for providing hints is vital to maintain the thinking during a lesson.

FAQ

Q Why bother with the banner? Wouldn't it just be easier to give the students all the tasks at once and let them work through them at their own pace?

A It is incredibly important that students feel present when they are working on the thinking tasks. Being present means that they are in the moment, focused on whatever they are doing, and using their empathy to care for their group mates. The research shows that it is very difficult for students to be present if we keep reminding them of the future. One of the ways we remind students of the future is to give them the whole task sequence all at once. It is incredibly difficult for students to be present on task 3 when they can see tasks 4–9. Using the banner allows students to see the tasks one at a time and will help them to stay present on the task at hand.

Incidentally, some of the other ways that we prevent students from being present are we set a timer, show them an agenda, tell them that they all have to complete the same amount of work, or tell them that, when complete, they will have to present their solution to the whole class. In thinking classrooms, we do not do any of these things.

Q I have a problem with students copying what other groups have done. How do I fix this?

A When we saw this in our research, it was a strong indicator that we had somehow incentivized speed in the classroom. The most common routines that provoke these behaviors are

1. giving students the whole task sequence all at once, and

2. allowing students to sit down when they are done.

Together, these incentivize speed as it shifts the goal of the activity from learning and understanding to compliance and completion. Copying is only beneficial to students in a setting where being done is an option (or a goal!). Giving all the tasks at once tells the students where the finish line is.

We understand why there is an urge to develop such norms in our classrooms; it comes down to efficiency and motivation. Giving students the whole list of tasks at once is very efficient—for the teacher. But very ineffective—for students. This is a tension we always have to grapple with—efficiency vs. effectiveness. Things that are more efficient for us are rarely more effective for learners, and vice versa. We want to skew toward effective, but not at the cost of becoming so inefficient that it becomes untenable. Sometimes there is no good alternative. But here there is—use the banner.

Allowing students to sit down when they are done can be very motivating as it rewards productivity. Or does it? It actually rewards speed. And speed can be accomplished through copying. What behaviors do you want to motivate? Do you want to encourage collaboration, empathy, perseverance, and so on? None of these is motivated by letting students sit down when they are done. We need different tools for this—tools that will be discussed in Chapter 8.

Q The banner seems to work great if all the groups are working at more or less the same speed. What if we have groups that are way faster or way slower? How will they know which task is next?

A The short answer to this is, it just works. The medium answer is it really doesn't matter. Once students develop perseverance and patience (see BTC, Chapter 9), it is not a big deal if a group takes a task out of order. However, this is only true if the task they pick to do next is not *way* out of line with your intended task sequence.

This brings us to the long answer. When using the banner there are two things you can do to make sure that no group picks a task that is way out of line with your intended task sequence:

1. If one or two groups are getting far ahead of the other groups, you give them the next task in the sequence, but you ask them not to write it on the banner. This will narrow the number of options for other groups.

2. If there are one or two groups that are falling behind the other groups, you need to be there as soon as they finish a task to direct them to the next task, or to give them the next task. You can also step in and write on the bottom of their board a list of three or four tasks for them to progress through to keep them in the correct sequence.

Both of these are easily achievable because of the time you have saved not having to run around giving each group their next task.

Q If I am using the banner, wouldn't it just be easier to number each task, so students know which one is next?

A We tried that. There are two negative consequences to numbering in this fashion. The first was that about 20% of the students started racing to be first. When this happened, empathy for their group disappeared as their goal shifted from being present in the learning to being first. The second thing that happened was that groups that were further behind became very discouraged and gave up. Do not number the tasks. Instead, use the tools provided in the answer to the previous question to keep everyone engaged.

Q I try to get my students to look around at other boards, but they won't look. Instead, they just wait for me to come and give them what is next—whether that is a hint or the next task.

A We have seen this as well. Usually this happens for one of three reasons. First, waiting is rewarded. If they wait long enough, we eventually give them what they need. So, they learn that they do not need to look around. This is an easy fix. Never give them something that is already visible on another board. Instead, point at a board where they can get what they need—whether that is a hint or the next task.

The second reason they do this is that they are unsure what is the correct hint or the correct next task. This is a sign that they are more concerned with being correct than thinking. Keep emphasizing that trying anything is better than standing still. Even if the hint or the next task is the wrong hint or task, they will learn something.

The third reason is specific to not wanting to steal the next task from a banner and comes down to the fact that they want to receive your validation before moving on. In this case, what they are looking for is either validation that they have the right answer or validation that you are seeing them being good students, or both. Regardless, the solution is the same—ask them what they are supposed to do when they are done. This tells them two things:

1. It is up to them to decide when they are done.

2. You value their ability to mobilize knowledge more than their being done.

Q What if I am doing word problems, or we are doing work with data sets or geometric shapes? None of these types of tasks work well with the banner. What do I do then that is both efficient and effective?

A As mentioned in Chapter 2, it is best to put these types of tasks on paper. But, how do you reduce the burden on you to be running around giving out slips of paper? The easy answer is to have a central location where a member of a group goes to get the next task. Some teachers use a table in the center of the room for this. But there are things to think about to make sure this doesn't devolve into a need for speed. First, never put out all the tasks at once. Instead, put out just the first two tasks to begin with. When everyone has picked up the first task, remove the leftovers of this and add a third. And so on. In this way, no one knows how many there are, and no one knows how far they have gotten. Second, if a group is way ahead, you can give them the next one without putting out the whole pile. Likewise, if a group is falling behind, be there to give them the next one when they are ready. Some teachers have found that putting the stacks of slips for each task into separate bins helps keep the stacks organized both for the teacher and the students. Whether you use bins or not, remember what was mentioned in Chapter 2—tasks on paper should have a small font and very little white space.

Questions to Think About

1. What in this chapter feels immediately correct?

2. What in this chapter challenges you?

3. If you have ever had students working at VNPSs on a sequence of tasks, think about a sequence that would have worked well with a banner. Now think of a sequence that would not have worked well with a banner. What are the differences between the nature of the tasks that make them good or bad candidates for a banner?

4. In this chapter we talked about the way that letting students be done can incentivize copying. What other behaviors does letting students be done incentivize? Are these the kinds of behaviors you want to see in your classroom?

5. What are some other things that you do in your teaching that may actually incentivize behaviors that you do not value?

6. What are some things you do that incentive behaviors that you do value?

CHAPTER 4

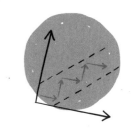

HOW TO USE HINTS AND EXTENSIONS TO MAINTAIN FLOW

• •

In this book, so far, we have used the words *thinking* and *engagement* almost interchangeably. Are they the same thing? It turns out that they are not. Thinking is a cognitive process and, as such, invisible to the observer. We cannot see whether you are thinking. We cannot see what you are thinking. Engagement, on the other hand, is an embodied process—it manifests through physical actions. We can see engagement in your eyes, your gestures, the way you lean into the board, and we can hear it in your voice and your words. You cannot hide it from us. Despite being different ideas, there is a very strong association between thinking and engagement. If your students are thinking, they are engaged. And if they are engaged, they are thinking.

HOW ARE THINKING AND ENGAGEMENT CONNECTED?

What do we really mean by *engagement*? It turns out that this is a term that is used in education a lot, and often without precise definition. This is true in research as well. We tend to use engagement as a modifier to indicate that what is being observed is good. But we rarely define it or delineate it from other behaviors. One of the rare exceptions to this is a Hungarian psychologist by the name of Mihály Csíkszentmihályi. He worked at the University of Chicago and 50 years ago he became interested in something he called the *optimal experience*. The optimal experience is that experience when we are so engaged in what we are doing that we don't want to disengage:

> a state in which people are so involved in an activity that nothing else seems to matter; the experience is so enjoyable that people will continue to do it even at great cost, for the sheer sake of doing it. (Csíkszentmihályi, 1990, p. 4)

Csíkszentmihályi wanted to understand this phenomenon better, so he studied people he thought were mostly likely to have this optimal experience. He studied artists, musicians, athletes, scientists, and mathematicians. And when he had enough data, he began to analyze them to see if there were any common patterns between these experiences—and patterns he found (Csíkszentmihályi, 1998, 1996, 1990).

He found that whenever someone was having an optimal experience, the following happened:

1. They lost track of time and much more time passed than the person realized.

2. They were un-distractible and unaware of things in their environment that would otherwise interfere with their focus.

3. They became less self-conscious, stopped worrying about failure, and began doing the activity for the sake of doing it and not for the sake of getting it done—engagement became an end unto itself rather than a means to an end.

These three characteristics, like thinking, are all internal to the doer. It is how they live the optimal experience. However, Csíkszentmihályi also noticed that whenever there was an optimal experience, there were also three things present in the environment in which the optimal experience was taking place:

1. clear goals every step of the way

2. immediate feedback on one's actions

3. a balance between the ability of the doer and the challenge of the task

The third of these—balance between challenge and ability—is central to Csíkszentmihályi's (1998, 1996, 1990) analysis of the optimal experience and comes into sharper focus when we consider the consequences of having an imbalance in this system. For example, if someone's ability far exceeds the challenge, they are likely to experience boredom. Conversely, if the challenge of the activity far exceeds a person's ability, they are likely to experience a feeling of frustration. And boredom and frustration both lead to disengagement. However, when there is a balance in this system, a state of what Csíkszentmihályi refers to as *flow* is created (see Figure 4.1). Flow is a state of engagement that is accompanied by enjoyment, positive self-efficacy, and a sense of accomplishment.

Figure 4.1 | Balance and imbalance between challenge and ability

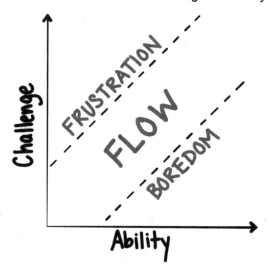

Source: Liljedahl, 2018

From that point forward, Csíkszentmihályi stopped talking about the optimal experience and only talked about flow. He wrote a number of books on the topic (e.g., Csíkszentmihályi, 1998, 1996, 1990), and then his work went in a different direction.

But this is where the BTC work comes in. If we want our students to think, then there needs to be a balance between ability and challenge. This is where flow happens. This is where the optimal experience happens. This is where engagement happens. And this is where thinking happens. There isn't a lot of thinking when students are bored and frustrated.

MAINTAINING FLOW THROUGH TIMING AND SEQUENCE TYPES

The challenge with this is that flow is a dynamic state. What we mean by this is that students don't live in one location on this ability-challenge graph. This is because when they work on something, their ability increases. And in order to keep them from getting bored, there now needs to be an increase in challenge, and so on (see Figure 4.2). Both the non-curricular and the curricular tasks in this book are accompanied by extensions to help you maintain flow.

Figure 4.2 | Maintaining the balance between challenge and skill as a dynamic process

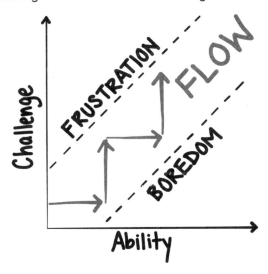

Source: Liljedahl, 2018

This is the essence of the work of the teacher in a thinking classroom—to keep students in flow by increasing the challenge as their ability grows. Here's the problem, though—timing matters. If we increase challenge before the ability has fully developed, rather than keep students in flow, we push them into frustration (see Figure 4.3). Luckily, there are some things inherent in thinking classrooms that help us get the timing right.

Figure 4.3 | Getting the timing wrong

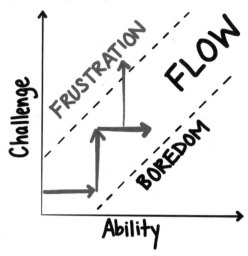

Source: Liljedahl, 2018

First, the VNPSs help us get the timing right. They help us to see everything at the same time. We can see where a group is in their work, so we know when they will be ready for the next challenge. We could not get the timing right if the students were sitting down and working at their tables or desks. We need to see what they are doing to get the timing right. Second, the random groups of three helps us to get the timing right. We could not monitor 30 students if they were working individually—regardless if they were working at a VNPS or at their desk. It is just too many things to keep track of. We cannot monitor 30 students, but we can monitor 10 groups. The fact that they are in groups helps us get the timing right. Finally, the students themselves help us get the timing right. Their autonomy to mobilize knowledge and to steal tasks from each other when they are ready—when their ability has fully grown—helps us get the timing right. The banner is instrumental in this. We can get the timing right.

Because we can get the timing right, we can build a sequence of tasks that get incrementally more challenging as the ability of the students increases. This is called *thin-slicing* and is what all of Part 3 of the book (curricular tasks) is based on—keeping students in flow through small incremental increases in challenge (see Figure 4.4).

Figure 4.4 | Thin-slicing sequence of tasks

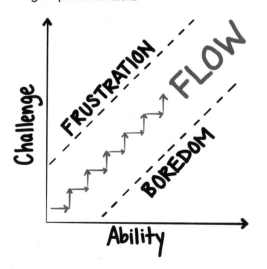

Adding two-digit numbers can be approached through thin-slicing.

1. 10 + 10 =	**6.** 34 + 20 =
2. 11 + 10 =	**7.** 21 + 30 =
3. 12 + 10 =	**8.** 21 + 31 =
4. 22 + 10 =	**9.** 33 + 31 =
5. 11 + 20 =	**10.** 42 + 26 =

Each task in this sequence is marginally more challenging than the task that came before it. But the tenth task is significantly more challenging than the first task. And we get there by maintaining a balance between challenge and ability. We get there by getting the timing right. We get there by maintaining flow—by avoiding boredom and frustration.

But there is more to thin-slicing than this. We cannot keep making these incremental increases in challenge forever because adding two-digit numbers involves more than what is exemplified in Tasks 1–10. At some point we are going to have to move on to different types of adding two-digit number tasks. And when we do this, the increase in challenge is not going to be incremental.

The previous sequence of tasks are all of the same type. This is not to say that the tasks don't get more challenging as they progress. The numbers get larger, and we shift away from having one of the addends being a multiple of ten. But in all the tasks, the sum of the ones is less than 10, which means that regrouping is not needed. This does not remain true when we move to Tasks 11–20. For Tasks 11–20, the sum of the ones is now greater than or equal to 10. This will require the students to regroup the sum of the ones into tens and ones. This is significantly more challenging.

11. 42 + 28 =	**16.** 47 + 26 =
12. 42 + 29 =	**17.** 56 + 18 =
13. 25 + 16 =	**18.** 29 + 16 =
14. 38 + 14 =	**19.** 38 + 29 =
15. 19 + 14 =	**20.** 48 + 49 =

Each of these sequences—Tasks 1–10 and Tasks 11–20—is built on the *principles of flow* (Csíkszentmihályi, 1998, 1996, 1990) and, as such, each is designed to have incremental changes in challenge as the students' abilities grow. But the transition between the two sequences is not incremental. The shift from Task 10 to Task 11 marks a significant increase in challenge. It will require the students to make a shift in their thinking—to make a cognitive jump. To help them notice that this shift or jump is needed, these sequences are also built on *principles of variation theory* (Marton & Tsui, 2004).

Variation theory tells us that we notice things that are varying, set against a backdrop of things that are invariant. For example, consider a tree in a meadow. If there is no wind and all the leaves are still, our attention is not really drawn to the leaves. If the wind is blowing and all the leaves are rustling, our attention is, likewise, not really drawn to it. However, if there is no wind so all the leaves are still, but all the leaves on only one branch are rustling, perhaps from a squirrel running along the branch, then our attention is drawn to it. Our attention is drawn to the moving leaves against a backdrop of leaves that are not moving.

Getting back to the sequences of tasks, for Tasks 1–10 there is an invariance (sum of the ones is less than 10). When students get to Task 11, that which was until now invariant suddenly varies (sum of the ones is now greater than or equal to 10). They will notice the variance between Task 10 and 11—their attention is drawn to variance against a backdrop of invariance—and this will signal to them that they need to think differently. This is also true when they get to Task 21 where there is a new variance (sum of the tens is now greater than or equal to 100) against the backdrop of an invariance for Tasks 11–20 (sum of the tens is less than 100).

21. 96 + 43 =

22. 81 + 66 =

23. . . .

This is the nature of mathematics. Adding two-digit numbers is not one type of task. It is made up of multiple types.

Type 1: adding two-digit numbers where the sum of the ones is less than 10 and the sum of the tens is less than 100 (Tasks 1–10).

Type 2: adding two-digit numbers where the sum of the ones is greater than or equal to 10 and the sum of the tens is less than 100 (Tasks 11–20).

Type 3: adding two-digit numbers where the sum of the tens is greater than or equal to 100 and the sum of the ones is either less than or greater than or equal to 10 (Tasks 21–30).

In this book, we use the labels *Type 1, Type 2,* and *Type 3* to distinguish between these different types of tasks, with each type holding something invariant that then varies when we move on to the next type. This is the complete picture of what thin-slicing is—a series of tasks with incremental increases in challenge punctuated by occasional significant increases in challenge (see Figure 4.5).

When these significant increases in challenge occur, we are throwing off the balance between challenge and ability, and students will get stuck. But getting stuck is not a bad thing—getting stuck is where the learning happens. When students get stuck, they will either persist or they will get frustrated. If the former happens, they have entered into a state of productive struggle, and they will increase their ability to get themselves

Figure 4.5 | Flow and variation together

Figure 4.6 | Two types of hints

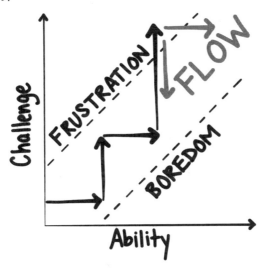

back into flow. If the latter happens, our job, as teachers, is to step in and give them a hint. Except, there are two types of hints—hints that decrease challenge and hints that increase ability (see Figure 4.6).

Hints that decrease challenge are quicker to give and either require you to give a partial answer to the question students are working on or shift them to an easier task. The second type of hint—increase ability—takes longer and requires you to either remind them of a strategy they already know or give them a new strategy. Other than how long it takes to give these hints, the main difference is that hints that decrease challenge are only useful in that moment, whereas a hint that increases ability continues to be useful even as they move on to the next task. Both the non-curricular and curricular tasks in this book are accompanied by hints to help you increase ability.

For example, consider the *Open Middle* task from Chapter 1:

> Using the digits 1 to 9 at most one time each, place a digit in each box to create an expression with the greatest possible value.
>
> □□ + □□ - □□ =

For this task, hints that decrease challenge could be, "The first box needs to be a 9" or "the third box needs to be an 8." Hints that increase ability, on the other hand, are more subtle and designed to help them see something they aren't yet seeing. For example, if a group thinks they can maximize the value by adding 98 and 76, you might prompt them with, "If I told you that you still need to use the digits 1 to 9 at most one time each, but you also HAVE to use 3 zeros, where would you put the zeros and why?" After they have done that, you would come back and ask, "Ok, what digits would you put in the remaining three boxes?" And when they are done with that, "Ok. Let's go back to the original task without the zeros. Where are you going to put the digits now?" This series of prompts will, hopefully, get students to see that you maximize the value not with 98 + 76, but with 97 + 86. But it takes time, and we have to come back to the group after each prompting question. But in the end, our hints help the group to see something they didn't see to begin with.

Through a combination of hints and extensions, you will be able to maintain flow and also engagement. More importantly, through hints and extensions, you will help your students figure things out. We provide both hints and extensions for each task in this book—both non-curricular and curricular. And using them, you will be able to help your students stay in flow, stay engaged, figure things out, and begin to make meaning. To help them finish making that meaning, however, you will also need the next three practices—how to consolidate the task(s), how to have students make meaningful notes, and how to use check-your-understanding questions.

FAQ

Q In thin-slicing, the order really seems to matter. If we are not numbering the tasks for the groups (see Chapter 3), groups will inevitably get the order wrong sometimes. What do we do if this occurs?

A Yes, sometimes this happens. And it can happen in one of two ways:

1. **WITHIN TYPE:** This happens when the students mess up the order within one type of task. This is not a problem. Does it really matter if they skip one of 22 + 10, 11 + 20, or 34 + 20, or do them out of order? No. Within a type there is so much redundancy that skips or sequence issues do not much matter.

2. ACROSS TYPE: This happens when students skip ahead to a new type of question too early. For example, they have just begun adding two-digit numbers where the sum of the ones is greater than 10 (42 + 29) when they accidentally skip ahead to a task where the sum of the tens is more than 100 (96 + 43). This is a big jump and they may not be ready for it—or they may be. If they are not, you can simply step in and either give a hint or say, "Oops. That task is for later. Do this one first." Then give them the correct task in the sequence.

Regardless of the type of skip that can happen, it is important to remember that your students will develop perseverance and patience with more and more experiences with BTC. At the same time, they will also become more and more likely, when faced with a challenge, to enter into a state of productive struggle. And with the emergence of these competencies, they will be more tolerant of tasks coming at them out of sequence.

Q Is there any harm in giving students the entire sequence of tasks all at once?

A Yes, there is harm! As mentioned in the FAQ in Chapter 3, this incentivizes speed and creates a motivation to be done rather than to be present in the thinking and learning. We need students to be present, and giving them the whole list reminds them of the future.

Q I know that this book has 30 thin-sliced lessons, but I also know that this is not enough for me to teach my curriculum. And it seems like a lot of work to figure out thin-slicing. Is there a way I can get access to ready-made thin-sliced sequences of tasks?

A You are correct; it *seems* like it is a lot of work. But in reality, it isn't. In Part 4 we dedicate an entire section to how to thin-slice as well as provide links to resources in which people are archiving thin-sliced lessons.

Q In this chapter, you talk about flow as though a group is a single entity. But it is not. There is not just diversity between groups, but also within a group. How do we maintain a balance between challenge and ability within a group when their abilities are so different?

A You are correct. There is diversity within groups. And this is key. In the original BTC research we found that diverse groups were much more productive than homogeneous groups. Diverse groups ask better questions of each other, show more empathy toward each other, and have access to a larger repertoire of ideas. Diversity is something to be celebrated, not something to be afraid of. This is not to say that all diverse groups are going to function flawlessly. You, as the teacher, will still need to intervene, provide hints, and support to keep groups on track. The main BTC book has several strategies to help with this scattered throughout. But the important thing is to realize that you already have the teacherly craft to do this. One of the main tenets of a thinking classroom is it does not run on its own. Like all classrooms, it still needs its teacher.

Q In this chapter you talk a lot about how important engagement is. Sometimes in my lesson I am not sure if they are engaged or not. How do I know?

A If they are engaged in the tasks at hand, you will know. Engagement is an embodied process that manifests in their actions, gestures, words, and posture. They cannot hide their engagement from you. So, if you look at your students and you do not see engagement, then there isn't any. They're not hiding it from you. They can't hide it from you.

Q What if a group gets all the way to the end of my thin-sliced list? Are they done?

A As mentioned, it is incredibly important that as students are working on the thinking tasks they feel present. Being present means that they are in the moment, focused on whatever they are doing, and using their empathy to care for their groupmates. It is very difficult for students to be present if we keep reminding them of the future. Some of the ways we do this, as teachers, is we set a timer or refer to a clock in the room, show them an agenda, give them all the tasks at once, or let a group be finished. Letting a group be done tells everyone else that done is a possibility, and now the focus is getting done rather than being present for the learning. In a thinking classroom, no one is ever allowed to be done. In normative classrooms, we assign the same amount of work but students or groups complete it in different amounts of time. In a thinking classroom, students work for the same amount of time but complete different amounts of work. And this is absolutely OK.

> It is very difficult for students to be present if we keep reminding them of the future.

Letting a group be done is also problematic for a different reason. Working at the VNPSs is incredibly safe because everyone is working at them—there is no audience. If we let a group be done and sit down, there is now an audience. It is a small audience, but it is an audience. And then another group gets done. Then another. And then the groups that are not yet done begin to worry that they might be the last group not done and everyone will be watching them. There are very few things in education that we know for sure, but one of them is that when anxiety goes up, learning goes down. No one ever gets to be done.

Q If everyone works for the same amount of time, how do I keep everyone busy? Some groups are going to go further than others.

A Yes. This is why you are going to have to over-plan and over-prepare. You need to have more tasks than you think you will need. And the last few are going to have to be more challenging than you anticipate your students will be able to do. This way you are ready for the group that makes meaning quickly and, as a result, moves through lots of tasks in a short period of time. So, for the adding two-digit numbers sequence, you might want to have a couple of tasks of the type 259 + 344 and 867 + 486 to keep those groups who blow through the Type 3 tasks engaged.

At the same time, you need more of each type of task than you think. In the adding two-digit numbers sequence, we provided 10 tasks for each type of task. This is more than most groups will likely need before they figure out how to do each type. But some groups will need all of them, and maybe even more, before they see the pattern.

This doesn't mean that every group needs to do every task, but it is better to have them and skip them than it is to not have them and need them.

Q Thin-slicing seems to be heavily predicated on students having some prior knowledge that we can use to start with. We can use the fact that they know what 10 + 10 is to get them thinking about 10 + 11, and so on. What if there is no prior knowledge on a topic? How do we introduce new content in a thinking classroom?

A As mentioned in Chapter 2, this is rarely the case. Math is inherently spiraled and it is very rare that we are introducing something that is absolutely brand new to them. But if we are, you just tell them what they need to know to start. But you need to keep two things in mind:

1. You have five minutes. That is, you have five minutes from the time you start talking until they are at the VNPSs thinking. So, keep it short.

2. Don't tell them everything. It is our tendency to want to tell them every detail and show them how to do every variation. Don't. If there is something they need to know to start, tell them the minimum needed to help them start—the first task. Resist the urge to tell them how to do the third or sixth task. Just tell them what they need to start the first task.

Questions to Think About

1. What in this chapter feels immediately correct?

2. What in this chapter challenges you?

3. In this chapter, we talk about the close relationship between thinking and engagement. Think back to the last time your students were really engaged. Were they thinking? If not, were they just entertained?

4. When you see the thin-slicing sequence of tasks in this chapter, do the three types make sense to you?

5. Think about the last unit you taught. Can you identify three types of tasks within that unit?

6. Think about the next unit you are going to teach. Can you identify three types of tasks within that unit?

CHAPTER 5
HOW TO CONSOLIDATE THE TASK(S)

W hether students are working on non-curricular or curricular tasks, flow creates a powerful state wherein students can spot patterns, make conjectures, and test and refine those conjectures. It is a space wherein students can begin to make meaning. At the same time, however, all of that activity is very situated in the here and now. Students' ideas, although powerful, are emergent and fleeting. They are working in and with unorganized, unstructured, and informal ideas, and if students walk out of the room without an opportunity to organize, structure, and formalize their thinking, their ideas are apt to drift away before their next math lesson. To turn the pattern-spotting, conjecturing, and meaning-making into retained learning, students need to have opportunities to organize, structure, and formalize their thoughts. The next three practices help students to do just that—organize, structure, and formalize their ideas.

THREE KINDS OF CONSOLIDATION

This organizing, structuring, and formalizing begins with consolidation—a teacher-led activity to close out the lesson. There are three ways in which consolidation can take place.

1. **CONVERSATION:** The teacher leads a general discussion about the task(s) and solution(s) but writes nothing down (see Figure 5.1).

Figure 5.1 | Conversation to consolidate a task

Photo credit: Maegan Giroux

2. **TEACHER-SCRIBES:** The teacher leads a detailed discussion of the task(s) and solution(s) while recording on the board what is being discussed (see Figure 5.2).

Figure 5.2 | Teacher scribes to consolidate a task

Photo credit: **Maegan Giroux**

3. **GUIDED GALLERY WALK:** The teacher leads a detailed discussion of the task(s) and solution(s) using student work on the vertical surfaces to work through the different layers of the solution (see Figure 5.3).

Figure 5.3 | Teacher does a guided gallery walk to consolidate a task

Photo credit: **Maegan Giroux**

The first of these three methods, *conversation*, is most useful when talking about big ideas and general strategies that have emerged out of the student activity. For example, recall the *Open Middle* tasks from Chapter 1:

> Using the digits 1 to 9 at most one time each, place a digit in each box to create an expression with the greatest possible value.
>
> □□ + □□ – □□ =

We may choose to consolidate this by just talking about how to make answers big when adding and subtracting.

The second method, called *teacher-scribe*, is suitable when more detail is required, such as when consolidating ideas around how to add two-digit numbers. To be clear, the first and second method are not lectures where the teacher does most of the talking. They are discussions where the teacher asks very focused questions and the students contribute ideas—ideas that are reified and formalized through the teacher's reframing of things that are being offered by the students. The difference between the two is that the teacher records these ideas in the second method whereas in the first they exist only as a discussion.

The third method, *guided gallery walk*, is used in the same circumstances as the second method, but rather than having the teacher writing on the board, the existing work of students is used to demonstrate the details. Regardless of the method, it is very important that consolidation follows a sequence that goes from the simplest ways of thinking to the most complex, from the most concrete ways of thinking to the most abstract, and from the most common ways of thinking to the most uncommon (see Figure 5.4). This is called *consolidation from the bottom* and allows all students to enter the conversation at the level that their doing and thinking got to during their VNPS work.

Figure 5.4 | Consolidation from the bottom

Since the main BTC book was published, we have learned that the guided gallery walk is better for consolidating *divergent* tasks and teacher-scribe is better for consolidating *convergent* tasks. Divergent tasks are tasks that, when given to students, produce a lot of different thinking to solve them. And these different ways of thinking are represented on different vertical surfaces around the room. This diversity of thinking is worth exploring through a guided gallery walk. Rich tasks are often divergent tasks. Convergent tasks, on the other hand, are tasks that every group thinks about in more or less the same way, and often this thinking is not represented on the vertical surfaces. Instead, the thinking lives in discussion within the group, and what is on the boards is often just the answer. In this case, a guided gallery walk will not work as there is nothing to

> We have learned that the guided gallery walk is better for consolidating *divergent* tasks and teacher-scribe is better for consolidating *convergent* tasks.

really look at and, even if there was, everyone did it the same way. These types of tasks are better consolidated through a teacher-scribe method. Thin-sliced tasks are often convergent tasks. As such, in this book, we lean into the guided gallery walk for the consolidation of non-curricular tasks and teacher-scribe for the consolidation of thin-sliced curricular tasks.

CONSOLIDATION THROUGH A GUIDED GALLERY WALK

Preparation for a guided gallery walk involves three steps: *selecting, seeding,* and *sequencing. Selecting* involves watching for different strategies and ways of thinking to emerge and locking these in by using your red marker to draw a box around them (shown here as a green box) and asking students to not erase what is inside it (see Figure 5.5). This will ensure that these ideas are still present in the room should you wish to include them in the gallery walk. We call this form of selecting *boxing.* If the work you want to box takes up too much of the students' workspace, we us a different method called *fill-the-box.* Fill-the-box involves drawing the box in a corner and asking them to rewrite specific work inside that box (see Figure 5.6). This will free up board space for further tasks.

Figure 5.5 | Selecting student work through boxing

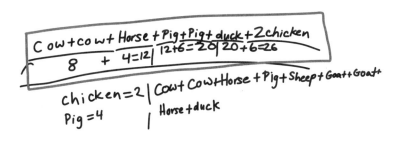

Figure 5.6 | Selecting student work through fill-the-box

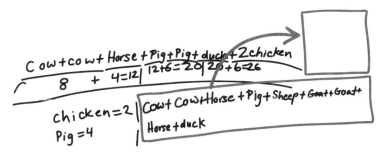

Seeding is what we do when something that we want to share in the gallery walk is not appearing among the work in the room—we plant a seed. From the student perspective, a seed is not different from a hint. From the teacher's perspective, however, it serves very different purposes. A hint is what helps a group move to the next stage of their thinking. A seed is what helps *a group* produce the work that you will use to move *the whole class* to the next level of thinking. In essence, a hint is for the group and a seed is for the class. Some seeds grow well no matter where you plant them. For example, a seed to have students organize their ideas in a table is a form of hint that easily takes root anywhere you plant it. Others are

> A hint is for the group and a seed is for the class.

more difficult to get to take root. For example, students will do just about anything to avoid actually performing symbolic subtraction. They would rather count up, reference benchmarks, use manipulatives, and so on. If you really want to see a solution that involves subtraction you will need to give that seed lots of water—"How is the subtraction coming?" "I have all these different colored whiteboard markers. Which ones do you want to use to do subtraction?" Once a seed takes root, however, you select it—either by boxing or fill-the-box—and ask them to not erase it.

Sequencing is the last step and occurs just before we begin the consolidation. This involves going around and deciding which of the selections you have made are going to comprise the gallery walk and in what order they should occur. To ensure that we are consolidating from the bottom, we want to make sure that this sequence is going from simplest ways of thinking to the most complex, from the most concrete ways of thinking to the most abstract, and from the most common ways of thinking to the most uncommon.

This preparation of selecting, seeding, and sequencing all takes place during the lesson while the students are working in their groups at their VNPSs. If you wish to do some of this preparation prior to the lesson, you can work to try to anticipate what kinds of things they will do. But the reality is that anticipation will only account for a small amount of what will happen in the classroom. This is because when we try to solve a task we come up with one or maybe two ways to think about the task, and it is difficult for us to break away from these ways of thinking to consider other possibilities. In psychology, this is called *functional fixedness* (Ashcraft, 1989) and is known more colloquially as getting stuck in rut. This will happen to your students as well, but they all get stuck in different ruts. So, although you and each of your students may come up with one or two ways of thinking, between all of you, you will come up with many different ways of thinking about the problem. This is why a gallery walk is so useful—it shares out all of the different ways of thinking that are possible and connects them to each other in a powerful narrative from simple to complex, from concrete to abstract, from common to uncommon.

This selecting and sequencing in a thinking classroom is similar to Smith and Stein's (2018) notion of selecting and sequencing in their book, *5 Practices for Orchestrating Productive Mathematics Discussions*. They are similar in that they both try to achieve a sensible sequence that moves the learners through various ways of thinking about a task or tasks. The big difference is that Smith and Stein have students present their own work, whereas in the thinking classroom, the decoding of students' work is left to the others in the room.

CONSOLIDATION THROUGH TEACHER-SCRIBE

Consolidation of thin-sliced tasks, as mentioned, leans more into the teacher-scribe method of consolidation. More specifically, it relies on a specific form of teacher-scribing called *noticing and naming variation*. This still involves the teacher scribing ideas given to them from the students in the classroom, but by leveraging very specific tasks in a very specific order—or disorder. The process begins by having students look at and discuss three exemplars—one from each type of task encountered in the thin-slicing sequence. This is introduced by having them first sort the three exemplars into the correct order in a turn-and-talk.

Teacher: I have written three adding questions on the board, but I may have put them in the wrong order. Turn to your neighbor and discuss what the order should be and why.

A. $89 + 36 =$

B. $12 + 34 =$

C. $29 + 37 =$

[Students turn and talk]

Teacher: OK. Which task should be first?

Students: B!

Teacher: OK. Why?

Student A: B is the easiest because we don't have to regroup. We can just add the numbers.

Teacher: Add what numbers?

Student B: Add the tens to the tens and the ones to the ones.

Teacher: OK. Which task should be second?

Students: C!

Teacher: OK. Why?

Student C: Because the ones adds to more than 10. So, we have to regroup.

Teacher: OK. That makes A last. Why?

Student D: The answer is more than 100.

Student E: And the ones is more than 10.

The request to have them order the three types of tasks and the subsequent discussion help them to make explicit what varies between the tasks—we are helping them to *notice and name variation.* After this, we shift to a discussion of how to solve each type of question.

Teacher: OK. So let's do B first. Is there something I can do right away without thinking too much?

Students: You can write them on top of each other.

Teacher: Like this?

$$12$$
$$+\underline{34}$$

Students: Yeah!

Teacher: Can I do that for all of them?

Students: Yeah!

[Teacher rewrites each question with the numbers "on top of each other."]

Teacher: OK. Come back to the first question. What Do I do next?

Student E: Add the ones first.

Student F: Add the tens first.

Teacher: Does it matter?

Student F: Not in this one.

Teacher: Not in this one? When does it matter?

Student G: On the other two. When you add the ones for those ones you will get more than 10.

The prompt, "Is there something I can do right away without thinking too much?" creates a focus on what aspects of the task are routine. The prompt, "Can I do that for all of them?" really emphasizes how the steps that are routine are invariant—requiring not too much thinking. These prompts do not only draw attention to the steps that are routine, however. By delineating the steps that do not require much thinking and are invariant, we also draw attention to the fact that there are steps that require more attention—more thinking—and are not invariant. And like the guided gallery walk, this form of consolidation goes from simple to complex, concrete to abstract, common to uncommon.

> The *noticing and naming variation* type of consolidation helps students to notice and name salient features of solving the tasks that may have been, during the collaborative time, unnoticed and unnamed.

Taken together, the *noticing and naming variation* type of consolidation helps students to notice and name salient features of solving the tasks that may have been, during the collaborative time, unnoticed and unnamed. As mentioned, when students are working in their groups, they are sometimes operating in informal and unstructured ways. They are just solving the current task, and then the next one, and so on. They will notice as they work that the tasks are getting more challenging. And, through careful use of variance against a backdrop of invariance, they will notice tasks that are suddenly more challenging. But they may or may not notice and name what it is about the tasks that is making them more challenging. This type of consolidation helps them to notice and name the aspects of the tasks that make the types different from each other and how to think about them appropriately.

Whether you are consolidating a non-curricular or a curricular thin-sliced sequence of tasks and whether you are doing that consolidation through conversation, teacher-scribe, or guided gallery walk, consolidation helps students begin to organize, structure, and formalize their thoughts and turn their experiences working through tasks in their random groups into retained learning.

Q Do I always have to consolidate a lesson?

A No. There will be times that you feel that consolidation is not necessary. Maybe you have observed and talked to every group, and you sense that everyone has already organized and structured their thinking. So, you may feel that consolidation is not necessary. Having said that, you should always do something to close the lesson—whether that is consolidation, meaningful notes, or check-your-understanding questions.

Q What if the students are working well at the boards? Shouldn't I just leave them at it?

A No. It turns out that there is a difference between collective knowing and doing and individual knowing and doing. The fact that the students are working well at the boards does not mean that they can all do it individually. Closing out the lesson through consolidation, meaningful notes, or check-your-understanding questions helps transfer that collective knowing and doing into individual knowing and doing.

> Closing out the lesson through consolidation, meaningful notes, or check-your-understanding questions helps transfer that collective knowing and doing into individual knowing and doing.

Q How do I know if I should be doing a gallery walk or a noticing and naming variation type of consolidation?

A The answer to this lies in whether or not there is anything on the vertical boards worth looking at. If not, do not do a gallery walk. Instead, do a noticing and naming variation consolidation.

Q There isn't a lot of time in the launch (five minutes) to introduce vocabulary. Is consolidation a good time to do so?

A Yes! Consolidation is an ideal time to introduce vocabulary. One of the goals of consolidation is to help students to formalize their learning. Vocabulary, as well as notation, are formalizations.

Q How am I supposed to have time to prepare for a gallery walk while I am trying to manage flow?

A It is challenging. In fact, preparing and executing a good gallery walk is, in our opinion, the most challenging practice in BTC. And it is exactly for the reason mentioned. Preparation for a gallery walk happens at the same time as you are trying to manage flow. The answer to this is that as students become more autonomous and their proficiency with knowledge mobility improves, this will get easier. The less they need you, the more time you have for this sort of thing.

Q It feels like to be able to lead a good gallery walk, I need to really know the math behind the task and have anticipated all the ways to solve it. This seems like more prep work than I have time for.

A Yes and no. Yes, you need to know a lot of different ways to solve it. No, you do not need to figure all these out ahead of time. You should attempt the task on your own before giving it to your students. But doing the task yourself will only enable you to anticipate a small fraction of what will happen in your classroom when you use a divergent task. You are going to have to watch, listen, and talk to your students as they emerge ideas and ways of thinking that never occurred to you. Doing so will help you to anticipate many more possibilities the second time you use the task—the second time you use a task is way better than the first but not nearly as good as the third. In essence, anticipation of what will happen in your classroom is enhanced far more by experience than it is by preparation.

Q What is the difference between consolidation and *direct instruction*?

A It depends on how you define direct instruction. If you view it as an opportunity for you to now tell the students the *correct* way to do something, then no, consolidation is not direct instruction. Consolidation is not about telling; it is about asking. No matter which form of consolidation you are doing, the research showed that it is about engaging students in discussion to help them organize, structure, and formalize their understanding. It is not about giving them your already organized, structured, and formalized ways of thinking.

> Consolidation is not about telling; it is about asking.

Q Does one of the types of consolidation work better with very young students (K–1)?

A They all work as well with younger students as they do with older students. The key is to remember that it is harder to hold young students' attention for long periods of time. So, the younger they are, the shorter the consolidation needs to be.

Q Is there ever value in doing a whole class consolidation in the middle of a lesson and then sending them back to the boards? I am thinking about situations where I need to introduce a new piece of information to everyone or every group is stuck in the same place.

A No! You will be tempted to do this, but it just does not work well. First, not every group will be ready for the same piece of new information at the same time. Second, it takes a lot of time and effort to break the groups away from the boards and to focus their attention on you. When you finally achieve this, tell them the thing you want to tell them, and then send them back to their boards, they have just lost a tremendous amount of momentum. You will see a marked decrease in energy, enthusiasm, and focus after you have broken the flow. It is actually better to go speak with each group separately, or to pull two or three groups that are ready for new information or in need of a hint together, than to do the whole class at once.

Q When consolidating using the *noticing and naming variation* form of consolidation, what does the "wrong order" mean, and should I specify that for my students?

A Our experience is that, for Grades 3 and above, we do not need to specify what we mean by "wrong order." The students will interpret this to mean either the order they saw the tasks in during the lesson or simple to complex. Either way, they will get the order you are looking for correct. Our experience is also that, for K–2, it doesn't matter if we are explicit. Some will still pick as the first tasks the task with their favorite number in it ("I like 7s"), or the most complex ("That one was hard"), or whatever. So, for K–2, just ask everyone to call out which task should come first and then pluck the correct answer out the cacophony of answers.

Questions to Think About

1. What in this chapter feels immediately correct?

2. What in this chapter challenges you?

3. Think about a task that you have done with your students that was *divergent*. Now think of one that was *convergent*. Can you come up with a description of the types of tasks that are divergent versus the ones that are convergent?

4. Think about a time when you learned from your students while they were doing a divergent task. What did you learn?

5. Think about a lesson you recently taught on a topic that was convergent. If you had to do it again, what would the three tasks for consolidation look like?

CHAPTER 6

HOW TO HAVE STUDENTS MAKE MEANINGFUL NOTES

• •

Up until this point in a lesson, everything that students have experienced, whether through their group work or consolidation, has happened at the VNPSs. And by its very nature, is temporal, situated, and nonpermanent. All the work will be erased. This is troubling to a lot of teachers, and we often get asked about student notes. Historically, note-taking is one of the most consistently practiced parts of mathematics education. And it definitely has a role to play, but *how* your students engage with notes makes all the difference in a BTC classroom.

COMMON BELIEFS ABOUT THE VALUE OF NOTES

From the BTC research, we know that there are two reasons teachers want students to write notes:

1. They want students to have a record—something they can look back at when doing check-your-understanding questions and studying for tests.

2. They believe that the act of writing things down helps students build understanding of ideas as well as helping to remember them.

The first reason is something that we never hear from primary teachers and always from upper-grade math teachers. The need for students to have a record is, for the most part, unimportant to kindergarten teachers and very important for Grade 12 teachers—and the importance grows almost linearly from K to 12. Regardless of where you are *on the line*, if the only reason for students to *take* notes is for them to *have* notes, then we recommend that you post notes *online*. This ensures that everyone has equal access to notes, that they are correct, and they are exactly as you want them to be. Our research shows that, by and large, students do not use them as much as you would expect. But our research also shows that parents love them. Parents see them as a product of learning and a tool for test preparation, and they like to know that if their child is absent, or does a poor job writing notes, they will still have access to good notes. Notes also give them something to learn from should they need to help their children at home. Despite not accessing them often, students also gain peace in knowing that notes are online should they need them. Taken together, if students having a record is important to you, we highly recommend online notes.

The second reason—increases understanding and memory—is a common assumption about the value of note taking. You likely have direct lived experiences that tell you that this is true. You may have taken notes at the last professional development session you attended, and you could feel how the act of writing notes was helping you to organize and formalize your thoughts. We do not disagree with this. But let's contrast your experience of *note making* with students' lived experience of *note taking*.

By far, the most common form of note taking we see in schools is *I-write-you-write*. This is where we, as teachers, write on the board what we want students to copy down in their notebooks. The BTC research (BTC, Chapter 11) showed that having students simply taking notes through this method did not achieve the intended outcomes. Less than 20% of students were cognitively engaged while taking the notes and, once taken, less than 20% of them used these notes in meaningful ways. They were not making any gains of understanding and memory through the mere act of copying down what the teacher was writing. In many cases, they weren't even reading what it was they were writing down.

The fundamental difference between your experience writing notes in a PD session and the lived experience of many students is that you were cognitively present in the process while the students were not. You were *note making* while they were *note taking*. To achieve the desired outcome of using notes as a way to help students to organize, structure, and formalize the thinking that began in the collaborative work at the VNPSs and was noticed and named in the consolidation, students need to be cognitively present. They need to be note making.

NEW RESEARCH ON STUDENT NOTE MAKING

The main BTC book offered a number of templates that could be used for student note making, with a key feature being that students have autonomy over what to write. The problem with autonomy, however, is that the research showed that 20%–40% of students may exercise this autonomy to write nothing down. This was still better than having upwards of 80% of students mindlessly copy notes and then never refer to them. But better was not good enough. This created inequitable access to learning. Students choosing to not seize the opportunities we provide them does not absolve us of the responsibility to make learning equitable.

> Students choosing to not seize the opportunities we provide them does not absolve us of the responsibility to make learning equitable.

Since the main BTC book was published, we've continued to do research on note making. What has emerged out this research is a template (Figure 6.1) and a practice that has shown to be effective for 100% of students. That is, in more than 70 K–12 classrooms, 100% of students participated in the note-making activity and 100% of students had access to the notes as a record afterwards.

Most important about this new structure is that this is not something you have your students do individually. Instead, it's something that they do collaboratively. In essence, after you have completed the consolidation, you simply draw this template on the board or project it on a screen for your students to reproduce and fill in back at their VNPSs in their random groups of three.

The template is broken into four quadrants: A, B, C, and D. You do not need to name or label the quadrants for your students. We do it here for the sake of being able to explain what each quadrant is meant to do. Quadrant A is a fill-in-the-blank note. Your students

Figure 6.1 | New meaningful notes template for Grades 2–12

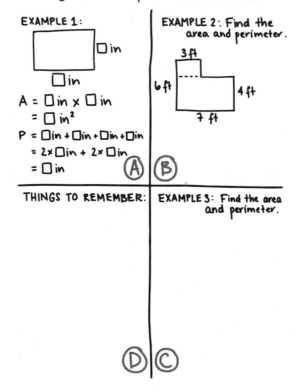

will, in essence, work through and complete an example you have created and partially completed for them. Giving them a fill-in-the-blank ensures that their notes contain an organized, structured, and formalized representation of some of the ideas that were present during your consolidation but may not have been present as they worked in unorganized, informal, and unstructured ways through the thin-slicing tasks. It also provides them with a structure that they can use for quadrants B and C. Usually, the fill-in-the-blank note in quadrant A is a Type 1 task from your thin-slicing sequence.

Quadrant B gives students a task to solve on their own—hopefully with the structure from quadrant A. This task is usually a Type 2 task from your thin-sliced lesson. It is important to make sure the students understand that this is not homework. It isn't an exercise or practice. It is a task with which they can showcase their learning from the day. It is, in the end, a worked example. Worked examples are a very effective way for students to capture and hold information. A good, worked example can carry organization, structure, and formalism. The problem is that when we create the worked example and the students just copy it down, they do not attend to, or extract from it, the meaning that a worked example can carry. Students need to be cognitively present when writing notes. They need to be note making, not note taking. Quadrant B gives them an opportunity to do this.

Quadrant C likewise gives them the opportunity to be note making. The difference here is that, in quadrant C, they choose their own task to become a worked example. One of the ways to ensure that students remain cognitively present in note making is to create opportunities for them to select and sequence information. When you are taking meaningful notes at a conference, this is what you are doing. You are selecting what to write down, and you are sequencing your selections so as to give your notes meaning—both when you write them and, later, when you read them. Quadrant C gives students an opportunity to select. Hopefully, they will look at the nature of the two worked examples they already have (usually a Type 1 and Type 2) and choose to include a worked example for a task that is different from what they already have (Type 3). In the case of the template presented in Figure 6.1, they may or may not notice that neither example involves a shape they need to subtract area from. They may or may not notice that quadrant A was a Type 1 task and quadrant B was a Type 2 task. Or they may notice this and feel more comfortable with Type 2. The important thing is that, as they select what to put in quadrant C, they feel like they are capable of completing it and that the completion of it can showcase their learning. If they didn't get to Type 3 problems during the thin-slicing, or didn't fully understand them, then they shouldn't be including a Type 3 task in quadrant C. Meaningful notes are meaningful because they are a record of the meaning students have made, not a record of the meaning you have made.

> Meaningful notes are meaningful because they are a record of the meaning students have made, not a record of the meaning you have made.

This is not to say that if you observed a group doing, with confidence, Type 3 tasks you cannot suggest to that group that they include one of those in quadrant C. Lots of groups are going to need help selecting what task to exemplify in quadrant C—especially when you first introduce this note template. This is one of the things you will need to be doing while they are working on their meaningful notes.

From a formative assessment perspective, it is important for you to remember that if they do not choose a Type 3 task for quadrant C, it does not mean that they do not know how to do a Type 3 task. As mentioned, there are lots of reasons why a group who knows how to do Type 3 tasks does not choose one. Just like Carl Sagan's aphorism, "Absence of proof is not proof of absence," in this case, an absence of evidence does not mean that there is evidence of absence.

Quadrant D is called *Things to Remember* and is just that. This is a place where each group can put into words the things that they took to be important in these tasks. This could be something they struggled to make meaning of or something they know they are likely to forget. This is the quadrant you will need to provide the most amount of support for—especially for young learners. There are two things that you can do to support them.

First, have them write their thoughts in complete sentences. They will want to write things like "remember units," "perimeter is adding," and so on. These statements make perfect sense to them in the moment, when all their thoughts are on the examples they just produced. But such statements will make little sense three weeks from now when they look back at them. Second, have them look at other groups' Things to Remember and steal ideas from them. Sometimes they just need to see other things to realize that this is something they hold as important as well.

As mentioned, this is a structure that has been shown to be very effective for Grades 2–5. If you teach K–1 and you want them to do meaningful notes, you would only use quadrants A and B (Figure 6.2). The mere act of trying to recreate what you have written on a board or projected on a screen is a lot of work for such young learners. And you will need to spend some time getting them to understand what it means to fill in the boxes in quadrant A. But they are capable. Likewise, they are capable of copying the structure of quadrant A when they complete the example in quadrant B. Eventually you can get them to quadrant C and, if you act as a scribe, quadrant D. But this is not of the same importance for such young learners. Remember, they do not need to have a record to the same extent as Grade 5. The purpose here is to help them organize, structure, and formalize their thoughts, and that can be achieved in just quadrants A and B.

Whether you are using the first two quadrants (K–1) or all four (Grades 2–5), once complete, you take a picture of their board and either post it online or print it out for them to include

Figure 6.2 | New notes template for Grades K–1

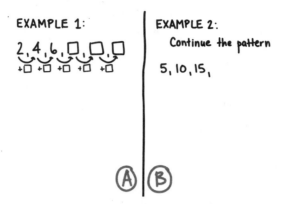

in their notebook. As mentioned, this four-quadrant structure has been shown to be an effective way to have all students contribute to, and walk away with, meaningful notes. After a period of time doing these exclusively in groups at the VNPSs, you can transition to a two-phase practice wherein they first do the notes in groups at the VNPSs and then, during the same lesson, sit down and create their own individual notes based on the notes on the boards. What is interesting about this is that students don't necessarily just copy what they did in their groups. They may select, for example, to take an example from a different board for quadrant C or to have quadrant D be an amalgam of things to remember from a variety of boards.

When transitioning to using this two-phase method of note making, it is important that you resist the urge to print the organizers for your students to fill out with the fill-in-the-blank task in quadrant A and the question to turn into a worked example in quadrant B already in place. The notes they make have to be reflective of the learning they achieved in that lesson, and your class does not always achieve everything that you anticipated that they would. It is OK for you to anticipate what the meaningful note will look like ahead of time, but you need to be nimble and responsive to what is actually happening in the lesson. Printing the organizer for your students makes you less nimble and less responsive.

Whether you stay with the one-phase method of having the students do the notes only at the VNPSs or you move to a two-phase structure where they first do the notes in groups at the VNPSs and then individually in their notebooks, this method of making meaningful notes creates access and opportunities for all students to participate in, and have, meaningful notes. It is this increased level of access and opportunity that is the big improvement over the meaningful notes methods in the main BTC book because it is not strictly an individual activity: Everyone can participate, contribute, and have meaningful notes. And through this, everyone has access to opportunities to organize, structure, and formalize their thinking at the end of the lesson.

Q Should we have students do meaningful notes at the end of every lesson?

A No. There will be times that you feel that notes are not necessary. Maybe you feel that not enough variance was experienced in one lesson to warrant having them make notes. Or maybe you are short of time. Or maybe you would rather spend the time you have doing a consolidation or check-your-understanding questions. Having said that, you should always do something to close the lesson—whether that is consolidation, meaningful notes, or check-your-understanding questions.

Q I feel like there should be a third phase of note making where we stop doing the notes in groups at the VNPSs and just go straight to having them make their own notes. Don't they need to learn to do this on their own?

A Yes and no. After seeing the effectiveness of one-phase and two-phase note making, we tried having the students go straight to making their own meaningful notes using the template presented in this chapter. And then 20%–40% of students immediately opted out. We were back to the issue we saw previously. There was a marked improvement in the number of students who were cognitively engaged in note making over note taking. But we excluded a significant number of our students from this experience. This is inequitable. If you are teaching an elective Grade 12 math course like AP Calculus then, yes, they need to learn how to make notes on their own. But in K–5, definitely not.

Q I teach primary. Do I really have to have the students make meaningful notes?

A No. You do not need to do anything in this, or any other, BTC book. But if you want students to have opportunities to organize, structure, and formalize the learning that happened at the VNPSs, then note making using the templates mentioned in this chapter will help.

Q Can I prepare the note template on a slide (for one-phase notes) or paper (two-phase notes) for the students?

A No! This cannot be stated emphatically enough. As with consolidation, you can anticipate what will happen and prepare for it. But things don't always go to plan, and you need to be responsive to what happens in the room. The note template needs to be a reflection of what happened in the lesson, not a reflection of what you wanted to happen in the lesson. Putting the template on a slide or paper prevents you from being able to respond properly.

Questions to Think About

1. What in this chapter feels immediately correct?

2. What in this chapter challenges you?

3. Think back to the last math course you took—whether in high school or in post-secondary. What did the instructor value more: note having or note making?

4. To what degree do you want your students to have notes? Is note having more important to you than note making?

5. What would have to change in the way you currently close your lessons to make room for students to make notes?

CHAPTER 7
HOW TO HAVE STUDENTS DO CHECK-YOUR-UNDERSTANDING QUESTIONS

Homework, like I-write-you-write notes, was something that showed incredibly low engagement in the original BTC research. When homework was graded, only 22% of students did it with fidelity. This number jumped to 31% when homework was not graded. Homework is not working. But teachers don't need data to tell them that.

WHY HOMEWORK DOESN'T WORK

Homework is a broken construct, and it has been for a long time. When we asked teachers, "How is homework working for you?" their typical response was to roll their eyes and then say, "It's not" or "Students who don't need to do their homework are the ones who do their homework." When prompted to explain why, if this is the case, they still do it, the number one response was, in some shape or form, "faint hope." They hoped that this would be the year that homework is going to *work* for them. But what does *work* mean? What do they want homework to achieve?

When we push past ideas like "parents want us to assign homework," "grading homework means there are fewer grades assigned to tests," "it's departmental policy," "students need practice," or "this is how it has always been done," what teachers want homework to achieve—what it means for homework to *work*—boils down to one of three things:

1. I want homework to be a safe place for students to make mistakes and learn from their mistakes.

2. I want homework to be a way for students to see whether they can do on their own what they were able to do in groups during the lesson.

3. I want homework to be a way for students to check their understanding.

These are great reasons to have students do homework. But when students were asked why they did homework, no one said, "Homework is a safe place to make mistakes and learn from my mistakes." No one said, "Homework is a way for me to see whether I can do on my own what I did in groups that day." No one said that. What did they say when asked why they do homework?

1. It's for grades.

2. My parent/guardian (usually mom) makes me.

3. My teacher makes me.

None of them said that homework is a way for them to "check their understanding." The reason that homework doesn't work is that the gulf between what teachers want to achieve with homework and why students do it is massive. If we want homework to work, we need to narrow this gulf.

It is because of this gulf that in the original BTC research (BTC, Chapter 7), homework was rebranded as check-your-understanding (CYU) questions—calling it what we want it to achieve. It is not practice. It is not exercise. It is not an-easy-way-to-get-grades. The purpose of homework is for students to check their understanding. So, we call it check-your-understanding questions. We do not grade it. We do not check it. And we do not assign it. Instead, we give students opportunities to do them. And as much as possible, we give these opportunities during class time.

When this rebranding and these practices were put into place, we saw students doing CYU questions for the right reason—to check that they understood rather than for grades. They would take ownership of their own work while at the same time they made use of the knowledge of the students around them as resources to check their answers and get help when stuck. We called it *working on their own together*. They didn't divide up the tasks among themselves or copy from each other. With CYU questions not being graded, there was no incentive to do so. Having an opportunity to do CYU questions incentivized learning over grading. And the students seized these opportunities in the best ways possible.

Like with meaningful notes, the original research showed a huge improvement in the ways in which students engaged in CYU questions over homework. But not for all students. Between 20% and 40%, and higher in some settings, did not seize the opportunities to check their understanding that CYU questions afforded them and, instead, used the autonomy that came with CYU questions to opt out of doing anything. The students who were doing CYU questions were now doing them for the right reason, and the ones who were not doing them were likely the same students who, when homework was graded, either did not complete it, cheated on it, or did it purely for the grade and not for the learning. So, overall, CYU questions were still better than homework.

But as with meaningful notes, the fact that students do not seize the opportunities we give them does not absolve us of the responsibility to find ways to make education more equitable. Children will make bad decisions—decisions that are counter to their self-interest. This is the nature of childhood. It is the job of the adults in these children's lives to not only encourage them to make better decisions, but to create situations where they are more likely to make better decisions. In many ways, this is what the BTC research is all about—creating situations that make it more likely that students make the right decision, take the correct action, and engage in thinking and learning in more authentic ways.

RESEARCH-BASED IMPROVEMENTS ON CHECK-YOUR-UNDERSTANDING QUESTIONS

So, the research continued. And since the publication of the main BTC book, a more effective CYU practice has emerged. This new practice is built on the same foundation of giving students opportunities to check their understanding. We still do not assign it, grade it, or check it. We just create a situation that makes it more appealing for students to make the right decision. Figure 7.1 is an example of what this looks like.

Figure 7.1 | CYU questions for adding two-digit numbers

Mild	Medium	Spicy
$13 + 25 =$	$15 + 18 =$	$65 + 82 =$
$23 + 31 =$	$23 + 39 =$	$84 + 49 =$
$41 + 58 =$	$58 + 27 =$	$87 + 68 =$

These questions are written on the board and then the students are told the following:

Teacher: These are your CYU questions. You are all going to sit down and do some of these. But, there are three things for you to keep in mind. First, do your own. Second, you choose where you want to start. Third, check your work with the students around you and if you need help, get help. And if someone else needs help, give help.

Telling students to check their work with their peers explicitly promotes and normalizes an environment of *working on their own together*. This is an environment, like at VNPSs, where students continue to feel safe making mistakes, feel supported when they do so, and feel successful. Being explicit in our language that we want this matters.

So, too, does the language around which questions they are to do. We found that when we said, "Which ones are you going to choose?" students behaved differently than when we said, "Where are you going to start?" With the former, students would pick some finite number of questions to do, do them, and then stop. With the latter, however, they would keep going. "Which ones?" implies a quantity, but "Where are you going to start?" implies a direction, and the students keep moving in that direction. And, even if they don't keep moving, it is easy enough to prompt them with "OK. So, where are you going next?" We still want students to do CYU questions, and we want them to keep doing them.

> To promote a growth mindset, then, we need to make sure that activities such as self-assessment help students understand where they are instead of who they are.

In the last few years, there has been a big focus on developing a growth—as opposed to fixed—mindset in math education. One of the big differences between how growth and fixed mindset manifests is in assessment and evaluation. Students with a fixed mindset view evaluation and assessment as a description of *who* they are, whereas students with a growth mindset view evaluation and assessment as a description of *where* they are. To promote a growth mindset, then, we need to make sure that activities such as self-assessment help students understand where they are instead of who they are. We need to STOP *who*ing and need to START *where*ing. Statements such as "Where are you going next?" do this—they are *where*ing rather than *who*ing statements.

We need to do more than just adding *where*ing language. We also need to stop using *who*ing language. The headings we choose for CYUs helps with this. At its core, the three columns of CYU tasks are just the different types of tasks from Chapter 4. The first column is Type 1, the second column is Type 2, and the third column is Type 3. We often see curricula, rubrics, and performance scales using headings like "novice, master, expert" to delineate different levels. This is *who*ing language. They describe the students. What they need to do is describe the tasks. The headings matter. And "mild, medium, and spicy" works better than any headers we have tried. First, they describe the tasks, not the students. Second, mild, medium, and spicy, in colloquial language, are preferences. They are non-evaluative, nonjudgmental.

We have been using these headings to label the CYU questions for more than a year, in more than 100 different classrooms from K to 12, and they have a huge impact on students' desire to do the tasks. Students are excited by them.

"I'm doing one mild, one medium, and then I'm going straight to spicy."

"Can we have another spicy one?"

"I think I'll start with mild and see where I go from there."

"I got to medium."

They are engaged. In fact, we have observed numerous lessons where students wanted to stay and keep working well after the bell to leave has gone. Why is that? In Chapter 1 we talked about productive struggle as a state rather than a trait and that, in order to enter this state, students need to have encountered challenge after success. Once this state is entered, however, it begins to feed itself. With every success comes the desire to take on more challenge. And the greater the challenge, the greater the feeling of success. The students are enjoying feeling successful at things that are challenging and they want to keep it going—they want to go from mild to medium to spicy.

That is not to say that all students enter this state. These CYU questions are about creating a situation that makes students more likely to do them. Mild, medium, spicy, along with language like "Where are you going to start?" help with this, but sometimes they still need a nudge. "Where are you going next?" helps move them to the next one. But how do we nudge them when they haven't even started? Interestingly, the data tell us that the number one reason students don't start is that they don't know where to start. They are paralyzed by choice. In such circumstances, the best thing to say is, "How about if you start with this one?" and point at one of the mild ones. In many cases, by the time you get back to them they have actually moved through three or four questions in sequence from your suggested starting point.

For other students, they may not be starting because even the mild is too spicy. This is often the case with students who, for a multitude of reasons, were not able to make sufficient meaning out of the VNPS work, the consolidation, and/or the meaningful notes. Maybe there are gaps. Maybe they were in a group that underperformed. Or maybe they were just inattentive. Whatever the reason, we still need to help them to feel success, and one of the ways to do this is to offer them some CYU questions that they can do, that they can succeed at, so they can begin to feel the desire to challenge themselves. For these students, we lower the floor on mild. But we still call them mild.

At the other end, some students may need help toning down the heat on their chosen starting point. They are so eager to get to spicy that they don't take the time to reify their understanding on the mild and the medium. When you see this happening, it is important that you coach them to start with a different one. They can become discouraged at their lack of immediate success—they need success to stay in the state of productive struggle.

You may also have students who jump directly to spicy and rightfully so. This is where they are in their learning, and they need to be checking their understanding at this level. As a teacher, you are going to be tempted to add a fourth category for these students—called extra spicy, habanero, or flaming hot. Do NOT do this. Our research showed that when we have three categories (mild, medium, and spicy) almost 100% of students strived to get to spicy. When we had four categories, 50%–70% of students stopped at medium. The reason they go for spicy with three categories is it is just one level past medium AND it is the last level. They can get to the last level. They want to get to the last level. When there are four categories, it is clear to many students that the last level is not for them. They cannot get to the last level. So, why bother getting to the second to the last level? This is not to say that you can't add more challenging tasks for those students who jump straight to spicy—the spicy tasks can get spicier. But do not make a fourth category.

Students will need support, encouragement, and challenge. A lot of this will come from their peers as they *work on their own together*. But you still need to be present. CYU questions is a great time for you, as the teacher, to work the room to see where students need the individual support, encouragement, and challenge necessary to complete the learning for the day. Along the way you will gather a ton of informal information about where individual students are in their learning that you can use to either inform your teaching or to inform your grading (BTC, Chapter 14). Of course, this means that CYU tasks are best done in class—at the end of the lesson. If students choose to take some home and work on them there, great. But, relying on them doing CYU questions at home is a losing proposition. Some will do them. Some will not. Regardless, doing them at home means they are away from the guidance and encouragement that you can provide.

One of the reasons that homework has traditionally been graded is the belief that grades serve as either the stick or the carrot that motivates students to do the work—students are held accountable. This is not the case for CYU questions. Students are given the opportunity to do them, not made to do them with the threat or reward of grades. And, under the circumstances described in this chapter, students seize these opportunities. And in so doing, they take responsibility for their learning.

More than that, however, meaningful notes and CYU questions, coupled with consolidation from the bottom, help students to first organize, structure, and formalize the thinking that emerged during the VNPS work, then turn this organization into a record of their thinking, and finally to check their thinking. In so doing, it helps students turn their collective knowing and doing into individual understanding and to turn their unstructured and informal collaborative work into retained learning. In this book, both the non-curricular and curricular tasks are accompanied by sets of mild, medium, and spicy CYU questions.

Q I teach K–1. The idea of homework isn't really relevant to me. Is this true of CYU questions as well?

A We agree that, for a K–1 teacher, math homework is not necessarily relevant. But CYU questions are. As opposed to homework, CYU is not about practice or compliance. CYU questions help students finish the meaning-making process, transfer their collective knowing and doing to individual knowing and doing, and check their understanding. This is relevant for students of all ages.

Q If students are working in this state of *on their own together*, won't they just copy off each other?

A They will if you grade it or make it an exit ticket. In doing so, you are incentivizing getting done more so than thinking, learning, and understanding. When getting done is the goal, then copying is a great strategy to meet that goal. If the goal is thinking, learning, and understanding, copying makes no sense. The essential difference is whether students are held accountable for CYU questions or they take responsibility for CYU questions.

Q I have tried doing mild, medium, and spicy and some of my students only do one question—and it is usually a mild one.

A Try adopting more *where*ing language—"Where are you going to start?" "Where are you going next?"

Q Should I do CYU questions at the end of every lesson?

A No. As mentioned, you should always do something to close the lesson—whether that is consolidation, meaningful notes, or check-your-understanding questions. You may close different lessons differently. Different lessons lend themselves more to consolidation or meaningful notes as a way to close the lesson than CYU questions. One of the things about CYU questions that is different from consolidation and meaningful notes is that students do them sitting down. Sometimes they need that.

The bottom line is, you need to be responsive to the needs of the students. Read the room and decide for yourself what is the best way to close a lesson.

Q Should I send some of these CYU questions home for students to do?

A No! If they wish to take them home and do them, they can. But if you expect everyone to do them at home, you will be disappointed. And when we get disappointed, sometimes we turn what is otherwise a rich learning activity into an accountability activity. Do them in class.

Q I have parents asking for homework. What do I tell them?

A In general, what we tell parents is that we would rather have students do CYU questions in class where they can be supported, and we can see what they are capable of. Homework doesn't achieve this. If parents are insistent that their child has work to do at home, direct them to some resources where they can find and assign work for their child to do for them—not you. Parents' desire to have homework should not affect your professional judgement of what is best for your students.

Q One of the reasons I have always graded homework is that it gives my students a chance to get some easy points and reduces what the quizzes and tests are worth. If I stop grading homework, won't that stress out the students with respect to tests and quizzes?

A It will if you keep using point-gathering methods of grading. But if you move to a data-gathering method of grading (BTC, Chapter 14), this is not a problem.

Q Can I have the mild, medium, and spicy questions printed out on paper ahead of time?

A No! Doing so creates two major problems. First, having questions on paper looks like a worksheet, and this will trigger a very specific response from students. They will begin to behave like it is a worksheet—something that they are accountable for rather than responsible for. The second problem is that, just as with consolidation and meaningful notes, CYU questions need to be a reflection of what happened in the lesson, not what you wanted to happen in the lesson. Mild, medium, and spicy is relative to what occurred that day. Putting CYU questions on paper restricts your ability to be responsive and prevents mild, medium, and spicy from being reflective of what was achieved in the lesson. This means that what is spicy today might be medium tomorrow.

Questions to Think About

1. What in this chapter feels immediately correct?

2. What in this chapter challenges you?

3. Think back to your time as a K–12 student when you were assigned homework. Why did you do it and who did you do it for?

4. What about this chapter feels counterintuitive? Why?

5. Whether you call it homework or just in-class assignments, why do you want your students doing math questions?

6. What are some things you have done to "make" students do their work? What message does this send to them?

CHAPTER 8

HOW TO USE TASKS AS THE CONTEXT TO IMPROVE STUDENT COMPETENCIES

BTC can have a transformative effect on your class as a whole, on students as individuals, and on you as a teacher. Data on student and teacher satisfaction and enjoyment in thinking classrooms are positive, as are data on students' self-efficacy, mathematical identity, and growth mindset. What all of these have in common is that they are ways in which participation in a thinking classroom changes a person's (both students and teachers) affect—beliefs, attitudes, and emotions. But the lived experience of a thinking classroom doesn't just change how students experience mathematics; it also changes their behaviors in mathematics. The data show that after a full school year of BTC, students show noticeable improvements in competencies such as perseverance (88%), collaboration (89%), and willingness to take risks (95%). These sorts of improvements are not only by-products of participation in a thinking classroom, but also contribute to how well a student functions in a thinking classroom and how well a thinking classroom functions as a whole. Students' perseverance, collaboration, and willingness to take risks are pivotal in a thinking classroom.

> Students' perseverance, collaboration, and willingness to take risks are pivotal in a thinking classroom.

For some time, there has been a great push in math education to help develop competencies with mathematics. Some of these, such as the five NCTM (2000) process standards, the eight Common Core Standards for Mathematical Practices (Common Core State Standards Initiative, 2010), and the five NRC (2001) mathematical proficiencies, are aimed at developing student competencies as learners and users of mathematics. Others, such as the *5 Practices for Orchestrating Productive Mathematics Discussions* (Smith & Stein, 2018) and the NCTM (2014) *Principles to Actions* eight mathematical teaching and learning practices are aimed at developing teacher competencies. The competencies we are talking about in this book certainly overlap with these, but they come from, and serve, a related but different purpose. And although they do develop naturally from the day-to-day immersion in a thinking classroom, the speed, breadth, and depth with which competencies develop is enhanced by explicitly attending to them.

HOW DO WE REINFORCE THE COMPETENCIES WE WANT TO SEE IN A THINKING CLASSROOM?

As we've said before in this book and elsewhere, students don't listen to what we say. They listen to what we do. We may tell students that thinking is important, but if what we do is I do-we do-you do, what they hear is that mimicking is important. Likewise, we may tell students that collaboration is important, but if what we do is always evaluate our students individually, what they hear is that individual work is important. Evaluation is a double-edged sword. When we evaluate our students, they evaluate us. What we choose to evaluate tells them what we value. They listen to what we do—not what we say. So, if we value competencies such as perseverance, collaboration, and risk taking, we need to find a way to evaluate them. But how?

> Evaluation is a double-edged sword. When we evaluate our students, they evaluate us.

In Chapter 12 of the main BTC book, you were shown how student behaviors such as perseverance, collaboration, and risk taking could be improved in the thinking classroom through evaluation using rubrics. But these are not the typical four-column rubrics like the one in Figure 8.1.

In the original BTC research, these kinds of rubrics were shown to be hugely problematic. Teachers found them laborious, and students did not attend to the details of what was trying to be communicated through them. Some of the problems with these types of rubrics were the following:

1. **TOO MUCH LANGUAGE:** Although detailed, students did not attend to the details because they were overwhelmed by the number of words. When it comes to communicating with students—especially young students—less is more.

2. **TOO-SOPHISTICATED LANGUAGE:** The rubric in Figure 8.1 is designed for Grade 3 students. But this is not Grade 3–friendly language. Consider the bullet, "In familiar situations, most estimates and predictions are within the bounds of logic." This is not how Grade 3 students speak. And it is not language they understand.

3. **TOO-AMBIGUOUS LANGUAGE:** Despite the copious detailed and sophisticated language, these types of rubrics somehow still manage to be ambiguous. Consider the following two statements:

   I. "Work is hard to follow in places"

   II. "Work may be unclear, confusing"

   How are these different? Which of these indicates better performance? Could you put these in order of proficiency? Could a Grade 3 student? For the record, in the rubric in Figure 8.1, statement I is deemed to indicate greater accuracy than statement II. The purpose of a rubric is to give students the kind of feedback that can help them to improve. How does a student take feedback from this rubric and move from, for example, *work may be unclear* to *work is hard to follow*?

4. **TOO MANY COLUMNS:** The main culprit behind problems 1 to 3 is that there are too many columns. To describe poor performance in a rubric is relatively easy. As is describing very good performance. These are the first and last column of a rubric, respectively. The problem described in points 2 and 3 arises when we try to parse mediocre performance into two categories—low mediocre and high mediocre. This artificial divide not only necessitates more language (problem 1), but also very sophisticated language (problem 2). And yet, ambiguity still abounds (problem 3).

Figure 8.1 | An existing four-column rubric

Aspect	Not Yet Within Expectations	Meets Expectations (Minimal Level)	Fully Meets Expectations	Exceeds Expectations
Snapshot	• *The student is unable to meet basic requirements of the task without close, ongoing assistance. Unable to provide a relevant extension.*	• *The work satisfies most basic requirements of the task, but it is flawed or incomplete in some way. May produce a simple extension with help.*	• *The work satisfies basic requirements. If asked, the student can produce a relevant extension or further illustration.*	• *The work is complete, accurate, and efficient. The student may volunteer an extension, an application, or a further illustration.*
Concepts and Applications* • recognizing mathematics • grade-specific concepts, skills • patterns, relationships	• unable to identify mathematical concepts or procedures needed • does not apply relevant mathematical concepts and skills appropriately; major errors or omissions • often unable to describe patterns or relationships	• identifies most mathematical concepts and procedures needed • applies most relevant mathematical concepts and skills appropriately; some errors or omissions • may need help to describe and use patterns and relationships	• identifies mathematical concepts and procedures needed • applies mathematical concepts and skills appropriately; may be inefficient, make minor errors or omissions • describes and uses basic patterns and relationships	• identifies mathematical concepts and procedures needed; may offer alternatives • applies mathematical concepts and skills accurately and efficiently; thorough • independently describes and uses patterns and relationships
Strategies and Approaches • procedures • estimates to verify solutions	• appears unsystematic and inefficient • results or solutions are often improbable	• generally follows instructions without adjusting or checking • may need reminding to verify results or solutions; estimates are generally logical	• follows logical steps; may be inefficient • makes logical, relatively accurate estimates to verify results or solutions	• structures the task efficiently; may find a shortcut • makes logical estimates to verify results or solutions
Accuracy • recording, calculations	• often includes major errors in recording or calculations	• may include some errors in recording or calculations; generally "close"	• recording and calculations are generally accurate; may include minor errors	• recording and calculations are accurate; may use mental math

Aspect	Not Yet Within Expectations	Meets Expectations (Minimal Level)	Fully Meets Expectations	Exceeds Expectations
Representation and Communication • presenting work • constructing • charts, diagrams, displays • explaining procedures, results	• work is often confusing, with key information omitted • often omits required charts, diagrams, or graphs, or makes major errors • explanations are incomplete or illogical	• most work is clear; may omit some needed information • creates required charts, diagrams, or graphs; some features may be inaccurate or incomplete • explanations may be incomplete or imprecise	• work is generally clear and easy to follow • uses required charts, diagrams, or graphs appropriately; may have minor errors or flaws • explains procedures and results logically in own words	• work is clear, detailed, and logically organized • uses required charts, diagrams, or graphs effectively and accurately • explains procedures and results clearly and logically; may include visuals

Source: British Columbia Ministry of Education, 2020.

5. **THE HEADINGS ARE WHOING:** Despite there being a temporal element to the headings, these headings are clearly describing *who* they are rather than *where* they are (see Chapter 7). To help develop and maintain a growth mindset, we need to stop *who*ing and start *where*ing. We looked at 20 different four-column rubrics and all but one used *who*ing headings.

The research in the main BTC book showed that these problems could be remedied with an alternative rubric (see Figure 8.2).

Figure 8.2 | Example of a collaboration rubric

• closed to others' ideas • disrespectful of others • actively excluding • hogging the marker • discouraging		• open to others' ideas • respectful of others • actively inclusive • sharing the marker • encouraging

This rubric avoids all the problems that the typical four-column rubrics tend to have. This is not too wordy, the words are not overly sophisticated or ambiguous, there are only three columns and the middle one is empty, and the arrow instead of column headings is *where*ing. The research showed that students were much more receptive to these types of rubrics. More importantly, the research showed that these types of rubrics shifted student behavior—in this case, collaborative behavior—in the classroom.

The research also showed that in order for these rubrics to have the biggest impact, they needed to be co-constructed with students at the end of one lesson and then used as a group self-assessment tool for several subsequent lessons. To co-construct these rubrics, the teacher would wait for a negative behavior—lack of collaboration, lack of perseverance—to manifest during a lesson. Then at the end of that lesson they would call students to the board and talk about what they observed.

Teacher: So, I saw a lot of good math today. But, your collaboration was not the best. Can you tell me what good collaboration looks like? [teacher draws T-chart on the board and labels the right-hand column as good]

Student 1: Sharing the marker. [teacher writes that under good]

Student 2: Being inclusive.

Teacher: Do you mean that the other person is allowed to be there and participate or that you want them there and you want them to participate?

Student 2: You want them there.

Teacher: Ok. So, like actively including them?

Student 2: Yes. [teacher writes that under good]

After a period of time gathering ideas of what good collaboration looks like, the teacher does the same for bad collaboration (see Figure 8.3)

Figure 8.3 | T-chart for collaboration

The teacher then produces a rubric like the one in Figure 8.2 for older students (grades 3*ish*–12) or Figure 8.4 for younger students (K–2*ish*). The difference between these two rubrics goes beyond the icons. Very young students are still viewing the world in binary structures—black and white, good and bad, yes and no. They are either listening or not listening to each other. There is no middle ground; there is no nuance. As students get older, they move from seeing the world as binary opposites to seeing it as a continuum. They could be sharing the marker well or not at all. But they can also be sharing the marker sometimes. These nuances are reflected in the presence of a middle column in the rubric in Figure 8.2 and the absence of a middle column in the rubric in Figure 8.4. Having said that, the words and icons in Figure 8.4 are spread to the extreme left and right of the rubric to give room for the idea of a middle ground when the students begin to develop this sense of continuum.

Regardless of whichever rubric is more appropriate for your students, once co-constructed, they get used in the same way. When the students come in the next day, one of these rubrics will be posted at every VNPS. It is preferable that they are printed on colored paper to stand out better against the white background of the VNPS. You then gather them at one of these workstations and discuss the rubric.

Figure 8.4 | Collaborative rubric for younger students

did not listen	listened well
did not share	shared
argued	took turns talking
worked alone	worked together
unhappy group	happy group

Teacher: At the end of last class, we made a T-chart of what makes good and bad collaboration. Well, I took that T-chart home and made it into a rubric like this one. [teacher points at the rubric on the VNPS where they are gathered]

Teacher: You will see that there is a rubric just like this one at each workstation around the room. [teacher gestures to the rest of the room]

Teacher: I am going to pass out a couple of copies for you to look at more closely with your neighbors [passing out examples]. Take a look at these for a few minutes and then we will discuss them.

[...]

Teacher: Ok. Let's discuss what each of these things means.

[...]

Teacher: Today, I am going to use this rubric to evaluate three groups on how well you collaborate.

You then give them their tasks, put them into random groups, and send them off to their VNPSs. At some point toward the end of the lesson, you call everyone to some neutral location in the room.

Teacher: Ok. I saw much better collaboration from all of you today. In a minute I am going to send you back to your groups to talk about how you think you did as a group collaborating today. Then I am going to come around and give each group a highlighter so that you can highlight on the rubric how you, as a group, think you did.

Teacher: [teacher explains how this is to be done]

The students then go back to their workstations and self-evaluate how they did (see Figure 8.5). While they are working on this, you go around and share the evaluation you did with the three groups that you evaluated.

Figure 8.5 | Collaborative rubric after groups have self-evaluated

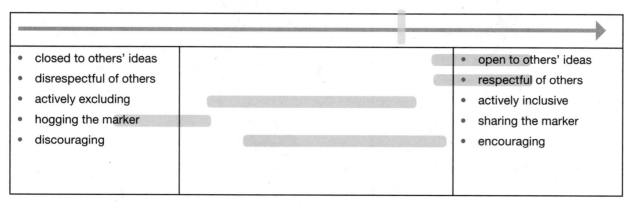

Moving forward, the norm that is established is that students self-evaluate at the end of each lesson. After the second or third time doing this, you no longer need to also evaluate them. That move proved useful the first few times to show them that you are evaluating what you value—to communicate your values. But after a few iterations, the students begin to see the value themselves. You may also wish to establish a norm that the students self-evaluate part way through the lesson with one color highlighter and then a different color at the end. This serves to adjust behaviors early on in the lesson that can then be beneficial for the rest of the lesson. Regardless, if you see behavior that is not good, you can step into a group at any time and draw their attention to the rubric.

There are a few things that we have learned from the research into the use of rubrics that are worth noting. First, if the same rubric is used more than five to seven times in a row, its effect on student behavior begins to fade—its constant presence begins to make it invisible. After using it a few times, it needs to disappear for a few days. And then when it returns, it is on a different color paper. In Chapter 4 of this book, we learned that attention is drawn to things that are changing set against a backdrop that is not changing. If you want attention on these rubrics, they need to be the thing that is changing, not the backdrop that is not. Having said that, when the collaboration rubric disappears for a while, it can be immediately replaced by a rubric on perseverance or risk taking—on a different color paper.

In Parts 2 and 3 of this book, each of the non-curricular and curricular tasks is accompanied by an indicator of what competency that task can be used to accentuate and work on. If a task is good for perseverance, this means that you can use it either as the impetus to co-create a perseverance rubric or as the context in which to value perseverance through the use of a rubric. Most often, these are pulled from the three competencies that teachers have told us are most important to improve in their thinking classrooms: collaboration, perseverance, and willingness to take risks. But we list other competencies as well—competencies such as trial and error, organization, pattern spotting, and so on. This is not to say that you cannot co-create rubrics for other behaviors that you would like to develop—manners at the whiteboards, active inclusion, coming to class ready to learn, and so on. Any task, curricular or non-curricular, is a context to work on these competencies.

Q Should I be using a competency rubric every lesson?

A No. Competency rubrics are used every lesson for a while to change a behavior and then only occasionally to maintain or correct that behavior.

Q Can I have the students assess just themselves using these rubrics?

A Yes. Each rubric can be used as a group self-assessment or as an individual self-assessment. We found that group self-assessment was highly effective because it created a context in which to have conversation about behavior—which, in turn, changed behavior.

Q Can I use these rubrics to have students self-assess their participation in working on their meaningful notes or their CYU questions?

A Absolutely! Participation, irrespective of context, is a behavior that can stand to be improved—especially during note making and CYU questions.

Q Can I use a similar rubric to assess the quality of their meaningful notes?

A Yes and no. Notes are not a behavior. So, we have to do things a little bit differently. One of the interesting things in the research was that no matter how bad students were at some behavior, they could always tell us what good behavior was. This is because they could draw on the repertoire of recent experience from the lesson. The same is not true of producibles such as notes. They do not have a repertoire of recent experience to draw on. So, we have to create it for them. Begin the lesson with each group getting printouts of three different meaningful notes—a really good one, a really bad one, and one in the middle. Ask them to rank them in order from best to worst. When they are done with this, ask them to discuss, in their groups, what makes a good note and what makes a bad note. Then, when you call them to a board to co-construct the good/bad T-chart, they have a repertoire of recent experience to draw on—and they will have lots to say.

Questions to Think About

1. What in this chapter feels immediately correct?

2. What in this chapter challenges you?

3. Think about a time when you used a rubric like the one in Figure 8.1. Did you find it easy to use? Was it useful to your students?

4. The rubric in Figure 8.4 was designed for K–2*ish* students. Can you see older students also benefitting from it?

5. What are some behaviors that you want to work on in your classroom? What is the one you want to work on first?

Notes to My Future Forgetful Self

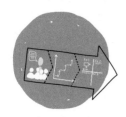

CHAPTER 9

WHAT LESSONS LOOK LIKE
IN A THINKING CLASSROOM
•••••••••••••••••••••••••••••••

Many teachers ask the question, "What does a lesson actually look like in a thinking classroom?" so we want to take some time to explicitly outline that for you. Part 1 of this book presents a summary and recent research results on eight of the practices that are discussed in the main BTC book.

Chapter Topic	Building Thinking Classrooms in Mathematics: K–12	Mathematics Tasks for the Thinking Classroom: K–5
what kinds of tasks to use	Chapter 1	Chapter 1
how to form collaborative groups	Chapter 2	
where students work	Chapter 3	
how to arrange the furniture	Chapter 4	
how to answer questions	Chapter 5	
how, when, and where tasks are given	Chapter 6	Chapter 2
how to use check-your-understanding questions	Chapter 7	Chapter 7
how to build and utilize student autonomy	Chapter 8	Chapter 3
how to use hints and extensions to maintain flow	Chapter 9	Chapter 4
how to consolidate the task(s)	Chapter 10	Chapter 5
how to have students make meaningful notes	Chapter 11	Chapter 6
how to use tasks as the context to improve student competencies	Chapter 12	Chapter 8
how to use formative assessment	Chapter 13	
how we grade	Chapter 14	

The chapters in the main BTC book are organized to correspond with the implementation framework for building a thinking classroom (see Figure 9.1). This is a developmental framework that emerged over a two-year period and involved research with more than 400 teachers—each of whom was given different thinking classroom practices to implement in different orders. The results revealed that, from an implementation perspective, the order mattered. That is, when we want to start the process of building a thinking classroom, we need to begin with thinking tasks, random groups, and VNPSs. We called this *toolkit 1* and the research clearly showed that we need to implement all three together. Once that is up and running, we move to *toolkit 2* where there are five practices, we implement them one at a time, and order does not matter. And so on. Following this sequence is how we grow our thinking classroom practice, transform our students into thinkers, and build our thinking classroom. This is why the main book is called *Building Thinking Classrooms in Mathematics* and not *Having a Thinking Classroom in Mathematics*. We have to build it. And we build it by disrupting the normative classroom practices, routines, and behaviors that keep students primarily in a non-thinking state of slacking, stalling, faking, and mimicking. For more details about this implementation model, we urge you to read Chapter 15 of the main BTC book.

Figure 9.1 | BTC implementation framework

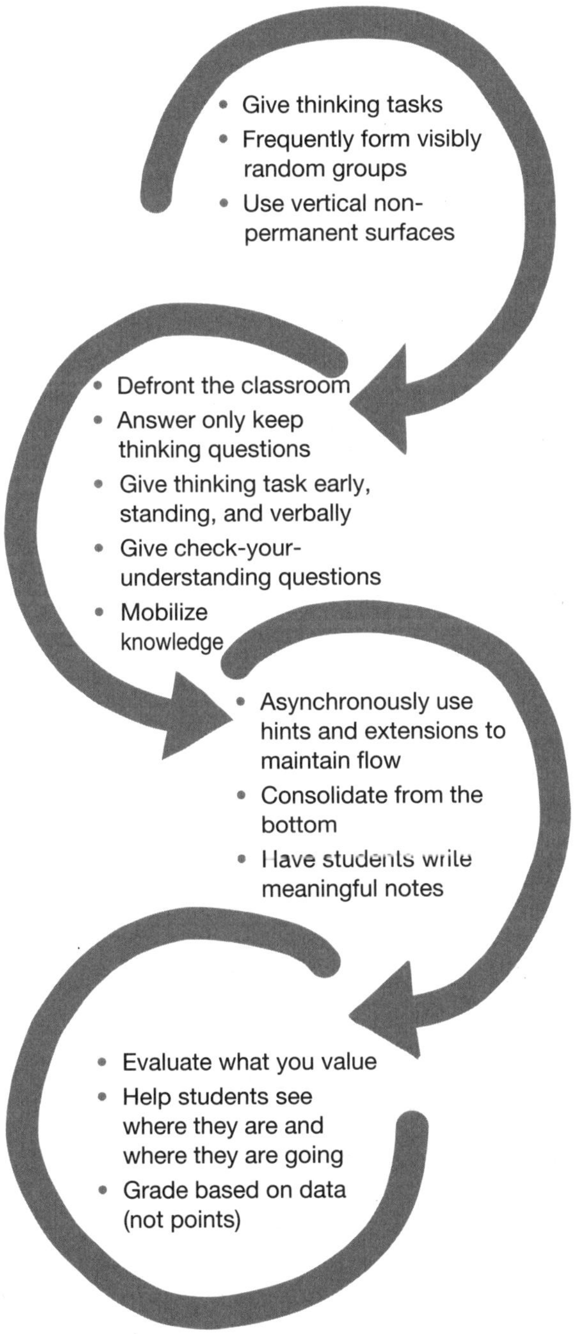

- Give thinking tasks
- Frequently form visibly random groups
- Use vertical non-permanent surfaces

- Defront the classroom
- Answer only keep thinking questions
- Give thinking task early, standing, and verbally
- Give check-your-understanding questions
- Mobilize knowledge

- Asynchronously use hints and extensions to maintain flow
- Consolidate from the bottom
- Have students write meaningful notes

- Evaluate what you value
- Help students see where they are and where they are going
- Grade based on data (not points)

The order of the chapters in this book, however, does not reflect this developmental implementation framework. The order in this book is representative of the order that the practices manifest in a lesson (see Figure 9.2).

Figure 9.2 | Sequence of practices in a BTC lesson

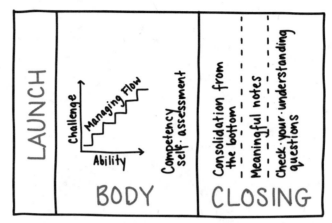

THE THREE-PHASE LESSON FORMAT

Every thinking classroom lesson can be broken into three phases—the launch, the body, and the closing. These main phases may seem familiar to you, as they have previously been described using terms like *launch, explore,* and *summarize.* So in many ways you aren't changing the structure of your lesson, but you are attending to specific details within each phase that may feel a bit different. It's the details that matter for thinking.

As you have read previously, the launch involves the following:

1. Call students to where you are in the room.

2. Verbally present the task in the first five minutes of the lesson, with the students standing in loose formation around you, the teacher. This can involve turn-and-talks to review past content, direct instruction of new content, as well as any instructions around routines.

3. Form visibly random groups and get students to their VNPSs.

Preparation for the launch begins with the selection of the task—curricular or non-curricular—readying any manipulatives you may need to have on hand, getting your cards ready to randomize (BTC, Chapter 2), and numbering the VNPSs. And long before this, you have defronted the room (BTC, Chapter 4).

After the launch we enter the body phase of the lesson. This is when you do the following:

4. Use hints and extensions to create and maintain flow.

5. Utilize and continue to build student autonomy to mobilize knowledge.

6. Prepare your consolidation, meaningful notes, and/or CYU questions.

Remember, if you are doing a divergent task, during which the class is likely to come up with many different solutions, you would use the body to prepare for a gallery walk style of consolidation. This would involve selecting, seeding, and sequencing. If you are doing a curricular thin-slicing activity, then you would use the body to select the three tasks you are going to use for your noticing and naming variation consolidation; for populating quadrants A and B for meaningful notes; and/or creating your mild, medium, and spicy CYU questions. The launch and the body together should take about two-thirds of the total time you have for your lesson. Having said that, you have to read the room. If your students are frustrated, tired, or too squirrely, you may want to transition to the closing sooner than this. Regardless, the body can end with a group self-assessment of whatever competency you were focused on, using a co-constructed rubric.

Like the launch and the body, which happen in every thinking classroom lesson, you need to close every lesson to ensure that students' unorganized, unstructured, and informal ideas that have emerged during their group work are somewhat organized, structured, and formalized, giving them the opportunity to finish their meaning making and retain their learning. Closing the lesson involves at least one of consolidation, meaningful notes, and check-your-understanding questions. Whatever the circumstances, we strongly recommend that you do at least one of these. You can do all three, but on any given day you may be doing one or two. For example, you may consolidate and do check-your-understanding questions, but not do meaningful notes. What you choose to do will depend a lot on where you are in your own development as a thinking classroom teacher, what happened in the lesson, and how much time you have. Maybe the students are really deep into flow and/or are demonstrating that they have good understanding of the concepts at hand, and you feel that it is more valuable to keep them in their groups. Alternatively, maybe they are running out of patience to work with each other, and you feel it is time to transition them into more individual activities like two-phase meaningful notes or check-your-understanding questions. Regardless, the order in which closing practices occur is important. Do whichever ones seem suitable, but do them in the order of consolidation from the bottom, meaningful notes, and check-your-understanding questions. The closing should take up to one-third of your lesson—the last third. But this is only a guideline. If your students are doing well in their groups, you may wish to give more time to the body. If they are not, you may wish to give more time to the closing.

All the best intentions aside, maybe your lesson is just not long enough to do everything you want to do. In this case, you may choose to extend the task—whether it is a rich task or a thin-sliced task—over two lessons (see Figure 9.3).

Figure 9.3 | Sequence of practices across two BTC lessons

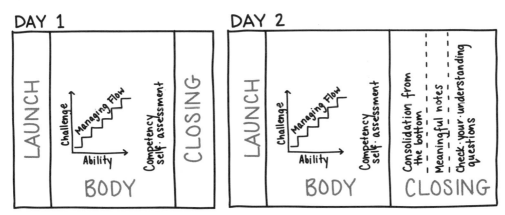

Figure 9.3 offers one way this can look—but only one. There are many variations to this. But one thing that stays constant is that every lesson needs to have a launch, a body, and a closing. The difference here is that the day 1 closing is very short, with maybe just a brief consolidation. Likewise, the day 2 body is much shorter to allow for more time to do a more thorough closing of the lesson. In general, you cannot close a lesson without first having a body. The purpose of closing the lesson is to help transfer unorganized thoughts into organized thoughts, unstructured ideas into structured ones, and informal ideas into formal ideas, and to begin to transfer collective knowing and doing into individual knowing and doing. We need some VNPS group work to re-create the constructs that we want to transform with the day 2 lesson closing.

> Re-randomizing the groups will create a natural jigsaw that will help mobilize the knowledge from day 1 around the room for day 2.

If you choose to break your lesson across two days, we strongly encourage you to still launch the same as you usually do—still ending with randomizing the groups. It is tempting to think that, since the class did not finish the task or task sequence the day before, we should keep the groups the same for day 2. Re-randomizing the groups will create a natural jigsaw that will help mobilize the knowledge from day 1 around the room for day 2.

Part 2 of this book contains 20 non-curricular tasks and Part 3 contains 30 thin-sliced curricular task sequences. Whether non-curricular or curricular, each task contains everything you need to enact a full lesson from launch, to body, to closing.

Q Once a week we have a double lesson of math. What would a really long lesson look like?

A It depends on how long a regular lesson is. If a regular lesson is long enough for you to comfortably get through the launch, the body, and the closing, then in a double lesson you would run two complete cycles of launch, body, and closing with a brain break in between. If, on the other hand, you feel rushed during a regular lesson, then a double lesson will give a nice opportunity to complete a single cycle of launch, body, and closing in a more relaxed and extended fashion.

Q What does a lesson look like if half my class is absent for some reason?

A It looks the same. You just have fewer groups and, if you have fewer than 15 students, you may wish to have groups of two. The issue is that the next day, you may want to repeat the lesson for those who were absent. Those who were present will now be dispersed throughout the groups, creating a nice opportunity to mobilize knowledge from the day before.

Q What does a lesson look like if half my lesson is going to be taken over by an assembly or something similar?

A If you know this is the case ahead of time, you may wish to do a non-curricular task that day with a very brief consolidation. If it is a surprise, like a fire alarm being pulled, then you just end the lesson where you are and start fresh the next day, maybe with a slight shift in the thin-sliced tasks.

Q One of the problems I have is that when the students get engaged, I get engaged. And just like they lose track of time, I lose track of time. And suddenly the bell is ringing, and I didn't get a chance to close the lesson. Any tips to help prevent this?

A We find that setting a timer for ourselves is an effective way to prevent this. Set the timer for the two-thirds point of the lesson. Then, when it goes off, do a quick check on how the students are progressing and decide at that point what you want your closing to look like. This may involve deciding which of the three closing practices you want to do. But it may also involve deciding how much time to dedicate to it. You may decide, for example, that the class needs five more minutes at the whiteboards in their groups and then you will close. Or you may decide that the closing needs to begin immediately. Regardless, setting the timer puts you in a position to make that decision rather than having the school bell make it for you.

Questions to Think About

1. What in this chapter feels immediately correct?

2. What in this chapter challenges you?

3. How will the lesson structures provided in this chapter fit into your specific context?

4. Which of the three closing practices—consolidation, meaningful notes, CYU questions—do you feel most comfortable to start with? Why?

5. Which of the three closing practices—consolidation, meaningful notes, CYU questions—do you feel least comfortable to start with? Why?

6. What strategy are you going to use to make sure you leave enough time for the closing?

PART 2

NON-CURRICULAR THINKING TASKS

It is clear that the chief end of mathematical study must be to make the students think.

—John Wesley Young
American mathematician

In this part of the book, you will find a collection of non-curricular tasks for use in your K through Grade 5 classrooms. Non-curricular tasks serve a very specific and important purpose in the building of a thinking classroom: They make math *fun*. The highly engaging nature of these tasks, coupled with visibly random groups and vertical non-permanent surfaces (VNPSs), constructs an environment that is unlike anything students may have experienced in the past and, as such, makes it *playful*. This can be disarming to students (and teachers). That is, by constructing an environment that is both different and fun, you will find students can get drawn into thinking mathematically before their normal studenting behaviors have a chance to kick in.

The playfulness of this environment is further enhanced by the fact that, by their very nature, non-curricular tasks are non-curricular. There isn't a curricular goal at the end of the activity to interfere with the enjoyment of the activity. We aren't trying to hit a target, an outcome, or a standard. It is not content students will be assessed on, so non-curricular tasks depressurize the environment for students and teachers alike. Students can just be in the moment, not worried about getting through some number of tasks or some number of pages in the workbook. They don't have to think about presenting or representing their work at the end of the activity. And they don't have to stress about being assessed on this work, now or in the future. They can just be in the moment. Be mathematical. They just have to think.

> Non-curricular tasks depressurize the environment for students and teachers alike.

The teacher, likewise, doesn't have to worry about achieving an outcome or a standard. They don't have to worry about what they are teaching, what the students are learning, or whether all of them are learning it. They can just be in the moment with their students, watching them be different. And they will be different. Non-curricular tasks, random groups, and VNPSs combine to create an environment that is radically different from what students are accustomed to. They break down the normative structures of the classroom. They make the classroom look, sound, and feel different. They change the classroom climate and environment. And when we change the environment, we change the behavior. Students who were accustomed to slacking, stalling, faking, and mimicking are suddenly thrust into an environment where that is not possible. So, they adapt. They change. They start thinking. And the teacher gets to see the students being different.

Taken together, non-curricular tasks are an essential element for building a thinking classroom. But their utility does not end there. The fact that they make mathematics playful, coupled with the way they depressurize the environment, provides three additional affordances. First, they can reinitiate students into thinking and the norms of a thinking classroom upon return from an extended absence such as a winter or spring break. We have to remember that regardless of how established the routines of a thinking classroom are in your practice, this is still a departure from the normative experiences students may have had over many years and many teachers. And time away from a thinking classroom may allow old studenting habits to surface.

Second, non-curricular tasks can serve as a break from the strain of moving through content—both for the students and the teacher. Even though a thinking classroom is reported by most teachers and students as being a more enjoyable way to teach and learn, there is still an intensity associated with the teaching and learning of math. And that intensity is amplified around things like assessment and evaluation. Spending the occasional lesson or part of a lesson doing non-curricular tasks serves as a break from the relentless march through content and grading for students and teachers alike.

Third, the purposeful use of non-curricular tasks creates the perfect environment for teachers to adopt new BTC practices. Building a thinking classroom starts with the first toolkit from the BTC framework: non-curricular tasks, visibly random groups, and vertical non-permanent surfaces. That first tool kit is about upending the norms of the classroom so that it looks different, so that students can be different—so they can begin to think. But the change to the environment does not end there. There are 11 more BTC practices to be implemented—one at a time—as you continue to build your thinking classroom. Each time you adopt a new practice, whether it is something as small as where you give the task (Chapter 2) or something as big as consolidating from the bottom (Chapter 5), it is best initiated without the specter of curriculum looming over you. Making changes to your practice is difficult enough. You do not need the added pressure of trying to hit a curriculum outcome or standard at the same time. Give yourself a break. Allow yourself the freedom to really explore the new practice, to rehearse and fine tune it, in an environment where the only goal is to think.

For all of these reasons, we need non-curricular tasks. But surprisingly, we don't need as many as you would think. You will need some to initiate the building of your thinking classroom. That is four to six tasks. You will need some to re-enculture your students to the norms of a thinking classroom when they come back from an extended break. That is an additional four to six tasks. And you will need some non-curricular tasks to use when you are introducing new BTC practices. That is another four to six tasks, depending on where you are in your journey. Altogether, you will need 12 to 18 non-curricular tasks—for a whole school year. Overall, most BTC teachers use non-curricular tasks for less than 10% of their lessons throughout the whole school year. More at the beginning, less at the end. The rest of the time they are using curricular tasks (see Part 3).

HOW DO I KNOW WHICH TASKS TO USE?

Anyone planning to, or in the midst of, building a thinking classroom needs non-curricular tasks. But not so many that it is difficult to choose. This part of the book contains 20 non-curricular tasks—a reasonable number to choose from. And to make choosing even easier, each task is accompanied by a set of six task- and BTC-specific indicators to help you quickly decide if a particular task is right for you and your students in your collective journey to build a thinking classroom (see the following example).

TASK 1: HEXAGON HAVOC

TASK

Write the numbers 1, 1, 2, 2, 3, 3 into 6 connecting hexagons without having hexagons with the same number touching one another.

Grades: K–1

Content Potential: patterning, counting, writing numbers

Perseverance Scale:

Grade Level	K	1
Perseverance Level	1	1

Macro-Moves: using hints and extension to maintain flow, consolidating from the bottom

Competencies: looking for patterns

Task

The first criterion is the task itself. It is written in a format similar to what you would see in a textbook or a website and in its simplest mathematical terms. For example, "If you write the numbers from 1 to 1000, how many times is the digit 7 used?" It is, however, not recommended that you present the task this way to your students. In Chapter 2, we talked about being verbal as much as possible when giving a task. And doing so needs a script (see the Launch Script indicator that follows). But having the question stated in this form allows you to quickly ascertain whether this is a task you have already done with your students, a task that you might be interested in doing with your students, and/or a task that your students might find engaging. What follows is a list of indicators that you might use to select tasks. But you might have your own criteria and easy access to the task, in simplistic terms, allows you to invoke your own criteria.

Grades

Although good non-curricular tasks are useful with a wide range of grade levels, there is often a limit to that range. And that limit is often set by the prerequisite mathematical topics that students need in order to engage with the task. Consequently, each non-curricular task is, first and foremost, accompanied by an indication of the grade levels that it is appropriate for. But this is just a guide. This range is dependent on the specific curriculum you are using and will change from jurisdiction to jurisdiction. You need to decide for yourself where your students are in their knowledge and abilities.

Having said that, this part of the book contains tasks where the recommended grades may include very young students—students that you may assume are not capable of this level of mathematics. When you feel yourself thinking this, please keep in mind that these tasks have been tested with a wide range of students and have been shown to be effective even with young students.

Likewise, there may be non-curricular tasks in here that you feel are actually curricular in your jurisdiction. This may be the case. But it is important to remember that a curricular task for a Grade 4 student is a non-curricular thinking task for a Grade 2 student. For example, we have done a ton of division tasks with kindergarten and Grade 1 students. These make amazing thinking tasks for these young learners, as they do not have the routines and strategies around this operation that older students have. And yet, division is completely approachable because they can think of it as *fair share*—something every child comes to school knowing. Division, although curricular for Grade 4 students, is non-curricular for K–1 students.

Content Potential

Although each of the tasks in Part 2 of the book purports to be non-curricular, they are still mathematical in nature and, hence, require mathematics to be solved. Some of the mathematics will, inevitably, intersect with outcomes and standards from curriculum. But given the nature of non-curricular tasks and how they are used, it just cannot be guaranteed that specific outcomes and standards will be met or that they will be met by every group of students. And even if every group does manage to hit on the specific outcomes and standards, there is no guarantee that those outcomes are actually part of the curriculum for the grade of students you are using the tasks with.

This lack of guarantees is OK. In fact, it is preferable. The alternative is problematic. Consider the typical word problem that you encounter in your textbooks. These are designed to ensure that every student who solves them does so using a narrow band of strategies and concepts, thereby ensuring that specific outcomes and standards are achieved. This often makes word problems inadequate thinking tasks. They are engineered and scaffolded to have the students use specific approaches and strategies and, as such, are not thinking tasks at all. They are just routine tasks shrouded in words. Thinking tasks are not like this at all. Thinking tasks are designed so that students need to use concepts from a variety of content strands and to combine these concepts in unique and varied ways to solve them. And, although there is a clearly stated task, and often only one solution, how they move from task to solution offers many different options. Thinking tasks are usually not open-ended. They are open-middle. This is what makes them good. But the price that needs to be paid for good thinking tasks is that there is no guarantee what path students will take and what content they will encounter. But they will encounter content. This is why we refer to non-curricular tasks as having *content potential*. As such, each non-curricular task is accompanied by a list of content that may potentially be encountered.

Perseverance Scale

Each task is also annotated with a perseverance scale. When you are first starting to build a thinking classroom, your students have little to no perseverance. So when starting out on your journey to build a thinking classroom, you will need tasks that require equally little perseverance. Level 1 tasks are ideal for this. They have been proven to be highly effective at engaging large numbers of students across a wide variety of contexts, so they are ideal to use as the first tasks that students encounter when you launch your journey into building a thinking classroom. Tax Collector (BTC, p. 107) and The Answers Are (BTC, p. 168) are examples of such tasks. They just work—every time. We recommend that you use a minimum of three Level 1 tasks when you begin to build a culture of thinking in your classrooms. Some classes will require more, but we have never encountered a class that needed less.

> We recommend that you use a minimum of three Level 1 tasks when you begin to build a culture of thinking in your classrooms.

It is still recommended to use four to six non-curricular tasks to begin to build a thinking classroom. They can all be Level 1 tasks, but after the first three tasks, they can also be Level 2 tasks. Level 2 tasks require some experience with the routines of thinking classrooms and some perseverance on the part of the students because the tasks have an evolving complexity that takes time and effort to fully complete.

As mentioned, non-curricular tasks are not only good for creating a thinking culture when beginning to build your thinking classroom. They are good for maintaining and fine-tuning that culture throughout the year and are also a safe place to explore new BTC practices. As your students become more and more accustomed and adept at thinking, they will be able to tolerate (even crave) more challenging tasks. And they will have developed greater perseverance (Chapter 4). Level 3 tasks are ideal for this. These tasks require greater perseverance than Level 2 tasks, yet are still approachable for all students.

Knowing what perseverance level is required for each task will help you to decide when to use various grade-level-appropriate tasks with your students as they grow into thinkers. As mentioned, each non-curricular task is appropriate for multiple grades, yet students in different grades will find varying degrees of challenge in each task. That is, the perseverance needed for a task varies by grade. The perseverance scale addresses this. For example, the perseverance scale here tells you that this particular task has a perseverance level of 2 for Grade 1 students and a perseverance level of 1 for Grades 2–4:

Grade Level:	1	2	3	4
Perseverance Level:	2	1	1	1

Macro-Moves

As mentioned, it is always good to expand into a new BTC practice with a non-curricular task. Doing so takes the pressure off the teacher to achieve an outcome or a standard while at the same time juggling the complexity of adopting new practices. In addition, it takes the pressure off the students to have to learn something from the curriculum while, as a result of the changes in your teaching practices, they are also experiencing changes in the way they work and learn mathematics. So, if you are looking for more tasks to accompany the introduction of a new-to-you or a new-to-your-students BTC practice, each of the non-curricular tasks is accompanied by an indication of which BTC practices it supports well. Some tasks are great for practicing consolidation from the bottom—others are not. Some tasks are better than others for practicing being verbal in your instructions. As such, each task is accompanied by a list of the macro-moves that are supported by the task.

Any teacher who has been using BTC practice knows that developing competency with these practices takes time. So, you can also use the macro-moves indicator to select BTC practices that you have previously introduced, but that you want to revisit through non-curricular tasks to continue developing familiarity and honing your expertise.

Competencies

In Chapter 8, we summarized the practice of co-constructing rubrics with students to improve student competencies that are specific to building a thinking classroom—competencies such as collaboration, perseverance, and willingness to take risks. The development of these competencies is important not only for functioning and contributing in the thinking classroom, but in education and life in general. Non-curricular tasks are a great context in which to accentuate and work on these competencies, so each task is accompanied by a list of competencies that are brought to the surface through engagement in that task. You can use this list as (1) a way to select tasks that introduce your students to a particular competency from which you can co-construct a competency rubric, or (2) a way to work on competencies you have previously established with your students.

WHAT ELSE DO THE NON-CURRICULAR TASKS INCLUDE?

After the six aforementioned task indicators comes ten sections to help you enact the task in your classroom. Which of these you make use of will depend greatly on where you are in your journey to build a thinking classroom. For example, if you are at the beginning, you might only make use of the launch script. If you are further along, you may want to consolidate the task and close out the activity with some check-your-understanding (CYU) questions. Regardless, the ten subsequent sections will help you to tap into the possibilities that each task offers in building your thinking classroom.

Launch Script

As mentioned in Part 1, as much as possible, tasks should be given verbally. But reading the task in its simplest mathematical terms as given in the indicators is not an adequate way to do this. Students need context and a gradual unfolding of the conditions, criteria, and constraints of a task. How you present the task matters, so each task is accompanied by a script to help you launch the task.

Each script has emerged from our multiple and varied experiences using each task with students. This is not to say they are the perfect script. What we can tell you, however, is that each script is better than the first (or second, or third) time we used a task. You may find ways to improve the script, which is great! Just know that how you launch the task matters—a lot. How you launch the task will determine how well it lands.

LAUNCH SCRIPT

Teacher: Each of these shapes is called a hexagon. How many hexagons do you see here? [teacher points at image]

Students: 6!

Teacher: I want to put one number in each hexagon, I have two 1s, two 2s, and two 3s. [writes 1, 1, 2, 2, 3, 3 on the board] Where could I put the 1s?

Students: [answers will vary but teacher picks an answer where the two 1s are side-by-side]

Teacher: Oh [snapping fingers], I forgot to tell you that none of the same numbered hexagons can be touching each other. So, where can the 1s go?

Students: [answers will vary but teacher picks an answer where the two 1s are not side-by-side]

Teacher: Where can the rest of the numbers go?

Each script is written for the specific version of the task as stated at the top of the page. Variations of the script are necessary if you are differentiating it for your students. But this is easy to do. Whether you follow the script verbatim or you make small differentiation adjustments or improvements to the script, try to make the script your own. Do not read it from the book or a page. Embrace it and tell it as if it is yours. Your students will see it as more genuine.

Creating Access

Most tasks can be made easier or harder simply by adjusting the numbers or some other facet of the task. As such, each launch script is followed by a set of notes on how to adjust the task to create access for learners who may be struggling to get started.

CREATING ACCESS

- For students who have no knowledge of numbers, laminate colored hexagons and make the problem about arranging the hexagons so that no two hexagons of the same color touch each other.

- For students who struggle with writing numbers, laminate numbered hexagons and have the students arrange the hexagons.

- For students who struggle with writing numbers, laminate numbers for them to place into the pre-drawn hexagons.

You will have to decide for yourself what is the best starting point for your students. But keep in mind that you can never go too easy. The only consequence of starting easy is that students are ready for something more challenging quickly. On the other hand, the consequences of starting too hard are frustration, disengagement, off-taskness and, for many students, a feeling that they cannot do math. Start easy.

Extension Scripts

The launch script is also followed by extension scripts. When groups finish the original task, as presented in the launch script, they need an extension. And when they finish the first extension, they need a second extension, and so on. The extension script provides these extensions. But this is more than a list of extensions. Each extension is embedded within a script that continues the narrative presented within the launch script.

EXTENSION SCRIPTS

1. What if it was 1, 1, 1, 2, 2, 2, and 3, 3, 3 and there were 9 hexagons. Where would the numbers go then?

2. What about 12 hexagons? Four 1s, four 2s, and four 3s?

Author Solution(s)

Unlike the main BTC book, each task in this book comes with solutions—both author solution(s) and student solutions. The author solution(s) is a concise summary of the solution(s) to the task. For some tasks there is just one way of thinking about the task, so only one solution is provided. For other tasks, however, there are many ways to come to the same answer, so many different solutions are provided. Regardless, the purpose of the author solution is two-fold. First, the author solution gives you important details of the task and its solution so that you can use the task confident in your own understanding of the nuances of both the task and its solution. Second, the author solution provides you insights into what features of the task and solution you need to draw attention to for your students to be able to get to the solution. Taken together, by being able to see clearly the nuances of both the task and its solutions, you will be better equipped to see and understand when students make mistakes and/or go off track and to better provide the hints necessary to get them back on track.

When you look at the solutions of 6, 9, and 12 hexagons next to each other, you begin to see a pattern—a pattern that underpins all the solutions. This is best seen when we replace numbers with colors, as shown here.

For 6 hexagons, like-colored hexagons are one line away from each other. This turns out to be true for 9 and 12 hexagons as well. In fact, this is true no matter how many hexagons you use. What numbers go into like-colored hexagons does not matter, as long as like colors have like numbers. This means that solutions can be generated by placing any number into one hexagon and then adding the same number to any hexagons that are one line away from it, and so on.

This is not to say that you should not attempt to solve the task on your own first. Our explanation of the solution is no substitute for the realizations you come to through your own problem-solving experience. In an ideal setting, you would read the task, either in its simplest form or in its launch script form, and then work to solve it on your own. Once you have played with the task and its possible solutions for a while, read the author solution as a way to consolidate your understanding of the task.

Student Solutions

Following the author solution(s) are the student solutions. This is a collection of renderings of work done by real students, each of which is accompanied by a commentary on that particular solution, highlighting what is important to notice about that solution and what makes it different from the previous solutions presented. These are mostly correct solutions, but there are also some incorrect solutions presented as well. Some of the solutions have aspects highlighted with a green box to alert you to the types of things you should be looking for in your students' solutions.

STUDENT SOLUTIONS

1.

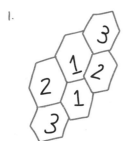

Commentary:

This incorrect solution shows that students started by putting numbers on the furthest points from each other and then realized the middle two hexagons are the most difficult to place.

Suggested hints:

Hmm ... Have you checked your work?

Let's erase the 3s and see if we can rearrange the 1s and 2s so that the 1s aren't touching each other and the 2s aren't touching each other.

It is unlikely that you will see all the solutions we share emerging from your students. But the list of solutions—correct and incorrect—with their green boxes and commentary will help you recognize the ones that do emerge. It is also unlikely that we have presented every solution that you will see emerging from your students. Every time we use a task with a new group of students, we see new ways to think about the task. Sometimes we see subtle variations of what we have seen before. Other times we see drastically different ways to solve the task. You need to always be open to the possibility that new solutions will emerge when using a task with your students.

Suggested Hints

Despite the fact that the author solutions provide you with a general sense of the solution and the student solutions provide you with very specific solutions you can expect to see in your classroom, you still need to know what kind of hints to use with your students. Embedded within the student solutions are hints to help you move a group of students from one solution, way of thinking, or way of representing their thinking to the next solution, way of thinking, or way of representing their thinking. In most cases, the hints are to help shift thinking within the same task. But in some cases, the hints are there to help them bring their thinking from one task to an extension task. Regardless, these hints sit beside the commentary and are presented as brief prompts to help you push your students' thinking.

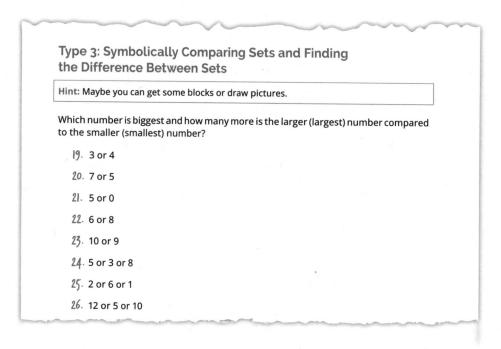

Type 3: Symbolically Comparing Sets and Finding the Difference Between Sets

Hint: Maybe you can get some blocks or draw pictures.

Which number is biggest and how many more is the larger (largest) number compared to the smaller (smallest) number?

19. 3 or 4
20. 7 or 5
21. 5 or 0
22. 6 or 8
23. 10 or 9
24. 5 or 3 or 8
25. 2 or 6 or 1
26. 12 or 5 or 10

The hints can also be used to prepare for consolidation by *seeding* (see Chapter 5) ideas that you want to emerge to make your consolidation more complete. For example, if during your consolidation you really wish to showcase a solution where the students worked backwards, but no group has used the method of working backwards, you may wish to seed this idea with some groups. From the students' perspective, there is no difference between hints and seeds. To them, they are all just hints. But there is a difference behind the intent of the two. Hints are for an individual group of students in the moment. Seeding is for the whole class to be showcased in the forthcoming consolidation.

Consolidation

Non-curricular tasks, by their nature, are usually rich tasks. Rich tasks will result in many different solution strategies emerging from the classroom, so the appropriate consolidation is most often to do a gallery walk, which you read about in Chapter 5. Embedded within the aforementioned list of possible student solutions lies the sequence you can use for doing a gallery walk. That is, the solutions are not presented in some haphazard order but rather laid out in an order through which the task can be consolidated. If you are at a point in your BTC journey where you are trying to consolidate tasks, then the green boxes, coupled with the commentary for each solution, will help you to select and sequence student work to facilitate an effective guided gallery walk.

CONSOLIDATION

The purpose of consolidation for this task is to move students from writing the numbers using trial and error to seeing that all the solutions to a given task have distinct patterns. This can be done by either looking at two or three correct, but different, solutions for 6 hexagons, or by looking at correct solutions for a 6 and a 9 hexagon and having them try to explain the patterns. The patterns will be easier to spot if you both get these multiple solutions next to each other and you color code the solutions. Alternatively, you can do a teacher-scribe where you start with a blank set of hexagons and have the students tell you where you need to start.

However, it is worth noting again that the set of solutions that emerge from your students will not be a perfect match with the solutions that are provided with each task. For those that do match, use the sequence of provided solutions to build your sequence for consolidation. If a unique solution not presented in this book comes up in your lesson, you need to decide whether you want to include it in the consolidation and, if so, where in the sequence it belongs. If a solution provided in the book does not emerge, you need to decide whether it is important that it does and, if so, how to plant the seeds that will help it to do so. The hints that accompany each task will help with this.

Check-Your-Understanding Questions

To close out the task, you may wish to transition your students into some check-your-understanding (CYU) questions. Depending on where you are in your BTC journey, and depending on the state the students are in, this may follow your consolidation, or you can go right from vertical work to CYU questions. Regardless, CYU questions are an important aspect of tasks, so we have included some CYU questions with each task—organized into the three categories of mild, medium, and spicy, which you read about in Chapter 7.

CHECK-YOUR-UNDERSTANDING QUESTIONS

MILD

If the first 3 is in the bottom left, where can't the other 3 be?

MEDIUM

If the first 2 is in the top center hexagon, where does the other 2 need to be?

It is important to remember to not set any accountability parameters—such as exit tickets, grading, checking—around these CYU questions. Instead, use the question, "Where are you going to start?" when offering the students the opportunity to do the CYU questions. Using this question naturally sets up the follow through of "What are you going to do next?" As mentioned in Chapter 7, the research shows that such phrasing positions CYU questions as something they are responsible to themselves for—rather than accountable to you for—and has been shown to engage students more. And, as a result, they actually do more questions and for the correct reason: as a way to check their understanding. This positioning also creates an environment where the students work in a balance of challenge and success that propels them into productive struggle (see Chapter 1).

It is also important to remember that, although the students take responsibility for their own work on CYU questions, they can make use of the knowledge around them, getting help from their peers as needed and giving help to their peers if needed. This is called *working on their own together* (see Chapter 7). Because there are no accountability measures around CYU questions, there is no incentive to copy from each other. They are not doing division of labor or cheating; they are learning from each other, and this is to be encouraged.

Author Notes

As much as we have tried to get everything organized into the above sections, the work that students do on non-curricular tasks does not always lend itself to the linear-textual format used in this section. There is often something that doesn't fit or doesn't fit well. In addition, there may be things we have learned from doing these tasks with students that we haven't been able to include in the categories above—acquired micro-moves, so to speak. It would be useful for you to know these, so we have included a section for author notes where we can include any important information that hasn't been included in the sections above.

Author Notes

An interesting situation that is likely to emerge with this task is students writing their numbers backwards and because of the VNPSs, other groups and students are likely to provide quick, effective feedback to each other.

We suggest you practice drawing hexagons before giving this task out and have the hexagons already drawn at each station. You might be tempted to substitute the hexagons for circles. This is fine, if you can really draw circles that touch each other—this is harder than you think. And the students care A LOT about this if the instructions are about touching.

Notes to My Future Forgetful Self

This is not to say that there isn't more to learn. Every time we do a task, students reveal something new to us. And, as a result, we learn something new about the students or about ourselves as teachers. You will, too, so we have also included a section where you can keep notes about your own experiences using each task. A place where you can make *notes to your future forgetful self.*

Notes to My Future Forgetful Self

THE 20 NON-CURRICULAR TASKS

Pulling all this together, what follows is a table of all the tasks and all their indicators. You can think of this as a hyper-detailed table of contents that will enable you to quickly look for, or come back to, tasks that you think are best for you and your students in your collective journey to build a thinking classroom.

#	Name	Grades	Content Potential	Perseverance Scale		Macro-Moves	Competencies
1	Hexagon Havoc	K–1	patterning, counting, writing numbers	Grade: K, 1 / Scale: 1, 1		using hints and extension to maintain flow, consolidating from the bottom	looking for patterns
2	Next Door Numbers	K–1	counting, addition, what makes 10?	Grade: K, 1 / Scale: 1, 1		giving tasks verbally, using hints and extensions to maintain flow	collaboration
3	Letters in a Name	K–2	counting, addition, subtraction, comparing sets of numbers	Grade: K, 1, 2 / Scale: 1, 1, 1		consolidating from the bottom	collaboration
4	Shape Race	K–2	patterning, counting, drawing, and recognizing shapes	Grade: K, 1, 2 / Scale: 2, 1, 1		consolidating from the bottom	organizing your work
5	Ice Cream Scoops	K–2	adding, counting, doubling, odds, and evens	Grade: K, 1, 2 / Scale: 2, 1, 1		using hints and extensions to maintain flow, consolidating from the bottom	representing your thinking
6	At the Fair	K–2	adding, counting, subtraction, make ten	Grade: K, 1, 2 / Scale: 2, 1, 1		giving tasks verbally, mobilizing knowledge, consolidating from the bottom	collaboration, showing your thinking pictorially and symbolically
7	Katha the Caterpillar	1–5	growing patterns, multiplication, skip counting, measurement, table of values	Grade: 1, 2, 3, 4, 5 / Scale: 3, 3, 2, 1, 1		giving tasks verbally, consolidation from the bottom	perseverance

#	Name	Grades	Content Potential	Perseverance Scale	Macro-Moves	Competencies
8	Carnival Conundrum	1–4	counting, adding, patterning	Grade: 1, 2, 3, 4 / Scale: 3, 3, 2, 1	using hints and extensions to manage flow	risk taking, trial and error, conjecturing and testing
9	Colored Boxes	2–5	comparative language, logic	Grade: 2, 3, 4, 5 / Scale: 3, 2, 1, 1	answering only keep-thinking questions	collaboration, risk taking
10	There's How Many Legs?	K–5	addition, subtraction, multiplication, division, patterning, linear relations	Grade: K, 1, 2, 3, 4, 5 / Scale: 3, 3, 2, 2, 1, 1	using hints and extensions to maintain flow	willingness to take risks, creativity, perseverance
11	Ways to Make 10	2–4	adding, doubling, halving, patterns, linear equations, linear relations	Grade: 2, 3, 4 / Scale: 2, 1, 1	how we foster autonomy, hints and extensions, how we give the task	collaboration
12	Tables at a Party	K–5	skip counting, repeated addition, multiplication/ division, commutative property, perimeter	Grade: K, 1, 2, 3, 4, 5 / Scale: 3, 3, 2, 2, 1, 1	using hints and extensions to maintain flow	risk taking, trial and error, organization
13	Squares on a Checkerboard	2–5	recognizing and discerning shapes, addition, square numbers, patterning, and equations	Grade: 2, 3, 4, 5 / Scale: 3, 3, 2, 2	consolidation from the bottom	perseverance, trial and error, organization
14	Prisms, Prisms, Prisms	2–5	2D and 3D shapes, edges, sides, faces, vertices, patterns, equations, multiplication	Grade: 2, 3, 4, 5 / Scale: 3, 2, 1, 1	mobilization of knowledge	organization, looking for patterns
15	Brianna the Birdy	3–5	multiplication, divisibility, table of values	Grade: 3, 4, 5 / Scale: 3, 2, 2	giving tasks verbally, answering only keep-thinking questions	perseverance, trial and error, risk taking

(Continued)

(Continued)

#	Name	Grades	Content Potential	Perseverance Scale			Macro-Moves	Competencies
16	When Is a Triangle a Square?	3–5	multiplication, addition, square numbers, triangular numbers, patterns	Grade: 3, 4, 5 / Scale: 3, 2, 2			consolidation from the bottom, knowledge mobility	looking for patterns, mobilizing knowledge
17	Outfit Choices	3–5	patterning, multiplication, counting	Grade: 3, 4, 5 / Scale: 3, 3, 2			use hints and extensions to maintain flow, knowledge mobility	organization, mobilizing knowledge, perseverance
18	How Many High Fives?	3–5	patterning, equations, addition, sequences	Grade: 3, 4, 5 / Scale: 3, 3, 2			how we give tasks, consolidation from the bottom	collaboration, risk taking, organization, looking for patterns
19	Folding Paper	3–5	multiplication, doubling, patterns, exponents	Grade: 3, 4, 5 / Scale: 3, 2, 2			consolidation from the bottom	communication, mobilizing knowledge
20	Twin Test	4–5	factors, division/ multiplication, fractions, decimals, percentages	Grade: 4, 5 / Scale: 3, 3			giving hints and extensions to maintain flow, knowledge mobility	perseverance, collaboration, mobilizing knowledge

We have included in this book 20 non-curricular tasks. We could have included many more, but then we would be back where we started. You do not really want an endless number of non-curricular tasks—you want good tasks. You want tasks that have been tried with students just like yours and that you can be confident will work to help you build a thinking classroom. That is what we have provided. But there are more tasks and there are resources for you to find more tasks. In Part 4, we provide you with a catalog of resources should you wish to look for more tasks. However, lists of resources are like lists of tasks—they can go on forever. And like with tasks, you do not want endless resources; you want a short list of resources that you can have faith in. This is what we provide in Part 4.

Alternatively, you may already have good non-curricular tasks that you have used in your thinking classroom. If you wish to format those tasks like the tasks in this book, in Part 4 we also provide a link to a template to help you do so. Whether you wish to do this for your own records or to share your good non-curricular tasks with colleagues, the template will help you to dissect and delineate tasks into their salient and actionable indicators and elements.

TASK 1: HEXAGON HAVOC

TASK

Write the numbers 1, 1, 2, 2, 3, 3 into 6 connecting hexagons without having hexagons with the same number touching one another.

Grades: K–1

Content Potential: patterning, counting, writing numbers

Perseverance Scale:

Grade Level	K	1
Perseverance Level	1	1

Macro-Moves: using hints and extension to maintain flow, consolidating from the bottom

Competencies: looking for patterns

LAUNCH SCRIPT

Teacher: Each of these shapes is called a hexagon. How many hexagons do you see here? [teacher points at image]

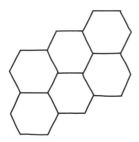

Students: 6!

Teacher: I want to put one number in each hexagon, I have two 1s, two 2s, and two 3s. [writes 1, 1, 2, 2, 3, 3 on the board] Where could I put the 1s?

Students: [answers will vary but teacher picks an answer where the two 1s are side-by-side]

Teacher: Oh [snapping fingers], I forgot to tell you that none of the same numbered hexagons can be touching each other. So, where can the 1s go?

Students: [answers will vary but teacher picks an answer where the two 1s are not side-by-side]

Teacher: Where can the rest of the numbers go?

CREATING ACCESS

- For students who have no knowledge of numbers, laminate colored hexagons and make the problem about arranging the hexagons so that no two hexagons of the same color touch each other.

- For students who struggle with writing numbers, laminate numbered hexagons and have the students arrange the hexagons.

- For students who struggle with writing numbers, laminate numbers for them to place into the pre-drawn hexagons.

EXTENSION SCRIPTS

1. What if it was 1, 1, 1, 2, 2, 2, and 3, 3, 3 and there were 9 hexagons. Where would the numbers go then?

2. What about 12 hexagons? Four 1s, four 2s, and four 3s?

AUTHOR SOLUTION(S)

When you look at the solutions of 6, 9, and 12 hexagons next to each other, you begin to see a pattern—a pattern that underpins all the solutions. This is best seen when we replace numbers with colors, as shown here.

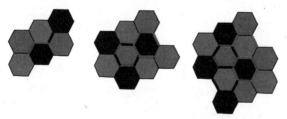

For 6 hexagons, like-colored hexagons are one line away from each other. This turns out to be true for 9 and 12 hexagons as well. In fact, this is true no matter how many hexagons you use. What numbers go into like-colored hexagons does not matter, as long as like colors have like numbers. This means that solutions can be generated by placing any number into one hexagon and then adding the same number to any hexagons that are one line away from it, and so on.

STUDENT SOLUTIONS

1.

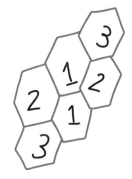

Commentary:

This incorrect solution shows that students started by putting numbers on the furthest points from each other and then realized the middle two hexagons are the most difficult to place.

Suggested hints:

Hmm ... Have you checked your work?

Let's erase the 3s and see if we can rearrange the 1s and 2s so that the 1s aren't touching each other and the 2s aren't touching each other.

2.

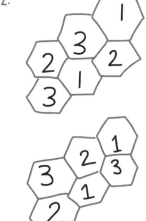

Commentary:

These solutions are good to pair together so that students can see that although there are different solutions, the placement of number pairs can only be (a) top middle and bottom left, (b) bottom middle and top right, and (c) top left and bottom right.

Suggested hints:

Where did you start? What happens if you start somewhere else?

What is the pattern here for 6 hexagons? Can you find a pattern with 9 hexagons?

3.

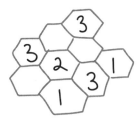

Commentary:

This solution is incomplete because the students know that it is not going to work out for them.

Suggested hints:

Look at the flower that I am outlining here. Now look at the center of that flower. You have put a 2 in the center. What does that mean for all the flower petals?

(Continued)

(Continued)

4.

3 1
2 3 2
2 1 3 1
3 2 3
1,1,1
2,2,2

Commentary:

This solution is a good representation for the students to see that, just like the original task, there is a clear pattern for how the numbers fit. All 3 of the same numbers make a triangle.

Suggested hints:

Can you see a pattern for how all the numbers fit? Are there any other ways to make the numbers fit?

Which hexagons are the most difficult to fit a number into?

Do you think there would be a pattern for 12 hexagons?

CONSOLIDATION

The purpose of consolidation for this task is to move students from writing the numbers using trial and error to seeing that all the solutions to a given task have distinct patterns. This can be done by either looking at two or three correct, but different, solutions for 6 hexagons, or by looking at correct solutions for a 6 and a 9 hexagon and having them try to explain the patterns. The patterns will be easier to spot if you both get these multiple solutions next to each other and you color code the solutions. Alternatively, you can do a teacher-scribe where you start with a blank set of hexagons and have the students tell you where you need to start.

CHECK-YOUR-UNDERSTANDING QUESTIONS

MILD

If the first 3 is in the bottom left, where can't the other 3 be?

MEDIUM

If the first 2 is in the top center hexagon, where does the other 2 need to be?

A. What is the pattern/rule for 6 hexagons?

B. What is the pattern/rule for 9 hexagons?

Author Notes

An interesting situation that is likely to emerge with this task is students writing their numbers backwards and because of the VNPSs, other groups and students are likely to provide quick, effective feedback to each other.

We suggest you practice drawing hexagons before giving this task out and have the hexagons already drawn at each station. You might be tempted to substitute the hexagons for circles. This is fine, if you can really draw circles that touch each other—this is harder than you think. And the students care A LOT about this if the instructions are about touching.

Notes to My Future Forgetful Self

_____

_____

_____

_____

_____

_____

_____

_____

_____

_____

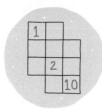

TASK 2: NEXT DOOR NUMBERS

TASK

Place the numbers 1 to 10 into 10 boxes, making sure that no consecutive numbers are side by side.

Grades: K–1

Content Potential: counting, addition, what makes 10?

Perseverance Scale:

Grade Level	K	1
Perseverance Level	1	1

Macro-moves: giving tasks verbally, using hints and extensions to maintain flow

Competencies: collaboration

LAUNCH SCRIPT

Teacher: [Teacher draws a row of boxes with the numbers from 1 to 10 on the board]

1	2	3	4	5	6	7	8	9	10

Teacher: This is a number line [pointing at the row of 1–10]. Did you know that these numbers are all brothers and sisters? They are. And every day when they come to school they have to sit on the number line in this exact order. And every day when they go home to their house, their house looks just like this, too. Yup, their house has 10 bedrooms all in a row, and their bedrooms are all in the same order as they are on the number line.

Teacher: And, because they are always together in this same order, they are starting to not like the numbers they are next to. 4 thinks that 5 smells funny. 8 thinks that 9 is too loud. And 2 thinks that 1 chews weird. They really don't like the numbers next door.

Teacher: Then one day, their parents buy a new house. [teacher draws new house]

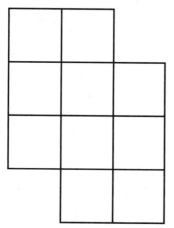

Teacher: Your job is to help the 10 numbers move into the new house so that the numbers that are next to each other on the number line [teacher points at number line] are *not* next to each other in the house.

CREATING ACCESS

- For students for whom the task is too difficult, reduce the problem to five boxes and numbers 1–5.

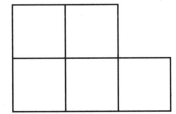

- For students having difficulty starting, draw the boxes for them.

- For students who are having difficulty understanding what the task is, ask students to put the numbers anywhere. Once they are done, ask them to identify places where "numbers that are next to each other on the number line are still next to each other when they are home."

EXTENSION SCRIPTS

1. I forgot to mention that number line neighbors REALLY don't like each other. When they are at home, number line neighbors don't want to be beside each other AND they don't want to be above or below each other either.

2. I forgot to mention that number line neighbors REALLY REALLY don't like each other. When they are at home, they don't want their bedrooms touching each other AT ALL. So, they can't be beside each other, and they can't be above or below each other, AND they can't be diagonal to each other either.

3. Do you know what ten-friends are? Ten-friends are numbers that add to 10. Well, ten-friends are not friends any more. They do not like each other. Can you keep ten-friends apart?

4. Their parents bought another new house and it's moving day. Now help them move into this new house so that the rooms of numbers that are next to each other on the number line don't touch.

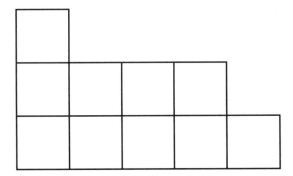

5. Now do ten-friends for the new house.

AUTHOR SOLUTION(S)

For any one of these tasks, there is no one solution. The trick to finding a solution that keeps number line neighbors apart is to put numbers that have only one neighbor on the number line (1 and 10) in bedrooms that have a lot of neighbors. Now place the 2 so it is touching the 10 but not the 1. Then place the 9 so it is touching the 1 but not the 10. Place the 3 so it is touching the 1 but not the 2. Place the 8 so it is touching the 10 but not the 9. With the six numbers 1, 2, 3, 8, 9, 10 placed, you then place 4 so it doesn't touch 3 and 7 so it doesn't touch 8, trying to keep two squares empty that are not touching for the 5 and 6. The placement of the last four numbers may have to be attempted more than once, but you will eventually get a solution. Possible solutions are as follows:

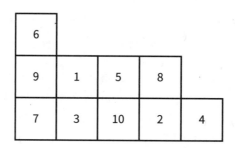

In the ten-friend problems, numbers are easier to place because we only have to keep two numbers apart (for example 3 and 7) and the 5 and 10 can go anywhere. So, place 5 and 10 last. Start by placing 1 and 9 only one square apart, then 2 and 8 one square apart. Then place 3 and 7 so they do not touch, making sure there are squares left that do not touch. Then place 4 and 6 in squares that do not touch. Finally place the 5 and 10. This is not hard. What makes this task tricky for K–1 is that they have to think A LOT about who are the ten-friends. Possible solutions are as follows:

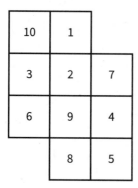

STUDENT SOLUTIONS

1.

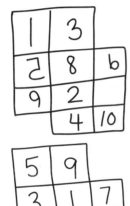

Commentary:

This solution is correct for the original task of having no consecutive (next door) numbers side by side. However, as the task has progressed, so have the constraints.

Suggested hints:

What if next door numbers couldn't be up or down from one another either? What if they couldn't be diagonal too?

2.

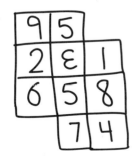

Commentary:

These two solutions are two potential options for the first and second extensions. The first is incomplete but could be completed during consolidation. The second is more of a complete solution.

Suggested hints:

What if the 10-friends couldn't be near each other?

3.

Commentary:

This is a solution for the ten-friend extension.

Suggested hints:

What if the numbers we used are only ten-friend numbers. What number can't we use? What number would we add instead?

4.

Commentary:

This is a different solution for the ten-friend extension. This group chose to have two 5s. This was a deliberate decision to make sure every number had a ten-friend. This actually makes the problem more challenging.

Suggested hints:

What if we wanted to keep the ten-friends apart AND we wanted to keep the numbers that are next to each other on the number line apart? Where are there going to be problems? Can you fix them?

CONSOLIDATION

The purpose of this consolidation is to demonstrate the different correct solutions while also looking at the various levels of tasks there were. You can do this by picking a rule and asking the class to verify that a solution is correct for that rule. Alternatively, you can pick a solution and ask the class to verify what rules are satisfied by that solution. For instance, the last two solutions presented above are incorrect for some rules but not other rules.

CHECK-YOUR-UNDERSTANDING QUESTIONS

MILD

Put the numbers 1–10 into the house so that number line neighbors don't touch.

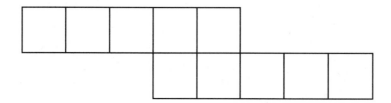

MEDIUM

Put the numbers 1–10 into the house so that number line neighbors don't touch.

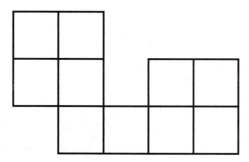

SPICY

Put the numbers 1–10 into the house so that number line neighbors don't touch.

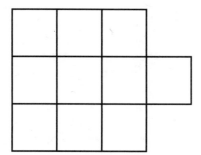

Author Notes

This task is a great opportunity for students to learn how to work on boards together and just practice writing their numbers. Many students will begin writing their numbers backwards, but with their learning visible, their partners or others will support them in correcting this. If they do not correct it, then you shouldn't. Drawing numbers correctly is not where you want the cognitive load for this activity. This task is about developing familiarity with which numbers belong together on the number line or in ten-friends and, thus, need to be apart in the house. This is where we want the cognitive load.

Notes to My Future Forgetful Self

TASK 3: LETTERS IN A NAME

TASK

Find out how many letters are in your name and who has a longer name.

Grades: K–2

Content Potential: counting, addition, subtraction, comparing sets of numbers

Perseverance Scale:

Grade Level:	K	1	2
Perseverance Level:	1	1	1

Macro-Moves: consolidating from the bottom

Competencies: collaboration

LAUNCH SCRIPT

Teacher: Today we are going to be working with our first names [teacher writes their first name on the board]. Whose name is this?

Students: Yours!

Teacher: How many letters do I have in my name? Let's count together.

Students: 1, 2, 3, 4, . . .

Teacher: Your job is for you and your partner to write your first names on the board and figure out how many letters you each have in your name.

CREATING ACCESS

• For students who don't know how to write/spell their first names, scribe it for them.

• For all students, you can have all the students' first names printed out on cards and you use these to make the random groups. Then the students can use these cards to write their first names on the boards.

EXTENSION SCRIPTS

1. In your group, who has the most letters in their name?

2. How many letters do you have in your names together? Can you write a number sentence for what you have found?

3. How many more letters does _____ have than _____? Write a number sentence for what you have found.

4. How many vowels do you each have? How many vowels do you have together? Who has more vowels in their name? How many more vowels do they have? Write a number sentence for what you have found.

5. In your group, what letter is used the most? The second most?

6. In your group, how many different letters are there?

7. My cat's name is *Super Fluff Monster* and my dog's name is *Mister Bif*. Can you write number sentences for their names?

8. How many letters does your group and the group next to you have together? Write a number sentence for what you have found.

9. Who has the most letters in the class? Who has the least number of letters in the class? How many more does the most have than the least? Write a number sentence for what you have found.

AUTHOR SOLUTION(S)

There is, of course, no one solution to these tasks.

STUDENT SOLUTIONS

1. | Maddex | Tennyson |

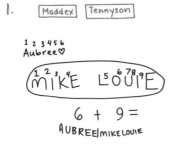

Commentary:

These examples are good discussion points around using the different ways to add or subtract. For instance, the top image shows a group using a number line and the bottom image shows that students numbered each letter.

Suggested hints:

What are other ways you could represent the sum or difference of the letters in your name?

2. | Kace | | Grace |

| Lex |

8 Brooklyn
6 Miguel

Commentary:

These two are addition tasks but are not explicitly written about. As an educator, you could push the students to be a bit clearer about showing their work.

Suggested hints:

What answer did you solve here? Could you show more of your math to make your thinking clearer?

What other ways can you look at the letters in your name?

(Continued)

(Continued)

3. M@CKE(N)Z(I)E9
    5 G@V(I)(n)

Commentary:

Here a group is looking at how many of the same letters they have. This solution is more complex than the other solutions for two reasons. It is focusing more on the "type of letters" compared to the number of letters. Second, the numbers are not easy to discern.

Suggested hints:

What can you add to your board that would help another group understand what you are doing?

How many different letters do you have?

CONSOLIDATION

The purpose of this consolidation is two-fold. First, use a gallery walk to discuss the various number sentences that are on the board and ask students to figure out what they represent. Second, use the gallery walk to look at different strategies for representing the sum and difference: counting on, counting backwards, one-to-one correspondence, using the number line.

CHECK-YOUR-UNDERSTANDING QUESTIONS

MILD

How many letters are in your name?

MEDIUM

A. Who has more letters in their name? You or me? Write a number sentence for this.

B. How many more letters did you (or I) have? Write a number sentence for this.

SPICY

A. My friend's cat is named *Morris* and her dog is named *Stinker*. Write a number sentence for this.

B. Write a name with 8 letters and a name with 3 letters. What number sentences can you make with these two names?

Author Notes

This task garners a lot of engagement from the students because the entry point is easy and the context of using their own names gets the students very excited. So make sure that everyone has their name on the board as soon as possible—whether they write it, you scribe it, or you use name cards.

This task also is a good approach to introducing subtraction because it is often introduced as "taking away" whereas this has students comparing two numbers.

Notes to My Future Forgetful Self

TASK 4: SHAPE RACE

TASK

Find all the different orders in which 3 shapes could finish if they raced each other.

Grades: K–2

Content Potential: patterning, counting, drawing, and recognizing shapes

Perseverance Scale:

Grade Level:	K	1	2
Perseverance Level:	2	1	1

Macro-Moves: consolidating from the bottom

Competencies: organizing your work

LAUNCH SCRIPT

Teacher: Have you ever had a race with one of your friends or family?

Students: Oh yeah! Of course!

Teacher: Have you ever come in first?

Students: I always win . . . I'm super fast! etc.

Teacher: Have you ever come in second or third?

Students: Yeah. . . . No. . . . etc.

Teacher: Today we are going to look at what might happen if some different shapes raced. If we had a circle [teacher draws a circle] and a square [teacher draws a square] racing [teacher draws a start line and a finish line], what could the results of the race be?

START   FINISH

Students: Circle could get 1st, then square would get 2nd or square could get 1st and circle could get 2nd.

Teacher: Oh! So, there are only two ways this race could end? Huh. What if triangle entered the race, too? [teacher draws triangle] How many ways could this three-shape race end?

CREATING ACCESS

- For students who are having trouble understanding the task, ask them to figure out how the circle could place in the race. Then say, "OK. Let's pretend that the circle won the race. How did the square and the triangle do?" If they give a single answer, ask them, "Could it have ended a different way for the square and the triangle?"

- For students who are having difficulty drawing the shapes, give them a bunch of different shapes to work with. They will need several of each shape to be able to show all the possible outcomes.

EXTENSION SCRIPTS

1. Look at this! Kite showed up for the race! And kite is very fast and won the race. How many results are there if the kite won?

2. Can you figure out how many total results there would be with circle, square, triangle, and kite racing?

AUTHOR SOLUTION(S)

The key to solving any problems of this sort is organization, and the trick to that is to keep one shape as the winner while varying the other two. For example, hold circle (C) as coming first and vary the position of the square (S) and triangle (T): CST, CTS. Then switch and hold the square as first: SCT, STC. Finally, hold the triangle (T) as first: TSC, TCS. So, there are two solutions if circle came first and two solutions if square came first, and so on. In essence, there are two possibilities for each shape coming first and there are three shapes that could have come first (3 × 2 or 3 × 2 × 1).

When adding the kite (K), you follow the same strategy, except this time you hold the kite as first while repeating what we just did above: KCST, KCTS, KSCT, KSTC, KTSC, KTCS. Then do it again holding a different shape first. So there are six possibilities if kite came first and there are six possibilities if circle came first, and so on. In essence, there are six possibilities once you decide which shape comes first, and there are four shapes that could have come first (4 × 6 or 4 × 3 × 2 or 4 × 3 × 2 × 1).

Setting up a table can help keep everything straight.

First	Second	Third
○	□	△
○	△	□
□	○	△
□	△	○
△	□	○
△	○	□

STUDENT SOLUTIONS

I.

Commentary:

This solution shows the first and second stage of students solving this problem. Students begin to write results almost at random but then begin to use a strategy (showing square winning in 2 ways). The next step is for the students to see that if there are two options for the square to win, this must also be true if another shape won.

Suggested hints:

Hmm ... so there are two options for square to win, but only one way for circle and triangle?

If there are two ways for square to win, how many ways would there be for circle/triangle?

2.

Commentary:

This solution shows students who provide all the possible results but in no particular order. Or they may not see the order. If the students can see circle winning twice, they might see how they can organize these results.

Suggested hints:

This is great! I see that you first have square winning, then triangle, then circle, and circle again. Can these results be written in a clearer order?

3. □ ○ △
   □ △ ○
   ○ □ △
   ○ △ □
   △ ○ □
   △ □ ○

Commentary:

This solution has the results in groups, but it may take some discussion for students to recognize it and see how to group all the results.

Suggested hints:

Why did you write the results in this order?

Can some of these be paired together because they have something in common?

4. ○ □ △   ②
   ○ △ □

   □ ○ △   ②
   □ △ ○

   △ ○ □   ②
   △ □ ○

Commentary:

This solution is a clear and organized illustration. It also shows the pattern that will be helpful with the kite extension.

Suggested hints:

How many groups will there be if there are four shapes racing?

How many different results will be in each group?

CONSOLIDATION

The purpose of consolidation for this task is to move students from writing out their answers randomly to creating some sort of organization that will enable them to see patterns. Organize a gallery walk to look at different representations and the patterns that emerge from them.

CHECK-YOUR-UNDERSTANDING QUESTIONS

MILD

If ○ □ △ have a race, how many results are there if ○ wins?

MEDIUM

If ○ □ △ have a race, how many total results are there?

SPICY

If ○ □ △ ♢ have a race, how many total results are there?

Author Notes

You will recognize that this is similar to the ice cream cone task in the main BTC book (BTC, p. 96). It is similar, but it's not the same. For one, in the ice cream task, groups naturally move toward a solution where all three scoops are chocolate. They do not do the same thing here. They do not naturally move to all three shapes winning in a tie. But some groups may decide that there can be ties. If they do, you will have to decide whether to allow it. The solutions we presented here do not cover this possibility.

You may be thinking that this seems like a weird task to use for having students count combinations. Compared to the ice cream task, it does seem farcical and maybe too abstract for our K–2 students. Rest assured; it is not. Students love this task. They love the context of a race. And, although having horses or cars race each other is more *real*, having the shapes race against each other gives them things that are easy to draw.

Finally, one of the things that we like about this task is that with minimal hints students can move from very random ways of counting possibilities to very ordered ways of counting.

Notes to My Future Forgetful Self

_____

_____

_____

_____

_____

_____

_____

_____

_____

_____

_____

_____

_____

TASK 5: ICE CREAM SCOOPS

TASK

Figure out how many scoops of ice cream each person has if you know the total number of scoops and that each person has the same number of scoops.

Grades: K–2

Content Potential: adding, counting, doubling, odds, and evens

Perseverance Scale:

Grade Level:	K	1	2
Perseverance Level:	2	1	1

Macro-Moves: using hints and extensions to maintain flow, consolidating from the bottom

Competencies: representing your thinking

LAUNCH SCRIPT

Teacher: Last weekend, I went for ice cream with *my son Jacob* [teacher says something relatable]. Now Jacob is all about everything being equal, and for him that includes having the same number of scoops of ice cream. So, we each got the same number of scoops. All together, we had four scoops. How many scoops did we each have?

CREATING ACCESS

- If students are struggling to begin, you can draw the cones and ice cream scoops for them.

- If students are struggling to draw the cones, you can give them triangles and circular discs to use when solving the task.

EXTENSION SCRIPTS

1. What if we had 6 scoops all together?

2. What about 8?

3. What about 12?

4. What if we had 9 scoops all together?

5. Is there a rule for how many scoops there can be in total?

6. Oops, I forgot to tell you that Jacob's cousin William came along, too. All three of us had the same number of scoops and all together we had 9 scoops. How many did we each have now?

7. What if we had 12 scoops all together?

8. What if we had 14 scoops all together?

9. Now that there are three of us, is there a rule for how many scoops there can be in total?

AUTHOR SOLUTION(S)

This task is about divisibility. Is the number divisible by two or three, depending on how many people there are? The answer for two people is obvious—there needs to be an even number of scoops. Depending on where your students are in their learning, they may know about even and odd numbers or they may know about skip counting by 2s, and they may express their answer in either of these ways. If they do not know about either, this is a great way for them to be introduced to these ideas.

For three people, the answer is not so obvious. Yes, it can be skip counted by 3s. But we doubt that any of your students are going to get to a point of seeing the divisibility rule for 3—*if the sum of the digits is divisible by 3 then the number is divisible by 3*. Nor should they. If they are skip counting by 3s and you were able to extend the task up into the 20s (3, 6, 9, 12, 15, 18, 21, 24, 27, ...) they may notice that this sequence contains every third even number and every third odd number. But it is unlikely that you will take this age group that far. In essence, for the students you are using this task with, the rule for three people is that there needs to be 3, 6, 9, 12, or 15 scoops in total.

STUDENT SOLUTIONS

1.

Commentary:

These solutions are something that students can create even if they don't understand doubling or anything really about addition. They may have just drawn one circle on each cone until they reached the desired number of scoops. However, they understood enough to the level of labelling each cone.

Suggested hints:

Look around at some of the other boards in the room. Do you notice what some of the groups are writing below or beside their drawings? Can you do the same?

2.

$2 + 2$
$= 4$

$3 + 3 = 6$

$3 + 3 + 3 = 9$

Commentary:

These solutions have students recognizing that they are adding the two (or three) cones together to create the total number of scoops. These are important to highlight when discussing the difference between doubling and tripling.

Suggested hints:

Does this work with every number? What if together we had 9 scoops in total?

3.

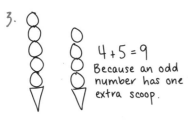

$4 + 5 = 9$
Because an odd number has one extra scoop.

7

$3 + 4 = 7$

7 is odd because an odd # has 1 more number sticking out.

Commentary:

These solutions show students who have attempted to make a "rule" for what numbers can and cannot be made from two of the same numbers.

Suggested hints:

Would the rule for odd numbers be true for three cones too?

CONSOLIDATION

The purpose of this consolidation is to begin with counting and addition and then to create collective *rules* around what can and cannot be a double. For instance, only even numbers can be doubles but odd numbers cannot. However, both odd and even numbers can be triples. You may also see students realize that it is skip counting. A guided gallery walk through the student solutions should work for this, but you may have to do a fair bit of seeding to get all the different ideas onto the boards.

CHECK-YOUR-UNDERSTANDING QUESTIONS

MILD

A. If two people have 3 scoops each, how many do they have together?

B. If two people split 8 scoops equally, how many does each person have?

MEDIUM

A. If two people split 14 scoops equally, how many does each person have?

B. If three people split 12 scoops equally, how many does each person have?

SPICY

A. Can two people split 11 scoops equally? Why or why not?

B. Can three people split 15 scoops equally? Why or why not?

Author Notes

This task has a very low entry point and gets into complex conversations about odd and even numbers, doubling, tripling, and skip counting. It also gets students into a process of *rulemaking* and then testing the limits of those rules. And kids love ice cream and care A LOT about fairness. So, this is a naturally engaging context.

Notes to My Future Forgetful Self

TASK 6: AT THE FAIR

TASK

Figure out how many rides you can go on if you have 10 minutes and three tickets (one ticket per ride) and the time for each ride varies.

Grades: K–2

Content Potential: adding, counting, subtraction, make ten

Perseverance Scale:

Grade Level:	K	1	2
Perseverance Level:	2	2	1

Macro-Moves: giving tasks verbally, mobilizing knowledge, consolidating from the bottom

Competencies: collaboration, showing your thinking pictorially and symbolically

Source: This task adapted from North Carolina Department of Public Instruction (n.d.) Problem Solving Cards Set A, card 45.

LAUNCH SCRIPT

Teacher: I went to the fair last weekend with my family, and I went on a bunch of rides. Turn to the person next to you and talk about what rides you really like and which ones you don't like.

Students: [talk among themselves]

Teacher: OK. Let's pretend you and your friends are at the fair. You have had a great day of going on rides, but your parents told you that it is soon time to go home, and they ask you how many tickets you have left. You look in your pocket and see that you have three tickets. That is enough to go on three more rides! If you have 10 more minutes before you leave, what rides could you go on before you need to leave?

Roller Coaster — 6 minutes

Ferris Wheel — 2 minutes

Bumper Cars — 5 minutes

Swings — 1 minute

Teacups — 4 minutes

Merry·Go·Round — 3 minutes

CREATING ACCESS

- For students who are struggling to start, you can tell them that you have already decided that the first ride will be the teacups. How much time do you have left and what other rides do you want to go on?

- For students who need help representing their thinking, Unifix cubes can be used to represent the time it takes for different rides. For example, a stack of two red cubes can be the ferris wheel.

EXTENSION SCRIPTS

1. Some other groups are having trouble deciding what to do. Can you come up with three different ride packages for them to choose from?

2. What if someone only likes one ride? What rides can they go on more than once? Which ride can they ride the most in 10 minutes?

3. What if you had 12 minutes and four tickets? What rides would you choose?

4. What if you had 20 minutes and six tickets?

5. How much time and how many tickets would you need to do your perfect ride combination?

6. What ride did we forget in our list? How long does it take? Come up with a solution for 15 minutes and four tickets with the new ride in it.

AUTHOR SOLUTION(S)

The number of combinations that solve this problem is massive. In essence, any combination that results in students not exceeding the number of tickets and the amount of time is an acceptable answer. Do keep in mind, though, that this task is driven by students' interest in going on rides, and interest trumps math for them. For example, for the extension task of 12 minutes and four tickets, some students may decide that going on the roller coaster twice is the way to go. They have used all their time, but not all their tickets. This is an acceptable answer. As is going on the same ride multiple times—even if this results in leftover time or leftover tickets. The goal here is not to optimize time or tickets, but to optimize fun.

STUDENT SOLUTIONS

1.

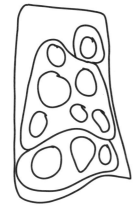

Commentary:

This solution is likely the first step students will use for keeping track of the time spent on each ride. This solution shows students clearly separating each ride to ensure that they go on 3 rides.

Suggested hints:

Can you indicate which rides you went on and how much time each took?

2.

$$S + B_c + M$$

Commentary:

This solution is quite complex as students as young as kindergarten are using symbols beyond numbers in operations. What is missing from this solution is the individual and total time for the rides.

Suggested hints:

How much time are you spending on each ride? Can you write a number sentence?

3.

$$1 + 5 = 6 + 3 = 9$$

Commentary:

This solution has students demonstrating the rides as numbers and using operations to indicate the cumulation of time. What comes next is to try to get the students to see that there is more than one solution.

Suggested hints:

Some other groups are having trouble deciding what to do. Can you come up with three different ride packages for them to choose from?

CONSOLIDATION

The purpose of this consolidation is threefold. First, we want students to see that the solution can be represented in many different ways—with pictures, with letters, and with numbers. Second, we want to showcase that the solution can be written as a number sentence (as in student solution #3) and that every solution can be represented as a number sentence. Finally, we want the students to see that there are multiple solutions and that some solutions can include the same ride multiple times. It is also good to show that, while some groups used all 10 minutes, others did not. And a solution that uses less than 10 minutes is still a solution. You can also take the time during consolidation to ask what a non-solution would look like. For example, "We have seen combinations that use all 10 minutes. And we have seen combinations that use less than 10 minutes. Can there be a combination that uses more than 10 minutes?"

CHECK-YOUR-UNDERSTANDING QUESTIONS

MILD

A. How much time does it take to ride the swings and teacups?

B. How much time does it take to ride the merry-go-round, ferris wheel, and swings?

MEDIUM

A. Can you ride the roller coaster, swings, and merry-go-round in 10 minutes?

B. If you have 14 minutes and four tickets, which rides would you go on?

SPICY

A. If you have 12 minutes and unlimited tickets, what is the most [or fewest] rides you can go on?

B. If you must go on three different rides in seven minutes, which rides can you NOT go on?

Author Notes

Students love this task because it is about going on rides. This is VERY real for them, and they have lots of stories. Trying to hold those back is difficult. This is why the launch script gives them a chance to get some of those stories out in a turn-and-talk. If you do not give this outlet, they will find a way to do it anyway. Give them time to vent that energy and then focus them on the math. But you can use this energy productively as well. The last task in the extension scripts taps into this energy to have them start expanding the problem to include other rides and how to use them in their solutions. The reason this is the last extension task is that once you open up this possibility you will not get them back into any sort of constrained task. In fact, we have seen many times students decide to create their own ride without prompting.

What is important to keep in mind is that not all students like all rides, so their solutions are going to be VERY situated. If one group does not like the roller coaster, it is not going to be a solution for them. This is why the first extension task is to design a ride package for a different group. This is also why the first Creating Access suggestion is to make the teacups the first ride—almost all students like the teacups.

Notes to My Future Forgetful Self

TASK 7: KATHA THE CATERPILLAR

TASK

Find out how many days it takes a caterpillar to reach the top of a tree, knowing how far it can travel in one day.

Grades: 1–5

Content Potential: growing patterns, multiplication, skip counting, measurement, table of values, division, algebraic equations

Perseverance Scale:

Grade Level:	1	2	3	4	5
Perseverance Level:	3	3	2	1	1

Macro-Moves: giving tasks verbally, consolidation from the bottom

Competencies: perseverance

Source: This task is adapted from *Problem Solving in Mathematics*, R.I.C. Publications.

LAUNCH SCRIPT

Teacher: Katha the caterpillar loves to climb trees. Every week she climbs a different tree. She climbs all the way to the top and when she gets there, she eats some leaves and enjoys the view. What do you think she would see if she climbed to the top of a tree?

Students: Lakes, mountains, other trees, etc.

Teacher: Well, one of the things that she sees every time she gets to the top of a new tree is Balveer the Big. Balveer is the name of the biggest tree in the forest and Katha has dreamed of climbing to the very top one day. But she is not sure she can do it. It would take a lot of strength. So, she keeps climbing smaller trees to build up her strength.

Teacher: Then one day, she thinks she is ready to climb Balveer. She is not very fast, but she is consistent. She climbs 2 feet (or meters) every day. The tree stands 36 feet (or meters) high. How many days will it take her to reach the top of Balveer?

CREATING ACCESS

- For students who have difficulty with big numbers, start with the height of the tree being 12 or 18. Whatever number you pick, you want it to be a multiple of lots of numbers. For example, 12 is a multiple of 2, 3, 4, and 6 and 18 is a multiple of 2, 3, 6, and 9.

EXTENSION SCRIPTS

1. What if she went up 3 feet (meters) every day? How long would it take her?

2. What if she went up 4 feet (meters) every day? How long would it take her?

3. What if she went up 6 feet (meters) every day? How long would it take her?

4. What if Katha climbed 3 feet (meters) every day, but then slides back 1 foot (meter) every night? What day would she reach the top of the tree?

5. What if Katha climbed 5 feet (meters) every day, but then slides back 3 feet (meters) every night? What day would she reach the top of the tree?

6. What if she went up 7 feet (meters) every day but slid back 2 feet (meters) every night? What day would she reach the top of the tree?

7. Every day she is twice as fast as she was the day before. If she climbs 1 foot (meter) on the first day, how many days will it take for her to reach the top?

AUTHOR SOLUTION(S)

Although this task may appear to be about division with and without remainders, students will not think about it in this way. They will think of it as multiplication, skip-counting, and so on. Regardless, you can use division to find the answers for the original task and each of the first three extension tasks. But you need to be careful with extension tasks 5 and 6. For example, Katha climbing 5 feet (meters) every day and sliding back 3 feet (meters) every night is not the same as climbing 2 feet (meters) every day. If you think of it as 2 feet (meters) every day then the answer is $36 \div 2 = 18$ days. This is not correct. After 16 days and nights, Katha will be at 32 feet (meters)—$16 \times 2 = 32$. But because she can climb 5 feet (meters) every day, part way through day 17 she will reach the top. The slide back that night is not relevant to the question—she has reached the top.

For extension question #7, the answer is that she will reach the top early on the sixth day. The sequence of climbs every day will be 1, 2, 4, 8, 16, 32. Therefore, at the end of any given day, she has climbed the sum of those numbers to that point. A table will help you see this.

Day	Climb that day	Total climb so far
1	1	1
2	2	3

(Continued)

(Continued)

Day	Climb that day	Total climb so far
3	4	7
4	8	15
5	16	31
6	32	63

There are some interesting patterns in this table. In particular, if you look at the total climb so far, you will notice that it is always 1 less than the climb that will happen on the next day. This is not important for students at this age to see, but they may if they can see their answers in an organized way.

Regardless, one of the solutions that you may want to emerge is to represent their thinking in some sort of algebraic expression. For example, for the first task, the height that Katha has climbed after any given day is $h = 2 \times d$, where h is the total height and d is the number of days that have passed. The only thing that will change for extensions 1–3 is the constant (in this case, 2) will change to be how far Katha climbs on any given day. The algebraic equations for extensions 4 and 5 are quite complex and well beyond the age of your students.

STUDENT SOLUTIONS

1.

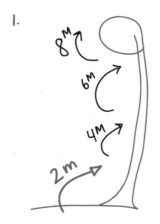

Each groups of 2

Commentary:

These solutions have students taking more of a literal, almost skip counting approach to finding the solution. This is a good starting point, regardless of which direction you want your students to go. These types of representation create an accessible entry point to discuss multiplication, division, patterns, or algebraic equations.

Suggested hints:

Are there other ways to represent this? [Seed a table of values or repeated addition]

2.

Day	2 m
1	2
2	4
3	6
4	8
5	10
6	12
7	14
8	16
9	18
10	20
11	22
12	24
13	26
14	28
15	30
16	32
17	34
18	36
19	

$36\,M = 18$ days

$2+2+2+2+2$
$2+2+2+2+2+2+2$
$+2+2+2+2+2+2$
$=36$

Commentary:

Depending on the direction you are hoping your students to go, you may see either or both of these solutions. Both are the next progression toward either building an algebraic equation or division.

Suggested hints:

Can you write this in a simpler way? Is there a way you could write this that includes f for feet (or m for meters) and d for days?

---

3. $d \times 2 = m$

$m / 2 = d$

Commentary:

These two solutions show students who have either discovered or noticed the multiplication and division strategy for the number of days. The top image even goes as far as to create an equation that can be used for different tree heights.

Suggested hints:

Would this work if Katha was going faster or slower each day? What would be the equation if Katha was going 4 m, 6 m, etc. per day?

CONSOLIDATION

The purpose of this consolidation is to get students to see the relationship between repeated addition, skip counting, multiplication, division, and algebraic equations. A guided gallery walk will enable you to do this. Depending on how far you want to push the students' understanding, you may wish to seed a table of values as well as use a variable to represent the total height and number of days.

CHECK-YOUR-UNDERSTANDING QUESTIONS

MILD

A. If Katha climbs 4 meters per day for 3 days, how far will she have climbed?

B. If Katha climbs 5 meters per day for 4 days, how far will she have climbed?

MEDIUM

A. How many days will it take Katha to climb 34 meters if she climbs 2 meters per day?

B. How many days will it take Katha to climb 36 meters if she climbs 7 meters per day but slides back 3 meters every night?

SPICY

A. Will Katha take more or less than 10 days to climb 40 meters at 3 meters per day?

B. Katha climbs twice as fast every day as she did the day before. If she climbs 2 meters on the first day, how far would she have climbed after 6 days?

Author Notes

This story really excites students, and every extension gets them more and more invested. For younger students, we stay with extensions that vary how far Katha climbs in a day and how tall Balveer is. For older students, we start adding in the fact that Katha slides down a bit every night. Either way, this task is extremely rich for moving students from skip counting to additive thinking to multiplicative thinking to algebraic thinking. And once they get an efficient representation, they can move quite quickly through the extension tasks.

Notes to My Future Forgetful Self

TASK 8: CARNIVAL CONUNDRUM

TASK

Place each of the numbers 1 to 5 into a V shape so that the two arms of the V have the same total.

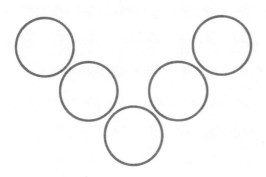

Grades: 1–4

Content Potential: counting, adding, patterning

Perseverance Scale:

Grade Level:	1	2	3	4	5
Perseverance Level:	3	3	2	1	1

Macro-Moves: using hints and extensions to manage flow

Competencies: risk taking, trial and error, conjecturing and testing

Source: This task was adapted from University of Cambridge (n.d.).

LAUNCH SCRIPT

Teacher: So, my family and I went to the carnival this weekend because Thayne loves to play carnival games, our kids love the rides, and I looooove the food. We were there all day Saturday, and I ate all kinds of amazing food, and the kids went on so many rides. Thayne also played lots of carnival games but never won. Every game he played, he just couldn't win; the bottles didn't get knocked down at one game, he couldn't shoot the water in the right spot at another, no matter what game he played, he couldn't win. So, after an exhausting day, we were about to leave the carnival but then Thayne saw a number game. At the game there were five circles and five numbers on a table [teacher points at diagram and numbers on the board].

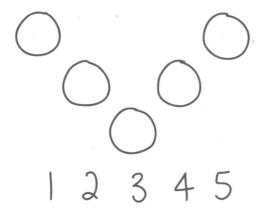

1 2 3 4 5

Teacher: The carnival worker said that all he needed to do to win was place the numbers into the circles so that each diagonal arm adds to the same sum. And it was $5 for two tries.

Teacher: Thayne was in a rush to win and go home so he put the numbers like this. [teacher writes the numbers 3, 1, 2, 4, 5 in the circles]

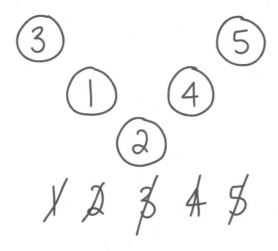

Teacher: When the worker checked he saw that 3 + 1 + 2 = 6 and 2 + 4 + 5 = 11 [teacher writes = 6 and = 11 on the diagram]

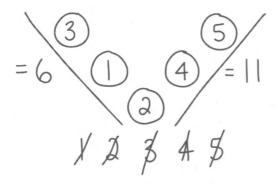

Teacher: Since 6 and 11 are not the same, he didn't win. But he has one more chance. So, how can Thayne arrange the five numbers to win the carnival game?

Teacher: As soon as you come up with one way to win, you need to put it in the *bank* and find another way to win. The *bank* is just a set of boxes down one side of your whiteboard [teacher shows a *bank*].

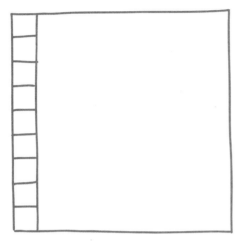

CREATING ACCESS

- For a group that is having difficulty adding, you can replace the numbers 1, 2, 3, 4, 5, with 1, 2, 2, 2, 3. Alternatively, you can use three circles and the numbers 1, 2, 2. Both of these options lower the floor significantly and you will need to move back to the original task pretty quickly. But it will give them success.

- For a group that is having trouble starting, or is ready to give up, you can place the 5 at the bottom of the V. This makes the rest of the solution pretty simple.

- Alternatively, you can place a 4 in one of the top circles. This gives them a starting point, but still keeps the task challenging. If they need another hint, place the 2 on the other upper circle.

- For a group that is struggling to understand the task, step in and redo the script above and then stay with them for a bit as they try it on their own.

EXTENSION SCRIPTS

1. Ok. You won the game. Let's save that up here [teacher redraws solution on the left of the board and boxes it in]. Now, can you come up with another way to win?

2. Can you come up with another way to win? [Keep asking this until they have three solutions with the numbers 1, 3, and 5 as the bottom number.]

3. Now I am changing the numbers on you. You still have five circles, but this time you are using the numbers 3, 4, 5, 6, 7. How do you win the game now?

4. Can you come up with another way to win? [Keep asking this until they have three solutions with the numbers 3, 5, and 7 as the bottom number.]

5. Do you notice anything about all the different ways to win? Is there a rule?

6. Now try to win with the numbers from 2 to 6. Does your rule hold?

7. What would be the new rule? Can you put it into a sentence?

8. Now let's do 7 circles and the numbers from 1 to 7. How do you win the game now? Does your rule hold?

9. What would be the new rule?

AUTHOR SOLUTION(S)

This is a task that prompts students to make a conjecture about a rule, test this rule, and then refine it. For five circles and numbers 1–5, students will notice that all the solutions have an odd number in the bottom of the V. When we move them to numbers 3–7, they conjecture that this will still be true, quickly finding the three new solutions. Shifting to numbers 2–6 breaks their rule, however, producing solutions where an even number needs to be at the bottom of the V. Their new conjecture will typically be one of three rules:

1. Whatever the first number is (odd or even) will determine whether the bottom of the V will be odd or even.

2. Whatever there are more of (odd or even) will determine whether the bottom of the V will be odd or even.

3. Whatever the middle number is (odd or even) will determine whether the bottom of the V will be odd or even.

For five numbers, these rules are all, in essence, the same. If the first number is odd, so too is the middle number, and there will be more odd than even. When we move to having seven circles and numbers 1–7, however, the first two rules no longer hold. But the third rule does. The numbers 1, 2, 3, 4, 5, 6, 7 starts with an odd, has more odd numbers, but the middle number is even. And, indeed, the solutions will all have an even number at the bottom of the V.

To understand why this is, we need to look at the sum of the numbers we are using. The numbers 1–7 add to 28. Whatever number we place in the bottom of the V will need to leave an even sum so we can divide the numbers evenly between the two wings of the V. For example, consider picking 6 to go at the bottom of the V as seen in this example. This leaves 22 (1 + 2 + 3 + 4 + 5 + 7 = 22), which can be split evenly into 11 for the left wing of the V and 11 for the right wing. Now we just need to pick numbers that add to 11 for the left wing. For example, we can choose 1 + 3 + 7 = 11. This leaves 2 + 4 + 5 = 11 for the right wing of the V.

$$1+2+3+4+5+6+7 = 28$$

$$1+2+3+4+5 + 7 = 22$$

Had we started with an odd number (like 5) for the bottom of the V, that would have left an odd number (in this case, 28 − 5 = 23) to try to split evenly between the left and right wing. This idea of whether to place an even or odd number at the bottom of the V based on the sum of the numbers also explains why 1–5 (sum = 15), 2–6 (sum = 20), and 3–7 (sum = 25) produce the rules that were discussed earlier.

What is interesting is that, regardless of the numbers we choose, the middle number will determine whether we need to start with an even or odd number. The reason for this is that the outer pairs will always add to an even number (see the next example), leaving the middle number to determine whether the sum will be even or odd.

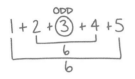

STUDENT SOLUTIONS

1. 1, 2, 3, 4, 5

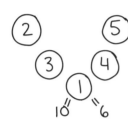

Commentary:

This is an incorrect solution. However, it is important to see what can be easily tweaked to make it correct. For example, they could switch the 1 and the 5. This will increase the value of the left arm by 4 while keeping the value of the right arm at 10. Alternatively, they could switch the 5 and the 3. This will decrease the value of the right arm by 2 while increasing the value of the left arm by 2.

Suggested hints:

How many more does the one side need and how many less does the other side need for them to be the same?

Can you rearrange the numbers on the right arm so that you get a solution?

Can you switch a number on the left arm with a number on the right arm so you get a solution?

2. 1, 2, 3, 4, 5

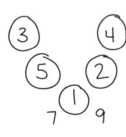

1, 2, 3, 4, 5

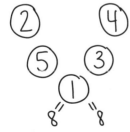

Commentary:

The top image is a solution where students were able to recognize that 7 and 9 are two apart, therefore the 7 needed one more and the 9 needed one less. They achieved this by switching the 2 and the 3, resulting in the bottom image. They could have also have switched the 5 and the 4.

Suggested hints:

Is there another move you could have made to get from your incorrect solution to the correct solution?

What if you put a 3 in the bottom of the V? What would the solution look like then?

What if the bottom of the V was a 2? Can you find a solution? Why or why not?

Is there a rule to be made to find a correct solution for numbers 1 to 5?

(Continued)

(Continued)

3. 2,3,4,5,6

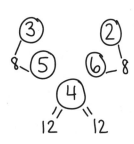

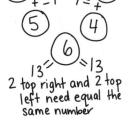

2 top right and 2 top
left need equal the
same number

Commentary:

This group is showing that the sum of the top two circles for each need to be equal and have written out the rule for that. What they have not yet figured out is that this is only possible for 2 to 6 if the number at the bottom of the V is even.

Suggested hints:

Come up with another solution for the numbers 2 to 6. What are you noticing about the numbers that are at the bottom of the V? Why?

What if the numbers are 3 to 7? What does the number at the bottom of the V have to be? Why?

CONSOLIDATION

The purpose of the consolidation is for students to first see that, for numbers 1 to 5 (and 3 to 7), the number at the bottom of the V needs to be odd. And, for numbers 2 to 6 it needs to be even. Looking at different groups' banks will help with this. More importantly, however, you want to look at some of the rules that groups have written to express the odd-even pattern. Every group who has gotten that far will have expressed the rule differently (see Author Solution(s)) and there is value in having students compare and contrast these different expressions to see if they are saying the same thing.

CHECK-YOUR-UNDERSTANDING QUESTIONS

MILD

A. Fit the numbers 1–5 into five circles so that both arms have the same sum.

B. Fit the numbers 2–6 into five circles so that both arms have the same sum.

MEDIUM

A. Fit the numbers 35–39 into five circles so that both arms have the same sum.

B. Fit the numbers 46–50 into five circles so that both arms have the same sum.

SPICY

A. Fit the numbers 1–7 into seven circles so that both arms have the same sum.

B. Fit the numbers 12–18 into seven circles so that both arms have the same sum.

Author Notes

This task is great because the entry point is low with several correct solutions, but there are interesting extensions that could be made to engage many learners. The use of the bank is vital for this task as students need to see multiple solutions at the same time to begin to see the pattern.

Notes to My Future Forgetful Self

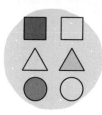

TASK 9: COLORED BOXES

TASK

Figure out the color of each of these shapes based on the given clues.

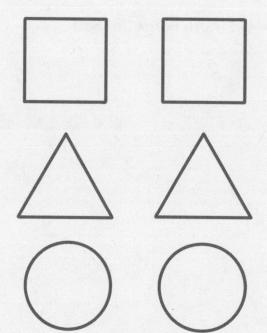

Grades: 2–4

Content Potential: comparative language, logic

Perseverance Scale:

Grade Level:	2	3	4	5
Perseverance Level:	3	2	1	1

Macro-Moves: answering only keep-thinking questions

Competencies: collaboration, risk taking

This task's images, extension scripts, and Check-Your-Understanding Questions are available for download at
https://companion.corwin.com/courses/BTCK5Tasks

LAUNCH SCRIPT

Teacher: How many shapes are drawn here?

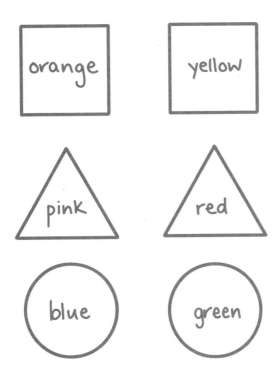

Students: Six!

Teacher: Great! Now tell me something about the color of these shapes.

Students: The square is orange.

Teacher: Which square is orange?

Students: The left square is orange.

Teacher: OK. Tell me something about a different shape.

Students: The right circle is green.

Teacher: OK. Now tell me something about the color of a shape using words like above, below, beside, etc.

Students: The red triangle is above the green circle.

Teacher: Good. Your job today is to label which color each shape is. The shapes are always the same and in the same order [teacher points at shapes].

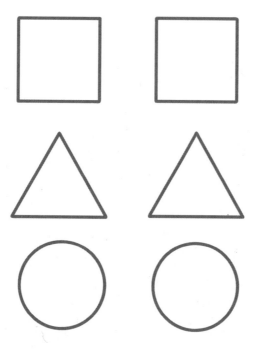

Teacher: But you can't just label it at random. I'm going to give you a series of clues to figure out where each color fits—clues like the triangle above the green circle is red.

Teacher: Once you are at your boards, I will come and give you your first set of clues [teacher holds up a piece of paper with the first set of clues on them].

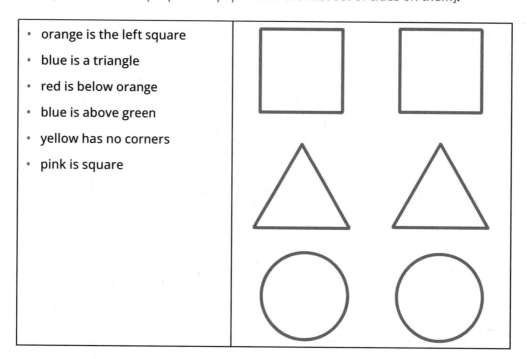

- orange is the left square
- blue is a triangle
- red is below orange
- blue is above green
- yellow has no corners
- pink is square

CREATING ACCESS

- For students who are having difficulty drawing the shapes, draw them for them.

- For students who are having difficulty reading the clues, have someone else in the group do the reading, or have them read together.

EXTENSION SCRIPTS
Print each of the extensions on a separate piece of paper.

1.
  - pink has three corners
  - green is between blue and orange
  - pink is to the right of green
  - orange has no corners
  - yellow is beside blue

2.
  - orange is above yellow
  - red is above orange
  - pink is to the right of yellow
  - pink is below green
  - pink is below blue
  - green has three sides
  - what shape is red?

3.
  - pink is between yellow and green
  - yellow is to the right of another color
  - red has no corners
  - blue is below orange
  - green is beside red

4.
  - pink is next to red
  - orange is between red and green
  - blue has no corners
  - yellow is on the left of orange

5.
  - red has no corners
  - green is between blue and yellow
  - orange is to the left of blue
  - what shape is pink?

6.
  - blue has no corners
  - green is between red and yellow
  - green is on the left of orange
  - pink is next to red

AUTHOR SOLUTION(S)

The key to finding the solutions for these is to label the possible effects of each clue on the diagram. For example, *orange is the left square* is unambiguous. Label the left square with an O. The second clue, *blue is a triangle*, could mean either triangle. So, label both triangles with a B. The third clue, *red is below orange*, could be referring to either the left triangle or the left circle. Label both with an R. And so on.

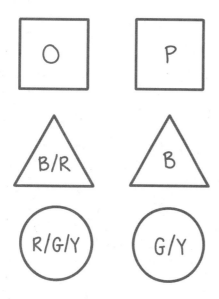

Once you have coded every clue, start circling the ones that must be true and the answer will emerge. You may have to go back to the clues for this. For example, once you realize the right triangle has to be blue then the clue, *blue is above green*, will reveal that the right circle is green.

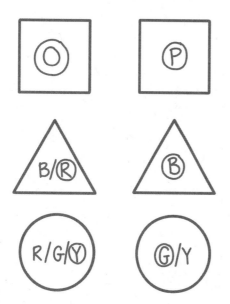

The complete list of answers for extensions 1–6 are as follows:

1	
• pink has three corners • green is between blue and orange • pink is to the right of green • orange has no corners • yellow is beside blue • what shape is red?	Y/B Y/B G P O/R O/R
2	
• orange is above yellow • red is above orange • pink is to the right of yellow • pink is below green • pink is below blue • green has three sides	R B O G Y P
3	
• pink is between yellow and green • yellow is to the right of another color • red has no corners • blue is below orange • green is beside red	O Y B P R G

4	
• pink is next to red • orange is between red and green • blue has no corners • yellow is on the left of orange	P R Y O B G
5	
• red has no corners • green is between blue and yellow • orange is to the left of blue • what shape is pink?	O B P G R Y
6	
• blue has no corners • green is between red and yellow • green is on the left of orange • pink is next to red	R P G O Y B

STUDENT SOLUTIONS

All of these solutions are based on the task in the launch script.

1.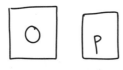

Commentary:

This solution is incomplete and incorrect. This group completed orange, pink, and red correctly but placed yellow preemptively. Blue needs to be above green and with the current configuration in this solution, that is impossible, thus why this group is stuck.

Suggested hints:

Look at your clues and put a check mark next to each color that the clues say is for sure. Which colors don't have a check mark next to them?

What are the clues mentioning blue and green? What does that tell you?

2.

Commentary:

This solution shows a group of students trying to use reminders (like left and right) to continue working. They are also encoding their shapes with possible colors.

Suggested hints:

If yellow is one of the circles, what would the other circle have to be? How do you know?

3.

Commentary:

This solution is complete and correct. These students are ready to move on to the next extension. The hints provided may create an opportunity for this group to understand why they were able to solve the task.

Suggested hints:

Which colors were the easiest to place? Why?

Which colors were the most difficult to place? Why?

What was an example where finding one color helped you find others?

CONSOLIDATION

This is an example of a *convergent* task. As mentioned in Part 1, this means that every group who gets the correct answer gets the same answer. In addition, the student work does not really show their thinking as much as other tasks. Taken together, this means that a guided gallery walk will not work well. However, *teacher-scribe* does. So, pick a task that students did not get to and write up the clues on a vertical surface and then solve it as a whole group. Use turn-and-talks as well as probing questions to drive the conversation. Use this as an opportunity to show how a shape can be labelled with more than one color until we know for sure where some colors need to be.

CHECK-YOUR-UNDERSTANDING QUESTIONS

Note: The images to the right of these CYUs are answer keys for reference.

MILD

What color would each shape be?

- pink is a square
- red is below green
- yellow is a circle
- green is to the right of pink
- orange is above yellow
- yellow is beside red
- what shape is blue?

MEDIUM

What color would each shape be?

- orange is between blue and green
- red is beside blue
- pink has no corners
- what shape is yellow?

SPICY

What color would each shape be?

- yellow is between red and orange
- green is on the left
- pink is to the left of orange
- blue is a triangle
- orange has no corners

Author Notes

Students love this task. They feel safe taking risks and they can check their answers to know if they got it right or not. Be ready for them asking for more and more spicy ones. You are either going to have to start making up your own or get them to make them. If you are going to get them to make them, make sure that they check that their clues cannot lead to more than one answer. Also make sure that they stay with the same colors. These are not random. Red, orange, yellow, green, blue, pink are all colors that start with a different letter. Introducing colors like purple can confuse this.

For you, this task is a great way to practice consolidation using *teacher-scribe* on a non-curricular task. It is also a good chance to practice giving extensions on slips of paper. You do not want to number these as you do not want students to start competing. But then it is easy for you to lose track of which one comes next for a group. Color coding the paper will help prevent this. For example, the first task is on red paper, the second on orange, and so on.

Notes to My Future Forgetful Self

_____

_____

_____

_____

_____

_____

_____

_____

_____

_____

_____

_____

_____

TASK 10: THERE'S HOW MANY LEGS?

TASK

Figure out how many animals are on a farm knowing the total number of legs.

Grades: K–5

Content Potential: addition, subtraction, multiplication, division, patterning, linear relations

Perseverance Scale:

Grade Level:	K	1	2	3	4	5
Perseverance Level:	3	3	2	2	1	1

Macro-Moves: using hints and extensions to maintain flow

Competencies: willingness to take risks, creativity, perseverance

LAUNCH SCRIPT

Teacher: Did you know that I grew up on a farm?

Students: Really?!

Teacher: Yup! And on this farm, we had cows and ducks. How many legs does a cow have?

Students: Four!

Teacher: And how many legs does a duck have?

Students: Two!

Teacher: Well, we had 2 cows and 2 ducks. How many legs in total is that?

Teacher: For this task we are going to be using the banner [see Chapter 4], so make sure you draw the banner and put the task in the banner. [Teacher draws the banner and writes *2 cows + 2 ducks* in the banner.]

CREATING ACCESS

- For students who struggle with understanding the task, have an image ready with 2 cows and 2 ducks.

- For students who understand the task but have difficulty with the arithmetic, providing different colored Unifix cubes (brown for cows and yellow for ducks), a list of skip-counted numbers (2s and 4s), a multiplication table, and/or a calculator—depending on grade—can help.

EXTENSION SCRIPTS

1. What if there were 3 cows and 4 ducks?

2. What if there were 5 cows and 5 ducks?

3. What if there were 10 cows and 10 ducks?

4. Good news! We got some different kinds of animals. What if I woke up one morning and saw that there were _____ (6 for kindergarten, 14 for Grades 1–2, 26 for Grades 3–5) legs on my farm? What could live there now?

5. Can you come up with a different answer? And another one? And another one?

6. What are all the possible ways I can have _____ (6 for kindergarten, 14 for Grades 1–2, 26 for Grades 3–5) legs on my farm?

7. What are all the possible ways I can have _____ (10 for kindergarten, 22 for Grades 1–2, 42 for Grades 3–5) legs on my farm?

8. Ok, you aren't going to believe this, but I think I just counted _____ (11 for kindergarten, 23 for Grades 1–2, 45 for Grades 3–5) legs on the farm. What could live there now?

AUTHOR SOLUTION(S)

The answers to the original or extension tasks 1–3 are relatively simple. Once we get to extension 4, things get a little bit more complex. Let's look at the scenario where the students are staying with cows and ducks. It is just a matter of coming up with a multiple of 2 and a multiple of 4 that add to the number of legs. So, for 26 legs, for example, we could have 6 cows (24 legs) and 1 duck (2 legs). But we could also have 5 cows (20 legs) and 3 ducks (6 legs) or 4 cows (16 legs) and 5 ducks (10 legs). This set of solutions sets up the pattern for how to find all the possible answers. We start with the largest number of cows we can have for 26 legs (6 cows = 24 legs) and add 1 duck (2 legs) to make up the difference. From there, we trade in one cow for two ducks repeatedly until we have only ducks (13 ducks = 26 legs). Putting all this into a table can help students see the pattern.

Cows	Cow legs	Ducks	Duck legs	Total legs
6	24	1	2	26
5	20	3	6	26

Cows	Cow legs	Ducks	Duck legs	Total legs
4	16	5	10	26
3	12	7	14	26
2	8	9	18	26
1	4	11	22	26
0	0	13	26	26

Of course, it could be argued that 13 ducks is not an actual answer because we specified that we had ducks *and* cows. So, there must be at least one cow. The same structure can be used for any mix of animals (e.g., horses, pigs, dogs, turkeys, and ducks) as long as all the animals have either two or four legs and you cluster all four-legged animals together in columns 1 and 2 and all two-legged animals in columns 3 and 4.

When we get into combinations of animals where the number of legs is not only two and four, the table gets a little more complex. For example, consider the case of cows, ducks, and three-legged dogs (see author notes) with a total of 25 legs. In this case, we need to add two columns to the table. The pattern is easier to see if we start with the animal with the greatest number of legs in the first two columns, and so on.

Cows	Cow legs	Three-legged dogs	Dog legs	Ducks	Duck legs	Total legs
5	20	1	3	1	2	25
4	16	3	9	0	0	25
4	16	1	3	3	6	25
3	12	3	9	2	4	25
3	12	1	3	5	10	25
2	8	5	15	1	2	25
2	8	3	9	4	8	25
2	8	1	3	7	14	25
1	4	7	21	0	0	25
1	4	5	15	3	6	25
1	4	3	9	6	12	25
1	4	1	3	9	18	25
0	0	7	21	2	4	25

(Continued)

(Continued)

Cows	Cow legs	Three-legged dogs	Dog legs	Ducks	Duck legs	Total legs
0	0	5	15	5	10	25
0	0	3	9	8	16	25
0	0	1	3	11	22	25

STUDENT SOLUTIONS

1.

Commentary:

This solution will be the first step for students creating what the farm might look like. This is the pictorial representation and shows students starting to count to make the correct number of legs.

Suggested hints:

How can you make sure that you have the right number of legs?

Is there a way to include numbers in your representation?

2.

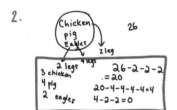

Commentary:

These solutions show the students moving from counting to adding (or subtracting) with numbers. There may still be some words or pictures, but they are accompanied with numerical operations.

Suggested hints:

Is adding (or subtracting) the only way to solve this task?

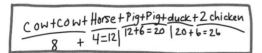

3.

26 Legs

5 Cows = 4L×5 = 20
3 chickens = 2L×3 = 6
20+6 = 26

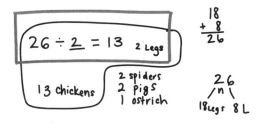

26 ÷ 2 = 13   2 Legs

13 chickens

2 spiders
2 pigs
1 ostrich

$\begin{array}{r} 18 \\ + \ 8 \\ \hline 26 \end{array}$

$\begin{array}{c} 26 \\ /\,n\,\backslash \\ 18legs \ \ 8L \end{array}$

Commentary:

These solutions show students moving from addition and subtraction to multiplication or division. The multiplication solution shows two different statements for the two different kinds of animals. With the division, the students only considered one animal and were able to divide total legs by number of legs per animal.

Suggested hints:

What if you couldn't use any animals with 2 or 4 legs?

What creative ways could you think of if there were an odd number of legs?

4.

15 legs

fox   chicin
        19
        Pig   Wlf

45 Legs
10 Sheep
1 Robin
1 dog if it's missing a leg !!

$\begin{array}{r} 40 \\ + \ 2 \\ \hline 42 \end{array}$

Commentary:

These solutions are examples of the creativity that students have found with finding an odd number of legs.

Suggested hints:

Using the same animals, can you come up with other combinations that add to 45 legs?

Can you organize this in some fashion so that you know you have all the solutions?

CONSOLIDATION

The purpose of consolidation is to first recognize and highlight that although some students may be drawing, adding, subtracting, multiplying, or dividing, everyone is applying mathematical content to the task. Having said that, this is an ideal task to do a gallery walk with. For K–3, this can be done to showcase a progression from drawing, to adding, to skip counting, and maybe to multiplying. For students in Grades 4–5, a gallery walk can showcase the progression from adding, to multiplying and/or dividing, to multiple solutions, to organizing solutions in a table.

CHECK-YOUR-UNDERSTANDING QUESTIONS

MILD

A. How many legs would there be with 4 ducks?

B. How many legs would there be with 3 cows?

C. How many legs would there be with 2 cows and 3 ducks?

MEDIUM

A. If I count 24 legs and there are only ducks, how many ducks is that?

B. If I count 24 legs and there are only cows, how many cows is that?

C. If I count 24 legs and there are ducks and cows, how many ducks and cows might that be?

SPICY

A. If I count 20 legs, and only have cows and ducks, what are all the possible solutions for cows and ducks?

B. What if I had spiders, cows, and ducks and I had 20 legs. What are all the possible solutions for spiders, cows, and ducks?

C. What is an animal with an odd number of legs? What if I only had this animal and ducks. What are all the ways I could have 23 legs?

Author Notes

This task is applicable to a wide range of grades and a wide range of fluency with numbers within any one grade. As such, it is important to use the banner to allow groups to move on as they finish with the launch task and the first few extensions.

This task is great if you are hoping to see more collaboration in your groups. The entry point allows students to just draw animals, but other students might look at it through adding, skip counting, or multiplication. Some might even look at it through the lens of division with and without remainder. Consequently, it is a great activity to practice operational fluency. And this is a great task for challenging students to find all possible solutions, which ladders nicely to linear relations.

The beauty comes when students are tasked with finding an odd number of legs because it relies on creativity not computation. We have seen students include a three-legged dog, a star fish, a flamingo, a snake, and our personal favorite: a cooked chicken leg from KFC. According to the Grade 1 student who came up with this, "You never said the animal had to be alive." This is not correct. We actually asked them, "What [animals] could live there now?" But, we do not want to squash creativity.

Quite the contrary—we want to encourage creativity. So, all students should get a chance to explore extension task #8:

> Ok, you aren't going to believe this, but I think I just counted
> _____ (11 for kindergarten, 23 for Grades 1–2, 45
> for Grades 3–5) legs on the farm. What could live there now?

You may wish to skip extension task #6 and/or #7 to ensure everyone gets to play with the idea of an odd number of legs. This may mean everyone skips extension tasks #6 and #7 or only some students do.

Notes to My Future Forgetful Self

TASK 11: WAYS TO MAKE 10

TASK

How many ways can you add to 10 with two whole numbers?

Grades: 2–4

Content potential: adding, doubling, halving, patterns, linear equations, linear relations

Perseverance Scale:

Grade Level:	2	3	4
Perseverance Level:	2	1	1

Macro-Moves: how we foster autonomy, hints and extensions, how we give the task

Competencies: collaboration

LAUNCH SCRIPT

Teacher: I have a super easy question for you today [teacher writes $\square$ + 2 = 5 on the board].

Teacher: What goes in the box?

Students: 3!

Teacher: OK. What about this one? [teacher writes $\square$ + 6 = 10]

Students: 4!

Teacher: OK. So, if I put a 4 into this box [teacher writes 4 into the box for $\square$ + 6 = 10], what does this mean?

Students: It means that 4 + 6 is equal to 10.

Teacher: Yes! It means that 4 + 6 is equal to 10. But it means more than that. It means that putting a 4 into that box makes this a true number sentence. Can I put anything else into that box to make this a true number sentence?

Students: No!

Teacher: OK. There is only one number that makes this true. What about if I give you this one? [teacher writes ☐ + 1 = 7 on the board] What can go in this box that makes this a true number sentence?

Students: 6!

Teacher: OK. Anything else?

Students: No.

Teacher: So, there is always only one number that can go into the box to make it true?

Students: Yes!

Teacher: OK. Well, what about this one? [teacher writes ☐ + ☐ = 6] Is there still only one number that can go into each box [teacher points at both boxes] to make this a true number sentence?

Students: No. This time it can be different numbers.

Teacher: OK. Give me one set of numbers that makes this true.

Students: 3 + 3 = 6. [teacher writes 3 + 3 = 6 on the board]

Teacher: Can you give me another set of numbers?

Students: 2 + 4 = 6 [teacher writes 2 + 4 = 6 on the board]

Students: 1 + 5 = 6 [teacher writes 1 + 5 = 6 on the board]

Teacher: Any others?

Students: 5 + 1 = 6 [teacher writes 5 + 1 = 6 on the board]

Students: 6 + 0 = 6 [teacher writes 6 + 0 = 6 on the board]

Teacher: OK. So there is more than one way to do this. We say that there is more than one solution to the task ☐ + ☐ = 6.

Teacher: What I want you to do in your groups now is to find all the solutions for ☐ + ☐ = 10. When doing so, however, let's not use 0. And let's also say that 1 + 5 is the same as 5 + 1.

CREATING ACCESS

- For students who struggle with adding to 10, start with ☐ + ☐ = 5.

- For students who struggle with adding numbers in general, offer them access to an addition table or a calculator.

- For students who are having difficulty understanding the task, offer them a stack of 10 Unifix cubes—preferably all the same color. This task is analogous to how many different ways we can split this stack of 10 Unifix cubes into two stacks.

- For students who are having difficulty tracking their answers, draw a table of values and put some of their answers into it for them.

EXTENSION SCRIPTS

1. How many solutions for $\square + \square = 15$?

2. How many solutions for $\square + \square = 20$?

3. What is one big difference between the solutions for $\square + \square = 15$ and $\square + \square = 20$?

4. How many solutions for $\square + \square = 22$?

5. How many solutions for $\square + \square = 21$?

6. How many solutions for $\square + \square = 20$?

7. Without writing them all out, how many solutions for $\square + \square = 100$?

8. Without writing them all out, how many solutions for $\square + \square = 99$?

AUTHOR SOLUTION(S)

The solution for this task depends on how we choose to interpret it. For example, $\square + \square = 6$ can have the following correct sets of solutions:

Set 1	Set 2	Set 3	Set 4
0 + 6 = 6	1 + 5 = 6	0 + 6 = 6	1 + 5 = 6
1 + 5 = 6	2 + 4 = 6	1 + 5 = 6	2 + 4 = 6
2 + 4 = 6	3 + 3 = 6	2 + 4 = 6	3 + 3 = 6
3 + 3 = 6	4 + 2 = 6	3 + 3 = 6	
4 + 2 = 6	5 + 1 = 6		
5 + 1 = 6			
6 + 0 = 6			

Each of these sets of solutions is based on a combination of assumed answers to two questions:

1. Are we allowed to use zero?

2. Is, for example, 1 + 5 different from 5 + 1?

Set 1 assumes that the answer to both of these questions is yes, while set 4 assumes that both answers are no. Sets 2 and 3 each assumes that the answer to one question is yes and the other is no—set 2 is no/yes and set 3 is yes/no, respectively. The students are likely to produce solutions according to what they assume to be true or not about these answers. For the purposes of having a uniform class discussion during the consolidation, we suggest you constrain the solutions by being explicit about what the answers to these two questions are. In the launch script we specified it as no to both—we are not using zero and 1 + 5 is the same as 5 + 1.

With these constraints in place, the number of solutions for an even number will be half that even number. For example, when we are adding to 6, there are 3 solutions. If we were adding to 8 there would be 4 solutions, and so on. For an odd number, the number of solutions is a little bit trickier. For example, if we are adding to 7, we can have 1 + 6, 2 + 5, 3 + 4. This is the same number of solutions as if we were adding to 6. The number of solutions when adding to an odd number is equal to the number of solutions for one less than that number. That is, the number of solutions for 7 equals the number of solutions for 6, the number of solutions for 19 equals the number of solutions for 18, and so on. If you constrain the problem differently you will get a different pattern, but there will always be some pattern between the number and the number of solutions.

STUDENT SOLUTIONS

1.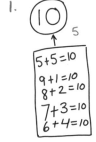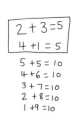

Commentary:

These solutions are demonstrating students beginning to organize "what makes 10," but the first group likely began with 5 + 5 because that was the most obvious one. From there, they recognized a pattern after. The second group did see the pattern faster.

Suggested hints:

Is there a reason that you began with 5 + 5 = 10? Can you use this strategy for what makes 20?

2.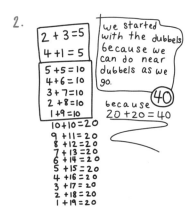

Commentary:

This solution shows a group who has organized their solutions into a pattern where they start with the double and then increases one addend by 1 and then decreases the other by 1 until they get to

1 + _____ .

Suggested hints:

So, doubles are important. What happens when you have a number that isn't a double, like 23?

(Continued)

(Continued)

3.

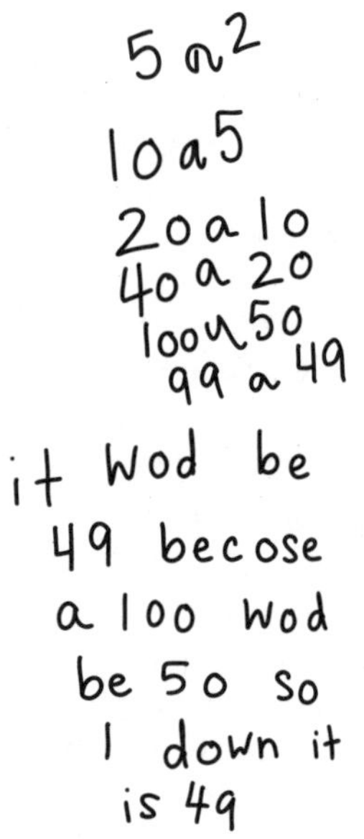

$5 \, a \, 2$
$10 \, a \, 5$
$20 \, a \, 10$
$40 \, a \, 20$
$100 \, u \, 50$
$99 \, a \, 49$

it wod be
49 becose
a 100 wod
be 50 so
1 down it
is 49

Commentary:

This solution shows students who have completed all the parts of the task and have proposed a possible solution for 99. During consolidation, the class can use their knowledge about beginning with doubles to see if their proposal is reasonable.

Suggested hints:

Can you make a formula (or rule) that someone could use for any number?

CONSOLIDATION

The purpose of this consolidation is to first recognize that any given answer can have many different combinations of addends. Second, these combinations can be organized into a pattern. And third, there is a way to predict how many solutions there will be given the number we are adding to. A gallery walk can showcase all these nuances.

CHECK-YOUR-UNDERSTANDING QUESTIONS

MILD

A. Show all the ways to add to 12.

B. Show all the ways to add to 13.

MEDIUM

A. How many ways can you add to get 35?

B. How many ways can you add to get 44?

SPICY

A. There are 25 ways to add to get a number. What number(s) could it be?

B. Can you make a rule for how many ways to add to make a number if you are allowed to use 0?

Author Notes

At face value, this task is about basic addition, but it develops into finding a pattern. Although the task can get quite complex for Grade 2 and 3 students, the students slowly build up to it and patterns can emerge. The extension scripts we include here can easily be varied to use smaller or bigger numbers for groups that are struggling or excelling. Make these changes as necessary. What is important is that you give them an even number and then one less than that even number. This will create the opportunity to begin to see a pattern between odd and even numbers.

Notes to My Future Forgetful Self

TASK 12: TABLES AT A PARTY

TASK

What size tables can you use to seat 12 guests, if every table is the same size and there must be the same number of guests at each table?

Grades: K–5

Content Potential: skip counting, repeated addition, multiplication/division, commutative property, perimeter

Perseverance Scale:

Grade Level:	K	1	2	3	4	5
Perseverance Level:	3	3	2	2	1	1

Macro-Moves: using hints and extensions to maintain flow

Competencies: risk taking, trial and error, organization

LAUNCH SCRIPT

Teacher: So, I decided that I want to have a party. Can you be my party planners?

Students: Yes!

Teacher: Great! Here are some details. I am going to rent tables for the party. The tables come in all different sizes. I can get tables that seat 1 person, 2 people, 3 people, all the way up to 100 people. But, even though the tables come in all different sizes, I want all the tables that I rent to be the same size. I just don't know what size tables to get.

Teacher: I also do not want any empty seats at any of the tables. So, if I order tables that each seat 4 people, I want there to be 4 people at every table.

Teacher: I have invited 12 people to my party. What size tables should I get? What are my options?

CREATING ACCESS

- For students who have difficulty representing numbers, give them round, square, or rectangular pieces of paper with numbers on them, each of which represents a table and how many people can sit at it.

- For students who have difficulty with skip counting, repeated addition, or multiplication, offer them a multiplication grid, a calculator, Unifix cubes, or the pieces of paper recommended above.

- This task can start at any number to increase or decrease the difficulty for different grades or groups with different abilities. For instance, you can start at 6 or 8, which will have fewer factors. Likewise, you can start at 20, 24, or 28 for more challenge. You can start with any number you wish as long as it is not a prime number or a square number. Regardless of what number you start with, the sequence of extensions (as seen in the extension scripts) should follow the following pattern before you jump to the noticing questions beginning at extension script 9:

  0. Even composite number [this is the launch script]

  1. Even composite number

  2. Odd composite number

  3. Composite number (odd or even)

  4. Composite number (odd or even)

  5. Square number

  6. Square number

  7. Prime number

  8. Prime number

EXTENSION SCRIPTS

1. Oh no! I just got an e-mail from some more friends saying they want to come to the party. I now have 20 people coming. What are my options now?

2. Oh no! Five of my friends just cancelled and I now only have 15 people coming. What are my options now?

3. What if there were 18 people at my party? What are my options now?

4. What if there were 24 people at my party? What are my options now?

5. What if there were 16 people at my party? What are my options now?

6. What if there were 25 people at my party? What are my options now?

7. What if there were 11 people at my party? What are my options now?

8. What if there were 17 people at my party? What are my options now?

9. OK. We have now tried a whole bunch of different numbers of guests, and I notice that sometimes you give me an even number of options and sometimes you give me an odd number of options. What kinds of numbers give me an even number of options and what kinds of numbers give me an odd number of options?

10. I notice that for some numbers of guests there are exactly two options and for others there are more than two options. What kinds of numbers produce exactly two options?

AUTHOR SOLUTION(S)

This task is fundamentally about factors and factor pairs. For example, with 12 guests, we can have 1 table of 12 guests (1 × 12), 2 tables of 6 guests (2 × 6), 3 tables of 4 guests (3 × 4), 4 tables of 3 guests (4 × 3), 6 tables of 2 guests (6 × 2), or 12 tables of 1 guest (12 × 1). These are all the factor pairs of 12. There are some things to notice just in these pairs. First, for every pair of factors there is an opposite pair. For example, we can have 3 tables of 4 guests (3 × 4) or 4 tables of 3 guests (4 × 3). For every $m \times n$ we can also have $n \times m$. This is the commutative property of multiplication: $4 \times 3 = 3 \times 4$. And because of this pairing, there is an even number of options for 12 guests. This is true for almost any number of guests.

But not all. If we start with a number of guests that is a square number, for example 16, we will have an odd number of options. We can see this if we arrange the options for 16 in a table.

Option	Tables	Guests per table
1	1	16
2	2	8
3	4	4
4	8	2
5	16	1

We can see that for every option there is an opposite pair—option 1 pairs with option 5 and option 2 pairs with option 4—except for option 3. Option 3 has no pair because 4 tables of 4 guests is the same as 4 tables of guests. This is true of all square number of guests. If we have 9 guests, we will have an option that is 3 tables of 3 guests. If we have 25 guests, we will have an option that is 5 tables of 5 guests. Square numbers, and only square numbers, have an odd number of factor pairs. And, the option that has no pair is the square root of the number of quests. That is:

- $\sqrt{9} = 3$

- $\sqrt{16} = 4$

- $\sqrt{25} = 5$

There is also something interesting that happens if the number of guests is a prime number. For example, if we have 13 guests, the only options are 1 table of 13 guests (1 × 13) or 13 tables of 1 guest (13 × 1). There are only two options. In fact, there are exactly two options. This is true of any prime number and occurs because a prime number has no factors other than 1 and itself.

STUDENT SOLUTIONS

1.

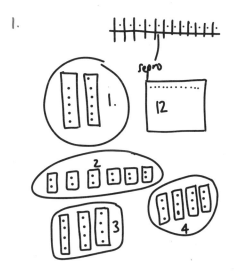

Commentary:

This solution is the first level of understanding that students will show. It shows they know the context and what is being asked but may not be connecting it to any specific mathematical concept.

Suggested hints:

This is interesting. Is there an easier way to represent, for example, 4 tables of 3 guests [teacher points at correct image] other than with dots?

2.

Commentary:

This solution shows the students beginning to bridge the pictorial to the abstract as they are aligning the tables as if to add them. These students may understand that they are creating groups, but they may not yet see connection to addition or multiplication.

Suggested hints:

Is there a way we can represent each of these images using multiplication (×)?

3.

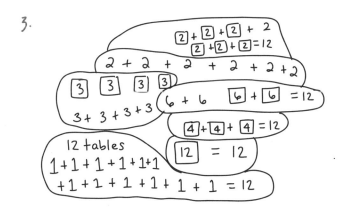

Commentary:

These students understand that these solutions can be found through repeated addition and are beginning to understand that the solutions can be paired up to represent the commutative property. You want them to connect their understanding to multiplication for cleaner notation and organization.

Suggested hints:

Is there a way we can represent each of these images using multiplication (×)?

(Continued)

(Continued)

4.

2
2
2   2×6=12
2   2 tables with 6 people
2   =12
6   6 tables with 2 people
6=12   6x2=12

3 × 4 = 12
4 × 3 = 12

3 tables with 4 People
4 tables with 3 people

1 × 12 = 12

table with 12 people

12×1=12
12 tables with one person

Commentary:

These students have grasped the concept that 2 tables with 6 guests is synonymous with 2 × 6. They also have clearly connected the solutions to commutative property and repeated addition. The next step for students would be to name and recognize each number as a factor of 12.

Suggested hints:

Can you put all your options into a list? How can you be sure you didn't miss any options?

CONSOLIDATION

The purpose of consolidation for this task depends on the grade you are doing it with. For all grades, you want to use consolidation to move them from the pictorial literal representation of tables at a party to the symbolic representation of multiplication and the commutative property. For older students, you also want to use consolidation to showcase the patterns that emerge in the relationship between the type of number (composite, square, prime) and the number of options that these types of numbers produce.

CHECK-YOUR-UNDERSTANDING QUESTIONS

MILD

A. 2 tables of 7 guests are ___ guests in total.

B. 4 tables of 6 guests are ___ guests in total.

C. 5 tables of 8 guests are ___ guests in total.

MEDIUM

A. How many options are there to seat 32 guests?

B. How many people sit at each table if there are 6 tables and 42 guests?

C. How many tables do I need if I have 56 guests total and 8 guests per table?

SPICY

A. What are all the options for 64 guests?

B. What number of guests can I invite if I want exactly 5 tables?

C. What numbers of guests have exactly 6 options?

Author Notes

This is a great task for almost any grade level. The context of tables and guests is one that every student can access. At the same time, it offers a very high ceiling with exploration of the types of numbers (composite, square, prime) and the effect that this has on the number of options. If you are moving toward having students notice the relationship between the number of options and the type of number, we recommend introducing the bank (see Task 8, The Carnival Conundrum) as a way for students to track their data.

Notes to My Future Forgetful Self

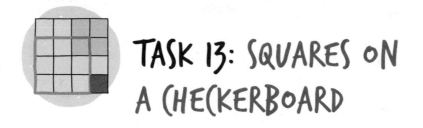

TASK 13: SQUARES ON A CHECKERBOARD

TASK

How many squares on a 4 × 4 checkerboard?

Grades: 2–5

Content Potential: recognizing and discerning shapes, addition, square numbers, patterning, and equations

Perseverance Scale:

Grade Level:	2	3	4	5
Perseverance Level:	3	3	2	2

Macro-Moves: consolidation from the bottom

Competencies: perseverance, trial and error, organization

LAUNCH SCRIPT

Teacher: How many squares are there on this checkerboard? [teacher points at a 4 × 4 checkerboard they have previously drawn on the board]

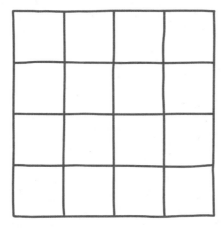

Students: 16!

Teacher: I can promise you there are more than 16. Your job is to figure out how many squares are on a 4 × 4 checkerboard.

CREATING ACCESS

- For students who are struggling with the complexity of the task, you can start with a 3 × 3 or even a 2 × 2 checkerboard.

- For students who are having difficulty seeing squares of different sizes, you can provide them with squares of paper of different size (1 × 1, 2 × 2, 3 × 3, and 4 × 4) that they can then hold up to the original 4 × 4 checkerboard.

- For students who are having difficulty keeping count, you can set up a T-chart for them in which to record their different counts:

Size of squares	Number
1 × 1	
2 × 2	
3 × 3	
4 × 4	

EXTENSION SCRIPTS

1. What about a 5 × 5 board?

2. What about a 6 × 6 board?

3. What about $n \times n$?

AUTHOR SOLUTION(S)

The solution to this task is almost entirely predicated on recognizing the patterns that exist for various sizes of squares. In the 4 × 4 example, there are 16 (1 × 1) squares. But there are also nine 2 × 2 squares, four 3 × 3 squares, and one 4 × 4 square. It is worth noting that each of these numbers of squares is, itself, a square number. Another pattern to recognize is how many squares there are of each size for different size checkerboards. This is best seen in a table.

		SIZE OF CHECKERBOARD				
		1 × 1	2 × 2	3 × 3	4 × 4	5 × 5
SIZE OF SQUARE	1 × 1	1	4	9	16	25
	2 × 2	-	1	4	9	16
	3 × 3	-	-	1	4	9
	4 × 4	-	-	-	1	4
	5 × 5	-	-	-	-	1
TOTAL		1	5	14	30	55

This task is a perfect example of how the patterns we are looking for are often not found in the answers to the question, but in the process. The answer to how many squares on a 4 × 4 checkerboard is 30. In and of itself, this is an uninteresting number. But how we got to the 30 is very interesting ($16 + 9 + 4 + 1 = 4^2 + 3^2 + 2^2 + 1^2$) and can be extended to any size checkerboard. For example, the answer to how many squares on a 8 × 8 checkerboard is $8^2 + 7^2 + 6^2 + \ldots + 1^2 = 64 + 49 + 36 + 25 + 16 + 9 + 4 + 1$. The sum of these consecutive square numbers is now inconsequential. The pattern has been found and the pattern is beautiful. And if need be, the pattern can yield an answer to the number of squares on any size checkerboard.

STUDENT SOLUTIONS

1.

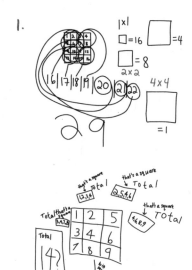

Commentary:

The solution on the top is an incomplete solution, and it is not clear which kind of squares they are counting (1 × 1, 2 × 2, etc.). The bottom solution is correct for a 3 × 3 but still does not name the types of squares, just indicates which small squares make up the larger ones.

Suggested hints:

What do each of these numbers represent?

Are you confident that you haven't missed any? Which ones are you sure are correct?

2.

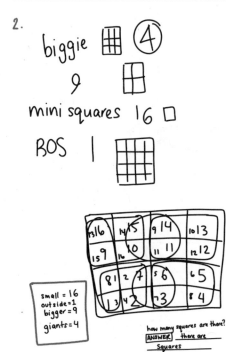

Commentary:

These two solutions are great boards for teachers to have students discuss what is meant by the various wording (mini, biggie, giant, etc.) of the different types of squares. The second solution also showcases nicely how the 2 × 2 squares can be seen on the 4 × 4 checkerboard.

Suggested hints:

Can you find a way to describe each type of square that would be easy for anyone to understand?

3.

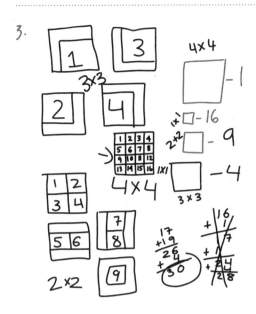

Commentary:

This solution offers visual clarity. First, the students have taken the time to clearly show each type of square. They also have separated each type of square to count them without overlaps. Finally, they provided a label for each type of square that is simple and mathematically relevant.

Suggested hints:

Do you see a pattern in the amount of each type of square? 1, 4, 9, 16 . . . What amounts are found in the 5 by 5?

CONSOLIDATION

The purpose of this consolidation is twofold. The first purpose is to use student work to showcase a progression of representation of the different solutions. This can include both how the parts of the solutions are named as well as how they present their solutions in an organized fashion. This will become evident through a gallery walk. Working toward a common language and a common representation will give you access to the second purpose of the consolidation: to help the students see the pattern that can emerge from the numbers of different-sized squares. Ultimately, we want them to see that patterns exist in the process and that they emerge more easily when the process is organized.

CHECK-YOUR-UNDERSTANDING QUESTIONS

MILD

A. How many of the smallest (1 × 1) squares are in a 5 × 5 checkerboard?

B. How many of the largest (4 × 4) squares are in a 5 × 5 checkerboard?

MEDIUM

A. How many total squares are in a 4 × 4 checkerboard?

B. How many total squares are in a 5 × 5 checkerboard?

SPICY

A. How many squares would there be in an 8 × 8 checkerboard?

B. A checkerboard has 91 squares on it. What size checkerboard is it?

Author Notes

This task has a lot of opportunities for rich discussion during consolidation. Due to the students age, very few of them are likely to name the squares mathematically, like 3 × 3. However, they will use words like *biggie* and *tiny,* which makes consolidating this much more enjoyable than it would be if the students were much older with more math knowledge. Having said that, they are likely going to need help getting organized with their solutions. Be ready to seed the idea of a T-chart and then mobilize that knowledge around the room.

Notes to My Future Forgetful Self

_____

_____

_____

_____

_____

_____

_____

_____

_____

_____

_____

_____

_____

_____

_____

_____

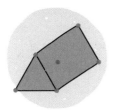

TASK 14: PRISMS, PRISMS, PRISMS

TASK

How many faces, edges, and vertices are there on a prism?

Grades: 2–5

Content Potential: 2D and 3D shapes, edges, sides, faces, vertices, patterns, equations, multiplication

Perseverance Scale:

Grade Level:	2	3	4	5
Perseverance Level:	3	2	1	1

Macro-Moves: mobilization of knowledge

Competencies: organization, looking for patterns

LAUNCH SCRIPT

Teacher: This is called a *triangular prism*. [teacher holds up a triangular prism and then draws it on the board]

Teacher: Can you tell me what these are called? [circle a vertex, an edge, and a face]

Students: A line, a corner, a side, etc.

Teacher: Those are all good names. In math, however, we can be very picky about names, and we want everyone to use the same name for things. So, in math, this is called a *vertex* [points at vertex], this is called an *edge* [points at edge], and this is called a face [points at face].

Teacher: Can you tell me how many vertices, edges, and faces are on a triangular prism?

CREATING ACCESS

- For students who are having difficulty drawing the shapes, draw them for them.

- For students who are having difficulty picturing the shapes from a drawing, provide them with physical 3D shapes.

- For students who are losing track as they count vertices, edges, and faces on a physical shape, let them mark on the shape with a nonpermanent marker.

EXTENSION SCRIPTS

1. What about a rectangular (4-sided polygon) prism?

2. What about a pentagonal (5-sided polygon) prism?

3. What about a hexagonal (6-sided polygon) prism?

4. What about a decagonal (10-sided polygon) prism?

5. What about a icosagonal (20-sided polygon) prism?

6. If I go from an octagonal (8-sided polygon) prism to a nonagonal (9-sided polygon) prism, how does that change the number of vertices, edges, and faces?

7. What is the relationship between the number of edges on the polygon's base and the number of vertices?

8. What is the relationship between the number of edges on the polygon's base and the total number of edges?

9. What is the relationship between the number of edges on the polygon's base and the number of faces?

10. What is the relationship between the number of vertices, edges, and faces of a prism?

AUTHOR SOLUTION(S)

A prism is basically two polygons connected by a number of rectangles. For example, consider the case of a pentagonal prism. In this case, the polygons are pentagons (5-sided).

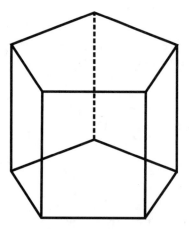

Each pentagon has 5 vertices. So, the total number of vertices is 10 (2 × 5). Each pentagon has 5 edges. In addition, there are 5 edges that go from one pentagon to the next. So, the total number of edges is 15 (3 × 5). Each polygon is a face and there are five rectangles (faces) connecting the two pentagons. So, there are 7 faces (5 + 2). This way of thinking is true for all prisms.

Prism	vertices (V)	edges (E)	faces (F)
triangular (3-sided polygon)	6	9	5
rectangular (4-sided polygon)	8	12	6
pentagonal (5-sided polygon)	10	15	7
hexagonal (6-sided polygon)	12	18	8
decagonal (10-sided polygon)	20	30	12
icosagonal (20-sided polygon)	40	60	22
n-gonal (n-sided polygon)	$2n$	$3n$	$n + 2$

The table reveals that for an n-gonal prism, the number of vertices is $2n$, the number of edges is $3n$, and the number of faces is $n + 2$. But there are other relationships discernable as well:

- the number of edges is related to the number of vertices according to

  $E = \frac{3}{2}V$ or $V = \frac{2}{3}E$.

- the number of faces is related to the number of vertices according to $F = \frac{V}{2} + 2$.

- the number of faces is related to the number of edges according to $F = \frac{E}{3} + 2$.

But the most famous relationship is called *Euler's Formula*: $V + F = E + 2$. This can be represented in a number of different ways, including $V + F - E = 2$ where $V + F - E$ is known as *Euler's Characteristic*. This formula (or characteristic) describes the relationship between vertices, edges, and faces for any polyhedral, of which prisms are a special case.

STUDENT SOLUTIONS

1.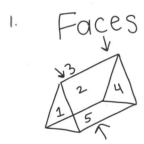

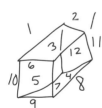

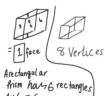

Commentary:

These are good examples of students simply counting the faces, edges, and vertices. This is often seen in the solutions to triangular and rectangular prisms, but by the hexagonal prism, the students realize they need to find a quicker way than counting.

Suggested hints:

Have you started to notice any pattern between how many edges are on the base [teacher points at the base] and the number of vertices, edges, and faces?

(Continued)

(Continued)

2.

1. faces - 5
   edges 9
   vertices - 6

2. faces - 6
   edges - 12
   vertices - 8

faces - 5
Edges - 9
vertices - 6

$3 \times 2 = 6$
$3 + 3 + 3 = 9$

Commentary:

These two images show groups that have started to look at different prisms and are beginning to try to find a pattern between the number of edges on the polygonal base and the number of vertices, edges, and faces. Although they may understand what the pattern is, they might not be able to make an equation to describe it mathematically.

Suggested hints:

Can you represent the relationships between how many edges are on the base [teacher points at the base] and the number of vertices, edges, and faces using formulas?

3.

$3 \times 2 = 6$

6 vertices

$3 + 3 + 3 = 9$

9 edges
5 faces

Faces : $n + 2$
Vertices: $n \times 2$
Edges : $n \times 3$

Commentary:

These images show how students are seeing the relationships and have represented these relationships with formulas.

Suggested hints:

Are there some relationships between vertices, edges, and faces?

Is there a relationship that combines vertices, edges, and faces together?

CONSOLIDATION

The purpose of this consolidation is to use student work to showcase the relationships between the number of edges on the polygonal base and the number of vertices, edges, and faces of any polygonal prism. You can do this through a combination of gallery walk and teacher-scribe where you set up a table and fill in the contents for different prisms as the gallery walk progresses. You may not get to Euler's Formula, but you do want to try to get to the three formulas that relate the number of sides in the polygonal base to the number of vertices, edges, and faces.

CHECK-YOUR-UNDERSTANDING QUESTIONS

MILD

A. How many vertices are on a triangular prism?

B. How many edges are on a triangular prism?

C. How many faces are on a triangular prism?

MEDIUM

A. How many vertices, edges, and faces are on a heptagonal (7-sided polygon) prism?

B. How many vertices, edges, and faces are on an octagonal (8-sided polygon) prism?

SPICY

A. How many vertices, edges, and faces are on a triangular (3-sided polygon) pyramid?

B. How many vertices, edges, and faces are on a pentagonal (5-sided polygon) pyramid?

Author Notes

This is a fun task to do with students because the patterns are easily identifiable and immediately usable to find the number of vertices, edges, and faces for *n*-gonal prisms where *n* is large. We have listed it as non-curricular because 3D shapes is not in the curriculum for most students in the Grade 2–5 range.

But even if 3D shapes is in the curriculum, the emergence of patterns and the establishment and use of relationships likely isn't. To do this, however, the students are going to need to organize their data. Helping one group to do this and then mobilizing knowledge will be vital in this regard.

Notes to My Future Forgetful Self

TASK 15: BRIANNA THE BIRDY

TASK

Brianna the Birdy has between 10 and 70 eggs. If she puts them into groups of 2, there is 1 left over. If she puts them into groups of 3, there are 2 left over. If she puts them into groups of 4, there are 3 left over. And if she puts them into groups of 5, there are no eggs left over. How many eggs could Brianna the Birdy have?

Grades: 3–5

Content: multiplication, divisibility, table of values

Perseverance Scale:

Grade Level:	3	4	5
Perseverance Level:	3	2	2

Macro-Moves: giving tasks verbally, answering only keep-thinking questions

Competencies: perseverance, trial and error, risk taking

LAUNCH SCRIPT

Teacher: Brianna the Birdy has a bunch of eggs. But she is very secretive about how many she has. Our job is to figure out how many eggs she could have given the clues she has given us.

Teacher: Clue 1 is that she has more than 10 but less than 70 eggs. [teacher writes *"more than 10 and less than 70"* on the board]

Teacher: Clue 2 is that if she arranges the eggs into groups of 2, there will be 1 egg left over. [teacher writes *"groups of 2 → 1 left over"* on the board]

Teacher: Clue 3 is that if she arranges the eggs into groups of 3, there will be 2 eggs left over. [teacher writes *"groups of 3 → 2 left over"* on the board]

Teacher: Clue 4 is that if she arranges the eggs into groups of 4, there will be 3 eggs left over. [teacher writes *"groups of 4 → 3 left over"* on the board]

Teacher: Clue 5 is that if she arranges the eggs into groups of 5, there will be no eggs left over. [teacher writes *"groups of 5 → 0 left over"* on the board]

Teacher: How many eggs could Brianna have?

CREATING ACCESS

- For students who are having difficulty starting, give them only clues 1 and 5 and ask them how many eggs *could* Brianna have? When they have that answer, give them clue 2 and ask how many eggs *could* Brianna have? Then give clue 3 and then clue 4. You may not get through all the clues, but at each stage the students will feel successful.

- For students who are having difficulty visualizing the problem, give them counters of some sort to represent the eggs.

- For students who are struggling with the arithmetic, give them a multiplication table.

EXTENSION SCRIPTS

1. Brianna lied to us about her first clue. She actually has more than 50 eggs, but less than 100 eggs. How many eggs does she have?

2. Brianna has an older sister named Bianca the Birdy. Bianca is also very secretive about how many eggs she has and has given us some clues:

   A. There are more than 70 and less than 170.

   B. In groups of 2, there is 1 left over.

   C. In groups of 3, there are 2 left over.

   D. In groups of 4, there are 3 left over.

   E. In groups of 5, there are 4 left over.

   F. In groups of 6, there are 5 left over.

   G. In groups of 7, there are 0 left over.

   H. How many eggs does Bianca have?

AUTHOR SOLUTION(S)

This problem can be approached in at least three different ways. The first is to use logic, coupled with knowledge of division properties. When we do this, it is useful to not follow the clues in the order that they are given. We begin with clue 1, clue 5, and clue 2. Clue 1 tells us that there are more than 10 and less than 70 eggs, clue 5 tells us that it must be a multiple of 5, and clue 2 tells us that it must be odd. This means that Brianna must have 15, 25, 35, 45, 55, or 65 eggs. Clue 3 tells us that it is not a multiple of 3. This eliminates 15 and 45. But this same clue also tells us that the number of eggs is 2 more than a multiple of 3. That eliminates 25 and 55. So, she can only have 35 or 65 eggs. Finally, clue 4 tells us that the number of eggs is 3 more than a multiple of 4. Well, 65 is 1 more than 64, which is a multiple of 4, so it is eliminated. This leaves only 35 eggs as a possible answer.

The second approach is to create lists of numbers that satisfy each clue independently. When we have all the lists, we look for what numbers are in all the lists. This method, although laborious, really helps students see what is going on.

Clue 1: 11, 12, 13, 14, 15, 16, . . . , 33, 34, 35, 36, 37, . . . , 69

Clue 2: 11, 13, 15, 17, 19, . . . , 31, 33, 35, 37, . . . , 69

Clue 3: 11, 14, 17, 20, 23, 26, 29, 32, 35, . . . , 68

Clue 4: 11, 15, 19, 23, 27, 31, 35, 39, . . . , 67

Clue 5: 15, 20, 25, 30, 35, 40, 45, 50, 55, 60, 65

The third method is to run a sieve on all the numbers from 11 to 69, eliminating numbers that are obviously excluded by each clue. If we are to take the clues in the order they are given, we begin by writing out all the numbers from 11 to 69 (clue 1).

11, 12, 13, 14, 15, 16, 17, 18, 19, 20, . . . , 30, 31, 32, 33, 34, 35, 36, 37, 38, 39, 40, . . . , 69

Clue 2 tells us that it cannot be even. So, we cross out all even numbers.

11, ~~12~~, 13, ~~14~~, 15, ~~16~~, 17, ~~18~~, 19, ~~20~~, . . . , ~~30~~, 31, ~~32~~, 33, ~~34~~, 35, ~~36~~, 37, ~~38~~, 39, ~~40~~, . . . , 69

Clue 3 tells us that it cannot be a multiple of 3. So, we cross out all multiples of 3.

11, ~~12~~, 13, ~~14~~, ~~15~~, ~~16~~, 17, ~~18~~, 19, ~~20~~, . . . , ~~30~~, 31, ~~32~~, ~~33~~, ~~34~~, 35, ~~36~~, 37, ~~38~~, ~~39~~, ~~40~~, . . . , 69

Clue 4 tells us that it cannot be a multiple of 4. So, we cross out all multiples of 4. (FYI, these were already crossed out by clue 2).

11, ~~12~~, 13, ~~14~~, ~~15~~, ~~16~~, 17, ~~18~~, 19, ~~20~~, . . ., ~~30~~, 31, ~~32~~, ~~33~~, ~~34~~, 35, ~~36~~, 37, ~~38~~, ~~39~~, ~~40~~, . . ., 69

Clue 5 tells us that it must be a multiple of 5. So, we cross out anything that is not a multiple of 5.

~~11~~, ~~12~~, ~~13~~, ~~14~~, 15, ~~16~~, ~~17~~, ~~18~~, ~~19~~, ~~20~~, . . . , ~~30~~, ~~31~~, ~~32~~, ~~33~~, ~~34~~, 35, ~~36~~, ~~37~~, ~~38~~, ~~39~~, ~~40~~, . . . , 69

Of course, we would do all this crossing out on the same list of numbers—we have shown it here on separate lists to show the progression. When we run this sieve, we would be left with 25, 35, 55, and 65. The reason we have multiple possible answers is that at each stage we did not eliminate all ineligible numbers, just those that were obviously eliminated. For example, clue 3 tells us that if we arrange the eggs in groups of 3 there will be 2 left over. This means that it cannot be a multiple of three. But it also tells us that it cannot be 1 more than a multiple of 3. We have only eliminated the multiples of 3. Nonetheless, with the four possible answers remaining, we then fully run each clue on them to eliminate 25, 55, and 65. Notice that this third method is similar to the first method, just less efficiently so. The third method would be identical to the first method if we ran the sieve in a different order—clue 1, 2, and 5 all at once, then clue 3, then clue 4.

STUDENT SOLUTIONS

1.

Commentary:

This solution shows the students looking for the pattern within the task. They clearly understand that there is a pattern to be found but are looking at multiples instead of multiples plus a remainder.

Suggested hints:

Brianna can't have 2, 4, 6, 8, etc. eggs because when she arranges it in 2s there is 1 egg leftover. So, what should the numbers in the 2s column be? What would the 3s column look like? What about the 4s column?

2.

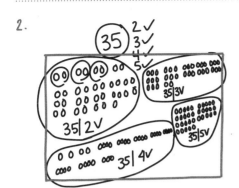

Commentary:

This solution is a realistic image of what the story could look like. This is a good solution to highlight because it shows that students understand how their solution satisfies the clues while staying with the context of the eggs.

Suggested hints:

How can you represent this solution using number sentences?

---

3. $35/2 = 17 r 1$

$35/3 = 11 r 2$

$35/4 = 8 r 3$

Commentary:

This solution, like solution 2, shows that the students know that 35 satisfies all the clues. But it does so with number sentences. The challenge is that it is completely devoid of the context of the eggs.

Suggested hints:

What does *r* mean in these number sentences? How is that related to Brianna?

4.

[1] $35 \div 2 = 1$ left

[11] $35 \div 3 = 2$ left

[8] $35 \div 4 = 3$ left

Commentary:

This solution demonstrates students' understanding of division and what remainders actually mean in the context of the story.

Suggested hints:

Is there another way to solve this without using division?

Could Brianna have a different number of eggs? How do you know?

CONSOLIDATION

The purpose of consolidation in this activity is twofold. First, you want to highlight some of the different ways that the problem could have been solved. Second, and the purpose we have emphasized here, is to showcase the different representations of what the solution can look like and how we can verify it. Many students will justify their work through images (actual eggs) while others may divide right away. An interesting phenomenon is that students who divide may not understand what a remainder means in the context of the story. Showcasing pictorial and symbolic solutions will help to link division with remainder to the story.

CHECK-YOUR-UNDERSTANDING QUESTIONS

MILD

A. Can 13 eggs be put into equal groups of 2?

B. Can 18 eggs be put into equal groups of 3?

C. Can 22 eggs be put into equal groups of 4?

A. Can you think of a number larger than 30 that could be put into equal groups of 2 and can also be put into equal groups of 3?

B. Can you think of a number larger than 30 that could be put into equal groups of 4 and can also be put into equal groups of 5?

C. Can you think of a number that can be put into equal groups of 3, can also be put into equal groups of 4, and can also be put into equal groups of 5?

SPICY

A. If a number can be put into equal groups of 2 and can also be put into equal groups of 3, does that mean that it can also be put into equal groups of 6?

B. If a number can be put into equal groups of 8, what other equal groups can it be put into?

Author Notes

This task is a great task to have students play with numbers. Whether they are doing so through addition, skip counting, multiplication, or division, the complexity of the clues is going to challenge them. Even students who are well-versed in division find this task challenging as it doesn't use division in the usual way. Students are used to finding the quotient and the remainder, not having the remainder and looking for the dividend. As a result, you expect most students to only use division to verify their solution.

Notes to My Future Forgetful Self

_____

_____

_____

_____

_____

_____

_____

_____

TASK 16: WHEN IS A TRIANGLE A SQUARE?

TASK

What numbers are both triangular numbers (1, 3, 6, 10, etc.) and square numbers (1, 4, 9, 16, …)?

Grades: 3–5

Content: multiplication, addition, square numbers, triangular numbers, patterns

Perseverance Scale:

Grade Levels:	3	4	5
Perseverance Levels:	3	2	2

Macro-Moves: consolidation from the bottom, knowledge mobility

Competencies: looking for patterns, mobilizing knowledge

LAUNCH SCRIPT

Teacher: You know we describe some numbers as odd and even. Well, we can also describe them as square and triangular based on the shape they can make. For example, four is a square number because it can be made into the shape of a square [teacher points at 4 dots arranged into a square] and 3 is a triangular number because it can be made into the shape of a triangle [teacher points at 3 dots arranged into a triangle]. Can you find a number that is both a square number and a triangular number?

CREATING ACCESS

- If you have students who are struggling to understand how to make square numbers and triangular numbers, give them manipulatives. Although any manipulative will work, cubes work best for making square numbers and circular disks are best for making triangular numbers just because of how they fit together.

- If you have students who are having difficulty tracking their data, make a T-chart for them to put their numbers into.

EXTENSION SCRIPTS

1. If I tell you that the 10th triangular number is 55, what would be the 11th triangular number?

2. If I tell you that the 15th triangular number is 120, what would be the 16th triangular number?

3. If I tell you that the 10th square number is 100, what would be the 11th square number?

4. If I tell you that the 15th square number is 225, what would be the 16th square number?

5. What happens if I add the 4th and the 5th triangular numbers together?

6. Will that always be true? Can you show me why?

AUTHOR SOLUTIONS

To solve the original task, you will need to list the triangular and square numbers and look for a number that is in both lists.

Number	Square Numbers	Triangular Numbers
1	1	1
2	4	3
3	9	6
4	16	10
5	25	15
6	36	21
7	49	28
8	76	36
9	81	45
10	100	55

By doing this, you will see immediately that there are two numbers that are both square and triangular—1 and 36. The next number that is both square and triangular is 1225.

Looking at the list of square numbers, we can see the pattern in one of two ways—through addition and through multiplication.

$$1 \xrightarrow{+3} 4 \xrightarrow{+5} 9 \xrightarrow{+7} 16 \xrightarrow{+9} 25 \xrightarrow{+11} 36 \xrightarrow{+13} \dots$$

$$1, 4, 9, 16, 25, 36, \dots$$
$$1\times1 \quad 2\times2 \quad 3\times3 \quad 4\times4 \quad 5\times5 \quad 6\times6$$

The first of these ways of looking at it is how your students are more likely to see it as they are used to finding the next term in a pattern by considering the previous terms. Anne Watson (2000) refers to this as *going with the grain*. In this way of thinking, we see the pattern growing by successively increasing odd numbers: +3, +5, +7, +9, +11, +13, . . . The second way of looking at the pattern is multiplicative and involves recognizing that the 1st square number is 1 × 1, the 2nd is 2 × 2, the 3rd is 3 × 3, and so on. This involves seeing a given term in relation to its position. This is called *across the grain* thinking (Watson, 2000). Although with the grain thinking is more natural for students, across the grain will enable you to quickly find the 25th square number (25 × 25). To find this using with the grain thinking would require you to calculate the first 24 square numbers to find the 25th square number.

The relationship between the two ways of seeing this pattern can be seen in how we go from the 4th square number to the 5th square number. The 4th square number is 16, and with the grain tells us that we need to add 9. This will then give us the 5th square number of 25. But when we deconstruct 25 to show where the 16 is, we can see why we are adding 9.

$$16 + \underbrace{(4 + 4 + 1)}_{9}$$

Here we can see that we are actually not just adding 9. We are adding a new row and a new column, both of length 4, plus a 1 to fill in the missing corner. This will then give us the 5th triangular number. If we wanted to get the 6th triangular number, we would again add a row and a column (this time of length 5) plus the missing corner piece for a total of 11, and so on.

The pattern for triangular numbers can also be seen with the grain and across the grain. With the grain, it is just +1, +2, +3, +4, +5, etc. as we add another row to the bottom of the triangle. Each time we do this, the row we are adding gets longer by 1. Using this method, we can always find the next triangular number provided we know, at least, the previous two.

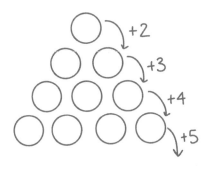

But there is also an across the grain way of seeing triangular numbers that will allow us to quickly determine a triangular number without knowing the previous terms. This comes from the recognition that the 1st triangular number is $\frac{(1 \times 2)}{2}$, the 2nd is $\frac{(2 \times 3)}{2}$, the 3rd is $\frac{(3 \times 4)}{2}$, and so on. This means that the 10th triangular number is going to be $\frac{(10 \times 11)}{2} = 55$. To understand where this comes from, we need to think of triangular numbers in a staircase representation and then think about what happens when we add two of the same triangular number together.

Here we can see that if we add the 3rd triangular number to itself, we actually get a rectangle. The number of disks in this rectangle is easy to calculate ($3 \times 4 = 12$). This will happen with any triangular number added to itself—we get a rectangle whose width is equal to the base of the triangle and the height is one more than the height of the triangle. So, if we add the 10th triangular number to itself, we would get a rectangle that is ($10 \times 11 = 110$). But this is double what we need. So, we divide by 2 – $\frac{(10 \times 11)}{2} = 55$.

This same thinking can be used to combine consecutive triangular numbers to show that this will make a square number.

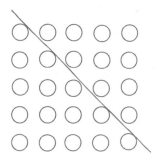

In this case, we see that the 4th (10) triangular number added to the 5th (15) triangular number will produce the 5th square number (25). Any time we add consecutive triangular numbers you will get a square number.

STUDENT SOLUTIONS

1.

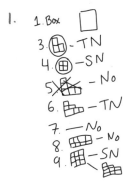

Commentary:

This is an example of students starting with a number and then seeing if it is square or triangular based on if they can create one or the other shape out of the numbers.

Suggested hints:

Rather than starting with a number and seeing if it is square or triangular, try building square and triangular numbers and see what kinds of numbers you get.

2.

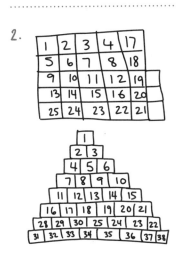

Commentary:

In this example, the students are building triangular and square numbers. The numbering strategy for the triangular numbers is showing us what the triangular numbers are: 1, 3, 6, 10, 15, 21, 38, 36. However, the counting strategy for the square numbers is not as effective.

Suggested hints:

Let's build a square number together. Let's start with 1. Now, let's build the next one on its own. What will it look like? Now build the third one on its own.

3.

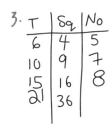

Commentary:

In these two examples, students have arranged their square and triangular numbers into a list. In the first case, they have made an error and listed 35 as a triangular number instead of 36. In the second case, they just need to keep going with their list of triangular numbers.

Suggested hints:

Check your work and keep going.

Is there a pattern to find square numbers?

Is there a pattern to find triangular numbers?

(Continued)

(Continued)

4.

St	Sq	
10	4	2x2
15	25	5x5
3	9	3x3
6	16	4x4
	36	6x6

□	△	
1	1	
4	3	+2
9	6	+3
16	10	+4
25	15	+5
36	21	+6
	28	+7
	36	+8

Commentary:

These are completed solutions and the left has indicated the pattern for finding square numbers. The right image shows students who have noticed and named the pattern for triangular numbers.

Suggested hints:

What would be the 10th square and triangular numbers?

What would be the 20th square and triangular numbers?

CONSOLIDATION

When consolidating this task, you want to use student work to showcase the different patterns that exist within the sequences of square and triangular numbers. Using a gallery walk will achieve this. You may also want to use the consolidation to push on to a task they may not have gotten to—like the sum of consecutive triangular numbers. To do this, you are better off to use the method of teacher-scribe to consolidate.

CHECK-YOUR-UNDERSTANDING QUESTIONS

MILD

A. Name 3 square numbers

B. Name 3 triangular numbers.

MEDIUM

A. What are some square and triangular numbers that are close to each other?

B. What do you notice about the pattern of odd and even numbers in the sequences of square and triangular numbers?

SPICY

A. What is the pattern for finding square and triangular numbers?

B. Take a triangular number and double it. How close is it to a square number? What pattern do you notice?

Author Notes

This task is rich with opportunities to share out different visual representations. You can really use these to seed knowledge in the room and then work on mobilizing that knowledge.

Notes to My Future Forgetful Self

TASK 17: OUTFIT CHOICES

TASK

How many outfits can be made with 3 shirts, 2 pairs of pants, and 1 pair of shoes?

Grades: 3–5

Content: patterning, multiplication, counting

Perseverance Scale:

Grade Levels:	3	4	5
Perseverance Levels:	3	3	2

Macro-Moves: use hints and extensions to maintain flow, knowledge mobility

Competencies: organization, mobilizing knowledge, perseverance

LAUNCH SCRIPT

Teacher: So, I had trouble deciding what to wear to school today. Not so much because I was worried about how I would look, but because I had so many choices of what to wear. You see, I have 3 shirts, 2 pairs of pants, and 1 pair of shoes. How many different outfits can I make?

CREATING ACCESS

• For students who are overwhelmed by the numbers, start with 3 shirts, 1 pair of pants, and 1 pair of shoes. Then go to 2 shirts, 2 pairs of pants, and 1 pair of shoes.

• For students who are having difficulty visualizing the problem, give the shirts specific colors—yellow, green, pink. Also give the pants specific colors—blue and black. And make the shoes white. Then, using different colored Unifix cubes, the student can actually build each outfit.

EXTENSION SCRIPTS

1. What if I had 4 shirts, 3 pairs of pants, and 2 pairs of shoes?

2. What about 10 shirts, 5 pairs of pants, and 2 pairs of shoes?

3. Can you find a pattern for any number of shirts, pants, and shoes?

4. What if I had 3 hats, 5 shirts, 4 pairs of pants, and 2 pairs of shoes?

AUTHOR SOLUTIONS

This is a counting problem. And like all counting problems, there are a number of ways it can be solved. For the purposes of this task, we are going to focus on using a tree diagram and we are going to label the 3 shirts as a S_A, S_B, and S_C, the 2 pairs of pants as P_A and P_B, and the shoes as F_A. So, when getting dressed, we have three choices for a shirt.

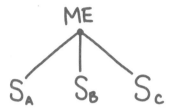

For each of these shirts, we can choose two pairs of pants.

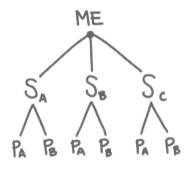

And for each of these shirt-pant combos, we can add a pair of shoes for a total of 6 different outfits.

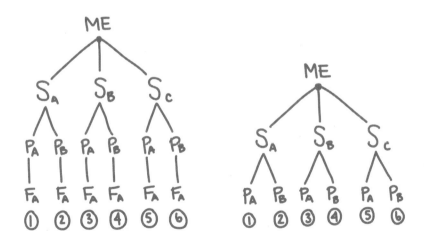

What is nice about a tree diagram, is that the order in which we get dressed doesn't matter. We can go shoes first, then shirts, and finally pants and still get the same number of outfits. Trying to get your pants on over your shoes would be tough, but the point is that the tree diagram can still tell you how many outfits there are and that each outfit is a unique combination of shirts, pants, and shoes. If I increase the number of shirts, pants, or shoes I would just add more branches at the relevant junctions.

What emerges from the tree diagram is that the number of outfits is equal to the number of shirts × the number of pants × the number of pairs of shoes = 3 × 2 × 1 = 6. We can see this in the tree diagrams. There are 3 shirts, each of which can be combined with 2 pairs of pants (3 × 2), each of which can be matched with 1 pair of shoes (3 × 2 × 1). This is called the *Fundamental Principal of Counting*, which states that the number of combinations is equal to the product of the choices. For example, if I had 7 shirts, 5 pairs of pants, and 3 pairs of shoes, the number of outfits I would have is equal to 7 × 5 × 3 = 105.

STUDENT SOLUTIONS

1.

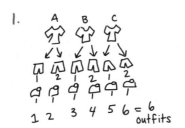

Shirt A $\big\langle$ PA+S 1, PB+S 2

Shirt B $\big\langle$ PA+S 3, PB+S 4

Shift C $\big\langle$ PA+S 5, PB+S 6

S = Shoes
PA = Pants A
PB = Pants B
6 outfits

Commentary:

These boards are examples of students creating a system to ensure every outfit is accounted for. This system is helpful, but it may become cumbersome when there are more types of clothing (like hats, scarves, etc.) and more of each type of clothing.

Suggested hints:

What if there were 4 shirts? How would that change your diagram and your answer?

Can you see the connection between the numbers 3, 2, and 1 and the fact that there are 6 outfits?

---

2. 3 shirts — 2 options for pants each
   2, 4, 6 = 6 outfits
   S1 S2 S3

   Only 1 pair of shoes

	Shirt 1	Shirt 2	Shirt 3
Pants 1	1+1	2+1	3+1
Pants 2	1+2	2+2	3+2

   6 outfits
   only 1 pair of shoes

Commentary:

This is an example of students who are trying to create a system that can be easily adapted for many more articles of clothing (such as 4 shirts, 3 pants, and 2 pairs of shoes).

Suggested hints:

How does 3 shirts, 2 pairs of pants, 1 pair of shoes connect to 6 outfits?

What is the pattern that could be used to find any number of outfits from the number of articles of clothing?

---

3. 3 shirts
   2 pairs of pants
   1 pair of shoes
   3 × 2 × 1 = 6 outfits

Commentary:

This image show students who have created a "rule" to be used for any set of outfits.

Suggested hints:

Are you sure this rule works? Could you test it with another set of outfits?

What if I added hats to the outfit? How would that change the rule?

CONSOLIDATION

The purpose of this consolidation is to look at and discuss the various methods students used to find out all the potential outfits. Your goal is to get them to see the connection between the tree diagram and a way of getting the answer by multiplying the choices. From here you would want to showcase a purely multiplicative strategy that a group found, test it by doing the tree diagram for it, and discuss whether it would work for all other scenarios. What you want to emerge out of the discussion is the *Fundamental Principal of Counting*.

CHECK-YOUR-UNDERSTANDING QUESTIONS

MILD

A. Use a tree diagram to show how many different outfits can be made with 1 shirt and 1 pair of pants.

B. Use a tree diagram to show how many different outfits can be made with 3 shirts and 1 pair of pants.

C. Use a tree diagram to show how many different outfits can be made with 2 shirts and 2 pairs of pants.

MEDIUM

A. How many different outfits can be made with 3 shirts, 2 pairs of pants, and 1 pair of shoes?

B. How many different outfits can be made with 4 shirts, 3 pairs of pants, and 2 pairs of shoes?

C. How many different outfits can be made with 5 shirts, 5 pairs of pants, and 3 pairs of shoes?

SPICY

A. How many different outfits can be made with 6 shirts, 5 pairs of pants, 3 pairs of shoes, and 2 hats?

B. If I have 100 different outfits made up of shirts, pants, and shoes, how many of each do I have? Is this the only solution?

C. What articles of clothing could I have, and how many of each, if I can make 80 outfits total? Is there another solution?

Author Notes

This is a task that has no quick mathematical solution. The students have to go through a process of creating different outfits before anything can begin to emerge. Be ready to help with naming and notating the different shirts, helping them to organize their outfits, and seeding and mobilizing a tree diagram. The nice thing about this task is that once order is brought to their thinking, they move quickly to a rule and then feel empowered to take on any set of numbers for each article of clothing.

Notes to My Future Forgetful Self

TASK 18: HOW MANY HIGH FIVES?

TASK

How many high fives are there for 12 people if every person high-fives every other person?

Grades: 3–5

Content Potential: Patterning, equations, addition, sequences

Perseverance Scale:

Grade Levels:	3	4	5
Perseverance Levels:	3	2	1

Macro-Moves: how we give tasks, consolidation from the bottom

Competencies: collaboration, risk taking, organization, looking for patterns

LAUNCH SCRIPT

Teacher: [Teacher asks for three volunteers to come to the front]

Teacher: The three of you just arrived at a party. You came in separate cars, so you need to say hi to each other—by high-fiving each other.

Students: [Students high-five each other]

Teacher: Awesome! How many high fives was that? Did anyone see how many there were?

Students: Three!

Teacher: OK, so three high fives for three people. How many high fives would it take for a party of 12 people?

CREATING ACCESS

- For students who are overwhelmed by the fact that there are 12 people, start with 5 people.

- For students who are struggling to visualize the task, give them manipulatives.

- For students who are struggling to keep track of their data, give them a representation that can help keep their thinking organized.

EXTENSION SCRIPTS

1. How many high fives are needed for 18 people?

2. How many high fives are needed for 24 people?

3. Can you come up with a representation that will help you figure out how many high fives for any number of people at the party?

4. Can you use this rule to find out how many high fives for 5, 6, 7, and 8 people?

AUTHOR SOLUTION(S)

Like so many of the non-curricular tasks, this task is best solved through organization. Although there are many ways to do so, we will focus on a very visual solution wherein people are dots and high fives are lines between people. From this representation, you can see that there will be 3 high fives for 3 people, 6 for 4 people, and 10 for 5 people.

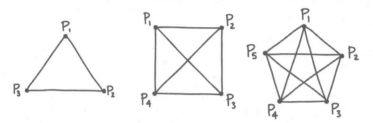

If you have read Task 16 (When Is a Triangle a Square?) you will recognize that these are triangular numbers.

5 people = 10 high fives = 4 + 3 + 2 + 1

4 people = 6 high fives = 3 + 2 + 1

3 people = 3 high fives = 2 + 1

2 people = 1 high five = 1

We can see why it is a triangular number if we look closely at how many high fives for 6 people. In this case, the first person (P_1) will high-five 5 people (P_2, P_3, P_4, P_5, P_6). P_2 will then high-five 4 people (P_3, P_4, P_5, P_6). P_2 does not have to high-five P_1 because P_1 already high-fived P_2. Then P_3 will high-five 3 people (P_4, P_5, P_6) and so on. So, for 6 people there will be 5 + 4 + 3 + 2 + 1 high fives = 15 high fives.

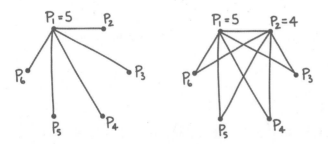

Another way to think of this task is that P_1 will high-five 5 people. P_2 will also high-five 5 people. And P_3 will high-five 5 people. And so on. That is, all 6 people will high-five 5 people = 6 × 5 = 30. But this then double counts every high five—P_1 high-fives P_2 and P_2 high-fives P_1. So, we have to divide 30 by 2 = 15.

STUDENT SOLUTIONS

1.

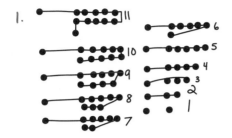

Commentary:

This solution is an interesting representation of what it looks like for 12 people high-fiving each person. This clearly shows that this group understands that the number decreases for every person who engages in a high five to avoid redundancy, but they may not see how this pattern could be used for other numbers of people.

Suggested hints:

How would you add all of these up? What order would you choose?

2.

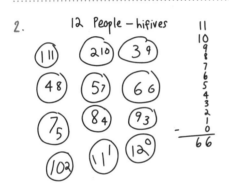

Commentary:

Similar to the first solution, this group has separated the high fives into people and represents them in descending order. They have also added on the right-hand side, which indicates they may have a strategy for other numbers.

Suggested hints:

Can you use that for another number of people?

3.

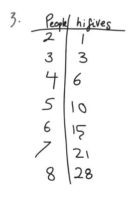

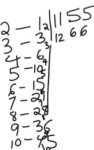

Commentary:

Both of these groups have organized their solutions into a table that tells us how many high fives (right column) for a specific number of people (left column). The work on the right shows that this group has recognized the difference between consecutive numbers of high fives. But neither group may actually see where the number of high fives comes from. They are thinking *with the grain* rather than *across the grain* (see Task 16).

Suggested hints:

Where did the numbers in the right column come from? For example, where did the 10 come from?

Can you make an equation that someone could use to figure out the number of high fives for any number of people?

CONSOLIDATION

The purpose of this consolidation is twofold. First, you will want to explore the different ways groups are visualizing and representing the high fives for 12 people. Second, you will want to look specifically at how these different representations can show how to calculate how many high fives for 12 people and how this can be used to come up with a general method for any number of people. A guided gallery walk will achieve both these goals.

CHECK-YOUR-UNDERSTANDING QUESTIONS

MILD

A. How many high fives would there be for 6 people?

B. How many high fives would there be for 8 people?

MEDIUM

A. How many high fives would there be for 9 people?

B. How many more high fives would there be for 10 people?

SPICY

A. There are 45 total high fives. How many people are there?

B. How would you find how many high fives there would be for 100 people? Do not solve it; just explain how to solve it and what numbers you would use.

Author Notes

What is fun about this task is that you get to model it with the kids. You should definitely do this in the launch, but you can also do it for parts of the consolidation. Although there are some tasks that are difficult for students to collaborate on, this one lends itself well to collaboration, so it is a great task after which to discuss what good collaboration looks like.

Notes to My Future Forgetful Self

_____

_____

_____

_____

_____

_____

TASK 19: FOLDING PAPER

TASK

How many sections will there be if a piece of paper has been folded in half 6 times?

Grades: 3–5

Content Potential: multiplication, doubling, patterns, exponents

Perseverance Scale:

Grade Level:	3	4	5
Perseverance Level:	3	2	2

Macro-Moves: consolidation from the bottom

Competencies: communication, mobilizing knowledge

LAUNCH SCRIPT

Teacher: If I fold a piece of paper in half [teacher folds a piece of paper in half] and then unfold it, how many sections have I made?

Students: 2!

Teacher: What if I folded it twice? [teacher redoes the first fold and then folds it in half again]

Students: 4!

Teacher: How many sections would there be after 6 folds?

Teacher: [teacher puts students into random groups and gives every group a piece of paper]

CREATING ACCESS

- For students who are overwhelmed by how many sections they are getting, start with 4 folds.

- For students who are having difficulty seeing a pattern, show them what is happening to a section when we add another fold. This can be done by unfolding the paper, having them pick one or more sections, and outlining those sections with a marker. Then, refold the paper and add one more fold. When you unfold it now, you will be able to see how the section became two sections.

- For students who are having difficulty tracking their data, set up a T-chart for them.

EXTENSION SCRIPTS

1. How many sections would we get if we folded it 8 times?

2. How about 10 times?

3. How about 20 times?

AUTHOR SOLUTION(S)

After we have folded the paper twice and unfolded it, there will be 4 sections. If we refold it and add a fold (3 folds), there will now be 8 sections. And so on.

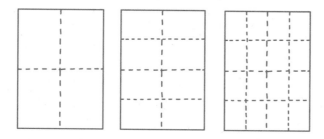

This is a doubling pattern, and we can think of it either additively or multiplicatively. So, for 7 folds, there are 128 sections. This means that for 8 folds there will be 128 + 128 = 128 × 2 = 256 sections. Whether you are thinking additively or multiplicatively, you are thinking *with the grain* (see Task 16). To think *across the grain*, you will need to think exponentially. That is, 8 folds is 2 × 128, but 128 = 2 × 64, but 64 = 2 × 32, and so on. So, 8 folds is 2 × 2 × 2 × 2 × 2 × 2 × 2× 2 = 2^8. And 9 folds will be 2^9 = 512.

Folds	Sections	Additive	Multiplicative	Exponential
0	1			2^0
1	2	1 + 1	2 × 1	2^1
2	4	2 + 2	2 × 2	2^2
3	8	4 + 4	2 × 4	2^3
4	16	8 + 8	2 × 8	2^4
5	32	16 + 16	2 × 16	2^5
6	64	32 + 32	2 × 32	2^6
7	128	64 + 64	2 × 64	2^7
8	256	128 + 128	2 × 128	2^8
9	512	256 + 256	2 × 256	2^9
10	1024	512 + 512	2 × 512	2^{10}
. . .	. . .	. . .	. . .	
20	1,048,576			2^{20}

This is called exponential growth—meaning that the terms grow exponentially in relationship to the previous term. It is difficult to imagine just how significant this growth is until you realize that after only 20 folds you have more than a million sections. And just one more fold will get you to more than 2 million sections.

STUDENT SOLUTIONS

1.

$1=2 \quad 2=4 \quad 3=8$
$4=16 \quad 5=32 \quad 6=64$
$7=128 \quad 8=256 \quad 9=512$
$10=1024$

Commentary:

This group clearly sees a pattern. Even if they were working with a paper, they did accurately, or in a timely fashion, count 128 sections. They may have been counting to begin with. What is not clear is whether they are thinking additively or multiplicatively.

Suggested hints:

Can you show your process for how you move from one number to the next?

2.

$2 + 2 = 4$
$4 + 4 = 8$
$8 + 8 = 16$
$16 + 16 = 32$
$32 + 32 = 64$
$64 + 64 = 128$
$128 + 128 = 256$
$256 + 256 = 512$
$512 + 512 = 1024$
$1024 + 1024 =$

$4 = 16$
$5 = 32$
$6 = 64$
$7 = 128$
$8 = 256$
$9 = 512$
$10 = 1024$

$\begin{array}{r} 64 \\ \times\ 2 \\ \hline 128 \end{array}$

$\begin{array}{r} 128 \\ \times\ 2 \\ \hline 256 \end{array}$

$\begin{array}{r} 256 \\ \times\ 2 \\ \hline 512 \end{array}$

$\begin{array}{r} 512 \\ \times\ 2 \\ \hline 1024 \end{array}$

Commentary:

These two solutions show doubling through adding and doubling through multiplication. They are also organizing their work in a way that makes it easy to follow and describe the pattern.

Suggested hints:

It would be pretty time consuming to just keep doubling from the previous one before. Is there an overall rule we can make to know the number of sections?

3. multiple by 2 that number of time

Commentary:

This group has formed a rule that can be used to find how many sections for any number of folds. However, the rule may not be clear enough that another person could easily use it.

Suggested hints:

What is meant by this statement? For 10 folds, does it mean 10 × 2? That would only be 20. Is that what you mean? Can you write this in a clearer way?

CONSOLIDATION

The purpose of this consolidation is to look at doubling through addition and multiplication. A gallery walk will achieve this, but you also want to get to a point where students see that multiplying by 2, for example, 5 times is different than multiplying 2 by 5. For instance, 5 folds is 64, which is $2 \times 2 \times 2 \times 2 \times 2$, not 2×5. To achieve this, you may need to consolidate through teacher-scribe.

CHECK-YOUR-UNDERSTANDING QUESTIONS

MILD

How many sections would there be in a paper folded in half 5 times?

MEDIUM

A. How many more sections are there if a paper is folded 7 times vs. 6 times?

B. How many sections are in a paper that has been folded 15 times?

SPICY

A. What is a rule that can be used for any number of folds?

B. If I fold a paper in 3, like a letter, I will get 3 sections. How many sections will I have if I repeat this process 6 times?

Author Notes

You may be wondering why this is classified as a perseverance level 2. This is because students very easily find the pattern in this task, but the difficulty begins when they have to create a rule. Their initial rules will be instructions for how to do it, but you can actually get students to understand the need for a new notation—exponential notation.

Notes to My Future Forgetful Self

_____

_____

_____

_____

_____

_____

_____

_____

TASK 20: TWIN TEST

TASK

Who did better on their test—Twin 1, who got 50/70, or Twin 2, who got 40/56?

Grades: 4–5

Content Potential: factors, division/multiplication, fractions, decimals, percentages

Perseverance Scale:

Grade Level:	4	5
Perseverance Level:	3	3

Macro-Moves: giving hints and extensions to maintain flow, knowledge mobility

Competencies: perseverance, collaboration, mobilizing knowledge

LAUNCH SCRIPT

Teacher: Did you know that I have a twin sister?

Students: What!?!

Teacher: And did you know that my sister has two twin girls the same age as you? Their names are Maya and Maisy. And they are super competitive!

Teacher: They are so competitive that their parents keep them in separate classes to stop them from competing against each other. This has worked really well until last week when they both had a science test on the same day.

Teacher: That night, my sister asked them how they did on their science tests. Naturally the twins wanted to see who did better. Here's the problem—they have different teachers, so they wrote different tests. And each test is out of a different number of points. Maya got 50 out of 70 and Maisy got 40 out of 56.

Teacher: Which twin did better?

CREATING ACCESS

- For students who struggle with such large numbers, you can call it a quiz and say that Maya got 15 out of 21 and Maisy got 10 out of 14.

- For students who are not fluent with 7s, you can use friendlier numbers and say that Maya got 6 out of 8 and Maisy got 3 out of 4.

- For students who do not understand equivalent fractions, you can provide them with fraction strips or other manipulatives and then say that Maya got 6 out of 8 and Maisy got 3 out of 4.

EXTENSION SCRIPTS

1. My son Taylor also took a science test last week. He got 35 out of 49. Did he do better than his cousins?

2. My nephew, the twins' brother, also wrote a science test last week. His test was out of 42 and he did better than the twins. What score could he have gotten on the test?

AUTHOR SOLUTION(S)

There are two main ways that this task can be solved—each of which requires us to think about the score as a fraction. That is, 50 out of 70 is equivalent to the fraction $\frac{50}{70}$ and 40 out of 56 is equivalent to the fraction $\frac{40}{56}$. The first method of solving this task involves dividing the numerator by the denominator.

$$\frac{50}{70} = 50 \div 70 = 0.7143 = 71.43\%$$

$$\frac{40}{56} = 40 \div 56 = 0.7143 = 71.43\%$$

The twins had the same percentage. So, they did equally well. The second way of solving the task involves finding equivalent fractions that have the same denominator. Usually, finding the same denominator involves finding the *lowest common multiple* (LCM) of the two denominators. For example, if we were comparing $\frac{3}{5}$ and $\frac{4}{7}$ the LCM of 5 and 7 is 35.

$$\frac{3}{5} = \frac{21}{35}$$

$$\frac{4}{7} = \frac{20}{35}$$

Once we have common denominators, we can then compare the fractions.

$$\frac{21}{35} > \frac{20}{35} \text{ which means that } \frac{3}{5} > \frac{4}{7}$$

In the case of our fractions, however, we are not going to find equivalent fractions by multiplying up to the lowest common multiple (which would be 280). Instead, we are going to reduce each fraction—find equivalent fractions with smaller denominators.

$$\frac{50}{70} = \frac{25}{35} = \frac{5}{7}$$

$$\frac{40}{56} = \frac{20}{28} = \frac{10}{14} = \frac{5}{7}$$

Once both fractions are represented with common denominators, we can see that the twins did equally well.

STUDENT SOLUTIONS

1.

$$70 - 50 = 20$$
$$56 - 40 = 16$$

$$50 \times 1.4 = 80$$
$$70 \times 1.4 = 100$$
$$A = 80/100$$

$$56 \times 1.94 = 100$$
$$40 \times 1.94 = 74$$
$$b = 74/100$$

$$b = 74/100$$
$$A = 80/100$$

Commentary:

Both of these solutions are incorrect but are reasonable starting points for students. In the first solution, the students compared the number of points that were lost by each twin. This group has yet to connect the idea of fractions, ratios, or proportions as a way of discerning who did better.

The second solution shows a group who understands that it is important to compare the twin's results with the totals being the same. The difficulty with this solution is simply that the calculations are wrong, which can be an easy fix by just asking them to show their process more.

Suggested hints:

Does the number of questions wrong always mean one person did better? What if someone got 1 out of 2 and someone else got 90 out of 100. Who did better?

Is 56 × 1.94 really 100? Can you check some of your calculations here?

2.

$$\frac{50}{70} \div 2 = \frac{25}{35} \quad \text{10 answers wrong}$$

$$\frac{40}{56} \div 2 = \frac{20}{28} \quad \text{8 answers wrong}$$

$$A \quad B \quad \text{Maybe}$$
$$\frac{5}{7} \quad \frac{10}{14}$$

Commentary:

These two solutions show students who have recognized they are dealing with fractions or proportions and can reduce the fractions. Interestingly, they have not recognized that it should be reduced until both fractions have the same denominator.

Suggested hints:

Hmmm ... is it possible to get these denominators (or numerators) even closer together or the same?

3.

$$A: 50 \text{ out of } 70$$
$$B: 40 \text{ out of } 56$$

$$\frac{40 \div 2}{56} = \frac{20}{28}$$
$$= \frac{10}{14} = \frac{5}{7}$$

$$\frac{50}{70} \div 5 = \frac{10}{14} \div 2 = \frac{5}{7}$$

Commentary:

This solution shows students who have worked through their respective processes and have been able to reach a conclusion.

Suggested hints:

Can you provide a rule that can be used to solve problems like this?

You reduced these fractions to make the denominators smaller. Does this strategy always work? If it doesn't work, what do you do then?

CONSOLIDATION

The purpose of this consolidation is to discuss the various approaches of comparing fractions. Many students may not reach a solution, so spending a lot of time on mistakes and different strategies groups tried is worthwhile. A gallery walk will achieve this.

CHECK-YOUR-UNDERSTANDING QUESTIONS

MILD

Who did better on their test?

A. 6 out of 10 OR 5 out of 10

B. 1 out of 2 OR 7 out of 10

C. 3 out of 4 OR 20 out of 40

MEDIUM

Who did better on their test?

A. 15 out of 20 OR 15 out of 21

B. 2 out of 5 OR 25 out of 50

C. 14 out of 21 OR 1 out of 3

SPICY

Maya did just a little bit better on her test than Maisy did.

A. Maya's test was out of 80. If Maisy got 36 out of 45, what could Maya have gotten?

B. Maya's test was out of 72. If Maisy got 49 out of 56, what could Maya have gotten?

C. Maya's test was out of 63. If Maisy got 23 out of 27, what could Maya have gotten?

Author Notes

It is hard to argue that this task is non-curricular, but it feels non-curricular for many students in Grades 4 and 5 who have not been exposed to two things: percentages and reducing fractions. For younger students, this is a level 3 perseverance task because it takes some creative thinking as the question is written as "out of" instead of representing it as a fraction or percentage.

As mentioned in the consolidation notes, this task will require you to look at student errors in the consolidation. Make sure you detach ownership from the boards before doing this (BTC, Chapter 10). That is, when you go to look at a board with errors on it, make sure there are no names on the work. Also use the prompt, "What was this group thinking?" to allow the students to talk about what the thinking was rather than what mistakes were made.

Notes to My Future Forgetful Self

PART 3
CURRICULAR THINKING TASKS

The essence of math is not to make simple things complicated, but to make complicated things simple.

—Stanley P. Gudder
American mathematician and artist

In this part of the book, you will find a collection of 30 tasks that you can use to explicitly address curricular topics such as counting, telling time, addition, subtraction, multiplication, division, factors, fractions, decimals, and so on. But before we describe in greater detail what this part of the book contains, let us begin by describing what it doesn't contain.

For a long time, the field of math education has been trying to generate instructional routines and resources that afford us the opportunity to explore, teach, and review mathematics content in ways that go well beyond the normative routines of I do-we do-you do. Some of the more fruitful routines are the following:

- Which One Doesn't Belong
- Estimate 180
- 3-Act-Tasks
- Open Middle
- Number Talks
- Problem Strings
- Visual Patterns
- Numberless Word Problems

Some of these activities were designed to be teacher directed with very set instructional routines, while others were designed to be more exploratory, with more autonomy given to students. Regardless of how they were designed, they can all be integrated into the BTC framework as curricular thinking tasks done in a random group at a VNPS. For example, as described in Chapter 1, you can use a sequence of progressively more challenging open middle tasks, given to groups one at a time to maintain flow, as a way to get students thinking about a particular mathematical concept. In Part 4 we provide a catalog of resources that include some of these routines and more. We encourage you to consider each of these resources as a rich source of curricular thinking tasks for use in your thinking classroom and highly recommend that you find ways to integrate them into your teaching. Students will love the uniqueness of these tasks, they will revel in the increasing challenge, and they will encounter so much curricular content.

In addition to the aforementioned instructional routines, there are a number of other resources that can serve as great sources of curricular tasks.

- *Engaging in Culturally Relevant Math Tasks, K–5* by Lou E. Matthews, Shelly M. Jones, and Yolanda A. Parker
- *Teaching Through Problems Worth Solving, Grades 2 and 3* by Alicia Burdess et al.
- *Math Tasks* by Kyle Webb and Maegan Giroux

The first of these (*Engaging in Culturally Relevant Math Tasks, K–5*) offers you ways to humanize mathematics for your students by bringing cultural relevance into the classroom. The second (*Teaching Through Problems Worth Solving*) is a set of tasks chosen for their easy integration into BTC teaching. The third of these (*Math Tasks*) is organized by grade and mathematical strand. All three of these resources provide tasks that are coded to math topics that are in your curriculum.

Finally, whatever textbook or program is available to you in your classroom is also a rich source of curricular thinking tasks for use in your thinking classroom. These come in three forms—rich curricular tasks, word problems, and, for lack of a better term, exercises. The first of these, rich curricular tasks, have become more and more prominent in textbooks and programs in the last 15 years and are an amazing resource for curricular thinking tasks. For example, consider this rich task:

8.   Use 2 or more of these numbers each time:

1, 2, 3, 4, 5, 6, 7, 8

Find ways to make 12.

How can you tell when you have found all the ways?

Show your work.

Source: Appel et al. (2009, p. 85).

This is a great thinking task. We are huge fans of these types of tasks, and many teachers have found success in using these in their thinking classrooms as a way to get students thinking about curriculum. Having said that, many teachers have reported that these take a long time for students to get through and that sometimes the learning that is hoped for from engaging in these tasks is not realized. There are two reasons for this. First, these rich tasks, used as curricular thinking tasks, do not follow a linear solution process. They may have multiple solutions (open end), they may have multiple ways to solve them (open middle), and they may even be open to interpretation (open beginning). As a result, there is no guarantee that the curricular outcome or standard you are hoping to hit is encountered in the solution process.

The second reason is that the student learning is not binary—we can't think of it in terms of "they don't understand it" vs. "they do understand it." It is a continuum, with students spending significant time in a state of, and operating with, partial understanding. So, just because a group of students manages to solve a rich task using the intended outcomes or standards does not mean that everyone in the group has constructed for themselves a full understanding of that concept. They more likely have a partial understanding of the concepts involved, and what they really need are further opportunities to work with those concepts in similar contexts. What they need is to solve a similar task in order for the partial understanding to move toward more complete understanding. In fact, they may need to solve multiple similar tasks. We are not talking about practice or routinization; we are talking about meaning making—the opportunity to grow their understanding and ability without being further challenged. An easy fix for this is for you to construct a similar, or a series of similar, problems to allow your students to complete their partial understanding.

8.1 Use 2 or more of these numbers each time:

1, 2, 3, 4, 5, 6, 7, 8

Find ways to make 12.

How can you tell when you have found all the ways?

Show your work.

8.2 Use 2 or more of these numbers each time:

1, 2, 3, 4, 5, 6, 7, 8, 9, 10

Find ways to make 12.

How can you tell when you have found all the ways?

Show your work.

8.3 Use 2 or more of these numbers each time:

1, 2, 3, 4, 5, 6, 7, 8, 9, 10

Find ways to make 14.

How can you tell when you have found all the ways?

Show your work.

The second type of curricular task that your textbook or program offers is word problems. Word problems are similar to the aforementioned rich tasks in that an element of decoding is needed to move from the words through which the task is communicated to the mathematics that students need to solve. The difference between word problems and rich tasks, however, is that once the decoding has been done, word problems do not really provide much mathematical challenge. They are basically an exercise obfuscated with words. Perhaps this is why they are called word problems—the problem is with the words (see BTC, Chapter 1 for more details).

> The difference between word problems and rich tasks, however, is that once the decoding has been done, word problems do not really provide much mathematical challenge. They are basically an exercise obfuscated with words.

In the men's long jump event, Marty jumped 8.26 m in the first trial and 8.55 m in the second trial. What is the difference of his jumps?

Source: Appel et al. (2008, p. 192).

Word problems are not, inherently, great curricular thinking tasks. But they are, in many places, a necessary evil that students need to become *proficient at* in order to be able to demonstrate their *proficiency with*. This is ironic. As discussed, word problems are basically mathematical exercises disguised with words. If the goal was to assess whether a student had understanding of, or skill with, a mathematical exercise, then we could simply assess their ability using such an exercise. So, when we use a word problem, what we are really assessing is their competency in solving word problems. We, as a field, have constructed a medium (word problems) to assess whether students are proficient in that medium (word problems).

Regardless, as long as students are assessed on their proficiency with word problems, we need to help them become proficient with word problems, and this will come through experience. However, the BTC research shows that text is a barrier (see BTC, Chapter 6 for more details). So, our recommendation on this is that you do not use word problems, as text that students read, while you are first building your thinking classroom. For the first few months, everything should be verbal (see Chapter 2). If you look back at many of the non-curricular tasks we offered in Part 2 of this book, they may be viewed as word problems. But they are not—at least not in the same sense as word problems that you find in your textbooks and programs. First, they are not something that students read—they are given verbally using the script that we provide. Second, they are not inert and discrete in the way that word problems tend to be. These are living tasks that grow through extensions as the students' abilities develop.

> Our textbooks and resources are dripping in curricular thinking tasks. We, as teachers, suck the thinking out of them through the use of *I do-we do-you do* instructional routines.

After the first few months, however, word problems can be integrated into your thinking classroom in their original text form in one of two ways. First, they can become part of your thin-sliced sequence of tasks. We often do this toward the end of the sequence of tasks. In this way, they are just another task in the sequence of progressively more challenging tasks, and students get repeated experiences to decode and solve them within the collaborative structures of a thinking classroom. Second, they can form their own thin-sliced sequence, moving from word problems that are easier to decode and solve to those that are more challenging to decode and solve. In this way, we are helping students to notice the nuanced differences in wording of word problems. We will discuss this more in Part 4.

The third source of thinking tasks in textbooks and resources are the mathematical exercises themselves. Asking students to figure out what's greater, $\frac{3}{5}$ or $\frac{4}{7}$, is an amazing thinking task—until we show them how to do it. Asking students to add two-digit numbers is an amazing thinking task—until we show them how to do it. Our textbooks and resources are dripping in curricular thinking tasks. We, as teachers, suck the thinking out of them through the use of *I do-we do-you do* instructional routines. We turn curricular thinking tasks into curricular mimicking tasks by showing students how to do it. But, if we do not show them how to do it, how will they figure it out? The answer to this is, through a carefully selected sequence of progressively more challenging tasks. We thin-slice them.

Rich tasks and word problems, as well as the other routines and resources mentioned previously, already exist and are easily accessible to all of you. And they are not difficult to integrate into your thinking classroom. For this reason, we do not include them in this part of the book. What we do include, however, are carefully constructed sequences of curricular tasks that adhere to the principles of flow, variation theory, and thin-slicing talked about in Chapter 4.

What this part of the book contains, then, is a collection of 30 thin-sliced curricular tasks for use in your already up and running thinking classroom. Each individual task in these sequences will look very much like an exercise from your textbook or resources. In fact, this is often all they are. But the sequence as a whole is more than just a collection of these exercises. They are carefully clustered and ordered in such a way that students will be able to see patterns and make meaning as they go.

Although not every thin-sliced sequence will be relevant to the grade(s) you are teaching, we urge you to look at each one. We hope that after seeing several examples of thin-slicing sequences you will begin to recognize how you can use the exercises in your resources to build your own sequences. But seeing them on the page is very different from seeing them in action in the classroom. As such, you need to also use some of these sequences with your students.

TASK SEQUENCE

Type 1: Adding Numbers Without Regrouping

What is the total?

1. 46 and 52	5. 51 and 41	9. 42 and 536
2. 19 and 70	6. 120 and 361	10. 5,044 and 3,924
3. 25 and 62	7. 569 and 320	11. 8,142 and 1,757
4. 18 and 81	8. 237 and 402	12. 440 and 2,539

Type 2: Adding Numbers by Regrouping Once

Hints: What happens when you add the ones together and the number is more than 10? What should you do?

What is the total?

13. 44 and 46	17. 208 and 353	21. 8,454 and 428
14. 53 and 27	18. 7,285 and 1,524	22. 271 and 8,541
15. 653 and 255	19. 8,048 and 1,748	23. 9,009 and 109
16. 716 and 193	20. 6,921 and 2,478	

Type 3: Two- and Four-Digit Addition by Regrouping Multiple Times

What is the total?

24. 56 and 87	28. 1,405 and 2,395	32. 7,239 and 2,861
25. 14 and 96	29. 6,099 and 801	33. 8,899 and 601
26. 852 and 168	30. 6,825 and 3,934	34. 995 and 2,982
27. 362 and 288	31. 5,493 and 9,597	35. 2,865 and 936

HOW DO I KNOW WHICH TASKS TO USE?

To begin implementing some of these curricular thin-sliced tasks, you will need to be able to quickly discern which sequences are relevant to you, your students, and your curriculum. To help with this, each task is accompanied by four salient task indicators.

TASK 21: STAR, STAR, MOON

TASK

This task will have students extending and completing repeating shape patterns.

Content: recognizing and completing a repeating pattern

Competencies: collaboration, communication, willingness to take risks

Seen Before: a basic AB repeating pattern

Before You Launch: Use the images available for download to create slips of paper that you give to groups to keep them in flow.

Task

The first indicator is the task itself. Thin-slicing is not one single task. It is a sequence of tasks—starting with something simple and getting progressively more difficult until students are working on quite challenging tasks. The task indicator does not only provide an example, and a context, it also provides the range of tasks that students will be exposed to. For example,

> This task moves students through sharing money (dividing) between people with various amounts. The students begin with sharing $36.00 between two people and conclude with $300.00 shared between nine people.

Stating the task in this way can help you to see if this task is right for your curriculum and your students.

Content

Unlike non-curricular tasks that can be used across a wide variety of grades and ability levels, thin-sliced curricular tasks are very curriculum specific. But curriculum varies greatly from region to region. What is a Grade 2 topic in one place is a Grade 3 topic elsewhere. And you may have students in your room who are at different grade levels in their understanding. So, it makes no sense to identify each thin-slice sequence by grade. Instead, they are identified by the content they cover. For example, some of the content indicators you will see are

- ▶ Division: Two- and three-digit numbers by a one-digit number
- ▶ Fractions: Estimating part of a whole
- ▶ Patterns: Identifying rules for increasing and decreasing patterns

Competencies

In Chapter 8, we reviewed the practice of co-constructing rubrics with students to improve their BTC competencies—competencies such as collaboration, perseverance, and risk taking. In Part 2 of this book, you were given the contexts for developing these competencies. Once developed, these competencies will make the curricular tasks run so much smoother in your thinking classroom.

This is not to say that, once developed, competencies are invariant. You don't develop them in October and then they function flawlessly for the rest of the school year. Vigilance and ongoing work is still warranted. So, each thin-slice sequence will be identified with a set of competencies that are instrumental in helping the sequence to go better. You can use these recommended competencies in two ways. First, you can use them as a reminder to yourself to be vigilant that students are using these skills within their collaborative groups. Sometimes all they need is a reminder, either in the launch of the lesson or while they are working, to use these competencies. Other times, more explicit reminders are needed by placing one of the co-constructed rubrics at a particular workstation if you see a group beginning to devolve, or even every workstation if you anticipate that a more tangible reminder is needed.

Alternatively, you can use the curricular tasks as the context to further develop, refine, and use competencies with your students. A particular sequence of tasks may show you a behavior that you deem to be destructive to your thinking classroom. For example, competition may rear its ugly head suddenly in the division sequence. At the end of that lesson is then a perfect time to have a discussion about this with your students and to use this as an opportunity to co-construct a (or refine a previously constructed) rubric on being cooperative.

Competencies for students, like the BTC practices for teachers, need constant attention and constant work. Transitioning to curricular tasks doesn't mean the work is done. You can reap the benefits of the culture you have sown during the use of non-curricular tasks—but vigilance and ongoing attention are still needed.

Seen Before

Each of the 30 thin-sliced task sequences assumes that students have some familiarity with prior content. For example, Task 40 Larger by a Fraction is a task sequence that takes students through comparing fractions. They need to have seen a fraction before they do this task. They do not need to know everything there is to know about fractions. If they are fluent in representing fractions pictorially, great. If not, the collective knowledge of the room coupled with knowledge mobility will fill in the gaps. This is why we are calling this indicator *Seen Before* rather than *Prerequisite Knowledge*. Each task is accompanied by a list of content the students need to have seen before you use the task.

Before You Launch

Each task will also have some things you need to know before you launch. Having done these tasks with students, we have come to realize that there are sometimes things that occur during the launch that are difficult to anticipate. This is a place where we alert you to them. For example, Task 40 Larger by a Fraction has context about two dogs and their dog food bowls. This context is inherently interesting to students, and they will want to share stories about their own dog(s). Just how important this was to students caught us by surprise the first time we used this task. But now we know. And we have left you a little note so that now you do as well.

 TASK 40: LARGER BY A FRACTION

TASK

This task moves students from comparing pictorial fractions with the same shapes, to comparing pictorial fractions with different shapes, to comparing fractions written symbolically.

Content: compare fractions pictorially and symbolically

Competencies: willingness to take risks

Seen Before: fractions

Before You Launch: With this intro story, be prepared for MANY interruptions and stories about each student's dog or some dog they know. You have been WARNED! Use the images available for download to create slips of paper that you give to groups to keep them in flow.

It was already mentioned that the indicator for grade level is missing and why that is. Also missing are indicators for perseverance levels and macro-moves. Perseverance indicators are missing because all thin-slicing tasks require the same amount of perseverance—very little to begin with and then more as the students proceed through the sequence. This is the nature of thin-slicing, so there is little point in indicating this for every task—perseverance is not a delineating indicator.

Macro-moves are missing from the list of indicators because all the thin-slicing tasks offer the exact same affordances for you to work on your BTC practices. By the time you get to thin-slicing you should have already started to build your thinking classroom through the practices in the first toolkit: non-curricular tasks (BTC, Chapter 1), visibly random groups (BTC, Chapter 2), and vertical non-permanent surfaces (BTC, Chapter 3). You should have started to explore or play around with some of the practices in the second tool kit: defronting the classroom (BTC, Chapter 4), answering only keep-thinking questions (BTC, Chapter 5), giving tasks verbally in the first five minutes while students stand around you (BTC, Chapter 6), and being deliberately less helpful (BTC, Chapter 8). This is not to say that you are a master of these practices yet. That takes time, practice, and experience. The shift to curricular thin-sliced tasks will give you this time, practice, and experience to refine these BTC practices while also giving you opportunities to develop your practice around the evolving BTC practices of consolidation, notes, and check-your-understanding questions.

WHAT ELSE DO THE CURRICULAR TASKS INCLUDE?

After the task, content, and competency identifiers comes the body of the thin-slicing tasks, laid out in nine sections, each of which is included to help you not only move through content, but to introduce and develop the BTC practices. Unlike the non-curricular tasks portion of the book (Part 2) where you pick and choose which sections fit where you are in your journey to build a thinking classroom, in this part of the book, we recommend that, time permitting, you try to enact all aspects of the lessons that are to follow.

Launch Script

As discussed in Chapter 2 and demonstrated in Part 2, as much as possible, tasks should be given verbally. And the simple statement of the task, as described previously, is rarely an adequate way to do this. Students need context and a gradual unfolding of the conditions, criteria, and constraints of a task. How you present the task matters. As a result, each task is accompanied by a script to help you launch the task. Most often, these are short and to the point:

> I just found some money! I want to share it with my friends, but I want to be fair and make sure that everyone has the same. Can I share $36.00 between me and (insert another teacher's name here)?

or they can also be longer and more embedded within a story:

> Hey everyone! So last night I was listening to some music with Jakester, my 5-year-old. We love listening to music in the evening. The problem is that my son is pretty impatient; he's only 5, right? So, during the first song, he asked how much of the song we have listened to, and I said, "We're about half done." Then we kept listening, and during the next song he asked again, and I said, "Oh, about three quarters done"; then during the third song he said, "Hey mom …" but I knew he was going to ask it, so I interrupted and said, "Jakester, the song is about a quarter done." He was about to say okay but then looked up at me and asked, "Is it exactly a quarter done?" I thought for a second and looked at my phone. I said, "I think it is a quarter done, but I'm not certain." He kept asking during every song after that but I felt pretty smart because I started to screenshot the songs last night so I could get your help today. Could you tell me exactly how much of each song we have listened to?

Regardless, each script has emerged from our multiple and varied experiences using each task with students. This is not to say they are the perfect script. Each script is a product of who we are and what feels natural for us as well as who the students are and what sorts of contexts are relevant for them. Students need context. Context not only gives them something to think *about*, it gives them something to think *with*. When students are doing the division task, they are not just dividing a two-digit number by a one-digit number—they are sharing money they found. They are not just estimating part of a whole—they are estimating what portion of a song has already played. They are not just thinking *about* these contexts, they are thinking *with* them.

Context offers opportunities for students to connect with the task—not generically, but specifically. Not all students are the same and, thus, not all connect with context in the same way. Some students like hockey. Others have never seen ice. For this reason, it is important that context be tailored to the lived, historical, and cultural experiences of your students. This is what it means, in part, to be culturally responsive to your students (Matthews et al., 2022). Being responsive in this way will help you to be actively inclusive of all your students. So, vary the scripts to make them more personally relevant for your students. Whatever modifications you make, however, do not think that the script doesn't matter. It matters. And the more culturally relevant the context is, the more connected students are to it. And the more likely they are to think about it and with it.

Task Sequence

After the launch script comes the actual sequence of tasks. As described in Chapter 4, this is a sequence of progressively more challenging tasks that can be used to keep students in flow—as their abilities grow, so too does the challenge of the tasks. But flow is not the goal. Having students develop proficiencies with more and more challenging tasks is the goal. Flow is the state within which they work that makes this possible.

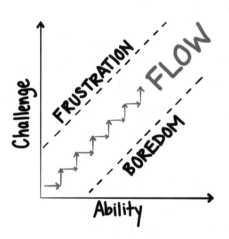

Although the sequence of tasks gets progressively more challenging from beginning to end, this is not necessarily as smooth a progression as this figure would imply.

Often there are unavoidable cognitive jumps—places where, by the very nature of the task similar to the one in Task 39, there is a bigger increase in the challenge of the task. For example, in the sharing money sequence, tasks 1 through 6 are all of the type where both the tens and the ones of the money are evenly divisible by the number of people. Among these, the tasks are getting marginally more difficult in that the dividend (the amount of money) and the divisor (the number of people) are getting bigger. These are Type 1 tasks.

Type 1

1 Share $26.00 between two of us? How much would we each get?

2 Share $42.00 between two of us? How much would we each get?

3 Share $68.00 between two of us? How much would we each get?

4 Share $69.00 between three of us? How much would we each get?

5 Share $88.00 between four of us? How much would we each get?

6 Share $66.00 between six of us? How much would we each get?

Next, tasks 7 through 13 are also getting more difficult in that dividend (the amount of money) and the divisor (the number of people) are getting bigger. But, tasks 7–13 are different in nature than tasks 1–6. Tasks 7–13 are Type 2 tasks in that the tens and ones of the money are not separately divisible by the number of people. There is a cognitive jump necessary for the students to make when moving between tasks 6 and 7—the increase in challenge between tasks 6 and 7 is greater than the increase in challenge between tasks 5 and 6 and between tasks 7 and 8.

Type 2

7 Share $32.00 between two of us? How much would we each get?

8 Share $76.00 between two of us? How much would we each get?

9 Share $42.00 between three of us? How much would we each get?

10 Share $51.00 between three of us? How much would we each get?

11 Share $64.00 between four of us? How much would we each get?

12 Share $80.00 between five of us? How much would we each get?

13 Share $84.00 between six of us? How much would we each get?

Likewise, there is a cognitive jump when we go from tasks 13 to 14. Now, we have a three-digit dividend (money) and a single-digit divisor (people). These are Type 3 tasks.

Type 3

14 Share $105.00 between five of us? How much would we each get?

15 Share $128.00 between four of us? How much would we each get?

16 Share $126.00 between six of us? How much would we each get?

17 Share $248.00 between four of us? How much would we each get?

18 Share $366.00 between six of us? How much would we each get?

19 Share $144.00 between four of us? How much would we each get?

20 Share $265.00 between five of us? How much would we each get?

21 Share $216.00 between six of us? How much would we each get?

Within Type 1, Type 2, and Type 3 tasks, the progression is relatively even—small increases in challenge. But between task types there are cognitive jumps. This is unavoidable. As much as we try to make the tasks smoothly increase in difficulty, math just doesn't work like that. The concept of dividing two- and three-digit numbers by one-digit numbers isn't a single concept. There are cognitive jumps in it, and we try to delineate these jumps by identifying it as a transition from Type 1 to Type 2 to Type 3 tasks.

As discussed in Chapter 4, we use the type designation to showcase these unavoidable cognitive jumps inherent in the nature of mathematics. We will be coming back to these type designations when we talk about hints, consolidation, and check-your-understanding tasks.

Hints

Unlike non-curricular tasks, which are often novel and have a wide variety of ways to solve them, curricular thin-sliced tasks will likely be more familiar to you and have a narrow set of approaches to solving. As a result, providing you with solutions is generally unnecessary. For example, you do not need us to tell you that $32 \div 2 = 16$. So solutions to the thin-sliced tasks are not provided, but hints are.

Type 2: Fill in the Blanks

Hint: If students are struggling, just verbalizing the pattern from the start helps students understand the pattern.

12. 5 6 __ 8

13. 3 4 __ __ 7

Type 3: Prequel to the Pattern

Hint: If students are struggling, just verbalize the pattern backward, especially if they have exposure to counting down beforehand.

In Part 2 (non-curricular tasks) we had the hints organized alongside the different solutions as a way to link one solution or way of thinking to another way of thinking. This made sense for non-curricular tasks where students worked on one task, and we used hints to move them from one way of thinking about the same task to a different way of thinking about the same task. This does not work for thin-sliced curricular tasks where students are working on a sequence of tasks. For curricular tasks, the thinking will remain the same within one task type, and then it will need to change slightly as they transition to a new task type. As mentioned in Chapter 4, these transitions are often not as smooth as the transition between tasks within a type. We have to be vigilant and anticipate that students may have difficulty. Being ready to offer a hint, or a series of hints, should a group struggle in making this transition is vital. In anticipation of this, we occasionally provide hints that you can use when students get stuck in the transition between task types.

Consolidation Tasks

In order to help your students organize, structure, and formalize their learning, you may wish to consolidate the lesson. Unlike non-curricular tasks, which often produce divergent ways of thinking within your classroom, thin-sliced curricular tasks tend to be more convergent—every group will, more or less, do the same things. At the same time, what the students show on their VNPS tends to not be representative of their thinking. As a result, consolidation through a gallery walk tends to not work well for curricular thin-sliced tasks. What works well in such circumstances, however, is to consolidate through *noticing and naming variation*.

As mentioned in Chapter 5, noticing and naming variation begins by having your students gather around one whiteboard with three very specific tasks written on it. Ideally, one of these is a Type 1 task from the lesson, one is a Type 2, and one is a Type 3. But this is only true if you managed to move the majority of the groups onto Type 3 tasks. If not, then do not include a Type 3 task in this list. Instead, you would have a Type 1 and two Type 2s. The tasks you use for noticing and naming variation need to be reflective of the tasks that the students managed to solve. Regardless, there are exactly three tasks written on the whiteboard.

What is also important is that these tasks are not in the same order as they would have occurred in the lesson. Perhaps they are in the order Type 3, Type 1, Type 2. The order can be anything as long as it is not Type 1, 2, and 3. This is because the first part of the consolidation activity is for students to turn-and-talk about what the correct order of the tasks is. After this, you will act as a teacher-scribe as you direct the class to talk you through solving the three tasks. What is important here is that you first focus on what is the same across solving all three tasks, and then what is different. See Chapter 5 for more details on what this looks like.

The consolidation section of each of the curricular tasks provides you with three tasks—a Type 1, a Type 2, and a Type 3—that you can use to facilitate the noticing and naming variation. The three tasks that we provide are not in order, but their type is indicated for your reference.

Meaningful Notes

After the consolidation, it might be desirable to continue to help your students organize, structure, and formalize their learning through meaningful notes. To achieve this, we need to shift our practice from *note taking* to *note making*. Chapter 6 showcases the most recent work on this practice, which has been shown to give 100% of students access to note making. This involves students returning to their VNPS in their random group and completing a four-quadrant template of notes (Figure 6.1). For more details on the different ways to use these templates with your students, see Chapter 6.

Each of the 30 thin-sliced curricular tasks in this part of the book is accompanied by a template that you can use to have your students do meaningful notes in their random groups. Like with consolidation, however, it is important that the exemplars chosen for quadrants A and B are reflective of the tasks that the students actually managed to solve during the lesson.

Figure 6.1 Four-quadrant template of notes on a student's VNPS

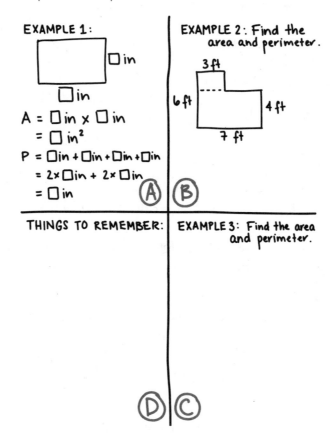

Check-Your-Understanding Questions

At some point after the students have finished working in random groups at the vertical whiteboards, you may wish to transition them into some check-your-understanding (CYU) questions. This may follow a consolidation and the students writing meaningful notes, or you can go right from vertical work to CYU questions. Regardless, CYU questions are an important aspect of tasks and, accordingly, we have included some CYU questions with each task. You will note that, as mentioned in Chapter 7, the emerging research on CYU questions indicated that it is advantageous to present these questions in three categories—*mild, medium*, and *spicy* (see the following examples).

Mild	Medium	Spicy
13 + 25 =	15 + 18 =	65 + 82 =
23 + 31 =	23 + 39 =	84 + 49 =
41 + 58 =	58 + 27 =	87 + 68 =

The research also shows that it is best to not set any accountability parameters—such as exit tickets, grading, checking—around these CYU questions. Instead, use the question, "Where are you going to start?" when offering students the opportunity to do the CYU questions. Using the question, "Where are you going to start?" naturally sets up the follow through of "What are you going to do next?" Our research is showing that such phrasing sets up CYU questions as something they are responsible to themselves for—rather than accountable to you for—and has been shown to engage students more. And as a result, they actually do more questions and for the correct reason—as a way to check their understanding. This positioning also creates an environment where the students work in a balance of challenge and success that drives them to want to do more and more questions.

When CYU questions become something students are responsible for, they will tend to work in a modality we call *alone together*. That is, although they take responsibility for their own work and their own understanding, they also use each other as support to verify their thinking and to get help from one another when there is something they do not understand. We have to be tolerant of that. Because there are no accountability measures around CYU questions, there is no incentive to copy from each other. They are not doing division of labor or cheating—they are learning from each other.

Author Notes

As much as we have tried to get everything organized into the above categories, the work that students do on curricular tasks does not always lend itself to the linear-textual format used in this section. There is often something that doesn't fit or doesn't fit well. In addition, there may be things we have learned from doing these tasks with students that we haven't been able to include in the categories already described—acquired tips, so to speak. It would be useful for you to know these tips. As a result, we have a section for author notes where we can include any important information that hasn't been included in the categories above.

Notes to My Future Forgetful Self

This is not to say that there isn't more to learn. Every time we do a task, students reveal something new to us. And, as a result, we learn something new about the students or about ourselves as teachers. You will, too. As such, we have also included a section for you to keep notes about your own experiences using each task. A place where you can make notes to your future forgetful self.

THE 30 CURRICULAR TASKS

Pulling all this together, what follows is a table of all the tasks and all their indicators. You can think of this as a hyper-detailed table of contents that will enable you to quickly look for, or come back to, tasks that you think are best for you and your students in your collective journey to build a thinking classroom.

#	Name	Content	Seen Before	Competencies
21	Star, Star, Moon	recognizing completing a repeating pattern	a basic AB repeating pattern	collaboration, communication, willingness to take risks
22	Grow Your Own Way	numerical patterns	repeating patterns, counting to 20, skip counting	collaboration
23	Up and Down We Go	identifying and continuing increasing and decreasing number patterns; identifying and communicating pattern rules	skip counting forward and backward, patterns	perseverance, willingness to take risks, guess and check
24	Red Skittle, Blue Skittle	adding numbers up to 10	counting	collaboration, tolerance for ambiguity
25	Fewer Than Most	comparing sets pictorially and symbolically, finding difference	sets, counting	perseverance, collaboration
26	Up to 20	counting, counting on, representing numbers to 20	counting on to 10	collaboration, patience
27	We're Frameous	adding and subtracting numbers up to 30	adding and subtracting up to 10	creativity
28	All About That Base	representing numbers up to 100 using base-10 blocks, composing, decomposing, regrouping numbers to 100	numbers to 50, decomposing numbers into tens and ones (e.g. 1 ten = 10 ones)	willingness to take risks, perseverance
29	Mo' Money, Mo' Problems	number operations involving quarters, dimes, nickels, and pennies	money and how much each coin is worth	collaboration, organization
30	Show Me Your Number	place value, number description and representation, number line	base-10 numbers, decomposing numbers	willingness to take risks
31	Oddly Even	addition, odd, even, place value	addition with regrouping	reasoning, guess and check
32	Sum Some More	adding 4-digit numbers	adding 1-digit and 2-digit numbers with regrouping	collaboration, perseverance

#	Name	Content	Seen Before	Competencies
33	Subtraction Is the Main Attraction	subtracting 4-digit numbers	subtracting 2-digit numbers with decomposition	collaboration, perseverance
34	Who's on First?	comparing and ordering decimals to the tenths	comparing and ordering whole numbers	collaboration, empathy
35	Deci-Line Dance	comparing and ordering decimals on a number line to the thousandths	decimals, comparing, and ordering whole numbers	collaboration, mobilizing knowledge
36	Grow by the Row	arrays, multiplication, repeated addition, area	skip counting, multiplication	collaboration, empathy
37	Garden Fences	perimeter, area, volume	addition, multiplication	perseverance, mobilizing knowledge
38	Track Day	repeated addition, skip counting, multiplication, repeated subtraction, division without remainder, division with remainder	repeated addition, skip counting	collaboration
39	Sharing Money	dividing two-digit and three-digit numbers by one-digit numbers, division with and without decimal quotients	multiplication, doubling, money, decimals	collaboration
40	Larger by a Fraction	compare fractions pictorially and symbolically	fractions	willingness to take risks
41	Musical Fractions	fractions, estimating fractions, fractions on a number line, time conversions	fractions, digital time	perseverance, knowledge mobility
42	What Time Is It?	reading and estimating analog clock	time, hours, minutes, skip counting	willingness to take risks
43	What Time Will It Be?	reading analog clocks, adding time, 24-hour time	analog time, AM, PM	collaboration, perseverance
44	How Many Paperclips in a Shoe?	measurement, measurement with referents (various objects), measurement using non-standard units	counting, estimation	willingness to take risks, tolerance of ambiguity
45	Formulas Arise	area of squares, rectangles, compound shapes, and parallelograms	area, parallelograms	creativity
46	Picture the Pictographs	reading graphs, reading pictographs, making inferences, estimation	basic pictographs, data	willingness to take risks
47	Baron von Graph	interpreting data, constructing bar graphs from data tables	data of some kind (pictographs, tables, charts, etc.)	willingness to take risks

(Continued)

(Continued)

#	Name	Content	Seen Before	Competencies
48	Keep the Balance	solving for an unknown value using a balance scale	equality	collaboration, empathy
49	I'm Thinking of a Number	solving one- and two-step equations	equality, adding, subtracting, multiplying, dividing, decimals	collaboration, empathy
50	What Are the Odds?	theoretical probability, fractions, percentages	coins, dice, spinners	willingness to take risks

We have included in this book 30 curricular thinking tasks. We could have included many more, but the reality is that it still would not have been enough. Each of you teaches a slightly different curriculum. And each curriculum is made up of a large number of curricular standards or outcomes—each of which needs its own thin-sliced sequence of curricular thinking tasks. We just cannot do this for every curriculum in the world. We have given you some. And we hope that some of what we have given you is relevant to what you teach. But the reality is that you are just going to have to make your own thin-sliced sequences of tasks. In Part 4, we provide you with a step-by-step guide for making your own curricular task sequences as well as how to use existing resources to help you.

Once you have made your own thin-sliced sequence of curricular tasks, you may wish to put them into the same format as is in this book. In Part 4 we also provide a link to a template to help you do so. Whether you wish to do this for your own records or to share your thin-sliced sequences of curricular tasks with colleagues, the template will help you to dissect and delineate the tasks into salient and actionable indicators and elements.

Notes to My Future Forgetful Self

TASK 21: STAR, STAR, MOON

TASK

This task will have students extending and completing repeating shape patterns.

Content: recognizing and completing a repeating pattern

Competencies: collaboration, communication, willingness to take risks

Seen Before: a basic AB repeating pattern

Before You Launch: Use the images available for download to create slips of paper that you give to groups to keep them in flow.

 This Task Sequence, Consolidation Tasks, and Check-Your-Understanding Questions are available for download at **https://companion.corwin.com/courses/BTCK5Tasks**

LAUNCH SCRIPT

Teacher: Hello my tremendous mathematicians. Do you remember what a repeating pattern means?

Students: [Various answers] A pattern that does the same thing again and again and again and again ...

Teacher: Could someone give me an example?

Students: [Various students answer] Circle, square, circle, square ... A, B, A, B ...

Teacher: Great! Do you know how to continue a pattern?

Students: Yes!

Teacher: So, □○□○, what would come next?

Students: □○

Teacher: Great, now how would this pattern continue? [Teacher writes ○△○△ _ _ _]

TASK SEQUENCE

Type 1: Extending the Pattern

1. ○△○△___ ___ ___
2. ○△△○△△___ ___ ___
3. □○□○□○___ ___ ___
4. ○○△○○△___ ___ ___
5. ○□△○□△___ ___ ___
6. □○□○□___ ___ ___
7. △○○△○___ ___ ___
8. ☆☆△☆☆___ ___ ___
9. △○□△○___ ___ ___
10. □△△□△___ ___ ___

Type 2: Writing the Prequel to the Pattern

11. ___ ___ ○△○△
12. ___ ___ □□○○
13. ___ ___ ___ △○○△○○
14. ___ ___ ___ ○○○△△△
15. ___ ___ ___ ○□○□
16. ___ ___ ___ □△○□
17. ___ ___ ___ △□△△
18. ___ ___ ___ △□□△△
19. ___ ___ ___ △○○○
20. ___ ___ ___ □△○○

Type 3: Fill in the Blanks of the Pattern

21. □○□○___ ___□___□
22. △○○___○○△___ ___△
23. ☆☆△☆___△___☆___☆
24. △○___△___□○△___
25. □□○___□___○○
26. △___ ___○△○___ ___ ___△○
27. ☆___ ___ ___☆☆___☆
28. △□___ ___□□△___□

CONSOLIDATION TASKS

Teacher: I have written on the board three questions like the ones you just did in your group, but I may have put them in the wrong order. Turn to your neighbor and discuss what the order should be and why.

A ___ ___ ___ □ □ ○ □ (Type 2)

B □ ___ ___ △ □ △ ___ ___ □ △ (Type 3)

C ○ □ △ ___ ___ ___ (Type 1)

STUDENT NOTES TO THEIR FUTURE FORGETFUL SELVES

Example 1:

Continue the pattern:

△ ○ △ ○ ___ ___ ___

Example 2:

Write the previous shapes in this pattern:

___ ___ ___ □ ○ ○ □ ○

CHECK-YOUR-UNDERSTANDING QUESTIONS

MILD

Continue the pattern:

A. □ ○ □ ○ ___ ___ ___

B. ☆ ☆ ___ ___ ___

MEDIUM

Write the previous shapes in the pattern:

A. ___ ___ ___ △ □ △ △

B. ___ ___ ___ ○ △ ○ △

SPICY

Fill in the blanks in the pattern:

A. □ ○ ___ □ ○ ○ ___ ○ ___

B. △ □ ___ △ ___ ○

Author Notes

Students at this age are used to seeing Type 1 tasks and are often adept at recognizing and continuing the pattern. One of the byproducts of this familiarity is that they come to believe that the first few symbols they see determine the pattern and they can run that forward at will. When they get to Type 2 and Type 3 tasks, this is no longer true. Be aware that if they are making mistakes, this is likely the reason.

Also note that we are not placing commas between shapes in the repeating pattern. Textbooks often do this. Our experience is that commas can be confusing to students at this age. Just use spaces between shapes and dashes instead.

Notes to My Future Forgetful Self

_____

_____

_____

_____

_____

_____

_____

_____

_____

_____

_____

_____

_____

TASK 22: GROW YOUR OWN WAY

TASK

This task will have students extending and completing growing number patterns.

Content: numerical patterns

Competencies: collaboration

Seen Before: repeating patterns, counting to 20, skip counting

Before You Launch: This task works well with the banner.

LAUNCH SCRIPT

Teacher: Hello my impressive mathematicians. Do you remember what a pattern is?

Students: Yes! [students offer various answers] A bunch of things (numbers, shapes, etc.), where we can figure out what will happen next.

Teacher: Can anyone give me an example?

Students: Blue, red, blue, red; square, triangle, square, triangle. [The students will likely give other repeating patterns]

Teacher: Fantastic! Those are called repeating patterns. There are also patterns that are called growing patterns. Do you know what that might mean?

Students: [students offer various answers; wait until you hear students saying that a growing pattern is where it gets bigger and bigger]

Teacher: [Teacher writes 1 2 3 4 __ __ __ on the board] This is an example of a growing pattern. What do you think the next three numbers in this pattern are?

Students: 5 6 7!

Teacher: Ok. What about [teacher writes 2 3 4 __ __ __]

TASK SEQUENCE

Type 1: Extend the Pattern

1. 2 3 4 ___ ___ ___
2. 4 5 6 ___ ___ ___
3. 6 7 8 ___ ___ ___
4. 8 9 10 ___ ___ ___
5. 10 11 12 ___ ___ ___
6. 11 12 13 ___ ___ ___
7. 2 4 6 ___ ___ ___
8. 1 3 5 ___ ___ ___
9. 4 6 8 ___ ___ ___
10. 5 7 9 ___ ___ ___
11. 9 11 13 ___ ___ ___

Type 2: Fill in the Blanks

> **Hint:** If students are struggling, just verbalizing the pattern from the start helps students understand the pattern.

12. 5 6 ___ 8
13. 3 4 ___ ___ 7
14. 9 ___ 11 12 13
15. 11 ___ ___ 14
16. 10 11 12 ___ ___ 15
17. 2 4 ___ 8
18. 1 ___ 5 7
19. 6 8 ___ 12
20. 7 ___ 11 ___ 15
21. 3 6 ___ 12 ___
22. 1 5 ___ ___ 17

Type 3: Prequel to the Pattern

> **Hint:** If students are struggling, just verbalize the pattern backward, especially if they have exposure to counting down beforehand.

23. ___ ___ 8 9 10
24. ___ ___ 5 6 7

25. _ _ _ 7 8 9

26. _ _ _ 11 12 13

27. _ _ _ 13 14

28. _ 4 6 8

29. _ 3 5 7

30. _ _ 8 10 12

31. _ _ 9 11 13

32. _ _ 9 12 15

33. _ _ 10 14 18

CONSOLIDATION TASKS

Teacher: I have written on the board three questions like the ones you just did in your group, but I may have put them in the wrong order. Turn to your neighbor and discuss what the order should be and why.

A   _ _ _ 5 7 9 (Type 3)

B   10 11 12 _ _ _ (Type 1)

C   11 12 _ _ 15 (Type 2)

STUDENT NOTES TO THEIR FUTURE FORGETFUL SELVES

Example 1:

Continue the pattern:

Example 2:

Fill in the blanks:

5 6 _ _ 9

CHECK-YOUR-UNDERSTANDING QUESTIONS

MILD

Extend the pattern:

A.   1 2 3 _ _ _

B.   11 12 13 _ _ _

C.   1 3 5 _ _ _

MEDIUM

Fill in the blanks:

A. 4 5 __ 7

B. 9 10 __ __ 13

C. 2 __ 6 __ 10

SPICY

Write the previous numbers in the pattern:

A. __ __ __ 7 8 9

B. __ __ __ 12 13 14

C. __ __ __ 8 10 12

Author Notes

You may be wondering why the fill in the blank questions are Type 3 for the Star, Star, Moon task but Type 2 for this task. The reason for this is that numerical growing patterns are much easier to fill in compared to repeating shape patterns. The students know the pattern is growing and just need to count or skip count on. Comparatively, writing the previous numbers can be more difficult as the focus is on looking at how the numbers change or counting/skip counting down, which can be tricky for our little mathematicians.

Also note that we are not placing commas between numbers in the growing patterns. Textbooks often do this. Our experience is that commas can be confusing to students at this age. Just use spaces between numbers and dashes instead.

Notes to My Future Forgetful Self

_____

_____

_____

_____

_____

_____

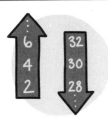

TASK 23: UP AND DOWN WE GO

TASK

This task will have students extending increasing and decreasing number patterns. They will also extend number patterns that have a combination of increasing and decreasing patterns.

Content: identifying and continuing increasing and decreasing number patterns; identifying and communicating a pattern's rules

Competencies: perseverance, willingness to take risks, guess and check

Seen Before: Skip counting forward and backward, patterns

Before You Launch: This task works well with the banner.

LAUNCH SCRIPT

Teacher: Hello my amazing mathematicians. I have three numbers here [teacher writes 2, 4, 6 … on the board]. Can you turn and talk to the person beside you about what the next three numbers would be?

Students: 8, 10, 12 [teacher scribes answer on the board]

Teacher: OK. Can you turn and talk to the person beside you and figure out what the pattern rule is?

Students: We add 2 each time.

Teacher: Great. We could say that we start at 8 and add 2 every time. [teacher writes START at 8 and ADD 2 each time on the board]

Teacher: What if the 3 numbers were 1, 3, 5? What would the next 3 numbers be and what would the pattern rule be?

TASK SEQUENCE

Type 1: Increasing Patterns

What would the next 3 numbers be and what is the pattern rule?

1. 2, 4, 6

2. 1, 3, 5

3. 13, 15, 17

4. 15, 18, 21

5. 49, 52, 55

6. 44, 49, 54

7. 62, 67, 72

8. 58, 63, 68

9. 45, 55, 65

10. 34, 45, 56

11. 41, 50, 59

12. 34, 43, 52

Type 2: Decreasing Patterns

Hint: If we are adding in the increasing patterns, what would we be doing in a decreasing pattern?

What would the next 3 numbers be and what is the pattern rule?

13. 32, 30, 28

14. 41, 39, 37

15. 61, 58, 55

16. 44, 40, 36

17. 69, 65, 61

18. 82, 77, 72

19. 74, 69, 64

20. 59, 50, 41

21. 84, 75, 66

22. 71, 62, 53

Type 3: Anticipating the Value of the 10th Number

Would the 10th number be bigger or smaller than the first number?

23. 35, 38, 36, 39

24. 47, 44, 46, 43

25. 56, 53, 55, 52

26. 32, 42, 38, 48

27. 57, 48, 56, 47

28. 23, 28, 22, 27

29. 34, 31, 28, 35, 32

30. 46, 41, 36, 45, 40

CONSOLIDATION TASKS

Teacher: I have written on the board three questions like the ones you just did in your group, but I may have put them in the wrong order. Turn to your neighbor and discuss what the order should be and why.

A   56, 60, 50 Would the 10th number be bigger or smaller than 56? (Type 3)

B   2, 4, 6 Write the next 3 numbers and the pattern rule. (Type 1)

C   83, 77, 71 Write the next 3 numbers and the pattern rule. (Type 2)

STUDENT NOTES TO THEIR FUTURE FORGETFUL SELVES

Example 1:

Write the next 3 numbers and the pattern rule:

1, 3, 5, ☐, ☐, ☐
   +☐ +☐ +☐ +☐ +☐

Start at __ , add __ each time

Example 2:

Write the next 3 numbers and the pattern rule:

41, 39, 37, __, __, __

CHECK-YOUR-UNDERSTANDING QUESTIONS

MILD

Write the next three numbers in the pattern and state the pattern rule:

A.   1, 2, 3, __, __, __

B.   2, 4, 6, __, __, __

C.   3, 6, 9, __, __, __

D.   10, 20, 30, __, __, __

MEDIUM

Write the next three numbers in the pattern and state the pattern rule:

A.   15, 13, 11, __, __, __

B.   44, 40, 36, __, __, __

C.   39, 30, 21, __, __, __

D.   50, 42, 34, __, __, __, __

Would the 10th number be bigger or smaller than the first?

A. 9, 14, 10, . . .

B. 50, 45, 48, . . .

C. 1, 5, 0, 4, . . .

D. 14, 6, 12, 4, . . .

Author Notes

The numbers in the three types of tasks can easily be adjusted based on your students' needs and abilities. For example, your students may only be comfortable with numbers up to 30. You can still do this task, but keep the numbers under 30. Your students may struggle to recognize the increasing patterns if the tens and ones place change at the same time (34, 43, 52). You can still do this task, but push those types of sequences to the end of Type 1 or Type 2.

Notes to My Future Forgetful Self

_____

_____

_____

_____

_____

_____

_____

_____

_____

_____

_____

_____

TASK 24: RED SKITTLE, BLUE SKITTLE

TASK

This task will have students finding what numbers (<10) could add to a given number (≤ 10) given some constraints.

> **Content**: adding numbers up to 10
>
> **Competencies**: collaboration, tolerance for ambiguity
>
> **Seen Before**: counting
>
> **Before You Launch**: Type 2 and 3 tasks are intentionally ambiguous to allow for multiple solutions and conceptual thinking. This task works well with the banner.

LAUNCH SCRIPT

Teacher: Hello my beautiful mathematicians! Last night, I was eating some red and blue skittles [or some other candy] out of a bag. When I reached in the first time, I opened my hands, looked down, and saw 3 blue and 1 red skittle. [teacher draws 4 circles, 3 with a B in the middle and 1 with a R in the middle] How many skittles did I grab out of the bag?

Students: Four!

Teacher: Wonderful! Now, the next time I grabbed 4 blue skittles and 1 red skittle out of the bag. How many skittles did I grab this time?

TASK SEQUENCE

Type 1: Adding Skittles Together

How many skittles did I grab?

1. 4 blue and 1 red
2. 3 blue and 2 red
3. 4 blue and 2 red
4. 3 blue and 3 red
5. 2 blue and 4 red
6. 3 blue and 5 red

7. 4 blue and 4 red

8. 1 blue and 8 red

9. 3 blue and 6 red

10. 5 blue and 5 red

11. 3 blue and 7 red

12. 9 blue and 1 red

Type 2: Decomposing Numbers Into 2 Addends

Hint: Why don't you draw out *x* number of skittles and then label the colors afterward?

How many blues and reds could I have if I have ...

13. 5 skittles

14. 5 skittles, but there are more red than blue [teacher writes 5: Red > Blue]

15. 7 skittles, but there are more blue than red [teacher writes 7: Red < Blue]

16. 8 skittles, but there are a lot more red than blue [teacher writes 8: Red > Blue]

17. 8 skittles, but there is the same number of red and blue [teacher writes: 8 R = B]

18. 9 skittles, but there are a lot more blue than red [teacher writes 9: R < B]

19. 10 skittles

20. 10 skittles, but there is the same number of red and blue [teacher writes 10: R = B]

21. 10 skittles, but there is just a bit more blue than red [teacher writes 10: R < B]

22. 10 skittles, but there is a lot more red than blue [10: R > B]

Type 3: Decomposing a Number Into 3 Addends

Teacher: Oh wow! I just bought a new bag and this one has some red, some blue, and some green skittles. How many of each color could I have if I have ...

23. 5 skittles

24. 7 skittles

25. 7 skittles but there are more blue than red or green [teacher writes 7: B > R, B > G]

26. 9 skittles but there is the same number of red, green, and blue [teacher writes 9: R = B = G]

27. 10 skittles

28. 10 skittles but there is only one green [teacher write 10: G = 1]

29. 10 skittles but there are 4 blues [teacher writes 10: B = 4]

30. 10 skittles but there are 8 green [teacher writes 10: G = 8]

CONSOLIDATION TASKS

Teacher: I have written on the board three questions like the ones you just did in your group, but I may have put them in the wrong order. Turn to your neighbor and discuss what the order should be and why.

A   How many blue and red skittles could I have if I have 9 skittles? (Type 2)

B   I have 10 skittles in total, some red, blue, and green. There are more red than green and more green than blue. How many of each color could I have? (Type 3)

C   I have 4 blue and 3 red skittles. How many do I have altogether? (Type 1)

STUDENT NOTES TO THEIR FUTURE FORGETFUL SELVES

Example 1:

I have 2 blue and 3 red skittles. How many do I have all together?

Ⓡ◯ + Ⓑ◯◯

Example 2:

I have blue and red skittles. How many blue and red do I have if I have 10 skittles in total?

CHECK-YOUR-UNDERSTANDING QUESTIONS

MILD

How many total skittles do I have if I grabbed:

A.   4 blue and 2 red?

B.   6 red and 1 blue?

C.   4 blue and 5 red?

MEDIUM

How many red and blue could I have if I grabbed:

A.   6 skittles: R > B

B.   7 skittles

C.   8 skittles: R = B

How many of each color could I have if I have red, blue, and green skittles and I grabbed:

A. 10 skittles

B. 8 skittles: G > R > B

C. 9 skittles: G = R = B

Author Notes

This task, like many others, can be adapted for higher numbers or more difficult addition like adding to 20, 100, etc. However, it cannot be overstated how important composing and decomposing numbers within 10 are to build a strong numeracy foundation.

You will notice that in the Type 2 and 3 tasks, the tasks move from explicitly writing Red and Blue to R and B. This is a very natural way for students to become comfortable with symbolic representation. You do not need to explain or define symbols. They will notice the shift from Red to R and just go with it.

One of the nice things about having tasks with multiple solutions is that you can ask groups that are moving faster to find multiple solutions—even all solutions—for a given task. This enables you to keep all the groups moving (close) together.

Notes to My Future Forgetful Self

_____

_____

_____

_____

_____

_____

_____

_____

_____

TASK 25: FEWER THAN MOST

TASK

This task will have students comparing sets pictorially and symbolically to decide which has more and how much more one set has than the other.

> **Content**: comparing sets pictorially and symbolically, finding difference
>
> **Competencies**: perseverance, collaboration
>
> **Seen Before**: sets, counting
>
> **Before You Launch**: Use the images available for download to create slips of paper that you give to groups to keep them in flow. For the Type 3 tasks, you should provide students with manipulatives (cubes, base-10 blocks, etc.) or encourage students to draw pictures to help connect the symbolic to concrete or pictorial representations.

This Task Sequence, Consolidation Tasks, and Check-Your-Understanding Questions are available for download at **https://companion.corwin.com/courses/BTCK5Tasks**

LAUNCH SCRIPT

Teacher: Hello my fantastic mathematicians! My son's friends, Asma and Fatima, came over last night to play. I noticed that they were always playing with the same toys, and both were making groups (or sets) with the toys. They called me over to see who had more. Do you think you could figure that out?

Students: Absolutely!

Teacher: Ok great! Here is the first set [teacher draws two circles, one with 5 triangles inside of it and one with 1 triangle inside of it. Teacher writes "Fatima" over the 5 triangles and "Asma" over the 1 triangle].

Teacher: Who has more?

Students: Fatima!

Teacher: Terrific! What about this set? [shows first prompt with apples and gets students into groups]

TASK SEQUENCE

Type 1: Comparing Sets—Who Has More?

Who has more? Fatima's set is always on your right:

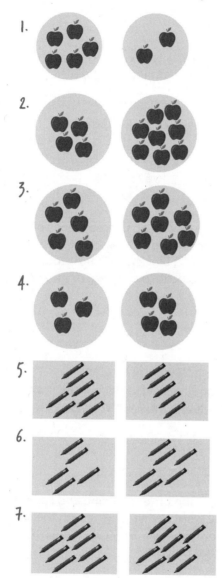

My son decided it was so much fun, so he joined now too! Which set has the most and the fewest?

Source: apples from iStock.com/AntonioFrancois; pencils from iStock.com/ksanagribakina

9.

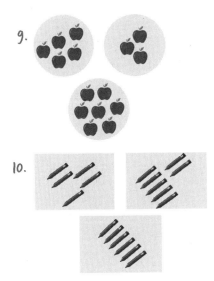

10.

Type 2: Comparing Sets and Finding the Difference Between Sets

Hint: The cars are lined up so nicely. How many are sticking out on the end of this row?

Which set has more and how many more?

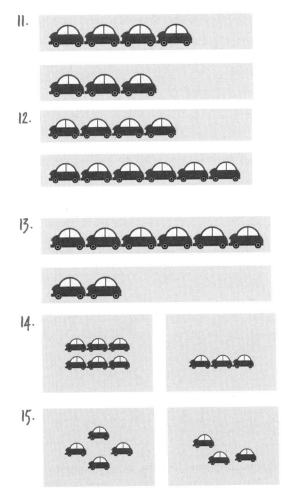

11.

12.

13.

14.

15.

Source: apples from iStock.com/AntonioFrancois; pencils from iStock.com/ksanagribakina; cars from iStock.com/yuwnis07

16.

How many more does the largest set have compared to the smallest set?

17.

18.

Source: cars from iStock.com/yuwnis07; apples from iStock.com/AntonioFrancois

Type 3: Symbolically Comparing Sets and Finding the Difference Between Sets

Hint: Maybe you can get some blocks or draw pictures.

Which number is biggest and how many more is the larger (largest) number compared to the smaller (smallest) number?

19. 3 or 4

20. 7 or 5

21. 5 or 0

22. 6 or 8

23. 10 or 9

24. 5 or 3 or 8

25. 2 or 6 or 1

26. 12 or 5 or 10

CONSOLIDATION TASKS

Teacher: I have written on the board three questions like the ones you just did in your group, but I may have put them in the wrong order. Turn to your neighbor and discuss what the order should be and why.

A Is 9 or 6 bigger? How many more is the larger number compared to the smaller number? (Type 3)

B Which set has more cars? How many more cars does it have? (Type 2)

C Which set has more? (Type 1)

Source: cars from iStock.com/yuwnis07; pencils from iStock.com/ksana-gribakina

STUDENT NOTES TO THEIR FUTURE FORGETFUL SELVES

Example 1:
How much does each set have? Circle which set has more.

Example 2:
Which set has the most and how many more?

CHECK-YOUR-UNDERSTANDING QUESTIONS

MILD

Which set has more?

A.

B.

MEDIUM

Which set has more and how many more does it have?

A.

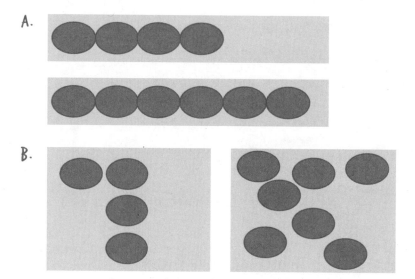

B.

SPICY

Which number is more and how many more is it than the smaller number?

A. 6 or 8

B. 9 or 5

Author Notes

This task is sliced in a way that helps students visually understand the difference between two sets. This task also provides a good reminder to students and educators that concrete, pictorial, and symbolic are not necessarily a linear path and that different representations can be used at various times to aid students and deepen their understanding.

Notes to My Future Forgetful Self

TASK 26: UP TO 20

TASK

This task has students count different sets of objects up to 20, represent numbers up to 20, and count on to a particular number.

***

Content: counting, counting on, representing numbers to 20

Competencies: collaboration, patience

Seen Before: counting on to 10

Before You Launch: Use the images available for download to create slips of paper that you give to groups to keep them in flow.

***

This Task Sequence, Consolidation Tasks, and Check-Your-Understanding Questions are available for download at **https://companion.corwin.com/courses/BTCK5Tasks**

LAUNCH SCRIPT

Teacher: Hello my awesome mathematicians! Today's focus will be on counting many different things. For instance, how many triangles did I draw here? [teacher draws 2 triangles]

Students: 2!

Teacher: Fantastic! This will be a snap for you guys! Now, how many dots do you see here? [give first image for students to take to boards]

TASK SEQUENCE

Type 1: Counting a Set

How many in the set?

1.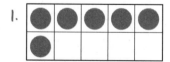

2.

3.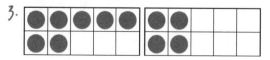

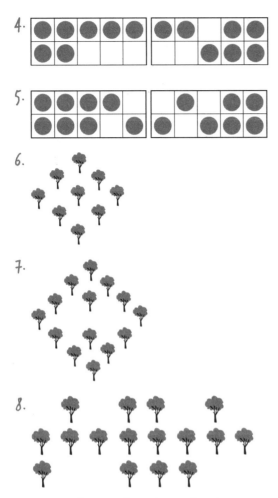

4.

5.

6.

7.

8.

Source: tree icons from iStock.com/Annandistock

Type 2: Creating Sets From a Given Number

Hint: Give the students the numbers from 1–20 or a number line for counting while drawing.

Draw the set:

9. 5 stars

10. 8 triangles

11. 11 circles

12. 14 squares

13. 12 circles

14. 16 triangles

15. 19 circles

16. 20 check marks

17. 18 triangles

Type 3: Adding to a Set and Counting On

18. How many more do I need to draw to get to 6?

19. How many more do I need to draw to get to 9?

20. How many more do I need to draw to get to 10?

21. How many more do I need to draw to get to 13?

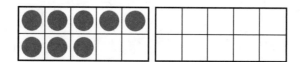

22. How many more do I need to draw to get to 17?

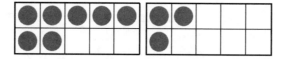

23. How many more do I need to draw to get to 15?

24. How many more do I need to draw to get to 20?

CONSOLIDATION TASKS

Teacher: I have written on the board three questions like the ones you just did in your group, but I may have put them in the wrong order. Turn to your neighbor and discuss what the order should be and why.

A   How many more squares do I need to have 17 squares? (Type 3)

B   Count the triangles. (Type 1)

C   Draw 16 circles. (Type 2)

STUDENT NOTES TO THEIR FUTURE FORGETFUL SELVES

Example 1:
How many △ do you see?

△   △
△△△△
△   △

Example 2:
Draw 14 circles.

CHECK-YOUR-UNDERSTANDING QUESTIONS

MILD

A. Count the circles.

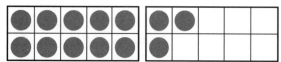

B. Count the hearts.

MEDIUM

A. Draw 15 triangles.

B. Draw 17 happy faces.

SPICY

A. How many more circles are needed to have 19 circles?

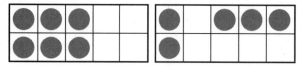

B. How many more  are needed to get to 15?

Author Notes

This task is a good lead in for Task 27 and can be easily adapted for a variety of purposes. For example, you could extend it to adding or subtracting mathematical statements or scale back to more basic counting or concrete representations.

Notes to My Future Forgetful Self

TASK 27: WE'RE FRAMEOUS

TASK

This task has students add and subtract different numbers on 10-frames based on the given mathematical statement.

Content: adding and subtracting numbers up to 30

Competencies: creativity

Seen Before: adding and subtracting up to 10

Before You Launch: Every group needs to have three 10-frames.

LAUNCH SCRIPT

Teacher: Hello my excited mathematicians! Have you ever used one of these? [teacher holds up a laminated 10-frame] This is called a 10-frame. Any guesses why?

Students: Because there are 10 boxes!

Teacher: Yep! We can use these to learn more about adding and subtracting numbers. To start, if I start with one dot, and add another dot, [teacher places two dots in a 10-frame] how many dots are there?

Students: 2!

Teacher: Great! We showed 1 + 1 = 2 on a 10-frame. Now, can you go to your boards [which already have 10-frames there] and show what 3 + 2 equals using 10-frames?

TASK SEQUENCE

Type 1: Adding and Subtracting With One 10-Frame

Show what __ + __ or __ – __ equals using a 10-frame:

1. 3 + 2	4. 1 + 9	7. 6 – 1	10. 10 – 7
2. 4 + 5	5. 3 + 7	8. 5 – 4	11. 10 – 8
3. 8 + 2	6. 5 + 5	9. 8 – 2	12. 10 – 5

Type 2: Adding and Subtracting With Two 10-Frames

Hint: What do you do if one 10-frame is full?

Show what __ + __ or __ − __ equals using 10-frames:

13. 7 + 4	16. 7 + 13	19. 15 − 6	22. 13 − 7
14. 10 + 5	17. 8 + 11	20. 17 − 10	23. 20 − 8
15. 14 + 5	18. 12 − 2	21. 19 − 6	

Type 3: Adding and Subtracting With Three 10-Frames

Show what __ + __ or __ − __ equals using 10-frames:

24. 20 + 4	27. 14 + 14	30. 24 − 2	33. 29 − 15
25. 19 + 6	28. 17 + 12	31. 26 − 7	34. 30 − 18
26. 24 + 4	29. 19 + 11	32. 24 − 12	

CONSOLIDATION TASKS

Teacher: I have written on the board three questions like the ones you just did in your group, but I may have put them in the wrong order. Turn to your neighbor and discuss what the order should be and why.

A   28 − 17 (Type 3)

B   3 + 6 (Type 1)

C   15 + 12 (Type 2)

STUDENT NOTES TO THEIR FUTURE FORGETFUL SELVES

Example 1:

What is 3 + 4?

Example 2:

What is 18 − 5?

CHECK-YOUR-UNDERSTANDING QUESTIONS

MILD

Show what __ + __ or __ – __ equals using a 10-frame:

A. 7 + 3

B. 8 – 2

C. 10 – 4

MEDIUM

Show what __ + __ or __ – __ equals using a 10-frame:

A. 8 + 9

B. 12 + 6

C. 19 – 7

SPICY

Show what __ + __ or __ – __ equals using a 10-frame:

A. 13 + 12

B. 22 – 15

C. 28 – 14

Author Notes

This task does not need laminated 10-frames, but it makes it more manageable. This task has the potential to go very fast, and if students are unable to redraw a 10-frame they may have erased, your time will soon be monopolized by drawing 10-frames instead of managing flow, giving hints, extensions, etc. You may also want to use two different-colored whiteboard markers so you can show adding numbers clearly.

Notes to My Future Forgetful Self

_____

_____

_____

_____

_____

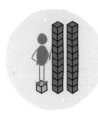

TASK 28: ALL ABOUT THAT BASE

TASK

This task has students explore base-10 representations for numbers up to 100 using base-10 blocks.

> **Content**: representing numbers up to 100 using base-10 blocks, composing, decomposing, regrouping numbers to 100
>
> **Competencies**: willingness to take risks, perseverance
>
> **Seen Before**: numbers to 50, decomposing numbers into tens and ones (e.g. 1 ten = 10 ones)
>
> **Before You Launch**: Make sure that every group has 10 one-blocks and 10 ten-blocks. This task works well with the banner.

LAUNCH SCRIPT

Teacher: Hello my magnificent mathematicians! [show base-10 blocks]. These are called base-10 blocks and they can be used to represent many different numbers. What do you think this represents? [teacher holds up a one-block]

Students: 1!

Teacher: Absolutely! What do you think this represents? [teacher holds up a ten-block]

Students: 10!

Teacher: Wonderful! Today, I will give you a number. Your job is to build that number with base-10 blocks and then draw what the blocks look like on your board. For example, how many tens do I need to make 11?

Students: 1!

Teacher: [teacher draws long rectangle to indicate a ten-block]

Teacher: How many one cubes would I need to make 11?

Students: 1!

Teacher: [teacher adds a small square to indicate a one-block]

Teacher: How many tens and ones do you need to make 14?

TASK SEQUENCE

Type 1: Constructing and Drawing Numbers With Base-10 Blocks Without Regrouping

Use the base-10 blocks to build each number and draw what you built on your board:

1. 14	4. 35	7. 67	10. 93
2. 17	5. 42	8. 78	11. 99
3. 29	6. 54	9. 83	

Type 2: Drawing Base-10 Blocks to Calculating Numbers With and Without Regrouping

> **Hints:** When you drew 93, how many tens did you use? Interesting; how many ones did you use? Could that help you solve this?

Draw these base-10 blocks and calculate what number they make:

12. 1 ten and 6 ones

13. 2 tens and 15 ones

14. 19 ones and 2 tens

15. 14 ones and 3 tens

16. 4 tens and 1 ones

Without drawing these, calculate what number they make:

17. 3 tens and 21 ones

18. 5 tens and 28 ones

19. 42 ones and 4 tens

20. 50 ones and 4 tens

21. 49 ones and 5 tens

Type 3: Drawing Numbers With Base-10 Blocks With Restrictions

Draw each number:

22. 15 using only one-blocks

23. 27 using less than 2 ten-blocks

24. 34 using more than 4 one-blocks

25. 50 using some one-blocks

26. 66 using less than 5 ten-blocks

27. 81 using more one-blocks than ten-blocks

28. 100 using ten-blocks and one-blocks

CONSOLIDATION TASKS

Teacher: I have written on the board three questions like the ones you just did in your group, but I may have put them in the wrong order. Turn to your neighbor and discuss what the order should be and why.

A   What number is made from 12 ones and 2 tens? (Type 2)

B   Draw 38 using more than 10 ones (Type 3)

C   Draw 25 using ones and tens (Type 1)

STUDENT NOTES TO THEIR FUTURE FORGETFUL SELVES

Example 1:

Draw 36 using base ten blocks

10

Example 2:

What number is made from 2 ten·blocks and 13 one blocks?

CHECK-YOUR-UNDERSTANDING QUESTIONS

MILD

Draw each number using ten-blocks and one-blocks:

A.   31

B.   68

C.   82

MEDIUM

What number is made from

A. 3 tens and 12 ones

B. 21 ones and 2 tens

C. 36 ones and 3 tens

SPICY

Draw:

A. 65 using more one-blocks than ten-blocks.

B. 72 with less than 7 ten-blocks

C. 84 with less than 6 ten-blocks

Author Notes

This task can be very beneficial to younger students because it lays a foundation for place value and leads into decomposing numbers in various ways. Students can utilize and expand upon a concrete understanding that 10 one-blocks are the same as 1 ten-block for many years. A good follow up to this would be showing your students exploding dots on Mathigon's Polypad at www.mathigon.org/polypad.

Notes to My Future Forgetful Self

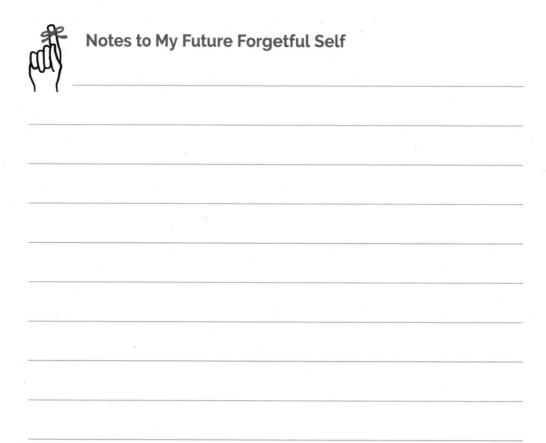

TASK 29: MO' MONEY, MO' PROBLEMS

TASK

This task has students solve a variety of number problems related to various kinds of money and change.

> **Content**: number operations involving quarters, dimes, nickels, and pennies
>
> **Competencies**: collaboration, organization
>
> **Seen Before**: money and how much each coin is worth
>
> **Before You Launch**: Prior to this task, you may need to do a quick review of what each coin is worth. You can weave this into the launch script. This task works well with the banner.

LAUNCH SCRIPT

Teacher: Hello my brilliant mathematicians. Last night, my son Jakester and I were looking through his piggy bank and he was trying to count the coins. But he doesn't know how to count money. Could you help him out?

Students: Of course!

Teachers: OK great! First, he had 7 pennies [teacher draws 7 circles with a 1 inside them]. How much money does he have?

Students: 7 cents!

Teachers: But wait, now he has 3 nickels. [Teacher draws 3 circles with a 5 inside]. How much is that?

TASK SEQUENCE

Type 1: Within a Dollar

How much money does Jakester have if he has

1. 3 nickels?
2. 4 dimes?
3. 2 quarters?
4. 3 quarters?
5. 2 nickels, 2 dimes, and 1 penny?
6. 10 pennies, 1 quarter, and 3 dimes?
7. 6 dimes and 2 nickels?
8. 1 nickel, 1 dime, and 1 quarter?
9. 2 quarters, 2 nickels, and 2 dimes?
10. 3 quarters, 3 pennies, and 3 nickels?

Type 2: More Than a Dollar

Hint: Could you draw each coin with the amount on it? Could that help?

How much money does Jakester have if he has

11. 7 dimes and 6 nickels?
12. 3 quarters, 3 nickels, and 10 pennies?
13. 6 dimes and 2 quarters?
14. 20 pennies, 4 dimes, and 4 quarters?
15. 5 quarters, 7 nickels, and 15 pennies?
16. 14 pennies, 5 nickels, and 5 quarters?
17. 100 pennies and 20 nickels?
18. 10 dimes and 13 nickels?
19. 22 pennies, 3 quarters, 15 dimes, and 2 nickels?

Type 3: Determining Coins for a Given Amount

What coins could Jakester have if he has

20. $0.34?
21. $0.55?
22. $0.75?
23. $0.90?
24. $1.00 with no quarters?
25. $1.41?
26. $1.85 with no nickels?
27. $2.10 with no dimes?
28. $2.51 with more than 1 penny?
29. $6.00 with at least 1 penny, 1 nickel, 1 dime, and 1 quarter?

CONSOLIDATION TASKS

Teacher: I have written on the board three questions like the ones you just did in your group, but I may have put them in the wrong order. Turn to your neighbor and discuss what the order should be and why.

A   How much money is 6 quarters, 17 pennies, and 2 nickels? (Type 2)

B   What coins can make $1.35? (Type 3)

C   How much money is 2 quarters and 1 dime? (Type 1)

STUDENT NOTES TO THEIR FUTURE FORGETFUL SELVES

Example 1:

How much money is 5 dimes?

(10¢) ◯ ◯ ◯ ◯

Example 2:

How much money is 3 quarters, 1 dime and 6 pennies?

Things to Remember:

Example 3:

CHECK-YOUR-UNDERSTANDING QUESTIONS

MILD

How much money is

A.   5 nickels?

B.   2 nickels and a dime and 6 pennies?

C.   12 pennies, 2 quarter, and 2 dimes?

MEDIUM

How much money is

A. 4 nickels, 4 dimes, and 4 quarters?

B. 6 quarters, 2 dimes, and 7 pennies?

C. 22 pennies, 8 nickels, and 4 quarters?

SPICY

What change could make each dollar amount using only quarters, dimes, nickels, and pennies?

A. $1.07

B. $1.58

C. $2.65

Author Notes

This task, like many others, can be adapted to fit the needs of specific students. For example, you could combine Type 1 and 2 questions to be able to extend further. The new Type 3 questions could be about making change at a store. It could and should be adapted for your money system. We are both Canadian, so our task could also include loonies ($1.00 coin) and toonies ($2.00 coin).

Notes to My Future Forgetful Self

_____

_____

_____

_____

_____

_____

_____

_____

TASK 30: SHOW ME YOUR NUMBER

TASK

This task has students represent whole numbers and then decimals in a variety of forms: expanded, number-word, word form, and place value charts.

> **Content**: place value, number description and representation, number line
>
> **Competencies**: willingness to take risks
>
> **Seen Before**: base-10 numbers, decomposing numbers
>
> **Before You Launch**: There are many suggestions here for representations. Use your professional judgement to highlight or pinpoint the ones that you want your students to work on. This task works well with the banner.

LAUNCH SCRIPT

Teacher: Hello my splendid mathematicians! Did you know that there are lots of different ways to represent a number? For example, I can show 24 as 20 + 4 [teacher writes 20 + 4 on the board]. You can show many numbers like that. Turn and talk to your partner about how we could represent 36.

Students: 30 + 6 [teacher writes 30 + 6 on the board]

Teacher: OK. What number is this? [teacher writes 300 + 80 + 5 on the board]

TASK SEQUENCE

Type 1: Representing Numbers, No Zeros

What number is this?

1. 300 + 80 + 5
2. 1,000 + 200 + 30 + 1
3. 6,000 + 400 + 80 + 8
4. 20 + 900 + 5000 + 4
5. 4 + 30,000 + 600 + 10 + 8000
6. 8 × 10,000 + 5 × 1,000 + 3 × 100 + 2 × 10 + 9 × 1
7. 3 × 100,000 + 4 × 10,000 + 8 × 1,000 + 4 × 100 + 4 × 10 + 8 × 1
8. Three thousand, seven hundred eighteen
9. Twenty-five thousand, eight hundred forty-one

10. Six hundred fifty-two thousand, one hundred twenty-seven

11. Fill in the table:

			tens	
5	1	8	2	3

12. Fill in the table:

		hundreds		
9	3	4	1	5

Type 2: Representing Numbers in Two Ways With Zeros

Hint: What happens when we show a number that has a zero in the middle of the number?

Represent these numbers in two ways:

13. 57,380   16. 14,056   19. 30,882   22. 250,011

14. 12,502   17. 28,077   20. 102,311   23. 904,005

15. 88,706   18. 90,414   21. 406,202

Type 3: Representing Numbers in Two Ways With Decimals

Hint: How can we show numbers that are smaller than 1 (to the right of the decimal)?

Represent these number in two ways:

24. 8.5   27. 14.28   30. 13.886   33. 0.084

25. 123.8   28. 24.06   31. 0.428   34. 625.026

26. 6.48   29. 123.08   32. 10.401

CONSOLIDATION TASKS

Teacher: I have written on the board three questions like the ones you just did in your group, but I may have put them in the wrong order. Turn to your neighbor and discuss what the order should be and why.

A   Represent 14.302 in two ways. (Type 3)

B   What number is 30,000 + 2,000 + 100 + 80 + 7? (Type 1)

C   Represent 9,033 in two ways. (Type 2)

STUDENT NOTES TO THEIR FUTURE FORGETFUL SELVES

Example 1:

What number is this?

30 000 + 6 000 + 200 + 10 + 1

Example 2:

Represent 702 894 in two ways:

Things to Remember:

Example 3:

CHECK-YOUR-UNDERSTANDING QUESTIONS

MILD

What numbers are these?

A. 200 + 50 + 6

B. 8 × 1,000 + 1 × 100 + 4 × 10 + 7 × 1

C. Fill in the table

		hundreds		
9	3	4	1	5

MEDIUM

Represent these numbers in two ways:

A. 240,348

B. 704,508

C. 904,006

SPICY

Represent these numbers in two ways:

A. 32.3

B. 154.04

C. 104.205

Author Notes

This is a very accessible task for the students. As students move through Type 1, they are seeing all the various ways to represent numbers that help them through Types 2 and 3. Discussing place values during consolidation is the most powerful part of this task. One student said, "Why is there no oneths?" This led into a great discussion about fractions to decimals, which connected nicely to our next unit.

Notes to My Future Forgetful Self

_____

_____

_____

_____

_____

_____

_____

_____

_____

_____

_____

TASK 31: ODDLY EVEN

TASK

This task moves students through adding odd and even numbers and determining whether the addends could be even or odd for a given sum.

Content: addition, odd, even, place value

Competencies: reasoning, guess and check

Seen Before: addition with regrouping

Before You Launch: Type 3 questions could be very easy for your students. If that is the case, you can have the students write multiple solutions for what the addends could be. This task works well with the banner.

LAUNCH SCRIPT

Teacher: Hello my sensational mathematicians! Today we will be working on some addition statements. Can anyone give me an example of an addition statement?

Students: [students give various responses]

Teacher: That is great. Let's start with 10 + 10.

Students: 20!

Teacher: Great! 20 is an even number. What if it was 15 + 13? Turn to your neighbor to discuss whether the answer will be odd or even.

Students: 28 and it is even.

Teacher: Ok. What about 24 + 22?

TASK SEQUENCE

Type 1: Adding to an Even Sum

What is the sum of __ + __ and is it odd or even?

1. 24 + 22	4. 37 + 21	7. 51 + 59
2. 25 + 23	5. 38 + 22	8. 66 + 54
3. 26 + 32	6. 45 + 47	9. 71 + 29

Type 2: Adding to an Odd Sum

Hints: What sums were you getting with the previous questions? What could you expect here?

What is the sum of __ + __ and is it odd or even?

10. 25 + 24	13. 41 + 12	16. 51 + 58	19. 43 + 58
11. 36 + 31	14. 48 + 33	17. 65 + 28	
12. 37 + 32	15. 37 + 46	18. 72 + 27	

Type 3: Using the Sum to Determine the Addends

Was this sum made by adding two evens, two odds, or an odd and an even, and how do you know?

20. 61	24. 77	28. 159	32. 241
21. 74	25. 90	29. 188	
22. 68	26. 107	30. 135	
23. 92	27. 136	31. 234	

CONSOLIDATION TASKS

Teacher: I have written on the board three questions like the ones you just did in your group, but I may have put them in the wrong order. Turn to your neighbor and discuss what the order should be and why.

A   What is the sum of 48 + 39? Is the sum odd or even? (Type 2)

B   Was the sum 85 made by adding two odds, two evens, or an odd and an even? How do you know? What 2 numbers could add to 85? (Type 3)

C   What is the sum of 21 + 27? Is the sum odd or even? (Type 1)

STUDENT NOTES TO THEIR FUTURE FORGETFUL SELVES

Example 1:

What is the sum of 10 + 11?
Is it odd or even?

10 + 11 = ☐ ☐ is odd

☐ is even

☐ + ☐ is _____

Example 2:

What is the sum of 42 + 35?
Is it odd or even?

Things to Remember:

Example 3:

CHECK-YOUR-UNDERSTANDING QUESTIONS

MILD

What is the sum and is it odd or even?

A. 26 + 22

B. 31 + 57

C. 48 + 34

MEDIUM

What is the sum and is it odd or even?

A. 47 + 38

B. 29 + 61

C. 47 + 56

SPICY

Were these sums made from adding two odds, two evens, or an odd and an even, and how do you know?

A. 75

B. 98

C. 137

Author Notes

Depending on students' prior knowledge, they may go through this thin-slicing task quickly. If that is the case, you can make the numbers larger in Type 1, 2, or 3. You can also encourage students to make rules if there are more than two addends.

Notes to My Future Forgetful Self

TASK 32: SUM SOME MORE

TASK

This task moves students through adding 2-digit to 4-digit numbers with and without regrouping.

Content: adding 4-digit numbers

Competencies: collaboration, perseverance

Seen Before: adding 1-digit and 2-digit numbers with regrouping

Before You Launch: This task works well with the banner.

LAUNCH SCRIPT

Teacher: Hello my incredible mathematicians! Last night my two sons [or any two people] were comparing how many cards [Pokémon, stickers, baseball cards, etc.] they had. Have you ever compared your stuff with someone else before?

Students: Yes!

Teacher: Well, when my sons got all of their cards together, they wanted to know how many they had when they combined all together. They each had counted their own cards but didn't want to start over and count all of them again. If they each started off with 10 [teacher draws 10 + 10 stacked on the board], how many would they have all together?

$$
\begin{array}{r}
10 \\
+10 \\
\hline
\end{array}
$$

Students: 20!

Teacher: All right, but then the next day when they looked, they say they had a lot more. Now they have 23 and 74; how many do they have all together now?

$$
\begin{array}{r}
23 \\
+74 \\
\hline
\end{array}
$$

TASK SEQUENCE

Type 1: Adding Numbers Without Regrouping

What is the total?

1. 46 and 52
2. 19 and 70
3. 25 and 62
4. 18 and 81

5. 51 and 41
6. 120 and 361
7. 569 and 320
8. 237 and 402

9. 42 and 536
10. 5,044 and 3,924
11. 8,142 and 1,757
12. 440 and 2,539

Type 2: Adding Numbers by Regrouping Once

Hints: What happens when you add the ones together and the number is more than 10? What should you do?

What is the total?

13. 44 and 46
14. 53 and 27
15. 653 and 255
16. 716 and 193

17. 208 and 353
18. 7,285 and 1,524
19. 8,048 and 1,748
20. 6,921 and 2,478

21. 8,454 and 428
22. 271 and 8,541
23. 9,009 and 109

Type 3: Two- and Four-Digit Addition by Regrouping Multiple Times

What is the total?

24. 56 and 87
25. 14 and 96
26. 852 and 168
27. 362 and 288

28. 1,405 and 2,395
29. 6,099 and 801
30. 6,825 and 3,934
31. 5,493 and 9,597

32. 7,239 and 2,861
33. 8,899 and 601
34. 995 and 2,982
35. 2,865 and 936

CONSOLIDATION TASKS

Teacher: I have written on the board three questions like the ones you just did in your group, but I may have put them in the wrong order. Turn to your neighbor and discuss what the order should be and why.

A 517 and 392 (Type 2)

B 429 and 273 (Type 3)

C 423 and 365 (Type 1)

STUDENT NOTES TO THEIR FUTURE FORGETFUL SELVES

Example 1:

120 + 361

$$\begin{array}{c}\square\ \square\ \square\\ +\ \square\ \square\ \square\\\hline \square\ \square\ \square\end{array}\quad\text{total}$$

Example 2:

What is 753 + 155

Things to Remember·

Example 3:

CHECK-YOUR-UNDERSTANDING QUESTIONS

MILD	MEDIUM	SPICY
What is the total?	What is the total?	What is the total?
A. 152 + 205	A. 341 + 758	A. 638 + 399
B. 1,421 + 3,446	B. 490 + 375	B. 2,322 + 6,780
C. 763 + 221	C. 5,105 + 2,786	C. 721 + 4,179
D. 8,105 + 1,453	D. 2,132 + 5,962	D. 956 + 3,284

Author Notes

The context for this task (combining cards, money, etc.) is accessible and engaging. It is interesting, though, because even though the story continues throughout the thin-slicing, the students quickly see it as simply adding two numbers, but they stay engaged due to the context. As well, whichever method you are encouraging your students to do is heavily reinforced throughout the task.

Notes to My Future Forgetful Self

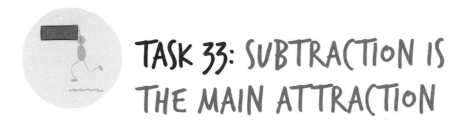

TASK 33: SUBTRACTION IS THE MAIN ATTRACTION

TASK

This task moves students through subtracting 2-digit to 4-digit numbers with and without decomposition.

Content: subtracting 4-digit numbers

Competencies: collaboration, perseverance

Seen Before: subtracting 2-digit numbers with decomposition

Before You Launch: This task works well with the banner.

LAUNCH SCRIPT

Teacher: Hello my delightful mathematicians! Do you remember how my two sons were comparing cards [Pokémon, stickers, baseball cards, etc.] the other night? They wanted to know how many they had all together. Sound familiar?

Teacher: Well, just as I suspected, finding out how many they had all together wasn't enough. It became a competition, and they now want to know who has more. This time, one had 14 and the other had 10 [teacher writes 14 and 10 on the board]. Which is more?

Students: 14!

Teacher: Turn and talk to someone beside you and talk about how much larger is 14 than 10.

Students: 4

Teacher: Okay, so 14 is 4 larger than 10. Well, the next time they had more than 10 and 14. One had 23 and the other had 74. [teacher draws 74 – 23 stacked on the board] Which is more and by how much?

$$\begin{array}{r} 74 \\ -\,23 \\ \hline \end{array}$$

TASK SEQUENCE

Type 1: Subtracting Numbers Without Decomposing

Which is more and by how much?

1. 23 and 74
2. 57 and 79
3. 320 and 559
4. 544 and 324

5. 7,285 and 4,165
6. 1,038 and 8,748
7. 7,654 and 4,552
8. 3,136 and 7,847

9. 4,208 and 6,438
10. 5,376 and 252
11. 414 and 2,966
12. 3,405 and 305

Type 2: Subtracting Numbers by Decomposing Once

> **Hints:** What happens if you are stacking to subtract, and the bottom number is bigger than the top? Can you make the top bigger?

Which is more and by how much?

13. 50 and 39
14. 66 and 47
15. 409 and 422
16. 367 and 348

17. 107 and 310
18. 3,557 and 3,438
19. 2,802 and 4,621
20. 7,239 and 1,338

21. 5,993 and 9,494
22. 8,872 and 653
23. 446 and 1,555

Type 3: Subtracting Numbers by Decomposing Multiple Times

Which is more and by how much?

24. 751 and 355
25. 265 and 461
26. 576 and 189
27. 685 and 196

28. 764 and 467
29. 1,995 and 2,982
30. 2,897 and 6,531
31. 1,738 and 4,000

32. 2,444 and 3,000
33. 9,000 and 6,758
34. 488 and 6,000
35. 259 and 8,000

CONSOLIDATION TASKS

Teacher: I have written on the board three questions like the ones you just did in your group, but I may have put them in the wrong order. Turn to your neighbor and discuss what the order should be and why.

A 431 – 256 (Type 3)

B 468 – 255 (Type 1)

C 816 – 534 (Type 2)

STUDENT NOTES TO THEIR FUTURE FORGETFUL SELVES

Example 1:

569 – 320

Example 2:

Subtract 4841 – 2702

Things to Remember:

Example 3:

CHECK-YOUR-UNDERSTANDING QUESTIONS

MILD	MEDIUM	SPICY
Subtract.	Subtract.	Subtract.
A. 768 – 435	A. 825 – 581	A. 7,032 – 5,972
B. 763 – 521	B. 8,341 – 8,332	B. 6,752 – 2,973
C. 4,659 – 3,446	C. 6,490 – 5,375	C. 4,000 – 1,964
D. 8,957 – 1,453	D. 5,883 – 2,791	D. 9,000 – 592

Author Notes

This task has the same elements as Task 32 Sum Some More. Although the math can be viewed as basic and formulaic, the context allows students to create meaning and strategies on their own. The consolidation and CYU are written as direct subtraction questions because after 30 questions, everyone understands they are subtracting. However, the thin-slicing questions force students to decide the order of subtraction, something that some students might struggle with at the beginning.

Notes to My Future Forgetful Self

_____

_____

_____

_____

_____

_____

_____

_____

_____

_____

_____

_____

_____

_____

_____

_____

_____

_____

TASK 34: WHO'S ON FIRST?

TASK

This task moves students through ordering decimal numbers to the tenths.

Content: comparing and ordering decimals to the tenths

Competencies: collaboration, empathy

Seen Before: comparing and ordering whole numbers

Before You Launch: This task can go very fast, which is why collaboration and empathy are the competencies. You might want to remind your students to work as a team, be patient with each other, and take care of each other. You might even want to use a collaboration rubric with this task. This task works well with the banner.

LAUNCH SCRIPT

Teacher: Hello, my marvelous mathematicians! Sometimes we need to compare numbers for many reasons.

Students: Why?

Teacher: Well, for instance, if you go to the store to buy something that is $10.00, [teacher writes $10.00 on the board] but you only have $8.00 [teacher writes $8.00], can you buy it?

Students: No. We don't have enough.

Teacher: Exactly! So that is you comparing numbers to know which number is larger. Can we put these numbers [teacher writes 14, 16, 13 on the board] in order from smallest to largest?

Students: 13, 14, 16

Teachers: Okay. What about 3, 7, 4.5?

TASK SEQUENCE

Type 1: Two Whole Numbers and One Decimal Number

Order these numbers from smallest to largest:

1. 3, 7, 4.5
2. 6, 8.3, 5
3. 5.9, 4, 10
4. 18, 20.5, 15
5. 28, 25.4, 32
6. 68, 14.7, 25
7. 51.1, 52, 50

Type 2: One Whole Number and Two Decimal Numbers

Hints: What digit in the numbers do you look at to know which is bigger? Could that help you here?

Order these numbers from smallest to largest:

8. 2, 1.5, 3.5
9. 6.4, 8, 5.9
10. 10.3, 15, 8.8
11. 16.0, 13, 15.8
12. 24, 23.6, 25.7
13. 62.5, 20.9, 84
14. 50, 51.6, 50.8

Type 3: Three Decimal Numbers

Order these numbers from smallest to largest:

15. 3.1, 3.5, 3.2
16. 7.6, 7.5, 7.0
17. 5.1, 5.8, 5.2
18. 11.0, 11.9, 11.3
19. 12.6, 12.1, 12.8
20. 15.2, 15.9, 15.5
21. 17.6, 17.1, 17.3
22. 8.2, 8.3, 8.1
23. 0.8, 0.5, 0.7
24. 6.8, 6.0, 6.2
25. 2.0, 2.9, 2.1
26. 3.1, 3.9, 3.8

CONSOLIDATION TASKS

Teacher: I have written on the board three questions like the ones you just did in your group, but I may have put them in the wrong order. Turn to your neighbor and discuss what the order should be and why.

Order these numbers from smallest to largest:

A   24.3, 22.1, 26 (Type 2)

B   5.8, 5.0, 5.9 (Type 3)

C   3, 5, 2.5 (Type 1)

STUDENT NOTES TO THEIR FUTURE FORGETFUL SELVES

Example 1:

Order these numbers from smallest to largest;
1.8 , 4 , 2

_____ , _____ , _____
smallest   largest

Example 2:

Order these numbers from smallest to largest:
2.5 , 4.1 , 3

Things to Remember:

Example 3:

CHECK-YOUR-UNDERSTANDING QUESTIONS

MILD

Order these numbers from smallest to largest:

A. 5.9, 4, 10

B. 6, 3, 9.5

C. 18, 20.1, 26

MEDIUM

Order these numbers from smallest to largest:

A. 1.7, 3, 1.2

B. 5, 4.7, 8.1

C. 16.8, 19.1, 14

SPICY

Order these numbers from smallest to largest:

A. 5.1, 5.6, 5.2

B. 9.3, 9.2, 9.8

C. 14.2, 14.9, 14.3

Author Notes

This task will seem very simple to both you and your students. But, at the end of the lesson, they are doing something they have never done before—ordering decimals. And making meaning with it. This is the beauty of thin-slicing.

Notes to My Future Forgetful Self

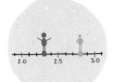

TASK 35: DECI-LINE DANCE

TASK

This task moves students through ordering decimals on a number line to the tenths, hundredths, and thousandths.

Content: comparing and ordering decimals on a number line to the thousandths

Competencies: collaboration, mobilizing knowledge

Seen Before: decimals, comparing, and ordering whole numbers

Before You Launch: There is a little bit of review built into this launch. That is all the review that is needed—the rest is for them to think about. This task works well with the banner.

LAUNCH SCRIPT

Teacher: Hello my collaborative mathematicians. The other day we were ordering whole numbers and decimal numbers. Let's do a little review. If I have these three numbers [teacher writes 5.1, 6, 5.5 on the board], how could I order these from smallest to largest? Turn and talk to the person next to you.

Students: 5.1, 5.5, 6 [teacher scribes on the board].

Teacher: Ok. Does anyone know what this is? [teacher draws on open number line with no numbers on it]

Students: A number line.

Teacher: Great. Your job is to take these numbers [teacher writes 1.9, 1.7, 2.1 on the board], make and label a number line, then place each number on it.

TASK SEQUENCE

Type 1: Ordering to the Hundredths With Same Number of Decimal Places

Place these numbers on a number line:

1. 1.9, 1.7, 2.1
2. 1.3, 2.9, 2.1
3. 0.9, 1.1, 1.0

4. 2.0, 1.8, 3.1

5. 4.24, 3.86, 4.70

6. 0.99, 4.03, 1.15

7. 6.59, 6.14, 6.87

8. 2.06, 0.99, 2.20

Type 2: Ordering to the Hundredths With Mixed Number of Decimal Places

> **Hints:** What should be at the start and end of your number line? Is there a digit that you look at first to know which number is bigger?

Place these on a number line:

9. 1.88, 1.9, 1.18

10. 0.09, 0.54, 0.7

11. 3.0, 2.07, 2.18

12. 1.58, 1.39, 1.6

13. 1.04, 1.19, 1.4

14. 5.09, 5.2, 5.3

15. 7.1, 7.09, 7.9

Type 3: Ordering to the Thousandths With Mixed Number of Decimal Places

Place these on a number line:

16. 2.199, 2.211, 2.337

17. 7.325, 7.911, 7.298

18. 1.461, 1.876, 1.552

19. 6.16, 6.161, 6.503

20. 0.098, 0.16, 0.201

21. 3, 3.088, 3.52

22. 6.072, 7, 6.1

23. 0.609, 1, 0.8

24. 5.1, 5.065, 5.37

25. 4.403, 4.080, 4

26. 0.50, 0.502, 0.5

27. 14.8021, 14.802, 15

28. 12.34, 12.340, 12.3

CONSOLIDATION TASKS

Teacher: I have written on the board three questions like the ones you just did in your group, but I may have put them in the wrong order. Turn to your neighbor and discuss what the order should be and why.

Order these decimals on a number line:

    A   7.08, 7.2, 7.28 (Type 2)

    B   1.50, 1.502, 1.6 (Type 3)

    C   3.7, 2.9, 2.4 (Type 1)

STUDENT NOTES TO THEIR FUTURE FORGETFUL SELVES

Example 1:

Place these numbers on a number line:

4.3 , 4.2 , 4.8

4.0   4.5   5.0

Example 2:

Place these decimals on a number line:

1.58 , 1.39 , 1.4

Things to Remember:

Example 3:

CHECK-YOUR-UNDERSTANDING QUESTIONS

MILD

Place these numbers on a number line:

A.   2.6, 2.3, 2.9

B.   9.9, 9.4, 9.0

C.   6.76, 6.53, 6.19

MEDIUM

Place these numbers on a number line:

A. 6.6, 6.90, 6.18

B. 8.09, 8.54, 8.7

C. 1.5, 1.39, 1.43

SPICY

Place these numbers on a number line:

A. 9.63, 9.097, 9.25

B. 7.082, 7.104, 7.32

C. 2.047, 2.1, 2.55

Author Notes

This task can be used as a follow-up task to Task 34 Who's on First, or it could be used in isolation, depending on the capacity or knowledge of your mathematicians.

Notes to My Future Forgetful Self

TASK 36: GROW BY THE ROW

TASK

This task has students finding out how many flowers are being planted based on how many rows there are and how many flowers are in each row.

> **Content**: arrays, multiplication, repeated addition, area
>
> **Competencies**: collaboration, empathy
>
> **Seen Before**: skip counting, multiplication
>
> **Before You Launch**: This task can go very fast, which is why collaboration and empathy are the competencies. You might want to remind your students to work as a team, be patient with each other, and take care of each other. You might even want to use a collaboration rubric with this task. This task works well with the banner.

LAUNCH SCRIPT

Teacher: Hello my terrific mathematicians. Today I want to plant a flower bed. I marked out my rows and where I want the flowers, but I'm not sure how many flowers I can fit. Can you help me?

Students: Sure!

Teacher: Great, so the first draft [teacher draws a grid with 2 rows of 3 on the board] I made was 2 rows of 3 flowers. Turn and talk to the person next to you. How many flowers could fit?

Students: 6.

Teacher: Ok. How many flowers could fit if it was 3 rows of 4 flowers? [teacher draws a 3 by 4 grid with 3 rows of 4]

TASK SEQUENCE

Type 1: Multiplying One Digit by One Digit

How many flowers are in the flower bed?

1. 3 rows of 4 flowers
2. 6 rows of 2 flowers
3. 6 rows of 4 flowers
4. 7 rows of 4 flowers

5. 7 rows of 5 flowers
6. 9 rows of 5 flowers
7. 9 rows of 7 flowers
8. 9 rows of 9 flowers

Type 2: Multiplying One and Two Digits by 10

Hints: What is 1 × 10? What is 2 × 10? What is 3 × 10? What is 7 × 10? What is 12 × 10?

How many flowers are in the flower bed?

9. 3 rows of 10 flowers
10. 5 rows of 10 flowers
11. 8 rows of 10 flowers
12. 9 rows of 10 flowers

13. 12 rows of 10 flowers
14. 10 rows of 15 flowers
15. 18 rows of 10 flowers
16. 10 rows of 22 flowers

Type 3: Multiplying One Digit by Two Digits

How many flowers are in the flower bed?

17. 4 rows of 12 flowers
18. 12 rows of 6 flowers
19. 15 rows of 6 flowers
20. 15 rows of 5 flowers
21. 18 rows of 5 flowers
22. 18 rows of 7 flowers

23. 7 rows of 21 flowers
24. 4 rows of 21 flowers
25. 4 rows of 36 flowers
26. 6 rows of 36 flowers
27. 6 rows of 42 flowers
28. 8 rows of 42 flowers

CONSOLIDATION TASKS

Teacher: I have written on the board three questions like the ones you just did in your group, but I may have put them in the wrong order. Turn to your neighbor and discuss what the order should be and why.

A 8 rows of 12 flowers (Type 3)

B 4 rows of 5 flowers (Type 1)

C 9 rows of 10 flowers (Type 2)

STUDENT NOTES TO THEIR FUTURE FORGETFUL SELVES

Example 1:

How many flowers are in 5 rows of 3 flowers?

□ + □ + □ + □ + □ = □

□ × □ =

Example 2:

How many flowers are in 10 rows of 7 flowers?

Things to Remember:

Example 3:

CHECK-YOUR-UNDERSTANDING QUESTIONS

MILD

How many flowers are planted if my garden is

A. 2 rows of 5 flowers?

B. 6 rows of 4 flowers?

C. 9 rows of 7 flowers?

MEDIUM

How many flowers are planted if my garden is

A. 7 rows of 10 flowers?

B. 10 rows of 8 flowers?

C. 10 rows of 13 flowers?

SPICY

How many flowers are planted if my garden is

A. 12 rows of 7 flowers?

B. 9 rows of 14 flowers?

C. 15 rows of 6 flowers?

Author Notes

Like many tasks, the engagement of this task will be high because the context is easy to understand and, at the very least, students can draw the flower bed to solve the task. The goal is that students move from counting, to skip counting, to multiplication.

Notes to My Future Forgetful Self

_____

_____

_____

_____

_____

_____

_____

_____

_____

_____

_____

_____

_____

_____

TASK 37: GARDEN FENCES

TASK

This task moves students through finding the length of wood around a planter box (perimeter), to what size felt is needed to block the weeds (base area), to how much dirt in units³ can fit into it (volume).

Content: perimeter, area, volume

Competencies: perseverance, mobilizing knowledge

Seen Before: addition, multiplication

Before You Launch: This task will require you to shift the narrative of the story as the task type changes. You can gather two to three groups together at a time to do this. For Type 2 tasks, it would be handy if the students had access to a nonpermanent grid at their VNPSs. This task works well with the banner.

LAUNCH SCRIPT

Teacher: Hello my superb mathematicians! I've decided to build a raised garden bed. I have all these ideas but I'm not sure of the amount of materials I need. I know I want it to be a rectangular shape, but can you help me figure out how much all my materials would be?

Teacher: I want to start by building the walls of the garden [teacher draws a rectangle] and I need to know how many feet of wood I need to go around my garden bed. How many feet of wood should I buy to go all the way around if it is 2 feet by 3 feet [teacher labels each side of the rectangle]?

3 ft

2 ft   2 ft

3 ft

Students: 10 feet of wood.

Teacher: OK. What if my garden bed was 3 feet long and 4 feet wide? [teacher draws out a rectangle]

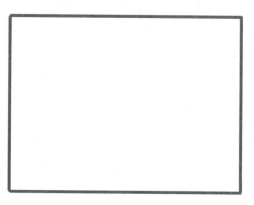

TASK SEQUENCE

Type 1: Perimeter

How many feet of wood do I need to go around the garden if it is

1. 3 ft long and 4 ft wide?
2. 6 ft long and 8 ft wide?
3. 5 ft long and 8 ft wide?
4. 10 ft long and 8 ft wide?
5. 10 ft long and 7 ft wide?
6. 9 feet by 7 feet?
7. 9 feet by 11 feet?
8. 14 feet × 11 feet?
9. 17 feet × 24 feet?

Type 2: Area

Hint: [Draw a 2 by 3 grid and have the students count the squares inside.]

10. **Teacher:** Now that I figured out how many feet of wood I need, I bought this black felt that covers the ground inside the garden bed to stop weeds from growing in the garden. It comes in square feet like this [teacher draws a rectangle with grid lines inside and colors in one square]. How many square feet of felt do I need if my garden is 3 feet long and 5 feet wide?

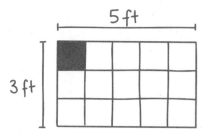

How many square feet of felt do I need if the garden is

11. 6 ft long and 8 ft wide?

12. 5 ft long and 8 ft wide?

13. 10 ft long and 8 ft wide?

14. 10 ft long and 7 ft wide?

15. 9 ft by 7 ft?

16. 9 ft by 11 ft?

17. 14 ft × 11 ft?

18. 17 ft × 24 ft?

19. 17 ft × 24 ft?

Type 3: Volume

Hint: [Show students a 1 × 3 × 4 prism built out of linking cubes and have them count how many linking cubes there are.]

20. This is great! I've got the wood (perimeter) figured out and the felt (area) figured out. Now I just need to figure out how much dirt to put in. We measure the dirt in cubic (cubed) feet. For example, if my garden is 2 feet long, 2 feet wide, and 2 feet high [teacher builds with linking cubes]. I will need [teacher counts each cube] 8 cubic feet of dirt.

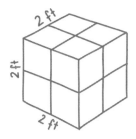

How many cubic feet of dirt will I need if my garden is

21. 4 ft long and 3 ft wide and 1 ft high?

22. 3 ft long and 2 ft wide and 2 ft high?

23. 4 ft long and 2 ft wide and 1 ft high?

24. 6 ft long and 2 ft wide and 3 ft high?

25. 7 ft by 5 ft by 2 ft?

26. 8 ft by 6 ft by 4 ft?

27. 9 ft × 11 ft × 6 ft?

28. 11 ft × 14 ft × 8 ft?

29. 12 ft × 20 ft × 7 ft?

CONSOLIDATION TASKS

Teacher: I have written on the board three questions like the ones you just did in your group, but I may have put them in the wrong order. Turn to your neighbor and discuss what the order should be and why.

A How much dirt in cubic feet (volume) is needed if the garden is 9 ft × 11 ft × 6 ft? (Type 3)

B How many feet of wood (perimeter) is needed to go around a 4 ft wide and 6 ft long garden? (Type 1)

C How many square feet of felt (area) is needed to cover the inside of an 8 ft by 12 ft garden? (Type 2)

STUDENT NOTES TO THEIR FUTURE FORGETFUL SELVES

Example 1:	Example 2:
What is the perimeter of a 3 feet × 6 feet rectangle? ▭ 3 ft 6 ft 3 ft + 6 ft + ☐ ft + ☐ ft = ☐ ft	What is the area of an 8 ft × 5 ft rectangle?
Things to Remember:	Example 3 :

CHECK-YOUR-UNDERSTANDING QUESTIONS

MILD

How many feet of wood (perimeter) is needed if my garden is

A. 4 ft wide by 6 ft long?

B. 3 ft wide by 9 ft long?

C. 10 ft wide by 7 ft long?

MEDIUM

How many square feet of felt (area) is needed if my garden is

A. 5 ft by 7 ft?

B. 4 ft by 8 ft?

C. 11 ft by 6 ft?

SPICY

How many cubic feet of dirt (volume) do I need if my garden is

A. 3 ft × 6 ft × 2 ft?

B. 10 ft × 7 ft × 3 ft?

C. 12 ft × 5 ft × 2 ft?

Author Notes

Students tend to understand how to solve these questions quite easily. It is important to note that by drawing the grid of the garden bed, the students have a visual aid to reason with to bridge the pictorial to abstract. With the Type 3 questions, linking cubes are incredibly helpful and should be used for everyone because the concrete promotes the abstract sense making. Each type of question eventually introduces the perimeter, area, and volume language to apply this task more widely later. This task could also easily be adapted to be only perimeter, area, or volume.

Notes to My Future Forgetful Self

TASK 38: TRACK DAY

TASK

This task has students finding out how many athletes there are in total, based on the number of groups (or heats), and how many athletes are in each group (heat).

Content: repeated addition, skip counting, multiplication, repeated subtraction, division without remainder, division with remainder

Competencies: collaboration

Seen Before: repeated addition, skip counting

Before You Launch: This task works well with the banner.

LAUNCH SCRIPT

Teacher: Hello my kind-hearted mathematicians. I was at a track event on the weekend and there were tons of athletes in each event. When there are a lot of athletes there isn't room for all of them to run at the same time. So, they run them in groups called *heats*. Unfortunately, I didn't have time to count how many athletes I saw in total. I only counted how many heats there were and how many athletes were in each heat. Could you help me find the total number of athletes?

Students: Sure!

Teacher: So, if I saw 2 heats of 3 athletes, how many athletes in total did I see?
[teacher draws two groups of three dots and makes a circle around it]

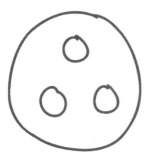 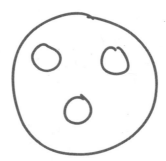

Students: 6!

Teacher: Ok. What about 3 heats of 5 athletes?

TASK SEQUENCE

Type 1: Multiplying One Digit by One Digit

How many athletes are there in total if there are

1. 3 heats with 5 athletes in each heat?
2. 4 heats with 4 athletes in each heat?
3. 3 heats with 6 athletes in each heat?
4. 6 heats with 5 athletes in each heat?
5. 7 heats with 5 athletes in each heat?
6. 7 heats with 8 athletes in each heat?
7. 9 heats with 8 athletes in each heat?
8. 9 heats with 9 athletes in each heat?

Type 2: Dividing Two Digits by One Digit, No Remainders

Hints: How did you solve the previous questions? Could that strategy help you solve these?

I eventually figured out that the program showed me how many athletes there were and how many heats there were. How many athletes are in each heat if there are

9. 10 athletes in 2 heats?
10. 28 athletes in 2 heats?
11. 28 athletes in 4 heats?
12. 48 athletes in 4 heats?
13. 48 athletes in 6 heats?
14. 72 athletes in 6 heats?
15. 72 athletes in 8 heats?
16. 96 athletes in 8 heats?

Type 3: Dividing Two Digits by One Digit, With Remainders

Sometimes, there aren't enough athletes to fill all the heats. So, the last heat has fewer athletes than the others. How many heats are there if there are

17. 25 people in heats of 4?
18. 42 people in heats of 4?
19. 42 people in heats of 5?
20. 68 people in heats of 5?
21. 68 people in heats of 6?
22. 75 people in heats of 6?

23. 75 people in heats of 7?

24. 90 people in heats of 8?

25. 95 people in heats of 9?

CONSOLIDATION TASKS

Teacher: I have written on the board three questions like the ones you just did in your group, but I may have put them in the wrong order. Turn to your neighbor and discuss what the order should be and why.

A If there are 80 athletes in 5 heats, how many athletes are there per heat? (Type 2)

B If there are 65 athletes with 7 athletes in each heat, how many heats are there? (Type 3)

C How many athletes are there if there are 3 heats of 6 athletes? (Type 1)

STUDENT NOTES TO THEIR FUTURE FORGETFUL SELVES

Example 1:

How many total athletes for 7 groups of 5 athletes?

$$\square + \square + \square + \square + \square + \square + \square = \square$$
$$\ \ \ 1 \quad\ \ 2 \quad\ \ 3 \quad\ \ 4 \quad\ \ 5 \quad\ \ 6 \quad\ \ 7$$

Example 2:

How many are in each group if I see 72 people in 6 groups?

Things to Remember:

Example 3:

CHECK-YOUR-UNDERSTANDING QUESTIONS

MILD

How many athletes are there if there are

A. 3 heats with 3 athletes in each heat?

B. 4 heats with 4 athletes in each heat?

C. 6 heats with 4 athletes in each heat?

MEDIUM

How many athletes in each heat if there are

A. 54 athletes in 6 heats?

B. 72 athletes in 9 heats?

C. 96 athletes in 8 heats?

SPICY

How many heats are there if there are

A. 52 people in heats of 5?

B. 66 people in heats of 7?

C. 90 people in heats of 8?

Author Notes

A focus of this task should be collaboration. Any time a task is related to simpler multiplication and division, some students tend to try and solve it themselves. A suggestion could be to have students show their math pictorially and symbolically.

Notes to My Future Forgetful Self

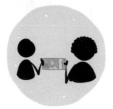

TASK 39: SHARING MONEY

TASK

This task moves students through sharing various amounts of money (dividing) between people. The students begin with sharing $36.00 between two people and conclude with $300.00 shared between 9 people.

Content: dividing two-digit and three-digit numbers by one-digit numbers, division with and without decimal quotients

Competencies: collaboration

Seen Before: multiplication, doubling, money, decimals

Before You Launch: This task works well with the banner.

LAUNCH SCRIPT

Teacher: Hello wonderous mathematicians! I just found some money! I want to share it with my friend Adeola, but I want to be fair and make sure that we both have the same, which means if I have $5.00, Adeola must also get $5.00. If I found $20.00, how much should we each get? Turn and talk to the person next to you.

Students: $10.00.

Teacher: OK. [teacher draws 10 twice and puts a box around each]

Teacher: What if I found $36.00? How much would we each get? [teacher draws a $36.00, puts a box around it and draws two diverging diagonal arrows below]

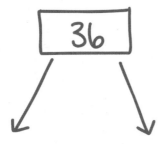

TASK SEQUENCE

Type 1: Dividing by 2 With and Without Decimal Quotients

1. Share $36.00 between two of us. How much would we each get?

2. Share $42.00 between two of us. How much would we each get?

3. Share $58.00 between two of us. How much would we each get?

4. Share $64.00 between two of us. How much would we each get?

5. Share $65.00 between two of us. How much would we each get?

6. Share $77.00 between two of us. How much would we each get?

7. Share $51.00 between two of us. How much would we each get?

Type 2: Dividing by 3, 4, and 5 With and Without Decimal Quotients

8. Share $51.00 between 3 people. How much would we each get?

9. Share $42.00 between 3 people. How much would we each get?

10. Share $63.00 between 3 people. How much would we each get?

11. Share $64.00 between 4 people. How much would we each get?

12. Share $84.00 between 4 people. How much would we each get?

13. Share $90.00 between 4 people. How much would we each get?

14. Share $66.00 between 5 people. How much would we each get?

15. Share $89.00 between 5 people. How much would we each get?

16. Share $91.00 between 5 people. How much would we each get?

Type 3: Dividing by 6, 7, 8, and 9 With and Without Decimal Quotients

17. Share $66.00 between 6 people. How much would we each get?

18. Share $80.00 between 6 people. How much would we each get?

19. Share $96.00 between 6 people. How much would we each get?

20. Share $96.00 between 7 people. How much would we each get?

21. Share $77.00 between 7 people. How much would we each get?

22. Share $147.00 between 7 people. How much would we each get?

23. Share $147.00 between 8 people. How much would we each get?

24. Share $240.00 between 8 people. How much would we each get?

25. Share $260.00 between 8 people. How much would we each get?

26. Share $279.00 between 8 people. How much would we each get?

27. Share $279.00 between 9 people. How much would we each get?

28. Share $290.00 between 9 people. How much would we each get?

29. Share $300.00 between 9 people. How much would we each get?

CONSOLIDATION TASKS

Teacher: I have written on the board three questions like the ones you just did in your group, but I may have put them in the wrong order. Turn to your neighbor and discuss what the order should be and why.

How much does each person get if they share

    A $156.00 between 7 people? (Type 3)

    B $28.00 between 2 people? (Type 1)

    C $61.00 between 5 people? (Type 2)

STUDENT NOTES TO THEIR FUTURE FORGETFUL SELVES

Example 1:

How much money does each person get if you share $36.00 between 2 people?

$$\boxed{36}$$
$$\square + \square = 36$$
$$\boxed{36} \div \boxed{2} = \square$$

Example 2:

How much money does each person get if you share $42.00 between 4 people?

Things to Remember:

Example 3:

CHECK-YOUR-UNDERSTANDING QUESTIONS

MILD

How much money would each friend get if they shared

A. $24.00 between 2 friends?

B. $30.00 between 2 friends?

C. $21.00 between 2 friends?

MEDIUM

How much money would each friend get if they shared

A. $57.00 between 3 friends?

B. $49.00 between 4 friends?

C. $71.00 between 5 friends?

SPICY

How much money would each friend get if they shared

A. $84.00 between 6 friends?

B. $91.00 between 7 friends?

C. $100.00 between 8 friends?

Author Notes

Although this task uses money, it can be adapted for any situation. It is possible to use similar numbers with sharing cookies, cupcakes, etc. It is also possible to differentiate this task up or down based on needs by only focusing on halving within 20. To start with 3-digit numbers, the situation could be a paperclip factory and they need to find out how many paperclips per box if they have 630 paperclips and 6 boxes.

This task is really about moving students into division with decimal quotients through their familiarity with multiplication. As a result, most of the representations you will see will be multiplicative in nature.

Notes to My Future Forgetful Self

_____

_____

_____

_____

_____

_____

_____

_____

_____

_____

TASK 40: LARGER BY A FRACTION

TASK

This task moves students from comparing pictorial fractions with the same shapes, to comparing pictorial fractions with different shapes, to comparing fractions written symbolically.

Content: compare fractions pictorially and symbolically

Competencies: willingness to take risks

Seen Before: fractions

Before You Launch: With this intro story, be prepared for MANY interruptions and stories about each student's dog or some dog they know. You have been WARNED! Use the images available for download to create slips of paper that you give to groups to keep them in flow.

This Task Sequence, Consolidation Tasks, and Check-Your-Understanding Questions are available for download at **https://companion.corwin.com/courses/BTCK5Tasks**

LAUNCH SCRIPT

Teacher: Hello, my outstanding mathematicians. Did you know that I have two dogs? One is a 10-year-old golden retriever named Sophie and she is the sweetest dog you have ever met! My other dog is one-year-old puppy named Jade. She is an energetic and adorable mixed breed. Sophie is a bigger dog, so she gets a lot more food. The colored portion is how much of their dog dish is filled with food. Can you tell which dish belongs to which dog? [teacher shows students the first question on a slip of paper]

TASK SEQUENCE

Type 1: Comparing Pictorial Fractions With the Same Shape

Which dish belongs to Jade (smaller dog) and which belongs to Sophie (bigger dog)?

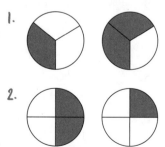

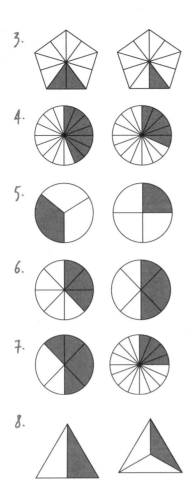

3.

4.

5.

6.

7.

8.

Type 2: Comparing Pictorial Fractions With Different Shapes

So, we recently took both dogs to the vet for their annual checkup. The vet told us that because Jade is a puppy and Sophie is 10 years old, they should not be eating the same dog food. She told us which dog food to buy for each dog. Now we buy two different brands that come in different sized and shaped bags. Which bag is closest to full?

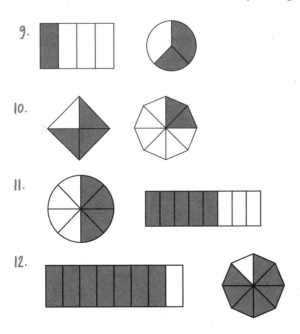

9.

10.

11.

12.

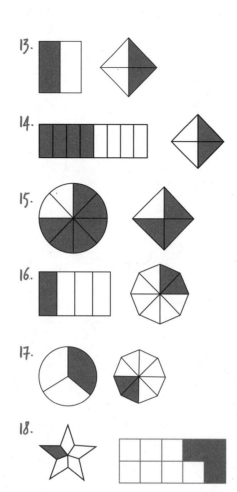

13.

14.

15.

16.

17.

18.

Type 3: Comparing Fractions With Different Denominators

Hint: Try drawing each fraction.

Which fraction is greater?

19. $\frac{1}{4}$ or $\frac{3}{5}$

20. $\frac{7}{10}$ or $\frac{3}{5}$

21. $\frac{3}{6}$ or $\frac{5}{8}$

22. $\frac{8}{10}$ or $\frac{5}{7}$

23. $\frac{4}{6}$ or $\frac{3}{5}$

CONSOLIDATION TASKS

Teacher: I have written on the board three questions like the ones you just did in your group, but I may have put them in the wrong order. Turn to your neighbor and discuss what the order should be and why.

Which fraction is bigger?

A 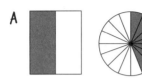 (Type 2)

B $\frac{2}{8}$ or $\frac{1}{5}$ (Type 3)

C  (Type 1)

STUDENT NOTES TO THEIR FUTURE FORGETFUL SELVES

Example 1:

Which is bigger?

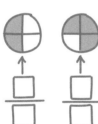

Example 2:

Which is bigger?
How do you know?

Things to Remember:

Example 3:

CHECK-YOUR-UNDERSTANDING QUESTIONS

MILD	MEDIUM	SPICY
Which fraction is bigger?	Which fraction is bigger?	Which fraction is bigger?

MILD

A.

B.

C.

MEDIUM

A.

B.

C.

SPICY

A. $\frac{1}{2}$ or $\frac{2}{5}$

B. $\frac{3}{6}$ or $\frac{5}{8}$

C. $\frac{4}{6}$ or $\frac{3}{5}$

Author Notes

This task can be a good lead-in to comparing fractions by finding equivalent fractions with common denominators.

Notes to My Future Forgetful Self

_____

_____

_____

_____

_____

_____

_____

_____

TASK 41: MUSICAL FRACTIONS

TASK

This task moves students through finding the fraction of a given time from a song. Example: 30 seconds is $\frac{1}{2}$ of a 1-minute song.

Content: fractions, estimating fractions, fractions on a number line, time conversions

Competencies: perseverance, knowledge mobility

Seen Before: fractions, digital time

Before You Launch: Use the images available for download to create slips of paper that you give to groups to keep them in flow.

This Task Sequence, Consolidation Tasks, and Check-Your-Understanding Questions are available for download at **https://companion.corwin.com/courses/BTCK5Tasks**

LAUNCH SCRIPT

Teacher: Hello my lovely mathematicians! So last night I was listening to some music with Jakester, my 5-year-old. We love listening to music in the evening. The problem is that my son is pretty impatient. He's only 5, right? During the first song, he asked how much of the song we have listened to. So I paused the song and said, "We're about half done." Then we kept listening and during the next song he asked again. And I paused the song and said, "Oh about three quarters done." Then during the third song he said, "Hey mom ..." But I knew he was going to ask it, so I interrupted and said, "Jakester, the song is about a quarter done." He was about to say okay but then looked up at me and asked, "Is it exactly a quarter done?" I looked at my phone and thought for a second and said, "I think it is a quarter done, but I'm not certain." He kept asking during every song after that but I felt smart because I started to screenshot the songs last night so I could get your help today. Could you help?

Students: Sure!

Teacher: Well, the first song was 2 minutes and I stopped it at 1 minute [teacher draws a number line that starts at 0:00 and ends with 2:00, then puts a dot in the middle and writes 1:00]. How far into the song are we?

Students: Half done.

Teacher: Ok. What about this one? [teacher shows students first question]

TASK SEQUENCE

Type 1: Fractions Using Denominators of 1 Minute or 2 Minutes

1.
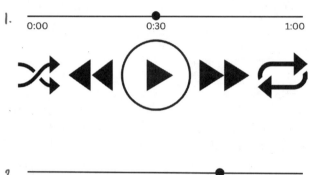

2.

3.

4.

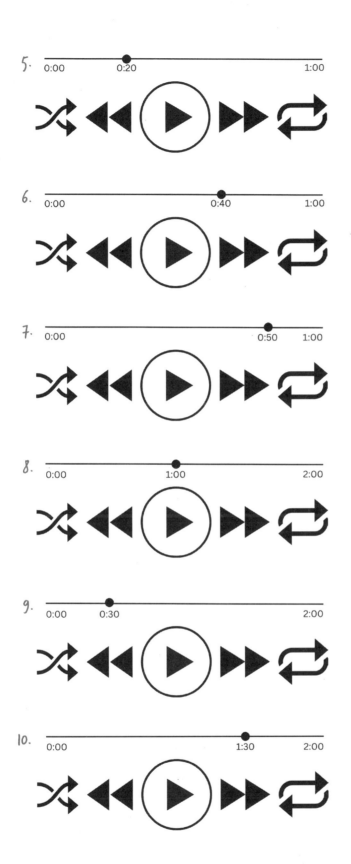

Type 2: Denominator Includes Minutes and Seconds—Easily Simplified Fractions

Hints: So one minute is 60 seconds, right? How can converting the minutes to seconds help you solve these?

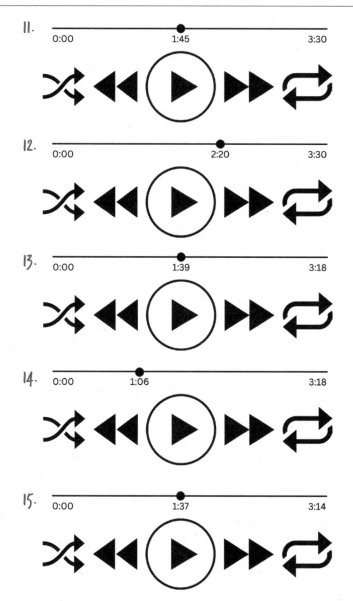

11.

| 0:00 | 1:45 | 3:30 |

12.

| 0:00 | 2:20 | 3:30 |

13.

| 0:00 | 1:39 | 3:18 |

14.

| 0:00 | 1:06 | 3:18 |

15.

| 0:00 | 1:37 | 3:14 |

Type 3: Denominator Includes Minutes and Seconds—Not Easily Simplified Fractions

16.

| 0:00 | 0:35 | 3:30 |

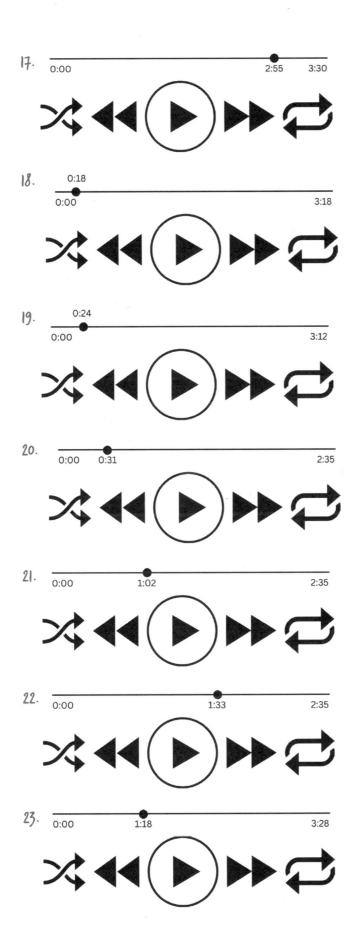

17. 0:00   2:55   3:30

18. 0:18 / 0:00   3:18

19. 0:24 / 0:00   3:12

20. 0:00   0:31   2:35

21. 0:00   1:02   2:35

22. 0:00   1:33   2:35

23. 0:00   1:18   3:28

CONSOLIDATION TASKS

Teacher: I have written on the board three questions like the ones you just did in your group, but I may have put them in the wrong order. Turn to your neighbor and discuss what the order should be and why.

How much of the song have I listened to if I heard

A   0:18 of a 3:12 song (Type 3)

B   1:06 of a 3:18 song (Type 2)

C   1:00 of a 2:00 song (Type 1)

STUDENT NOTES TO THEIR FUTURE FORGETFUL SELVES

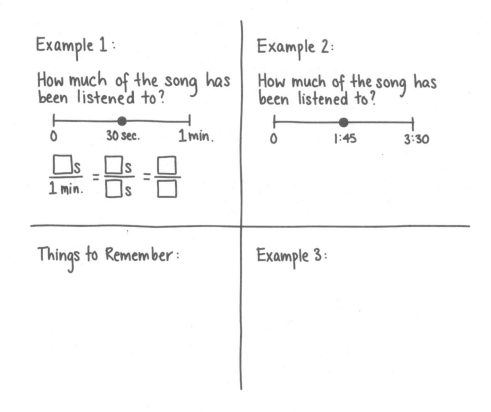

Example 1:

How much of the song has been listened to?

0   30 sec.   1 min.

$$\frac{\Box s}{1 \text{ min.}} = \frac{\Box s}{\Box s} = \frac{\Box}{\Box}$$

Example 2:

How much of the song has been listened to?

0   1:45   3:30

Things to Remember:

Example 3:

CHECK-YOUR-UNDERSTANDING QUESTIONS

MILD

How much of the song have I listened to if I heard

A.   0:30 of a 1:00 song

B.   0:15 of a 1:00 song

C.   1:30 of a 2:00 song

MEDIUM

How much of the song have I listened to if I heard

A. 2:05 of a 4:10 song

B. 1:05 of a 3:15 song

C. 1:45 of a 3:30 song

SPICY

How much of the song have I listened to if I heard

A. 2:22 of a 5:55 song

B. 1:15 of a 5:00 song

C. 2:10 of a 5:25 song

Author Notes

This task, though related to fractions, has a unique spin for two reasons. The first is using a number line to estimate and find a fraction of time, which students can struggle with. Second, the whole for the fraction is represented through two time-based units (minutes and seconds), which adds extra difficulty for students to work through.

Notes to My Future Forgetful Self

TASK 42: WHAT TIME IS IT?

TASK

This task has students estimate the time on the clock using only an hour hand and then telling the minutes using only the minutes hand and then a combination of both.

....

Content: reading and estimating time on an analog clock

Competencies: willingness to take risks

Seen Before: time, hours, minutes, skip counting

Before You Launch: Use the images available for download to create slips of paper that you give to groups to keep them in flow.

....

This Task Sequence, Consolidation Tasks, and
Check-Your-Understanding Questions are available for download at
https://companion.corwin.com/courses/BTCK5Tasks

LAUNCH SCRIPT

Teacher: Hello my clever mathematicians! What do you notice about this clock?
[teacher draws a clock with only an hour hand]

Students: It only has one hand.

Teacher: Yes. And it is the hour hand, not the minute hand. You can tell because the hour hand is shorter than the minute hand. So, with the hour hand here, what time would it be? [teacher points at clock]

Students: 5 o'clock.

Teacher: Great, but sometimes the hour hand isn't exactly on a number. If the hour hand was just past the 5, would the hour be 5 or 6?

Students: 5, it isn't 6 until the short hand reaches the 6 entirely.

Teacher: OK. So, your job is to tell me what hour this clock is showing. [teacher gives the first question]

TASK SEQUENCE

Type 1: Telling the Hour

About what time is this?

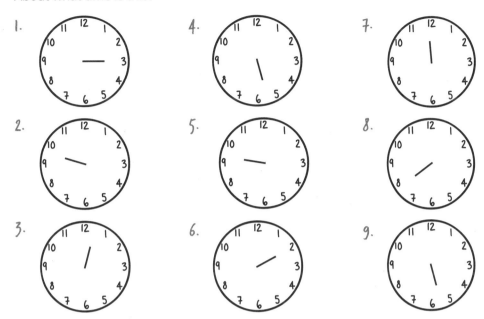

Type 2: Two Clocks—Hour and Minute

> **Hint:** Can the numbers that are going up by 5 on the outside help you understand the minutes?

So, if the shorthand is hours, the long hand is minutes. So now that you have both hands, what time is it?

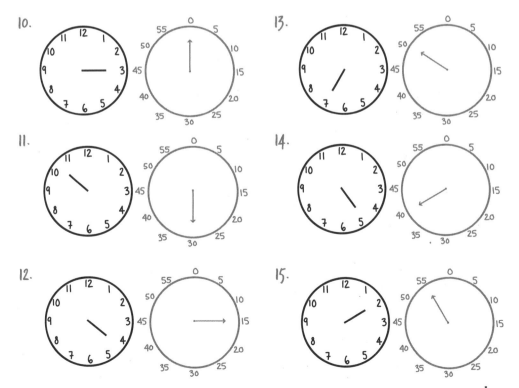

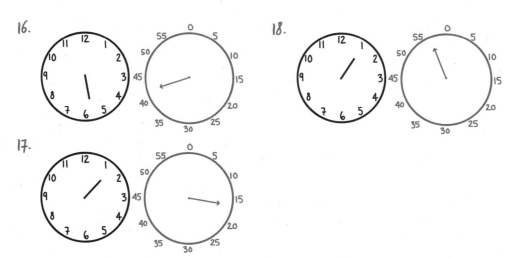

16.

17.

18.

Type 3: One Clock—Hours and Minutes

What time is it?

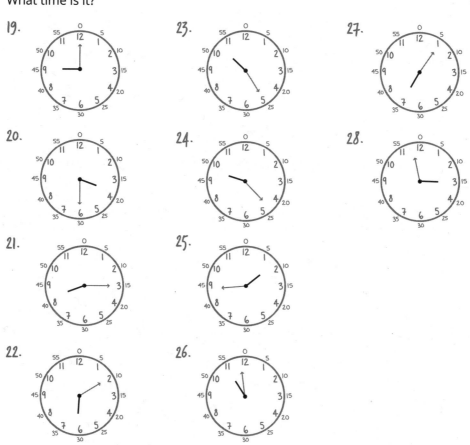

19.

20.

21.

22.

23.

24.

25.

26.

27.

28.

CONSOLIDATION TASKS

Teacher: I have written on the board three questions like the ones you just did in your group, but I may have put them in the wrong order. Turn to your neighbor and discuss what the order should be and why.

A What time is it? (Type 3)

B About what time is it? (Type 1)

C What time is it? (Type 2)

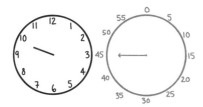

STUDENT NOTES TO THEIR FUTURE FORGETFUL SELVES

Example 1:

What hour is it?

 __ o'clock

Example 2:

What time is it?

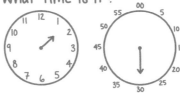

Things to Remember:

Example 3:

CHECK-YOUR-UNDERSTANDING QUESTIONS

MILD

About what time is it?

A.

B.

C.

MEDIUM

What time is it?

A.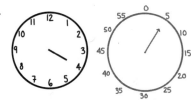

C.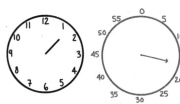

B.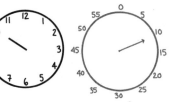

SPICY

What time is it?

A.

B.

C.

Author Notes

Learning to tell time using an analog clock is difficult for students because we are using the same instrument for two different measurements—hours and minutes. Splitting the clock into two separate instruments—one for hours and one for minutes—overcomes this challenge.

You can run this task actively as described here. Or you can run it passively in your classrooms over a period of weeks. To run it passively, simply put up an hours-only clock in your classroom and use that to discuss time throughout the day. You can talk about what time lunch is, when school ends, what time their dinner is, etc. You can even start to use relational language, like it is a bit past 2 o'clock, it is almost 10 o'clock, etc. Once they are comfortable with the hours-only clock, add the minutes-only clock right next to it. Now use both clocks to tell time more accurately. When they are comfortable with this, replace both clocks with the combined hours and minutes clock.

To make your own hours-only, minutes-only, and combined clocks, simply buy inexpensive clocks, open them up, and remove one or the other hands. When it is open, you can also edit or replace the face of the clock to contain only hours, only minutes, or combined. However, keep in mind that color coding matters. Make the hour hand and the hour numbers the same color. Then make the minute hand and minute numbers and minute marks the same color, but a different color than the hour hand and numbers. This will help when you move to the combined clock.

Notes to My Future Forgetful Self

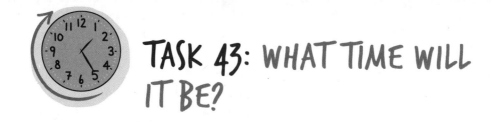

TASK 43: WHAT TIME WILL IT BE?

TASK

This task has students reading analog clocks, adding time, and reading 24-hour time.

Content: reading analog clocks, adding time, 24-hour time

Competencies: collaboration, perseverance

Seen Before: analog time, AM, PM

Before You Launch: Use the images available for download to create slips of paper that you give to groups to keep them in flow.

This Task Sequence, Consolidation Tasks, and Check-Your-Understanding Questions are available for download at **https://companion.corwin.com/courses/BTCK5Tasks**

LAUNCH SCRIPT

Teacher: Hello my insightful mathematicians. Today we are going to be reading analog clocks. Can someone give me a refresher on how we tell what hour it is?
[teacher draws a clock]

Students: The small hand

Teacher: What about the small hand? If it is in between 3 and 4, is the hour 3 or 4?
[teacher adds small line pointing in between 3 and 4]

Students: It is 3; it only becomes 4 when the small hand is on or past 4.

Teacher: OK. What about the longer hand?

Students: Each number counts as 5 minutes, 1 is 5 minutes, 2 is 10 minutes, etc.

Teacher: OK. So, my long hand is here. [teacher places long hand pointing to the 7] Turn and talk to the person beside you about what time it is and how you know.

Students: 3:35. It is 35 because 5, 10, 15, 20, 25, 30, 35.

Teacher: OK. Today we are going to push a little further. Today I want to know two things—what time it is and what time it will be in 30 minutes. [teacher gives out first question]

TASK SEQUENCE

Type 1: Reading Clocks With the Minute Hand at 00, 15, 30, and 45 Minutes

What time is it and what time will it be in 30 minutes?

Source: clocks from iStock.com/nutnai

10.   11.

Type 2: Reading Clocks to the Minute

Hints: Where will the minute hand be 30 minutes from now? Will that change the hour?

What time is it and what time will it be in 30 minutes?

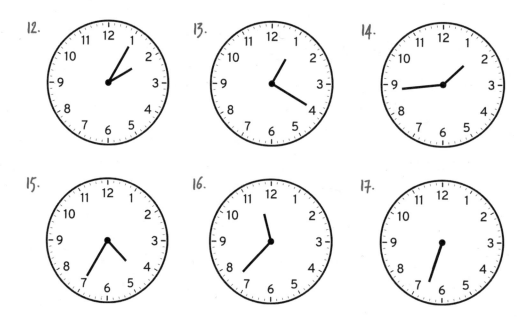

12.   13.   14.

15.   16.   17.

Source: clocks from iStock.com/nutnai

Type 3: Drawing a Clock With 12-Hour and 24-Hour Times

Hint: If 1:00 AM is 0100 hours, what would 1:00 PM be on a 24-hour clock?

In some places they work on a 24-hour clock. On a 24-hour clock, midnight is 0000 hours, 2:00 AM is 0200 hours, noon is 1200 hours, and 1:00 PM is 1300 hours. This continues until 11:59 PM, which is 2359 hours. For the following 24-hour times, what time would that be on a 12-hour clock? Will it be AM or PM? Draw the analog clock.

18. 0842 hours	22. 0930 hours	26. 1730 hours
19. 1235 hours	23. 1259 hours	27. 1615 hours
20. 0800 hours	24. 1301 hours	28. 2237 hours
21. 1115 hours	25. 1400 hours	29. 0026 hours

CONSOLIDATION TASKS

Teacher: I have written on the board three questions like the ones you just did in your group, but I may have put them in the wrong order. Turn to your neighbor and discuss what the order should be and why.

A   What time is it and what time will it be in 30 minutes? (Type 2)

B   Draw a clock showing 2240 hours. (Type 3)

C   What time is it and what time will it be in 30 minutes? (Type 1)

Source: clocks from iStock.com/nutnai

STUDENT NOTES TO THEIR FUTURE FORGETFUL SELVES

Example 1:

What time is it?
What time will it be in 30 mins.?

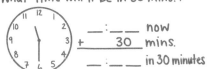

___:___ now
+ ___30___ mins.
___:___ in 30 minutes

Example 2:

What time is it?
What time will it be in 30 minutes?

Things to Remember:

Example 3:

CHECK-YOUR-UNDERSTANDING QUESTIONS

MILD

What time is this and what time will it be in 30 minutes?

A.

B.

C.

MEDIUM

What time is this and what time will it be in 30 minutes?

A.

B.

C.

Source: clocks from iStock.com/nutnai

SPICY

Draw these times on 12-hour analog clocks:

A. 0400

B. 1430

C. 2359

D. 0047

Author Notes

This task is great for both reviewing analog time and pushing students to think with analog time. Type 3 questions are designed intentionally to help guide students to understand a 24-hour clock, especially 12:59 hours to 13:01 hours.

Notes to My Future Forgetful Self

TASK 44: HOW MANY PAPERCLIPS IN A SHOE?

TASK

This task has students measure the length, width, and height of several classroom items using various referents, such as paperclips, linking cubes, shoes, etc.

Content: measurement, measurement with referents (various objects), measurement using nonstandard units

Competencies: willingness to take risks, tolerance of ambiguity

Seen Before: counting, estimation

Before You Launch: Some students are going to be anxious about the level of imprecision that is a natural consequence of using nonstandard units for measurement. Be ready to reassure them that precision is not important here. The Type 2 questions could be given to different groups in a different order to prevent every group being at the same place at the same time.

LAUNCH SCRIPT

Teacher: Hello my excellent mathematicians. Did you know that there is more than one way to measure? It's true. We can measure using standard measurements like miles (kilometers), inches (centimeters), and so on. However, we can also measure by using what are called referents. Referents are objects that can be used to estimate a measurement. For example, I'm 5 feet 6 inches (165 cm) tall in standard measurements, but using my dog as a referent I am about 2 and a half dogs tall. Do you guys think using a dog as a referent is good to estimate?

Students: No, we don't really know how tall they are because they can be different sizes.

Teacher: Exactly, and because of that, we will be using referents that we are familiar with. Here they are: [teacher shows at least 5 different objects to be referents, such as the following:

      paperclips, all the same length
      linking cubes
      base-10 blocks (ones or tens)
      pencils, unsharpened, all the same length
      uniform strips of paper]

Teacher: For this activity, you will be measuring things using two different referents. For example, my hand is ___ paperclips long, [teacher measures hand in paperclips and writes ___ paperclips] but it is also ___ linking cubes long [teacher measures hand in linking cubes and writes ___ linking cubes]. To start, measure the backpack of someone in your group using two different referents. Don't forget to record the different lengths and referents on the board.

TASK SEQUENCE

Type 1: Same Object, Different Referents

In your group, record your measurement and referents on your VNPS:

1. Measure a group member's backpack with 2 referents.

2. Measure a group member's shoe with 2 referents.

3. Measure a group member's hand with 2 referents.

4. Measure a group member from head to toe with 2 referents.

Type 2: Different Objects, Same Referent

> **Hint:** When measuring it is important that we measure every part of the length. Can you remeasure that, making sure to not miss any parts?

In groups, record your measurement and referents on your board:

5. Measure the length of the whiteboard (chalkboard, smartboard) and the length of the table with the same referent.

6. Measure the height of your table (desk) and the height from the floor to the bottom of a bulletin board (whiteboard) with the same referent.

7. Measure the width of the hallway and the width of the classroom with the same referent.

8. Measure the length and width of a textbook or notebook and a library book with the same referent.

Type 3: Find Object to Match Estimate

Find and measure (with the appropriate referent) an object that you and your partner(s) think is

9. about 11 paperclips long.

10. about 5 linking cubes tall.

11. 3 and a half rulers long.

12. 25 one-cubes (base-10 blocks).

13. 7 shoes long.

14. 1 and a half folders long.

CONSOLIDATION TASKS

Teacher: I have written on the board three questions like the ones you just did in your group, but I may have put them in the wrong order. Turn to your neighbor and discuss what the order should be and why.

A Measure the height of your desk (table) and chair using the same referent. (Type 1)

B Find and measure something in this room that is about 16 paperclips long. (Type 3)

C Measure a notebook with 2 referents. (Type 2)

STUDENT NOTES TO THEIR FUTURE FORGETFUL SELVES

Example 1:

How many linking cubes long is this rectangle?

Example 2:

How many paperclips is this quadrant?

Things to Remember:

Example 3:

CHECK-YOUR-UNDERSTANDING QUESTIONS

MILD

A. Measure your backpack with two different referents.

B. Measure your shoe with two different referents.

MEDIUM

A. Measure your hand and arm with the same referent.

B. Measure the height of your chair and desk (table) with the same referent.

SPICY

A. Find and measure something in this classroom that is 10 linking cubes long.

B. Find and measure something in this classroom that is 4 rulers tall.

Author Notes

We strongly recommend adapting this task as much as you need. The task sequence and materials depend heavily on what you have on hand, and this is meant to be a guide.

Notes to My Future Forgetful Self

_____

_____

_____

_____

_____

_____

_____

_____

_____

_____

_____

_____

_____

_____

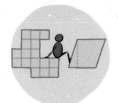

TASK 45: FORMULAS ARISE

TASK

This task has students finding the area of squares, rectangles, compound shapes, and parallelograms.

Content: area of squares, rectangles, compound shapes, and parallelograms

Competencies: creativity

Seen Before: area, parallelograms

Before You Launch: The focus of this task is on the conceptual understanding of area rather than formulas, so it is OK if students are counting squares or parts of squares. This task works well with the banner.

LAUNCH SCRIPT

Teacher: Hello my astonishing mathematicians! I just finished talking to the school admin and they finally agreed to let me put up a bulletin board for all my amazing jokes. You'll never be 'bored' with my joke board. Get it?

Teacher: The admin said that if I cover the board with paper, I can write all the jokes I want! Now I must figure out how many square feet of paper I need. If I had a 3 ft by 3 ft board, [teacher draws a 3 × 3 square grid] how many square feet would I need?

Students: 9!

Teacher: Okay, but what if it was a 5 ft by 5 ft board? [teacher draws a 5 × 5 square grid]

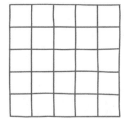

TASK SEQUENCE

Type 1: Areas of Squares and Rectangles

How many square feet of paper do I need if the joke board is

1. 5 ft by 5 ft?
2. 8 ft by 8 ft?
3. 12 ft by 12 ft?
4. 6 ft by 4 ft?

5. 6 ft by 8 ft?
6. 5 ft by 9 ft?
7. 10 ft by 4 ft?
8. 12 ft by 3 ft?

Type 2: Areas of Compound Shapes

> **Hint:** What if you drew the shape on a grid? Would that help you find the area?

Apparently some people don't like my humorous style, so the admin started giving me these weirdly shaped bulletin boards to cover with paper. How many square feet will I need for these shapes?

9.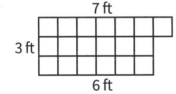

10.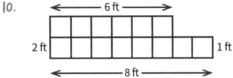

11.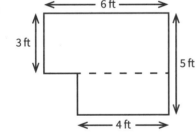

12.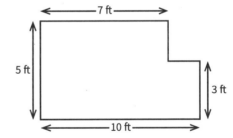

13.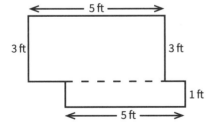

Type 3: Areas of Rhombuses and Parallelograms

> **Hints:** What if you drew the shape on a grid? Would that help you find the area? Is there a piece of the parallelogram that can be moved to somewhere else to make calculating the area easier?

The admin has given me some new shapes again. They must think this is hilarious that I'm having to do so much thinking for this joke board. They gave me these parallelogram boards; they look like a slanted rectangle. How many square feet of paper would I need now?

14.
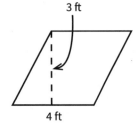
3 ft

4 ft

15.
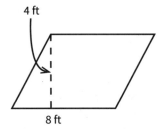
4 ft

8 ft

16.
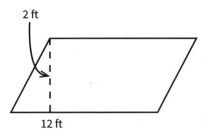
2 ft

12 ft

17.
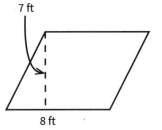
7 ft

8 ft

18. 9 ft tall by 9 ft wide

19. 6 ft tall by 13 ft wide

20. 5 ft tall by 20 ft wide

21. 4 ft tall by 20 ft high

CONSOLIDATION TASKS

Teacher: I have written on the board three questions like the ones you just did in your group, but I may have put them in the wrong order. Turn to your neighbor and discuss what the order should be and why.

How many square feet (area) do I need for each bulletin board?

A   6 ft high by 8 ft wide parallelogram (Type 3)

B   3 ft by 8 ft rectangle (Type 1)

C   (Type 2)

←— 4 ft —→

2 ft

←——— 6 ft ———→

STUDENT NOTES TO THEIR FUTURE FORGETFUL SELVES

Example 1:

What is the area?

4 ft

5 ft

___ × ___ = ___ ft²

Example 2:

What is the area?

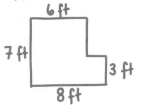
6 ft

7 ft

3 ft

8 ft

Things to Remember:

Example 3:

CHECK-YOUR-UNDERSTANDING QUESTIONS

MILD

How many square feet (area) do I need if my board is

A.   5 ft by 6 ft?

B.   7 ft by 4 ft?

C.   9 ft by 8 ft?

MEDIUM

How many square feet (area) do I need if my board looks like this:

A.
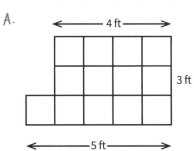
4 ft

3 ft

5 ft

B.
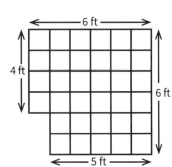
6 ft

4 ft

6 ft

5 ft

C.

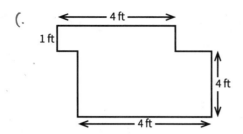

SPICY

How many square feet (area) do I need if my board is

A.

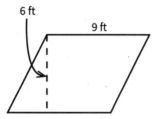

B. 3 ft high by 12 ft wide parallelogram

C. 4 ft high by 11 ft wide parallelogram

Author Notes

It is easy to increase or decrease the challenge for the students by drawing more or fewer grids and cut lines for the compound shapes and parallelograms.

Notes to My Future Forgetful Self

_____

_____

_____

_____

_____

_____

_____

MON	★ ★ ★
TUE	★
WED	★ ✓
THU	
FRI	★ ★ ★ ★ ✓

TASK 46: PICTURE THE PICTOGRAPHS

TASK

This task moves students through analyzing different parts of a pictograph to creating pictographs from data.

> **Content:** reading graphs, reading pictographs, making inferences, estimation
>
> **Competencies:** willingness to take risks
>
> **Seen Before:** basic pictographs, data
>
> **Before You Launch:** Use the images available for download to create slips of paper that you give to groups to keep them in flow.

This Task Sequence, Consolidation Tasks, and Check-Your-Understanding Questions are available for download at **https://companion.corwin.com/courses/BTCK5Tasks**

LAUNCH SCRIPT

Teacher: Hello my extraordinary mathematicians, have you ever seen a graph like this? [teacher shows graph]

Favorite Fruit	
Fruit	**Votes**
🍎	☺☺☺☺☺☺☺☺☺☺☺
🍐	☺☺☺☺☺☺☺
🍇	☺☺
🍌	☺☺☺☺☺☺
1 vote = ☺	

Source: apple from iStock.com/AntonioFrancois; pear from iStock.com/JDawnInk; grapes from iStock.com/MaksimYremenko; banana from iStock.com/Mykola Syvak; smiley faces from iStock.com/gmast3r

Students: Yes, no, etc.

Teacher: Well, someone gave me this graph [points at graph] but I'm not sure if I know how to read it. There are no numbers or anything. What do you think this graph is about? [teacher facilitates the conversation to have students say that this graph shows the favorite fruit of a bunch of people]

Teacher: So, which fruit do these people like best?

Students: Apples!

Teacher: OK. Do you think you could label how many votes each fruit got?

TASK SEQUENCE

Type 1: Extract Data From a Graph

What number does each row represent?

1.

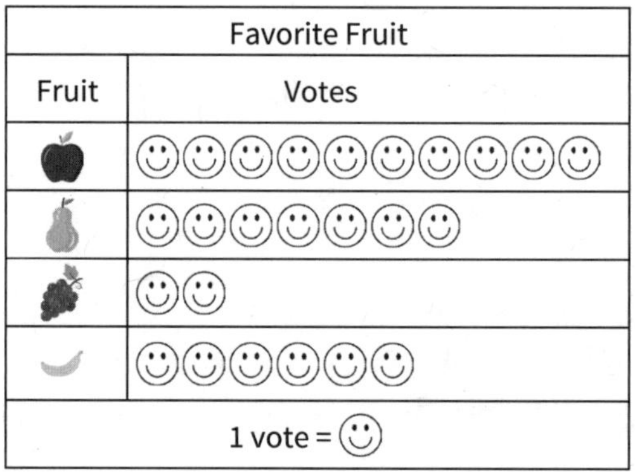

Favorite Fruit	
Fruit	Votes
🍎	☺☺☺☺☺☺☺☺☺☺
🍐	☺☺☺☺☺☺☺
🍇	☺☺
🍌	☺☺☺☺☺☺
1 vote = ☺	

2.

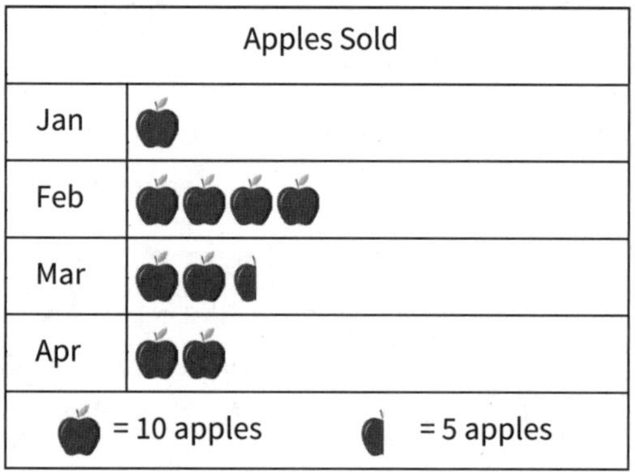

Apples Sold	
Jan	🍎
Feb	🍎🍎🍎🍎
Mar	🍎🍎🍎
Apr	🍎🍎

🍎 = 10 apples   🍎 = 5 apples

3.

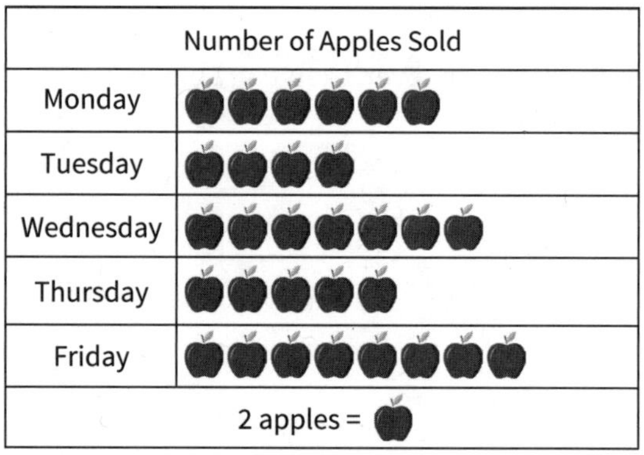

Number of Apples Sold	
Monday	🍎🍎🍎🍎🍎🍎
Tuesday	🍎🍎🍎🍎
Wednesday	🍎🍎🍎🍎🍎🍎🍎
Thursday	🍎🍎🍎🍎🍎
Friday	🍎🍎🍎🍎🍎🍎🍎
2 apples = 🍎	

4.

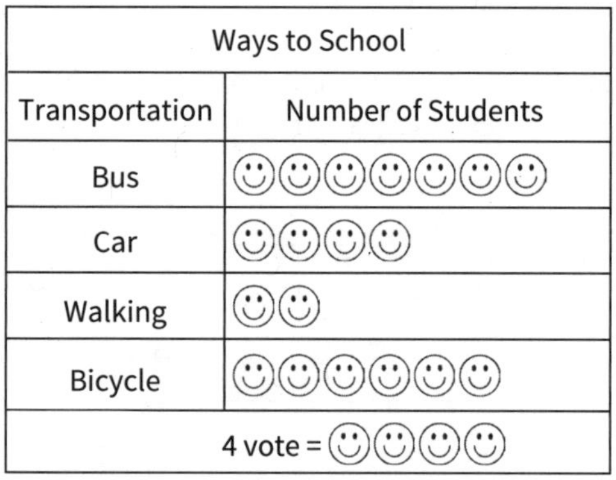

Ways to School	
Transportation	Number of Students
Bus	☺☺☺☺☺☺☺
Car	☺☺☺☺
Walking	☺☺
Bicycle	☺☺☺☺☺☺
4 vote = ☺☺☺☺	

Source: apple from iStock.com/AntonioFrancois; pear from iStock.com/JDawnInk; grapes from iStock.com/MaksimYremenko; banana from iStock.com/Mykola Syvak; smiley faces from iStock.com/gmast3r

Type 2: Add Data to a Graph

Add a row to the bottom of the graph representing an odd number:

5.

Students who like chocolate chip cookies best	
Grade 1	🍪🍪🍪
Grade 2	🍪🍪🍪🍪🍪
Grade 3	🍪🍪◖
Grade 4	🍪🍪🍪🍪🍪🍪
Grade 5	🍪🍪🍪◖
Grade 6	
2 students = 🍪	

Source: cookie from iStock.com/CandO_Designs

6.

Cupcakes Bought	
Monday	🧁🧁🧁🧁🧁
Tuesday	🧁🧁◖
Wednesday	🧁🧁🧁🧁
Thursday	🧁🧁🧁◖
Friday	🧁🧁🧁🧁🧁🧁🧁
Saturday	🧁🧁🧁🧁🧁🧁🧁🧁🧁
Sunday	🧁🧁🧁🧁🧁🧁🧁🧁🧁🧁
6 cupcakes = 🧁	

Source: cupcake from iStock.com/Stefan Ilic

7.

Ice Cream Cones Sold	
Flavor	Number of Ice Cream Cones
Vanilla	🍦🍦◖
Chocolate	🍦🍦🍦🍦
Strawberry	🍦🍦🍦◖
Butterscotch	🍦🍦🍦🍦🍦🍦
Pistachio	🍦🍦🍦🍦🍦🍦🍦🍦🍦
Cookie Dough	
Key: 🍦 = 50 cones	

Source: ice cream from iStock.com/Marina Parfenova

8.

Flavor	Number of Children
Cheese	🍕🍕🍕◖
Pepperoni	🍕🍕◖
Deluxe	🍕🍕◖
Veggie	
Key: 🍕 represents 4 children	

Source: pizza from iStock.com/subkontr

Type 3: Create a Graph From Data

Create a pictograph for the given data:

9. Time Spent on Activity

Sports	4 hours
Gadgets	4 hours
Read	1 hours
Sleep	10 hours
Other	5 hours

10. Trees Planted in a Week

Monday	3 trees
Tuesday	7 trees
Wednesday	6 trees
Thursday	8 trees
Friday	4 trees
Saturday	2 trees

11.	Sport Played		12.	Games Played	
	Cricket	22 Students		John	40
	Basketball	16 Students		Oke	45
	Football	19 Students		Shabnam	90
	Hockey	17 Students		Miguel	55

CONSOLIDATION TASKS

Teacher: I have written on the board three questions like the ones you just did in your group, but I may have put them in the wrong order. Turn to your neighbor and discuss what the order should be and why.

A Make a graph of the data below (Type 3)

Favorite Ice Cream

Chocolate	6 Kids
Vanilla	8 Kids
Cotton Candy	10 Kids
Cookie Dough	5 Kids

B Label each row of the pizza graph (Type 1)

Flavor	Number of children
Cheese	🍕🍕🍕🍕
Pepperoni	🍕🍕🍕
Deluxe	🍕🍕🍕
Veggie	
Key: 🍕 represents 4 children	

Source: pizza from iStock.com/subkontr

C Can you complete a row at the bottom so that it represents an odd number of children? (Type 2)

STUDENT NOTES TO THEIR FUTURE FORGETFUL SELVES

Example 1:

Label each row with a number:

Favorite Fruit

🍎	△ △ △ △ △	☐
🍌	△ △ △	☐
🍇	△ △ △ △ △ △	☐
🍐	△ △ △ △	☐

1 vote = △

Example 2:

Make a row for Saturday and a row for Sunday showing how many apples were sold each day. On Sunday they sold an odd number of apples.

🍎 = 2 apples sold

Things to Remember:

Example 3:

CHECK-YOUR-UNDERSTANDING QUESTIONS

MILD

Label each row for this pictograph:

Name	Number of Pizzas Sold
Monday	🍕 🍕 🍕 🍕 🍕
Tuesday	🍕 🍕 🍕 🍕 🍕 🍕 🍕 🍕 🍕 🍕
Wednesday	🍕 🍕 🍕 🍕
Thursday	🍕 🍕 🍕 🍕 🍕 🍕 🍕 🍕
Friday	🍕 🍕 🍕 🍕 🍕 🍕
🍕 = 5 pizzas	

Source: pizza from iStock.com/subkontr

MEDIUM

Add a row to the bottom for cotton candy ice cream that has an odd number of votes.

Flavor	Number of Votes
Vanilla	🍦 🍦 🍦 🍦
Chocolate	🍦 🍦 🍦 🍦
Strawberry	🍦 🍦 🍦 🍦 🍦 🍦 🍦
Butterscotch	🍦 🍦 🍦 🍦 🍦
Cookie Dough	
🍦 = 2 votes	

Source: ice cream from iStock.com/Marina Parfenova

Make a pictograph from this data.

Favorite Color

Red	15 Students
Blue	30 Students
Purple	24 Students
Green	21 Students
Other	18 Students

Author Notes

This task is a less traditional thin-slicing task because there is more asked of the students during each question. Type 2 questions do not need to be odd numbers that are added but should have some qualifier so that a student doesn't just draw one or two of a given object to complete the task.

Notes to My Future Forgetful Self

TASK 47: BARON VON GRAPH

TASK

This task has students interpret bar graphs, create data tables, and create bar graphs.

Content: interpreting data, constructing bar graphs from data tables

Competencies: willingness to take risks

Seen Before: data of some kind (pictographs, tables, charts, etc.)

Before You Launch: Use the images available for download to create slips of paper that you give to groups to keep them in flow.

This task's images, extension scripts, and Check-Your-Understanding Questions are available for download at **https://companion.corwin.com/courses/BTCK5Tasks**

LAUNCH SCRIPT

Teacher: Hello my fascinating mathematicians. Have you ever seen a bar graph before?

Students: Yes, no, etc. [teacher leads students to discussing what a bar graph is and what it does]

Teacher: Well, I've got this bar graph here and I was wondering if you could help me understand it. The first thing I want to know is, how many people voted in total?

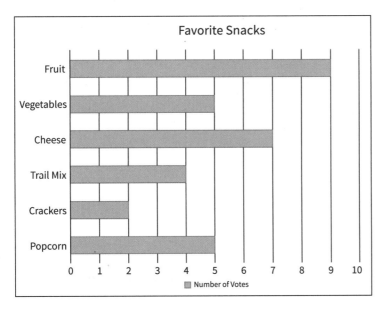

TASK SEQUENCE

Type 1: Interpreting a Bar Graph

Look at this bar graph:

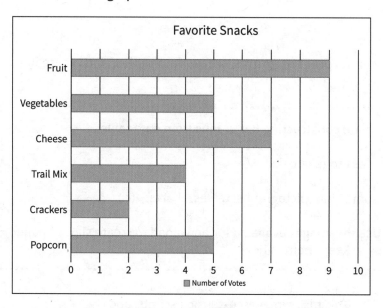

1. How many people voted in total?

2. Which snacks were the most and least popular?

3. How many more people voted for cheese than crackers?

Look at this bar graph:

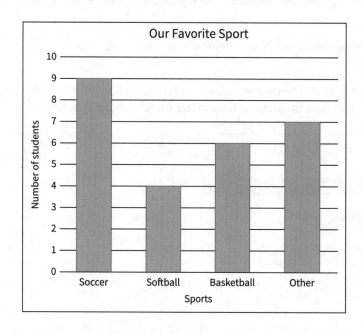

4. What is the total number of students?

5. What sport was the second most popular?

6. How many people's favorite sport isn't soccer or softball or baseball?

Look at this bar graph:

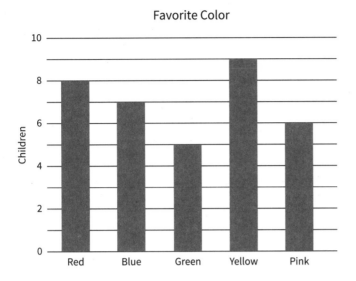

7. How many children were asked in total?

8. How many children's favorite color is red or pink?

9. How many children prefer yellow over green?

Look at this bar graph:

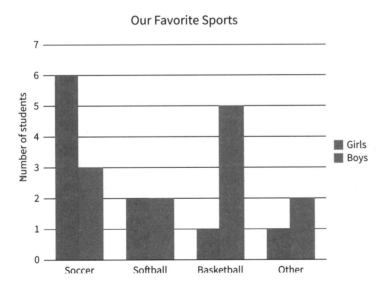

10. How many children are there in total?

11. Did more boys or girls vote?

12. How many more girls than boys prefer soccer?

Type 2: Create a Bar Graph From Data

Hint: Take a look at the elements in the graphs you looked at. What do you need to make your graph?

13. Create a bar graph from this survey data sheet:

Favorite Color	Blue	Green	Yellow	Red	Other
Number of Students	8	6	4	10	3

14. Create a bar graph from this survey data sheet:

What is your favorite
Subject?

Subject	Student votes
Math	＋＋＋ ＋＋＋ |||
English	＋＋＋ ＋＋＋
Science	＋＋＋	
Social	||||
Art	＋＋＋ ＋＋＋	
P.E	＋＋＋ ＋＋＋ ||||

15. Create a double bar graph from this data sheet:

Eye Color

Eye Color	Blue	Brown	Green	Hazel
Grade 4	＋＋＋		＋＋＋ ＋＋＋		|||	||
Grade 5	＋＋＋ ＋＋＋	＋＋＋ ||||	＋＋＋		

16. Create a double bar graph from this data sheet:

What is your favorite
season?

Season	Winter	Spring	Summer	Autumn
Grade 4s+5s	✓✓✓✓✓✓✓✓	✓✓✓ ✓ ✓	✓✓✓ ✓✓ ✓✓✓	✓ ✓✓ ✓
Grade 2s+3s	✓✓ ✓✓✓ ✓ ✓	✓✓✓✓ ✓✓✓	✓ ✓ ✓ ✓ ✓	✓✓ ✓✓ ✓

Type 3: Creating a Data Sheet From a Bar Graph

17. Create a data sheet from this graph:

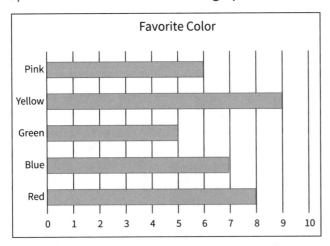

18. Create a data sheet from this graph:

19. Create a data sheet from this graph:

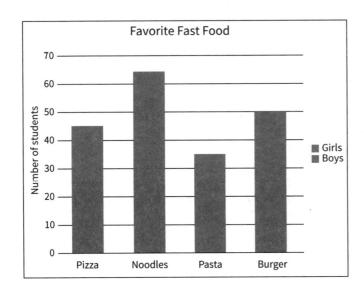

20. Create a data sheet from this graph:

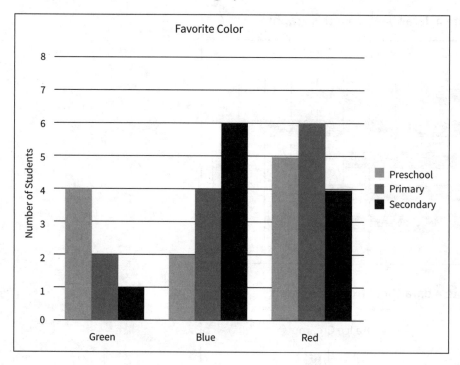

21. Create a data sheet from this graph:

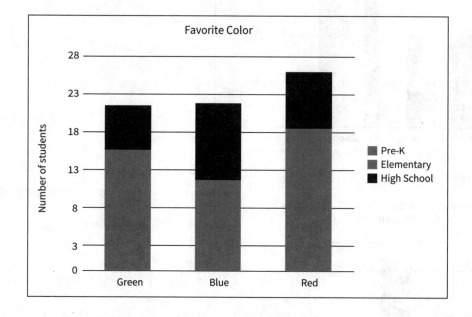

CONSOLIDATION TASKS

Teacher: I have written on the board three questions like the ones you just did in your group, but I may have put them in the wrong order. Turn to your neighbor and discuss what the order should be and why.

A   Create a data sheet from this graph. (Type 3)

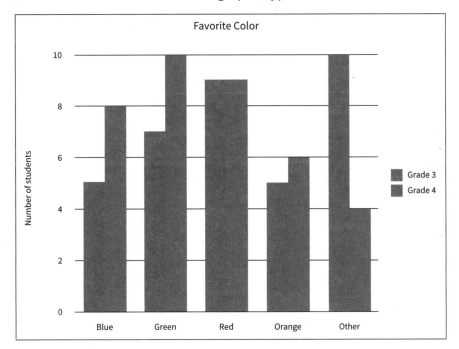

B   Based on the below graph, how many kids like soccer? (Type 1)

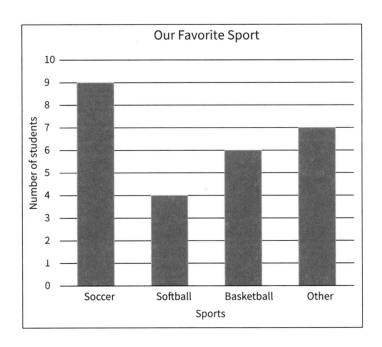

C   Create a bar graph from this data sheet: (Type 2)

Fruit	Apple	Orange	Banana	Kiwi	Blueberry	Grape
People	35	30	10	25	40	5

STUDENT NOTES TO THEIR FUTURE FORGETFUL SELVES

Example 1:

How many total votes were there?

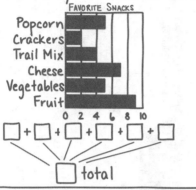

FAVORITE SNACKS

Popcorn
Crackers
Trail Mix
Cheese
Vegetables
Fruit

0 2 4 6 8 10

□ + □ + □ + □ + □ + □

□ total

Example 2:

Create a bar graph from this data:

Fruit	Apple	Orange	Banana	Kiwi	Blueberry	Grape
People	35	30	10	25	40	5

Things to Remember:

Example 3:

CHECK-YOUR-UNDERSTANDING QUESTIONS

MILD

Look at this graph and answer these questions:

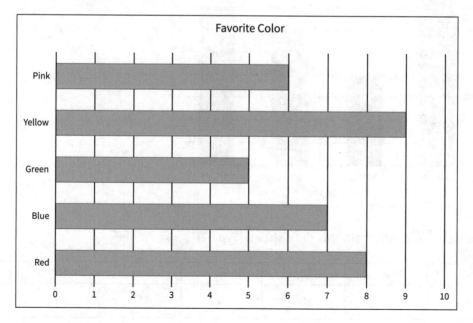

Favorite Color

Pink
Yellow
Green
Blue
Red

0 1 2 3 4 5 6 7 8 9 10

A. How many total votes were there?

B. How many people like yellow?

MEDIUM

Create a bar graph from this data sheet:

Eye Color

Eye Color	Blue	Brown	Green	Hazel
Grade 4	‖‖ I	‖‖ ‖‖ I	III	II
Grade 5	‖‖ ‖‖	‖‖ IIII	‖‖	I

SPICY

Create a data sheet from this graph:

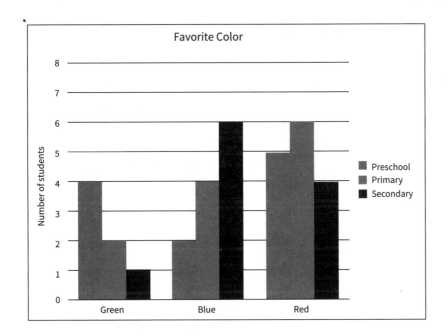

Favorite Color

(Legend: Preschool, Primary, Secondary)

Author Notes

Like Task 46 Picture the Pictograph, this is sliced thicker because of the time that a group will spend on one graph or data sheet. Although these graphs and data sheets are yours to use, you could also have students make their own surveys or graphs and have students investigate those.

Notes to My Future Forgetful Self

TASK 48: KEEP THE BALANCE

TASK

This task has students find the value of various objects by using clues from a balance scale. This task is the pictorial precursor to the next task, Task 49 I'm Thinking of a Number.

Content: solving for an unknown value using a balance scale

Competencies: collaboration, empathy

Seen Before: equality

Before You Launch: This task can go very fast, which is why collaboration and empathy are the competencies. You might want to remind your students to work as a team, be patient with each other, and take care of each other. You might even want to use a collaboration rubric with this task. Use the images available for download to create slips of paper that you give to groups to keep them in flow.

online resources

This Task Sequence, Consolidation Tasks, and Check-Your-Understanding Questions are available for download at **https://companion.corwin.com/courses/BTCK5Tasks**

LAUNCH SCRIPT

Teacher: Hello my talented mathematicians! Have you ever seen one of these? [teacher holds up a real or a picture of a balance scale] Turn and talk to the person beside you about what it is and what it does. [teacher facilitates discussion about balance scales and their use]

Teacher: This is called a balance scale, and it can help us figure out how much something weighs. When one side is heavier than the other side, it drops lower, but if both sides weigh the same, they balance in the middle. It is your job today to figure out the value of each object. Let's start here. If this scale is balanced, what is the value of this kitty? [teacher shows first image]

Source: balance clip art by istock.com/4evar; kitten icon by istock.com/Gastonbolivario

TASK SEQUENCE

Type 1: One-Step Equations

1. What is the value of this kitty?

2. Oh, I think his weight changed. What about now?

3. And now?

4. What about now?

5. Now?

6. Now?

7. Now?

Hint: What is the value of two puppies? Can that help you find the value of one puppy?

What is the value of **one** puppy for each of the following scales?

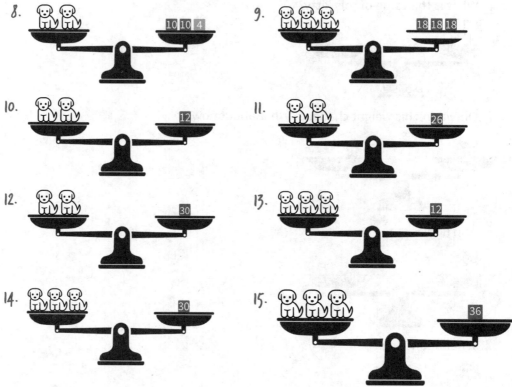

8.   [puppy][puppy]   [10][10][4]
9.   [puppy][puppy][puppy]   [18][18][18]
10. [puppy][puppy]   [12]
11. [puppy][puppy]   [26]
12. [puppy][puppy]   [30]
13. [puppy][puppy][puppy]   [12]
14. [puppy][puppy][puppy]   [30]
15. [puppy][puppy][puppy]   [36]

Type 2 Two-Step Equations

Hint: What would the value of both puppies be?

What is the value of **one** puppy or **one** gecko?

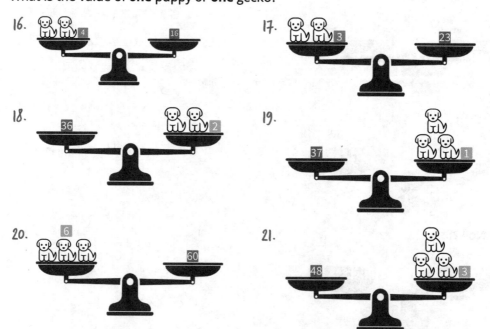

16. [puppy][puppy][4]   [16]
17. [puppy][puppy][3]   [23]
18. [36]   [puppy][puppy][2]
19. [37]   [puppy][puppy][puppy][1]
20. [6][puppy][puppy][puppy]   [60]
21. [48]   [puppy][puppy][puppy][3]

Source: balance clip art by istock.com/4evar; puppy icon by istock.com/sudowoodo;

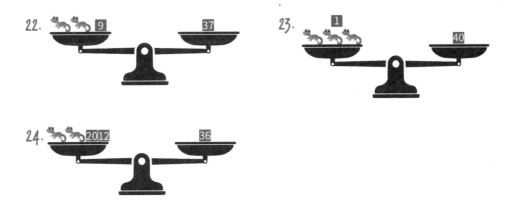

22.
23.
24.

Type 3: Three-Step Equations

What is the value of **one** gecko?

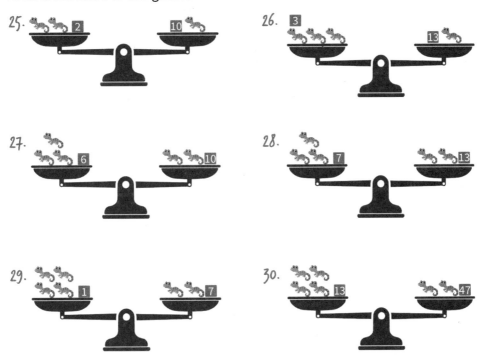

25.
26.
27.
28.
29.
30.

CONSOLIDATION TASKS

Teacher: I have written on the board three questions like the ones you just did in your group, but I may have put them in the wrong order. Turn to your neighbor and discuss what the order should be and why.

What is the value of one gecko?

A.

(Type 3)

Source: balance clip art by istock.com/4evar; gecko icon by istock.com/svaga

B. (Type 2)

C. (Type 1)

STUDENT NOTES TO THEIR FUTURE FORGETFUL SELVES

Example 1:

What is the value of one △?

$$\triangle + \triangle = 26$$
$$\triangle = \_\_\_$$

Example 2:

What is the value of one △?

19   △△5

Things to Remember:

Example 3:

CHECK-YOUR-UNDERSTANDING QUESTIONS

MILD

What is the value of one gecko?

A.

B.

MEDIUM

What is the value of one gecko?

A.

B.

Source: balance icon by istock.com/4zevar; gecko icon by istock.com/svaga

SPICY

What is the value of one gecko?

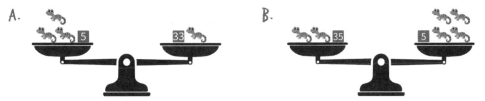

A.

B.

Source: balance icon by istock.com/4zevar; gecko icon by istock.com/svaga

Author Notes

Having an actual balance scale for the kids to work with concretely would be very beneficial for this task. If you are unable to during the task, giving students experience beforehand can help build conceptual understanding.

Notes to My Future Forgetful Self

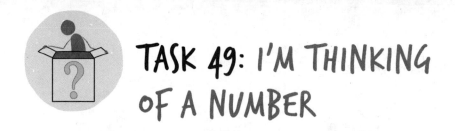

TASK 49: I'M THINKING OF A NUMBER

TASK

This task has students solving one- and two-step equations.

Content: solving one- and two-step equations

Competencies: collaboration, empathy

Seen Before: equality, adding, subtracting, multiplying, dividing, decimals

Before You Launch: This task can go very fast, which is why collaboration and empathy are the competencies. You might want to remind your students to work as a team, be patient with each other, and take care of each other. You might even want to use a collaboration rubric with this task. This task works well with the banner.

LAUNCH SCRIPT

Teacher: Hello my thoughtful mathematicians. Today we are going to play a game called *I'm Thinking of a Number*. The way it works is that I will think of a number. It can be any number. Your job is to guess my number. But because my number can be any number, I am going to give you one hint.

Teacher: Let's practice. I'm thinking of a number. Here is your hint—if you add 3 to my number, the answer will be 12. What is my number?

Students: 9!

Teacher: Great! Let's try another one. I'm thinking of a number. Here is your hint— if I multiply my number by 2 and then add 3, the answer will be 15. What's my number?

Students: 6!

Teacher: OK. Before we go on, we have to learn how to write what I just said.
[teacher writes $\boxed{?} \times 2 + 3 = 15$ on the board]

Teacher: There are three rules to this game. First, you can use a calculator—but there is only one calculator allowed per group. Second, if you use a calculator, you have to write on the board what you type into the calculator. Third, you have to check your answer.

Teacher: So, let's check your answer to the last one using a calculator. You said that the answer was 6. So, that means that 6 × 2 + 3 should equal 15 [teacher writes 6 × 2 + 3 on the board, then types it into a calculator]. Yes. The calculator shows that the answer is 15.

Teacher: OK. I am thinking of a new number. Here is your clue—if you add 3.44 to my number, the answer is 10.87. What's my number?

TASK SEQUENCE

Type 1: One-Step Equations—Adding and Subtracting

1. $\boxed{?}$ + 8.61 = 18.31

2. $\boxed{?}$ – 1.78 = 8.85

3. 12.92 + $\boxed{?}$ = 36.23

4. 8.3 + $\boxed{?}$ = 20.7

5. $\boxed{?}$ – 9.34 = 12.93

6. $\boxed{?}$ + 3.01 = 7.21

7. 18.36 – $\boxed{?}$ = 9.24

8. 13. 97 + $\boxed{?}$ = 25.98

Type 2: One-Step Equations—Multiplying and Dividing

> **Hint:** What did you do for adding and subtracting? Could the same method be used here?

9. $\boxed{?}$ × 0.3 = 0.9

10. 0.6 × $\boxed{?}$ = 1.8

11. $\boxed{?}$ ÷ 0.2 = 0.6

12. $\boxed{?}$ × 12.25 = 46.55

13. $\boxed{?}$ ÷ 2.06 = 3

14. 12.5 ÷ $\boxed{?}$ = 6.25

15. $\boxed{?}$ × 5.2 = 16.9

16. 14.05 × $\boxed{?}$ = 87.11

Type 3: Two-Step Equations

17. 0.5 × $\boxed{?}$ + 0.08 = 1.68

18. 1.5 × $\boxed{?}$ + 0.25 = 3.25

19. $\boxed{?}$ ÷ 3.2 – 1.6 = 5.4

20. $\boxed{?}$ × 2.4 – 1.2 = 8.1

21. $\boxed{?}$ × 0.1 + 0.9 = 2

22. $\boxed{?}$ × 0.75 + 0.25 = 4.75

23. $\boxed{?}$ × 0.2 + 99.4 = 108.9

24. $\boxed{?}$ ÷ 10.8 + 5.3 = 4.022

CONSOLIDATION TASKS

Teacher: I have written on the board three questions like the ones you just did in your group, but I may have put them in the wrong order. Turn to your neighbor and discuss what the order should be and why.

What's my number?

A 12.5 ÷ $\boxed{?}$ = 6.25 (Type 2)

B $\boxed{?}$ × 2.4 – 1.2 = 8.1 (Type 3)

C $\boxed{?}$ + 8.61 = 18.31 (Type 1)

STUDENT NOTES TO THEIR FUTURE FORGETFUL SELVES

Example 1:

What's my number?

$7.15 + \boxed{?} = 10.35$

$\boxed{?} = \boxed{} - \boxed{} = \boxed{}$

Example 2:

What's my number?

$4.16 \times \boxed{?} = 9.152$

Things to Remember:

Example 3:

CHECK-YOUR-UNDERSTANDING QUESTIONS

MILD

What's my number?

A. $\boxed{?} + 1.46 = 3.71$

B. $\boxed{?} - 7.5 = 7.13$

C. $13.24 - \boxed{?} = 3.04$

MEDIUM

What's my number?

A. $2.24 \times ? = 7.168$

B. $14.23 \div ? = 7.115$

C. $? \times 8.44 = 25.32$

SPICY

What's my number?

A. $? \times 0.1 + 0.9 = 2$

B. $? \div 3.2 - 1.6 = 5.4$

C. $1.5 \times ? + 0.25 = 3.25$

Author Notes

You will notice that we are not using whole numbers in this task. The reason is with whole numbers, students just do the math in their head and don't see a need to do inverse operations. We need them to do inverse operations on this task. Using decimals forces them to do so. Telling them that my number plus 7.22 is equal to 15.03 will prompt them to naturally begin to think about my number as being 15.03 – 7.22. They are using inverse operations to solve for the unknown.

The problem is that decimals can be challenging for students. This task is not about having them do a bunch of decimal arithmetic. That is not where we want the cognitive load. Hence, we give them a calculator. Having only one calculator per group ensures that they are collaborating—just like having only one marker does. Making them write on the board what they type into the calculator forces them to represent the inverse operation. And checking their answer helps them know they are correct, and then they use the banner to move on to the next task.

Notes to My Future Forgetful Self

TASK 50: WHAT ARE THE ODDS?

TASK

This task has students looking at probability (likely, not likely, certain, impossible) then finding out the exact probability of something happening.

Content: theoretical probability, fractions, percentages

Competencies: willingness to take risks

Seen Before: coins, dice, spinners

Before You Launch: The beauty of this task is that most of the groups will transition between the task types with ease. So, the knowledge is in the room. Help to mobilize that knowledge for groups that get stuck in the transitions between task types.

Note: For purposes of this printed book, the spinner used in this task is shades of gray and green. You can use a spinner with any colors you would like (e.g., red, green, blue, yellow) and adjust the task sequence accordingly.

LAUNCH SCRIPT

Teacher: Hello my fantabulous mathematicians. Today we are going to look at probability, which is the possibility of something happening. For instance, if I roll this dice, is it likely, not likely, certain, or impossible for me to roll a 6?

Students: Not likely.

Teacher: Perfect. Is it likely, not likely, certain, or impossible that I roll a number larger than 1?

TASK SEQUENCE

Type 1: Labeling Likelihood of Events Occurring

Is it likely, not likely, certain, or impossible to

1. Flip a coin and get heads?

2. Flip a coin and get tails?

3. Spin this spinner and get light gray?

4. Spin this spinner and land on a non-white section?

5. Spin the spinner and get dark green?

6. Spin the spinner and get dark gray OR light green?

7. Roll a number larger than 1?

8. Roll a number less than 3?

9. Roll a number more than 6?

10. Roll a 3?

11. Roll a number less than 5?

12. Roll an even number higher than 2?

Type 2: All Possible Outcomes

What are all the possible outcomes for

13. Flipping one coin?

14. Flipping two coins?

15. Spinning one spinner?

16. Spinning two of the above spinners?

17. Rolling one die?

18. Rolling two dice?

> **Hints:** What are all the possibilities? What are the possibilities you are hoping for?

Type 3: Theoretical Probability

What is the exact probability of

19. Flipping two coins and both are heads?

20. Flipping two coins and one is heads and the other is tails?

21. Spinning two spinners and getting light gray on one and dark green on the other?

22. Spinning two spinners and both ending up on dark gray?

23. Spinning two spinners and neither are light green?

24. Spinning two spinners and getting light gray on at least one?

25. Rolling two dice and both numbers are even?

26. Rolling two dice and both numbers are below 3?

27. Rolling two dice and both numbers are more than 2?

28. Rolling two dice and the sum of the numbers is less than 8?

29. Rolling two dice and both numbers are the same?

30. Rolling two dice and the numbers are consecutive (3, 4 or 2, 1, etc.)?

CONSOLIDATION TASKS

Teacher: I have written on the board three questions like the ones you just did in your group, but I may have put them in the wrong order. Turn to your neighbor and discuss what the order should be and why.

A What are the chances of rolling two dice and both dice being odd numbers? (Type 3)

B Is it certain, likely, unlikely, or impossible to roll a die and get a number greater than 4? (Type 1)

C What are all the possibilities when you flip 2 coins? (Type 2)

STUDENT NOTES TO THEIR FUTURE FORGETFUL SELVES

Example 1:

Rolling a number more than 1 on a dice; is that likely or not likely?

Dice 1, 2, 3, 4, 5, 6
      □ □ □ □ □
      are more than 1

Example 2:

What are all the possibilities when you flip 2 coins?

Things to Remember:

Example 3:

CHECK-YOUR-UNDERSTANDING QUESTIONS

MILD

Is it likely, not likely, certain, or impossible to

A. Roll a 4?

B. Roll a number more 2?

C. Roll a number more than 6?

MEDIUM

What are all the possibilities for

A. Flipping 2 coins?

B. Spinning 2 spinners?

C. Rolling 2 dice?

What is the exact probability of

A. Rolling two dice and both are the same number?

B. Flipping two coins and both are tails?

C. Rolling two dice and the sum is less than 6?

Author Notes

This task is a nice and easy entry point for students, starting with likelihood and then all possibilities. It may be beneficial to give students dice, spinners, and coins if they are having trouble conceptualizing the probability.

Notes to My Future Forgetful Self

PART 4
FROM PAGE TO PRACTICE

If less is more, just think how much more more would be.

—Dr. Frasier Crane
Frasier, Season 7, Episode 13

We have included in this book 20 non-curricular tasks and 30 curricular tasks. This is a lot. But it is not enough. These tasks are for students and teachers from kindergarten to Grade 5, and although each of the tasks can span multiple grades, they do not span all grades and all curricula. And although we believe that every task in this book can inform every teacher's BTC practice regardless of grade or curriculum, the reality is that not every task is relevant for the students you are currently teaching. You are going to need more tasks. This part of the book gives you access to more tasks— both by providing links to archives where you can find more tasks and by giving you the tools to make your own tasks. It is broken into five sections:

- Where to Find More Tasks

- How to Thin-Slice From Scratch

- How to Thin-Slice Existing Curriculum Resources

- How to Thin-Slice Word Problems

- How to Thick-Slice

Each section ends by providing you with access to downloadable task templates into which you can embed your work to build a living archive of tasks for your—and others'—thinking classroom(s).

WHERE TO FIND MORE TASKS

As mentioned, we have included in this book 50 tasks that can be used across a wide range of grades and differing perseverance levels, which is plenty for you to build and sustain a thinking classroom. You will be able to reuse many of these year after year. But, things change. The curriculum you teach may change. Or the grade you are teaching may change. And, for sure, your students will change. Whatever the reason, you may find yourself in need of different tasks—both curricular and non-curricular. In this section, we have provided you with a catalog of resources should you wish to look for more tasks. However, lists of resources are like lists of tasks—they can go on forever. And when they go on forever, choosing becomes difficult. For that reason, we have not provided you with a large catalog of resources. Instead, we have provided you with a small catalog of good resources—resources that we have drawn good tasks from, both curricular and non-curricular, and have used to both build and sustain our thinking classrooms.

These resources have two things in common. First, they are all archives of rich tasks— tasks that can be used across a wide range of grades, contexts, and curricula to invoke rich mathematical discussions that span multiple mathematical topics. This richness makes them ideal for use in a thinking classroom. Second, they are each indexed in a way that makes it easy for you to choose a task to use with your students. Most often, this indexing is based on curricular content. This is not to say that these can only be used as rich curricular tasks. Remember that all thinking math tasks invoke math content of some type. Whether or not that content is part of your curriculum is what determines whether a rich task is a curricular or a non-curricular task.

What follows is a limited catalog of resources from which you can get more good thinking tasks. Each resource is accompanied by a brief description of what the resource offers and how best to use it in your thinking classroom.

Open Middle

https://www.openmiddle.com/

Open middle tasks can be thought of both generally and specifically. In general terms, an open middle task is any task that has a well-defined beginning and a well-defined end but has a lot of options for how to proceed through the task. A specific version of open middle tasks is a collection of tasks called *Open Middle,* co-founded by Nanette Johnson and Robert Kaplinsky. You saw an example of an Open Middle task in Chapter 1.

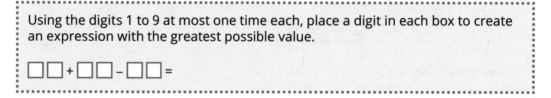

These tasks are a nice twist on routine or algorithmic work in that they require students to think deeply about the underlying ideas behind concepts as simple as two-digit addition and subtraction. Sometimes there is an ideal solution. Sometimes there is not. Regardless, the solution is not the important part. It's the process that is important. It's the middle that is important.

Open Middle tasks can be found on the Open Middle website and in Robert Kaplinsky's (2019) book, *Open Middle Math: Problems That Unlock Student Thinking, Grades 6–12.* The Open Middle website is nicely indexed by grade and by topic and contains large numbers of deep-thinking curricular tasks.

Which One Doesn't Belong?

https://wodb.ca/index.html

Which One Doesn't Belong? (WODB) is an idea that began with Christopher Danielson (2016) in his book *Which One Doesn't Belong? A Shapes Book,* and has lived on in the WODB website curated by Mary Bourassa. WODB tasks are always presented as a 2 × 2 grid with an object in each cell. The objective is to identify which of the four objects doesn't belong. For example,

(by Pam Wilson)

So, is it the 9 that doesn't belong because it is the only single-digit number? Or is it the 43 because it is the only non-square number, or the only prime number? Or is it the 16 because it is the only even number? Of course, there is no one right answer. But there are lots of things to notice. Like, did you notice that all the two-digit numbers have a sum of the digits equal to 7? Did you notice that 16 is the only square of a square? Did you notice that 43 is the only number where the tens-digit is larger than the ones-digit? And so on. With every noticing, students are propelled into a wider and wider assortment of mathematics. WODB are thinking tasks. They work great in a thinking classroom setting. They can be thin-sliced or thick-sliced. Some of them work great with a banner.

The WODB website is indexed by shapes, numbers, and graphs. And, although the website is not indexed by grade, each task is applicable across a wide range of grades. Students in different grades will just notice different things based on what they have learned so far.

NRICH

https://nrich.maths.org/frontpage

NRICH is an archive of rich math tasks aimed at "enriching the mathematical experiences of all learners." It is one of the Millennium Mathematics Projects at the University of Cambridge. It is indexed by early years (ages 3–5), primary (ages 5–11), and secondary (ages 11–18). Each of these age bands is further broken down into big ideas such as number, measurement, shape and space, geometry, algebra, and statistics, depending on the age band. Each of these big ideas is further broken down into specific math topics such as adding fractions, area and perimeter, and time, to name only a few. And each of these specific math topics leads to numerous tasks—each of which offers you links to the problem itself, tips on getting started, possible student solutions, and teacher's resources. In short, NRICH is an incredibly rich archive of rich tasks for getting your students to think.

3 Act Tasks

https://gfletchy.com/3-act-lessons/

The concept of a 3 Act Task is rather simple. In Act 1, students are shown an image or a video designed to engage and perplex them. For example, in *The Orange* task, students are shown a video of an orange being placed on one end of a balance scale, and then Unifix cubes are placed one-by-one on the other side of the balance scale. Before the question is even asked, the question that forms in students' minds is, "How many Unifix cubes will it take to balance out with the orange?" In Act 2, students work to answer the question from Act 1. During Act 2, they may ask for and be given more information, like the weight of one cube and the weight of the orange. Finally, in Act 3, students share their thinking and the teacher reveals how the scenario is resolved. In *The Orange,* there is a video of cubes being placed on the balance scale until it balances.

Although the idea of 3 Act Tasks originated with Dan Meyer, the production of video and resources has been taken up by several people in the math education community. The link we provide you here is to Graham Fletcher's website where he has archived more than 80 3 Act Tasks specifically for Grades K–7. Each task comes with the necessary videos and lesson plan and is indexed to the CCSS Standards as well as to the big idea that is addressed through the task.

Each 3 Act Task is a rich curricular thinking task that works great in a thinking classroom. They can be thick-sliced, and they are a great context in which to focus on consolidation.

Visual Patterns

https://www.visualpatterns.org/

Visual Patterns was started by Fawn Nguyen in 2013 and is a collection of 500 patterns for students to engage with. For example, consider pattern #3:

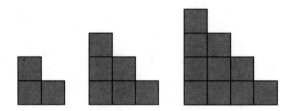

What you want to do with this is up to you. For example,

- ▶ Turn it into a number pattern (3, 6, 10, …).
- ▶ Have students draw the next shape or the next three shapes.
- ▶ Have students continue the number pattern for the next three terms.
- ▶ Have students figure out how many squares will be needed for the 10th shape in the pattern, or the 20th, or the 100th.

Each option is a rich task that integrates well into the thinking classroom. They can be thick-sliced and, like 3 Act Tasks, are a great context for you to work on the lesson closing.

Teaching Through Problems Worth Solving

http://aliciaburdess.weebly.com/problems-worth-solving-in-a-thinking-classroom.html

Teaching Through Problems Worth Solving is a collection of three books available online for free. Each book contains a collection of tasks archived by Alicia Burdess. Each book is indexed to a grade (2, 3, and 8), and they are written with the assumption that you are using them in a thinking classroom, so the tasks in each book are divided into two categories:

1. Problems to Create a Thinking Classroom

2. Problems to Target the Curriculum

The first of these is a collection of non-curricular tasks that you can use to build a culture of thinking while the second category contains tasks that are designed to address curricular content through a thinking classroom pedagogy. The curricular tasks include learner outcomes: Number Sense, Patterns and Relations, Shape and Space: Measurement, Shape and Space: 2D and 3D Shapes, and Statistics and Probability. This resource integrates seamlessly with the thinking classroom.

SK Math Tasks

https://tasks.kylewebb.ca/

This website is an archive of links to more than 800 curricular math tasks indexed by grade and topic. And for those who work in Saskatchewan, Canada, the tasks are also indexed by your provincial outcomes. SK Math Tasks was created by Kyle Webb and Maegan Giroux and, like Teaching Through Problems Worth Solving, was specifically pulled together to support the teaching of math content in a thinking classroom.

Because it as an archive of links, using this resource is going to expose you to a wide array of resources not mentioned in this list, from Menu Math to Desmos to Math Pickle, to name only a few. The content on this website integrates super well with thinking classrooms and will take you down the best kind of rabbit hole.

> Numeracy does not so much lead upwards in an ascending pursuit of abstraction as it moves outward toward an ever richer engagement with life's diverse contexts and situations.
>
> —Robert Orrill (2001)

Numeracy Tasks

buildingthinkingclassrooms.com/numeracy-tasks

On the Building Thinking Classrooms website there is a resource for Numeracy Tasks. Numeracy is about applying basic ideas from math across a wide array of contexts. This resource provides you with tasks indexed to grade bands to help you do just that. Each task will offer your students a context that has been shown to be engaging to them and ask them to resolve a dilemma. Because of the ambiguity inherent in real-life situations, each task is open to interpretation—each task is open beginning. And because of the varied places students can start, each task has multiple solutions—each task is open ended. Likewise, as students move from an ambiguous beginning to a varied ending, there are multiple solution paths they can take—each task is open middle. Taken together, these tasks are rich thinking tasks that intersect with wide arrays of content. They are also amazing tasks around which to develop students' competencies with everything from perseverance to tolerance for ambiguity.

BTC Facebook Group

https://bit.ly/3VRupE6

There are more than 40 different Facebook groups dedicated to BTC and you should definitely check out which ones are relevant to you. There is a K–2 group and a 3–5 group, both of which have more than 10,000 members. These are incredible spaces to get support from teachers who are willing to walk alongside you in their own BTC journeys. The main BTC group has nearly 60,000 members at the time of this printing who are likewise engaged in the pursuit of BTC and who are ready to provide support to anyone who asks.

The main BTC Facebook group has been archiving tasks for the thinking classroom for some time now and has built up an amazing repertoire of non-curricular and curricular tasks indexed by grade. This is a living document to which members of the BTC Facebook group are able to contribute tasks that have been used in their own classrooms. In addition to the tasks indexed by grade, each spreadsheet provides you with a list of resources for additional tasks. Like SK Math Tasks, this is a rabbit hole well worth going down.

***

Despite our efforts to keep this list short, the resources we have shared lead to, in some cases, massive archives of tasks. The indexing helps you to wade through them, but you will still have to make some effort to select tasks for your students. This will inevitably help you build a repertoire of good tasks that you have found and tested in your thinking classroom. If you wish to format these tasks as we have done in this book, we have provided templates to help you do so—one for curricular and one for non-curricular tasks. You can download them at https://companion.corwin.com/courses/BTCK5Tasks. Whether you wish to do this for your own records or to share your emergent good tasks with colleagues, these templates will help you to dissect and delineate the tasks into their salient and actionable indicators and elements.

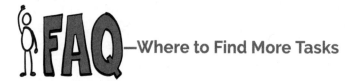 **—Where to Find More Tasks**

 How do I know if a task is good or not?

 The best way is to try it with students. You can try to anticipate what will happen, but to really see if it is good, you need to see how it works with real students in a real classroom. After a while, your ability to anticipate will get better. Also remember that tasks are not fixed. Every task can be edited to better suit a situation. It can be made easier or harder. You can add a launch script and extension scripts. You are the ultimate author of the tasks as enacted in your classroom.

Is the demarcation between curricular and non-curricular important? Wouldn't it be better to just do everything with curricular tasks?

Yes and no. Yes, demarcation is important. No, you cannot build a thinking classroom with only curricular tasks. The research showed that students need four to six experiences with non-curricular tasks when you are first building a thinking classroom. These tasks need to feel fun to students. Being non-curricular helps with that. Likewise, being non-curricular makes it safe for students to be different in the math classroom. Non-curricular tasks create a fun and safe context to build a culture of thinking. You also need some non-curricular tasks to reestablish this culture after a long break from school—like winter or spring break.

Q I don't have time to do non-curricular tasks. I have too much content to cover.

A You are correct. You have a lot of content to cover, and this takes time. And when students are not thinking, everything takes more time. When students are thinking, however, everything goes faster. Once you build a culture of thinking in your classroom and you begin to thin-slice, you will more than make up the time you lost doing non-curricular tasks. You have to go slow to go fast.

> You have to go slow to go fast.

HOW TO THIN-SLICE FROM SCRATCH

In Part 3 of this book, we provided you with 30 curricular thin-sliced sequences of tasks. Although these are not all relevant to you and your students, we hope that you have looked at all of them and seen how thin-slicing can be a platform on which you not only can enact several of the BTC practices, but also cover curricular content in your thinking classroom. Thin-slicing is important and effective to student learning in a thinking classroom.

Time and time again, however, we encounter requests for more information on, and more examples of, thin-slicing. Underpinning these requests is a belief that thin-slicing is some mysterious and magical process only achievable by those who are experts at BTC and have full mastery of the curriculum. We hope that having now seen 30 examples of thin-slicing, the mystique of thin-slicing has been somewhat dispelled. There is no magic or mystery here. You do not need mastery of either BTC or the curriculum to achieve it. What you need is a sense of what you are teaching and what your goals are as well as the courage to try, to have it not go perfect, and to try again.

Between the two of us, we can count on one hand the number of times we created a thin-slicing sequence that was so good, and worked so perfectly, that we felt it needed no editing after using it with students. For each of the other hundreds of times, we come out of a lesson saying things like,

- "OK. The transition from task 6 to 7 was too big. We needed to have more tasks in between."

- "There was too much redundancy from tasks 3 to 6 and the kids were getting bored. We need to cut some of those out."

- "We need to have more Type 2 tasks. Not for everyone, but some groups needed more experience with Type 2 before we move to Type 3."

And so on. Perfection comes from experience, not planning. This is not to say that planning is unimportant. You still want your first effort to be thoughtful and purposeful. Just don't expect perfection.

> So, keep records, take notes, and be willing to reflect and revise immediately after you have used a thin-slicing sequence.

There are two points to keep in mind here. First, you need to understand that the *second* time you use a thin-sliced sequence will be *way* better than the first. But not nearly as good as the third. As mentioned, perfection comes from experience, but not experience unexamined. High school teachers have the privilege of being able to reflect, revise, and retry almost immediately. However, most K–5 elementary teachers have to wait a whole year before you get to try a sequence again. But in a year's time, you will not remember what went well and what didn't the last time you used a sequence. So, keep records, take notes, and be willing to reflect and revise immediately after you have used a thin-slicing sequence. You may not get to retry right away, but you can still reflect and revise right away.

Second, if it goes badly, or less than perfectly, none of your students are sitting around the dinner table that night saying, "Wow! The teacher really screwed up her thin-slicing today." The only person who will know is you. You are your biggest critic. Your students only know that some tasks require more perseverance than others—but perseverance they have. You will see where you can improve and then you will. Next year's students will not know that they are receiving a better thin-sliced sequence than this year's students. They just know that this is fun, that they are learning, and that, sometimes, they will need to persevere. Only you will know whether the need to persevere is a result of a deliberate switch from Type 1 to Type 2 tasks or from an unanticipated increase in complexity within a type. You will work to smooth out the latter and be ready with hints for the former.

Having said all that, what follows is a beginner's guide to creating your own thin-slicing sequences. For the purposes of this discussion, we will consider the topic of division of two- and three-digit numbers by a one- and two-digit number (e.g., $48 \div 4$) using the area model. Generally, educators are more familiar with the area model as a powerful mediator for thinking about multiplying a two- or three-digit number by a single digit number—for example, 4×12. But, just like 4×12 can be thought of as $4 \times (10 + 2) = (4 \times 10) + (4 \times 2) = 40 + 8 = 48$, $48 \div 4$ can be thought of as $(40 \div 4) + (8 \div 4) = 10 + 2 = 12$ using the same model.

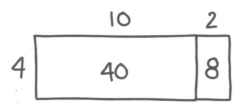

So, how do we build a thin-sliced sequence for this topic?

Step 1: Identify

The first step in creating a thin-sliced sequence is to identify the different types of tasks that your topic will divide into. In Part 1 of this book, we looked at an example of adding two-digit numbers. All tasks for this topic are not of the same type. There are tasks where no regrouping is needed (21 + 56), where regrouping the ones into tens and ones is needed (28 + 34), and where regrouping the tens into hundreds and tens is needed (85 + 42). There are also tasks where regrouping both the ones and tens are needed (45 + 97). Regardless of the topic, tasks always come in types. And types can often be identified by thinking about level of difficulty. For the example we are going to consider here, division of two- and three-digit numbers by a single digit using the area model, 48 ÷ 2 will be easier than 56 ÷ 4. Let's look at why that is.

The first task enables the students to break the 48 into a 40 and an 8, both of which are divisible by 2.

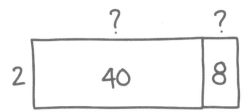

Breaking a two-digit number into its tens and ones is a natural action on the part of students and is, therefore, one type of task. Note that 48 ÷ 2 works well for this but 56 ÷ 4 does not. If the students perform the same action, they will get 50 + 6, neither of which is divisible by 4. To solve such a task, students would need to recognize that in order to get dividends that are divisible by 4, they need to break 56 into 40 and 16.

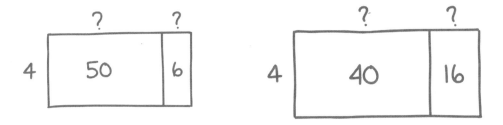

This is initially unnatural and requires them to make a cognitive jump. In other words, 56 ÷ 4 is a different type of task from 48 ÷ 2. And it is a more challenging type.

Now consider, 396 ÷ 3. Here, the dividend can be broken into 300 + 90 + 6, all of which are divisible by 3.

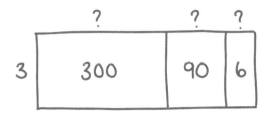

So, is this of the same type as 48 ÷ 2 because it follows the natural decomposition of the dividend? Or is it a different type because it has a three-digit dividend? And if it is different, is it more or less challenging than 56 ÷ 4? What about 258 ÷ 6? This is clearly not of the same type as 396 ÷ 3 because breaking it into its hundreds, tens, and ones produces 200 + 50 + 8, none of which are divisible by 6. It would need to be broken into 60 + 60 + 60 + 60 + 18, 120 + 120 + 18, or 240 + 18 in order for division using the area model to work nicely. So, is it of the same type as 56 ÷ 4 or is it different?

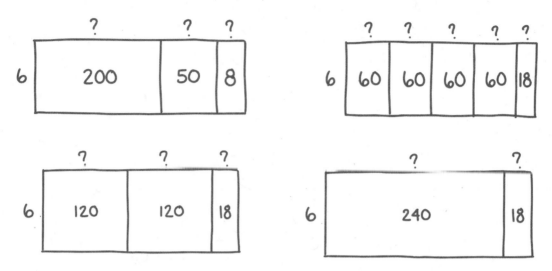

What about 192 ÷ 16? To solve this one, students would need to recognize that 192 can be broken into 160 and 32, both of which are divisible by 16.

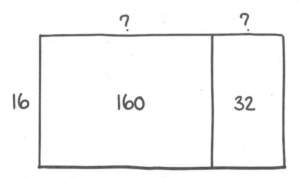

Step 2: Grouping

Once we have a list of possible types, we begin the process of grouping. Grouping is the process of deciding that what you may have thought were two types are actually just variations of the same type. Consider the examples we have seen so far:

A. 48 ÷ 2

B. 56 ÷ 4

C. 396 ÷ 3

D. 258 ÷ 6

E. 192 ÷ 16

We can decide that these are all different types or we can decide that A and B are of the same type because they are a two-digit number divided by a one-digit number. Likewise, C and D are of the same type, and E is its own type. Finally, we can decide that A and C are of the same type because these can nicely be broken into their base-ten parts (40 + 8 and 300 + 90 + 3, respectively) with each part still being divisible by the divisor. This is not true for B and D where they need to be broken into something other than their base-ten parts (40 + 16 and 240 + 18, respectively). In this way of thinking, E is more like B and D (160 + 32), but still different because the divisor is a two-digit number. We have to decide which of these types, if any, need to be grouped together.

Step 3: Sequencing

Regardless of the way we decide to group (or not) these types together, we then need to sequence them such that the tasks go from least complex to most complex. If we decide that these are all different types of tasks, then it seems reasonable to decide that the sequence would be A-B-C-D-E. If we have decided that A and B, as well as C and D, are the same types, then we would likely decide that the correct sequence is AB-CD-E. Finally, if we group A with C and B with D, then we would likely also decide that the correct sequence is AC-BD-E.

Having said all that, the reality is that we do not get to *decide* these things at all. It is not for us to decide how students perceive similarities and differences or how they experience variations in complexity. We can anticipate how they will react, but the only way for us to know is to try it. We have tried it. And we can tell you that students have an easier time transitioning from A to C than from A to B. Beginning with, and staying with, example tasks that can all be broken into their base-ten parts, is a natural place for us to introduce the idea of division using the area model—and the transition from two-digit dividends to three-digit dividends is an increase in complexity, not a change of types. As a result, we recommend the best lumping and sequencing to be AC-BD-E. But we did not get this right the first time. Our initial attempt was AB-CD-E. It wasn't bad. It could have been better, but it wasn't bad. We are certain that none of the students were sitting around the dinner table that night talking about how bad it went. But we learned from it, and the next time we did the same lesson, we tried AC-BD-E. This was better. Getting the grouping and the sequence wrong only means that the students have to exhibit more perseverance—which they will—and that we have to provide more hints—which we do.

This is, perhaps, the most important lesson with thin-slicing—it will not be perfect the first time, and we will learn from it. Preparation helps us to anticipate a little bit. Experience helps us anticipate a lot. We can only get to perfection through imperfection. We need to have the courage to be imperfect.

> Preparation helps us to anticipate a little bit. Experience helps us anticipate a lot. We can only get to perfection through imperfection. We need to have the courage to be imperfect.

Step 4: Filling

Once we have the anticipated grouping and sequencing—whether that is informed by preparation or experience—we need to now fill in each type with increasingly complex tasks for the students to solve. Having done this before and knowing that we want to go with AC-BD-E, we are going to need more tasks than what are listed above.

Type 1 (AC)	Type 2 (BD)	Type 3 (E)
1. 39 ÷ 3	11. 72 ÷ 3	21. 288 ÷ 12
2. 48 ÷ 4	12. 56 ÷ 4	22. 345 ÷ 15
3. 88 ÷ 8	13. 75 ÷ 5	23. 176 ÷ 16
4. 69 ÷ 3	14. 84 ÷ 6	24. 399 ÷ 19
5. 84 ÷ 4	15. 91 ÷ 7	25. 532 ÷ 14
6. 85 ÷ 5	16. 426 ÷ 3	26. 420 ÷ 28
7. 396 ÷ 3	17. 726 ÷ 6	27. 825 ÷ 33
8. 848 ÷ 4	18. 258 ÷ 6	28. 902 ÷ 41
9. 636 ÷ 3	19. 245 ÷ 7	29. 875 ÷ 35
10. 488 ÷ 4	20. 352 ÷ 8	30. 989 ÷ 23

This process of selecting, grouping, sequencing, and filling is how each of the thin-sliced task sequences in Part 3 were created. There is no magic or mystery to it. We basically start where the students are and finish with what it is we want them to learn. And then we fill in the difference between those two points with a thin-sliced sequence of tasks. Every step in the process is informed either by what we know of students, what we know of curriculum, or experience trying initial drafts of the sequence. It is definitely something you can do. And it is definitely something you get better at with experience. And before you know it, you will be able to produce initial drafts of sequences in a matter of minutes.

If you wish format these sequences into a structure like we use in Part 3, you can use the Curricular Task Template at **https://companion.corwin.com/courses/BTCK5Tasks.**

 **—How to Thin-Slice From Scratch**

Q I think my biggest concern with thin-slicing is getting it wrong. What if I get the sequence wrong or the gaps between tasks are too big or too small?

A Neither of these situations is a big deal. Getting these things right will make the sequences better. But this does not mean that having them wrong makes the sequences bad. Part of building a thinking classroom is starting with non-curricular tasks to build a thinking culture in the room. The more time students spend being in a thinking classroom the stronger this culture becomes, and with it emerges perseverance and patience. These, coupled with knowledge mobility, will more than compensate for imperfections in the thin-sliced sequences. The better your students get at thinking, the less good your sequences can be. This is not to say that you shouldn't try to make them good and that you shouldn't refine your sequences as you learn what works. You definitely should. But it is not the end of the world if they are not perfect to begin with. In essence, the rewards are high and the risk is low. Take the risk and reap the rewards.

Q I notice that every sequence in Part 3 as well as the example given here has about 10 tasks per type. Won't students get bored doing so many of the same type?

A Yes and no. Yes, you need this many. And yes, some students will get bored if you make them do all 10 per type. So, don't make every group do every task. When students encounter a new type of task, they will claw their way through the first one using what they know, perseverance, and thinking. They will do the same thing on the second task and the third task. Along the way, they will begin to see patterns in the math and in their way of thinking—they are beginning to make meaning. With more tasks of the same type, this meaning becomes more and more robust until they have full understanding and proficiency with the task. For some groups, this takes 5 tasks and for others it takes 8 to 10. As groups are making their meaning, you can skip redundant tasks within a type. When you feel a group has made their meaning you can move them on to the next type of task. The reason there are 10 tasks is for the groups who need all 10 to finish making their meaning. In fact, some groups may need more than 10, which means that you need to make more as you go. This is all part of using hints and extensions (Chapter 4) to maintain flow for each group.

Q What if we don't get through the entire sequence of tasks in a lesson? Do I just start where we left off the day before?

A No. Start with some Type 1 tasks to begin with. Doing so is a type of micro-spiraling that creates opportunities for built in review before moving on to Type 2 and Type 3 tasks. Students will move through these quickly and you can skip tasks and move on to the next type as warranted.

Q What do I do if I have a group that gets through the entire sequence? Are they just done?

A No. In a thinking classroom no one group is ever done. If a group gets through all the tasks and it is time to close the lesson anyway, then close the lesson for everyone with a consolidation, meaningful notes, and/or CYU questions. If it is not time to close the lesson, then you need to find more tasks for them to do. These can be curricular or non-curricular. But they are not done.

Q Aren't worksheets and textbooks already thin-sliced? Can't we just use those?

A Yes and no. This is what the next section is about.

HOW TO THIN-SLICE EXISTING CURRICULUM RESOURCES

Whatever resource you have, from textbooks to teacher manuals to old worksheets in your file cabinets, they are all full of tasks. What makes thin-slicing effective is not tasks, but the order of the tasks. Coming back to division using the area model, 56 ÷ 4 is nothing remarkable. This task, in and of itself, can be found in every teacher resource that covers division of a two-digit dividend by a one-digit divisor. The same is true of every task in that sequence. Every task in Part 3 of this book can be found in your resources. And, hence, every task in your resources has the potential to work well in a thin-sliced sequence. You just need to reorder them.

Thin-slicing is about getting students from where they are (what they know) to where you want them to be (what you want them to know). Achieving this requires selecting, grouping, sequencing, and filling. Your resources have already done the selecting for you—they are full of tasks that you can use with your students. What you still need to do, however, is grouping, sequencing, and filling.

> Practice is about using existing knowledge, whereas thin-slicing is about forming new knowledge.

The main work will be grouping and sequencing. Now your resources will already have tasks grouped and sequenced. The problem is that more often than not, they are grouped and sequenced for the purpose of having students practice. This is not the same as thin-slicing. Practice is about using existing knowledge, whereas thin-slicing is about forming new knowledge. Regardless, there will be times when the grouping and sequencing provided by your resources is adequate for thin-slicing. But there are times when it is not, and you will have to do it yourself. For example, a textbook may have the division-using-area model as five groups in the order A-B-C-D-E. Within each of these groups, the tasks are great and in a reasonable order. All you need to do is regroup and re-sequence the tasks into AC-BD-E. You may do this right away if you have experience with the topic. Or you may do it after running the sequence provided in your textbook and then realizing that a different grouping and/or different order is needed. Regardless, if you can thin-slice from scratch, then thin-slicing from a resource is easier.

Finally, you may need to do some filling. There are two types of filling—*adding to a type* and *adding a type*. Let's look at each one more closely:

Adding to a Type

Adding to a type is, basically, the same as the filling process described in the previous section. Once your grouping and sequencing is set, you just need to inflate each type with more tasks. If your textbook and worksheets have lots of tasks, you will not have any difficulty finding what you need to complete your thin-sliced sequence. If, however, your resource is comprised of rich curricular tasks, you may need to make your own tasks to add to a type. This is relatively easy as it is just a matter of making variations to the tasks already available to you. We gave an example of this in the introduction to Part 3, but here it is again.

8. Use 2 or more of these numbers each time:

    1, 2, 3, 4, 5, 6, 7, 8

Find ways to make 10.

How can you tell when you have found all the ways?

Show your work.

Source: Appel et al. (2009, p. 85).

This task may, in and of itself, constitute a type of task for whatever content you are teaching. The problem is that this one task may not be enough for your students to complete their meaning-making process and move from partial understanding to complete understanding. They need more tasks of the same type. And the resource may not have more of these types of tasks available. So, you will have to make them. You will have to fill in the type with tasks 8.1, 8.2, and 8.3:

8.1 Use 2 or more of these numbers each time:

   1, 2, 3, 4, 5, 6, 7, 8

Find ways to make 12.

How can you tell when you have found all the ways?

Show your work.

8.2 Use 2 or more of these numbers each time:

   1, 2, 3, 4, 5, 6, 7, 8, 9, 10

Find ways to make 12.

How can you tell when you have found all the ways?

Show your work.

8.3 Use 2 or more of these numbers each time:

   1, 2, 3, 4, 5, 6, 7, 8, 9, 10

Find ways to make 14.

How can you tell when you have found all the ways?

Show your work.

This is adding to a type and is comparatively easy because you already have an example to work from. This is not the case for *adding a type*.

Adding a Type

Adding a type is needed when, after grouping and sequencing from your existing resources, you realize that the gap between two types is too large for students to make—there is a type missing in between. For example, consider Task 45. Many resources will have students move from the areas of squares and rectangles straight to the areas of rhombuses and parallelograms. Mathematically, this makes sense. A rhombus is just a square, and a parallelogram is just a rectangle, with one of their constraints relaxed—adjacent sides no longer need to meet at a 90° angle. And to move from one to the other makes sense in a lecture where we, as teachers, will tell the students what to notice and how we calculate the area of a rhombus or parallelogram. But if we want students to think and figure this out for themselves, there needs to be a middle ground—a new type of task where they need to notice that the shapes are compound shapes—a line can be drawn and the area of a new shape can now be seen as a sum of the area of familiar shapes.

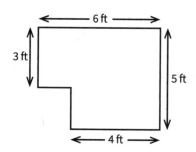

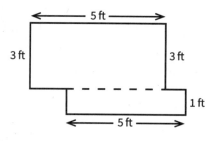

Students need to be familiar with this before moving on to the area of a rhombus or parallelogram. We need to add a type.

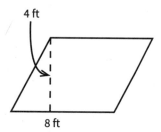

Once you have created a thin-sliced sequence from your resources, you may wish to use the Curricular Task Template. You can download the template at https://companion. corwin.com/courses/BTCK5Tasks

FAQ—How to Thin-Slice Existing Curriculum Resources

Q I get how to use my existing resources to create and fill my three types of tasks. The problem I am having is getting every one of the tasks from my resource to fit into one of the types. How do I do that?

A First of all, you don't need to force every task into a type. Remember that the tasks in your resources are often created for practice. Practice is about doing tasks that you already know how to do. This is different from thin-slicing where the purpose is to have students think, make meaning, and come to understand. As such, there is not a one-to-one correspondence between the tasks you have available in your resource and the tasks that you will end up using in thin-slicing. Think of the way a child eats. They eat the parts they like and leave behind the parts they don't like—usually vegetables. The same is true when you thin-slice from your resources. Take the parts that you like and are useful to you and leave the rest behind.

Q How do I know that a type is missing?

A Sometimes you don't know until you run a thin-slice sequence with your students and realize that you had to spend *a lot* of time and energy supporting groups as they moved from one type to the next. Just picture how much support students would need if we jumped straight from the area of a rectangle to the area of parallelogram. They would need *a lot* of hints and support. If you find yourself providing a lot of hints and support, that is an indicator that a middle step is missing—a type is missing. Ask yourself what task type you could slide in between the two types that will help students *notice* something or *learn* something that they can use on the next type.

Q I notice that you always have three types of tasks in this book. Do things always fall into three types?

A No. You can have more types or fewer. We have just found that if we have more, then we are often dealing with redundancy between types, and if we have fewer, then we are often missing an intermediary type that students need in order to make sense of a later type. Redundancy creates boredom and large gaps can create frustration.

HOW TO THIN-SLICE WORD PROBLEMS

As mentioned in the introduction to Part 3, there is a difference between rich tasks and word problems. Rich tasks are often given in words. Word problems, by definition, are always given in words. And both need decoding. The difference is that, once decoded, there is still a lot to think about with a rich task. Think back to the example from the previous section:

8. Use 2 or more of these numbers each time:

> 1, 2, 3, 4, 5, 6, 7, 8

Find ways to make 10.

How can you tell when you have found all the ways?

Show your work.

Source: Appel et al. (2009, p. 85).

The instructions are given in words. Once these have been decoded by the students, they are still left with a lot to think about. This is often not true with word problems.

In the men's long jump event, Marty jumped 8.26 m in the first trial and 8.55 m in the second trial. What is the difference of his jumps?

Source: Appel et al. (2008, p. 192).

Once the students decode this task, it reduces to $8.55 - 8.26$. If this comes at the end of a series of exercises where students are subtracting decimal numbers to the hundredths, then this is just an exercise with very little to think about.

Having said that, word problems are, in many places, a necessary evil that students are assessed on. Word problems have become a type of task that students need to become proficient at. There are number of ways that we can support the development of this proficiency in a thinking classroom:

1. Passive attention.
2. Active attention.
3. Thin-slicing.

Passive Attention to Word Problems

Passive attention occurs when you simply include word problems in your regular thin-sliced sequences. So, for example, coming back to the division-using-area model, the last task of every type might be a word problem.

Type 1 (AC)

1. $85 \div 5$
2. $396 \div 3$
3. $848 \div 4$
4. $636 \div 3$
5. Rasheda's mom has gone on a baking spree and has baked 488 gulab jamun (Indian milk donuts) for Rasheda to share at the volleyball tournament. If there are 4 volleyball teams, how many gulab jamun does each team get?

This word problem would be printed on a strip of paper, and when a group gets to that point in the sequence you just hand them the task. In this way, word problems become a ubiquitous part of the classroom, and students have the support of their peers in learning how to decode what is being asked. On the plus side, this passive approach is relatively nondisruptive to the flow of the lesson. On the downside, students can solve each of the word problems without actually decoding the task. In fact, they do not even need to read the task to know that they are meant to solve $488 \div 4$. Every task in the flow sequence has been about dividing two numbers using the area model. More specifically, it has been about dividing the larger number (the dividend) by the smaller number (the divisor). The word problem has exactly two numbers in it, one large and one small. What they are meant to do is pretty obvious—today. The problem is that next week, division word problems may be mixed up with addition, subtraction, and multiplication tasks, and decoding will no longer be a simple matter of extracting numbers and performing a single, well-defined operation.

Active Attention to Word Problems

A more effective method is to give more active attention to word problems. In order for the process to be more active, the word problems you give the students need to ask something different from what is happening in the rest of the task sequence.

1. $85 \div 5$
2. $396 \div 3$
3. $848 \div 4$
4. $636 \div 3$

5. Rasheda's mom wants to bake some gulab jamun (Indian milk donuts) for Rasheda to share at the volleyball tournament. If there are 16 volleyball teams, and each team has 12 players on it, how many gulab jamun does she need to bake?

Such a word problem will require the students to really think about what is being asked and actually read and decode the word problem. The downside is that it can disrupt the flow that you are building within the task type and between the task types. This is minor in relation to what is gained by having students collaboratively learning to decode word problems.

This learning can be further accentuated by giving a copy of the task to each member of a group and asking them to first think individually about what the task is asking, and then discuss collectively what is being asked before actually solving the task. This active process of "think individually, discuss collectively, solve" gives students immediate feedback on their individual competency to decode a word problem while at the same time providing the support to remediate any misunderstandings. This process is especially beneficial for complex word problems.

Thin-Slicing Word Problems

What both passive and active approaches have in common is that they involve the integration of word problems into sequences of thin-sliced curricular thinking tasks—word problems are add-ons. An alternative to this is to make the word problems the focus of the thin-slicing. That is, use the power of thin-slicing to help students notice and name salient aspects of what it is you want them to learn—in this case, how to decode word problems. Doing so involves the same process as thin-slicing—identifying, grouping, sequencing, filling. You can do this either from scratch or from your resources. Consider, for example, the following probability word problems that we created:

1. What is the probability of getting a sum of 8 when rolling two dice?

2. What is more likely to occur if you roll two dice, getting two 6s or getting a 1 and a 4?

3. Okeli and Sade are playing a board game with two dice—one red and one white. Okeli needs to roll a sum of 3 to win. Sade needs to roll a 1 with the white die and a 2 with the red die to win. Who is more likely to win?

4. What is more, the possible outcomes of flipping one coin three times or the possible outcomes of flipping three coins all at the same time?

5. What is the probability of rolling a 4 with a single die?

6. What are the possible outcomes of flipping one coin and rolling one die?

7. When I was in Grade 3, I was neighbors with a set of triplets—Ariana, Ariel, and Gertrude. They were the same age as me and we were all friends. We all got along great. The only thing is that these girls were all fiercely competitive—they raced and competed all the time. Only against each other, though. I was never invited to compete with them. Thank

goodness, as I hate competition. Instead, I got to be the finish line judge, the timekeeper, or the referee, depending on the competition. Sometimes they would run a race. Sometimes they would want to see who could eat their lunch the fastest. They would compete at everything, from standing on one foot the longest to shouting the loudest to holding their breath. Everything was a competition. And for every competition there had to be a first place, a second place, and a third place. That's where I came in. I had to determine who was first, second, and third. So, I printed up cards with different finish orders for the three girls. One card said Ariana, Ariel, Gertrude. Another said Gertrude, Ariana, Ariel, and so on. How many cards did I have?

8. Camila and Valeria are sisters, and they are trying to decide whose turn it is to do the dishes. Camila comes up with an idea for a fair way to decide. She puts 2 red blocks and 2 blue blocks into a bag and says to her sister, "Put your hand in the bag and pull out two blocks. If the blocks are the same color, I'll do the dishes. If the blocks are different colors, you do the dishes." Is the game fair?

9. What is the probability of flipping a coin and getting heads?

10. Every time your Uncle Alejandro comes to visit, he gives you a chance to win some money. You can win a lot of money, or you can win no money. The game is always the same. He pulls out of his pocket 10 dice. You can roll as many or as few dice as you want, and the sum of the dice is how much money he will give you. But, there is a catch. If any of the dice comes up with a 1, you get no money. How many dice would you want to roll?

These 10 word problems all deal with possible and desired outcomes. There are varying degrees of complexity in the mathematics and there are varying degrees of complexity in the wording. And these complexities do not correspond. For example, consider task 7. This is a very wordy word problem with relatively simple mathematics. On the other hand, task 4 is relatively easy to decode but is quite complex mathematically. For your information, tasks 8 and 10 are more than word problems. They are also rich tasks that can lead to really advanced discussion.

If I want to thin-slice these tasks, I can arrange them according to the complexity of the mathematics. To do this the grouping and sequencing would be as follows:

- Type 1: possible outcomes where order doesn't matter (tasks 5, 6, 9)
- Type 2: possible outcomes where order does matter (tasks 1, 2, 3, 4, 7, 8)
- Type 3: possible outcomes where weighting matters (task 10)

Type 1 and Type 2 are within the realm of content for K–5. Type 3 in its purest form is not. But by introducing the subjectivity of how many dice you would want to roll into the task, it can be seen as belonging to Grades K–5. From here, we could eliminate or add tasks to make a reasonable thin-sliced mathematical sequence.

However, we can also thin-slice this around the competency of decoding word problems. In such a sequence, the focus is on understanding the task more so than solving the task. Such a grouping and sequencing would be as follows:

- Type 1: simple language (tasks 5, 9, 1, 6, 2)
- Type 2: complex language (tasks 3, 4, 7)
- Type 3: language with rules (tasks 8, 10)

In having students move through the tasks in this order, the overarching instructions may be

> Decode each task and do something to show me that you know what the task is asking. You do not need to solve the task.

Just as with active attention to word problems, this process can be enhanced by having students first decode the task on their own, followed by a discussion with their group. Doing so will provide immediate feedback and the support needed to become proficient at decoding word problems.

Regardless of what method you use—passive attention, active attention, or thin-slicing—to introduce word problems into your thinking classroom, improvement in competencies can be achieved by attending to word problems as part of your consolidation, either through a gallery walk or by listing three tasks out of order and having students notice and name variation.

FAQ—How to Thin-Slice Word Problems

Q My curriculum resource is all word problems. What do I do with that?

A First, avoid word problems altogether in the first three weeks of building your thinking classroom. Turn them into launch scripts instead because being verbal gives access to the task to more students. Second, when you start to introduce word problems do it passively at first, then actively, and finally you can thin-slice it. Once the competency with decoding word problems is increased, use your resource as outlined in the section on thin-slicing from your existing resources.

Q Can I avoid word problems altogether?

A Yes and no. As mentioned in Part 3, word problems exist solely for the purpose of assessing whether students are competent with word problems. So, if you work in a jurisdiction where students are not being assessed on their ability to decode word problems, avoid them. Having said that, there is value in having students engage in rich tasks. And making students competent at decoding tasks presented in word form will give you and them access to more rich tasks.

Q Can I just read word problems out to my students as a way to turn them into launch scripts?

A No. A launch script is more than just telling students what the task is. It is dialectic in nature, involving the students in the situation and calling on them to participate in the unfolding of the narrative that brings them to the task. Having said that, it is easy enough to turn any word problem into a launch script.

HOW TO THICK-SLICE

Unlike thin-slicing, which begins with a clear goal to use a sequence of tasks to bridge the gap between where students are and where you want them to get to, thick-slicing usually begins with a rich task and then adds extensions. In part, these extensions exist because in a thinking classroom no one ever is allowed to be done and in part because it is through extensions that students can continue their meaning-making process and complete their understanding. We call it thick-slicing because, in contrast to thin-slicing, each task takes longer and we get through fewer tasks in any period of time—the slices are thicker.

Consider, for example, the How Many 7s task from Chapter 3 of the main BTC book.

> If I were to write the numbers from 1 to 100, how many times would I use the digit 7?

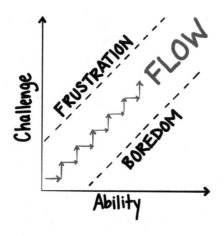 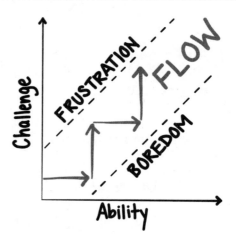

This is a great thinking task. Groups are going to think about it, and they will finish it at different times. What do we do with groups that are done? We give them an extension:

> What if I wrote 1 to 1,000?

And groups that finish that one get another extension:

> How many times would I use the digit 0?

Each of these extensions will take them time to solve. Each extension helps them continue their meaning-making process and complete their understanding. And each extension keeps them busy.

In Part 2, some of the non-curricular thinking tasks, coupled with their extension scripts, are examples of thick-slicing. Likewise, many of the tasks in the main BTC book, with their extensions, are examples of thick-slicing. Never go into a lesson without extensions in hand. It does not matter how rich you think your task is. And it doesn't matter how long you think students will take to solve it. Always have extensions—for their sake and yours.

> Never go into a lesson without extensions in hand.

Coming up with extensions for rich tasks is no different than filling when thin-slicing from existing resources. Start with the task at hand and add a slight variation to it. You can do this by increasing a number. For example, in the How Many 7s task we went from writing the first 100 numbers to writing the first 1000 numbers. We see this also in the Tax Collector task (BTC, Chapter 6).

> I have 12 envelopes, numbered 1 to 12. Each contains a number of dollars equivalent to the number on it. The game starts with you taking one of the envelopes—the money inside of which is yours to keep. The tax collector will then take all of the remaining envelopes whose number is a factor of the envelope you took. The tax collector must be able to take at least one envelope every turn. Play continues until you can no longer take an envelope, at which point the tax collector will take any remaining envelopes. What is the most amount of money that you can get? (adapted from Diane Resek task "The Tax Collector," 2007).

After they have solved it for 12 envelopes, we move them to 18, and then 24. We increase one of the numbers. Alternatively, we can create a thick-sliced extension by adding or changing a rule. For example, consider Task 2 Next Door Numbers.

> Your job is to help the 10 numbers move into the new house so that the numbers that are next to each other on the number line [teacher points at number line] are not next to each other in the house.
>
> ```
> 1
>
>     2
>        10
> ```

When they finish this task, the extensions are as follows:

1. I forgot to mention that number line neighbors *really* don't like each other. When they are at home, number line neighbors don't want to be beside each other *and* they don't want to be above or below each other either.

2. I forgot to mention that number line neighbors *really, really* don't like each other. When they are at home, they don't want their bedrooms touching each other *at all*. So, they can't be beside each other, and they can't be above or below each other, *and* they can't be diagonal to each other either.

3. Do you know what ten-friends are? Ten-friends are numbers that add to 10. Well, ten-friends are not friends any more. They do not like each other. Can you keep ten-friends apart?

Each of these thick-sliced extensions is an addition to, or a change of, the previously established rules.

Finally, we can flip the task. Consider, for example, the Country Road task (BTC, Chapter 12).

A country road is 27 miles long and goes all the way around a lake, connecting the six cottages that are next to the lake. Two of the cottages are 1 mile apart (along the road). Two cottages are 2 miles apart, two are 3 miles apart, two are 4 miles apart, ... two are 25 miles apart, and two are 26 miles apart. How are the cottages distributed along the road? Find a second way to distribute them.

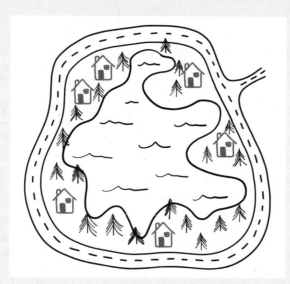

A thick-sliced extension to this task could be the following:

What is the longest road you could have for 5 cottages, where two cottages are 1 mile apart, two are 2 miles apart, etc.?

In this extension, we have gone from positioning the cottages around a 26-mile road to positioning the cottages and figuring out how long the road can be. We can use the same strategy on 1,001 Pennies (BTC, Chapter 11).

> There are 1,001 pennies lined up on a table. Starting at one end of the line, I replace every second coin with a nickel. I then go back to the beginning and replace every third coin with a dime. Finally, I go back to the beginning and replace every fourth coin with a quarter. How much money is now on the table?

An extension for this task could be the following:

> How many coins were there to begin with if, in the end, we have $47.76?

In both these examples, we flipped the task. We reversed what is given with what is asked. When thick-slicing, just like with thin-slicing, you always need to have an extension. Extensions maintain flow, keep students busy, and help them to continue their meaning-making process. You can easily make these by changing a number, changing a rule, or flipping the task.

FAQ—How to Thick-Slice

Q What if I go into a lesson with my thick-sliced extensions ready to go and a group goes through all of them? What do I do then?

A You have a couple of options in this situation. First, if the body of the lesson is more or less complete, you start your closing activities—consolidation, meaningful notes, and/or CYU questions. If you are not at that point,

1. Make up another thick-sliced extension on the spot.

2. You ask them to justify their answer to the last extension.

3. You ask them to explain their answer to the last extension.

4. You ask them to help a group that is struggling.

5. You ask them to come up with an extension for themselves or another group.

Each of these possibilities increases the challenge to the group by shifting their mode of engagement from doing to justifying to explaining to teaching to creating.

Q Instead of thick-slicing, can I just give them a different rich task?

A Yes. That will maintain engagement and keep them busy. But it does not allow the students to continue their meaning-making process and to complete their understanding.

Q My textbook is all rich tasks. Are they thick-sliced?

A Maybe. If task 2 is an extension of task 1, then yes. If, however, task 2 is not an extension of task 1, then it is not thick-sliced. What you have, instead, is a collection of rich tasks that could benefit from some grouping, sequencing, and filling. Luckily, you have the skills to do this.

Notes to My Future Forgetful Self

"Your ability to remain an unfinished math teacher is dependent on your willingness to admit you're imperfect."

— Chase Orton

Author of *The Imperfect and Unfinished Math Teacher:*
A Journey to Reclaim Our Professional Growth

EPILOGUE

The term *Building Thinking Classrooms*, like so many things in math and math education, often gets shortened to a three-letter acronym (TLA). But in shortening Building Thinking Classrooms to BTC, it is easy to lose sight of the fact that each of these letters stands for a word which, in turn, stands for something important. Building Thinking Classrooms is, first and foremost, about *thinking*. But it is not about students thinking on their own. It's about students thinking in a group—actually, in a group embedded within a collection of groups. We need to get our students to think. Not some of them. All of them. We need to get the whole *classroom* thinking. BTC is about *thinking classrooms*.

More than this, however, it is about *building* a thinking classroom. It is not called Shazam, You Have a Thinking Classroom. It is called *Building* Thinking Classrooms. You are building it. It is not built. It is never built. Which means that at every moment in time we have an imperfect version of what it is we are striving to achieve. And that is OK. Just like our students, we are thinking, making meaning, and learning. We have to accept the fact that we are imperfect and draw from this acceptance the will and the courage to always try to be better—to do better, for our students and ourselves.

Building Thinking Classrooms began as an idea—a question, actually—20 years ago, and it has never stopped evolving. The main BTC book was published in 2020. And it was imperfect. In that moment of time, it was a record of what we knew best. But it was unfinished. The book you now hold in your hands is less unfinished. Less imperfect. It is the best of what we know in this moment in time. But it is still evolving. As are you.

We hope that the latest research and tasks we offer you in these pages can help you to continue to evolve into a more competent and more confident thinking classroom teacher. But remember, you are *building* your thinking classroom. Be patient with yourself and your students. And know that every bit you do to get your students to think will be of great benefit to them and to us.

> Could there be anything more important and pressing than teaching students how to think?
>
> —Tracy Johnston Zager

REFERENCES

Appel, R., Brown, T., Chichak, D., Harcourt, L., Jeroski, S., Kinsman, L., Morrow, P., Pratt Nicolson, C., & Wortzman, R. (2008). *Math makes sense 5*. Pearson Education Canada.

Appel, R., Brown, T., Galvin, D., Gibeau, L., Jeroski, S., Morrow, P., Weight, W., Wood, & Wortzman, R. (2009). *Math makes sense 3*. Pearson Education Canada.

Ashcraft, M. (1989). *Human memory and cognition*. Scott, Foresman and Company.

British Columbia Ministry of Education. (2020). *BC performance standards—Numeracy (grade 6)*. https://www2.gov.bc.ca/assets/gov/education/administration/kindergarten-to-grade-12/performance-standards/numeracy/numerg3.pdf

Burdess, A., et al. (2016). *Teaching through problems worth solving*. http://aliciaburdess.weebly.com/problems-worth-solving-in-a-thinking-classroom.html

Common Core State Standards Initiative. (2010). *Standards for mathematical practice*. Retrieved online on Aug 1, 2022 from https://corestandards.org/wp-content/uploads/2023/09/Math_Standards1.pdf

Csíkszentmihályi, M. (1990). *Flow: The psychology of optimal experience*. Harper and Row.

Csíkszentmihályi, M. (1996). *Creativity: Flow and the psychology of discovery and invention*. Harper Perennial.

Csíkszentmihályi, M. (1998). *Finding flow: The psychology of engagement with everyday life*. Basic Books.

Danielson, C. (2016). *Which one doesn't belong? A shapes book*. Stenhouse.

Kaplinsky, R. (2019). *Open middle math: Problems that unlock student thinking, grades 6–12*. Routledge.

Kaplinsky, R. (2022). *You must read Building Thinking Classrooms by Peter Liljedahl*. Retrieved online on August 10, 2022 from https://robertkaplinsky.com/you-must-read-building-thinking-classrooms-in-mathematics-by-peter-liljedahl/

Lesh, R., Cramer, K., Doerr, H., Post, T., & Zawojewski, J. (2003) Using a translation model for curriculum development and classroom instruction. In R. Lesh & H. Doerr (Eds.), *Beyond constructivism. Models and modeling perspectives on mathematics problem solving, learning, and teaching* (pp. 449–464). Lawrence Erlbaum Associates.

Liljedahl, P. (2021). *Building thinking classrooms in mathematics (grades K–12): 14 teaching practices for enhancing learning*. Corwin.

Marton, F. & Tsui, A. B. M. (2004). *Classroom discourse and the space of learning*. Lawrence Erlbaum Associates.

Matthews, L., Jones, S., & Parker, Y. (2022). *Engaging in culturally relevant math tasks*. Corwin.

National Council of Teachers of Mathematics. (2000). *Principles and standards for school mathematics*.

National Council of Teachers of Mathematics. (2014). *Principles to actions*.

National Research Council. (2001). *Adding it up: Helping children learn mathematics*. The National Academies Press.

Orrill, R. (2001). Mathematics, numeracy, and democracy. In L. A. Steen (Ed.), *Mathematics and democracy: The case for quantitative literacy* (pp. xiii–xix). National Council on Education and the Disciplines.

Papert, S. (1980). *Mindstorms—Children, computers and powerful ideas*. Basic Books.

SanGiovanni, J., Katt, S., & Dykema, K. (2020). *Productive math struggle: A 6-point action plan for fostering perseverance*. Corwin.

Smith, M., & Stein, M. K. (2018). *5 practices for orchestrating productive mathematics discussions* (2nd ed.). National Council of Teachers of Mathematics.

University of Cambridge. (n.d.). Magic vs. *NRICH Project*. https://nrich.maths.org/6274

Vardabasso, N. (Host). (2023, May 15). #EESummit23 Debrief (No. 82) [Audio podcast episode]. In *#EduCrush*. https://podcasts.apple.com/ca/podcast/educrush/id1529486348?i=1000613091570

Watson, A. (2000). Going across the grain: Mathematical generalisations in a group of low attainers. *Nordic Studies in Mathematics Education*, 8(1), 7–20.

Webb, K., & Giroux, M. (2022). *Math tasks*. https://tasks.kylewebb.ca/

INDEX

Keep learning...with Peter Liljedahl and his BTC team

Whether you're looking for keynotes, professional development workshops, model teaching in classrooms, or coaching in the BTC model, Peter Liljedahl and his hand-picked team of highly-experienced BTC educators will have your needs met. Select from a range of highly engaging and interactive workshop experiences, including

- Introduction to the Thinking Classroom
- Building Thinking Classrooms Across the Curriculum
- Increasing Student Responsibility in a Thinking Classroom
- Tasks for the Thinking Classroom
- Closing a Thinking Classroom Lesson
- Assessment for a Thinking Classroom
- Equity and Access in a Thinking Classroom

Each of these topics can be pursued through a single workshop or series of workshops, in-person or virtually.

Building Thinking Classrooms in Mathematics, Grades K–12
ISBN: 9781544374833

Modifying Your Thinking Classroom for Different Settings
ISBN: 9781071857847

Mathematics Tasks for the Thinking Classroom, Grades K–5
ISBN: 9781071913291

Coming Soon

Mathematics Tasks for the Thinking Classroom, Grades 6–12
ISBN: 9781071877210

Visit **buildingthinkingclassrooms.com/consulting/** for further information and contacts.

A Sage Company

Helping educators make the greatest impact

CORWIN HAS ONE MISSION: to enhance education through intentional professional learning.

We build long-term relationships with our authors, educators, clients, and associations who partner with us to develop and continuously improve the best evidence-based practices that establish and support lifelong learning.